教育部人文社会科学规划基金项目《当代美国南方文学主题研究》[10YJA752008]
兰州大学中央高校基本科研业务费专项资金项目[09LZUJBWZY047]

20th Century American South Literature

20世纪美国南方文学

20th Century American South Literature

高红霞 张同俊 编著

兰州大学出版社

图书在版编目(CIP)数据

20 世纪美国南方文学 = 20th American South Literature：汉英对照 / 高红霞，张同俊编著. —兰州：兰州大学出版社，2010. 12

ISBN 978-7-311-03638-6

Ⅰ. ①2… Ⅱ. ①高… ②张… Ⅲ. ①文学研究—美国—20 世纪—汉、英 Ⅳ. ①I712. 065

中国版本图书馆 CIP 数据核字(2010)第 259739 号

策划编辑　锁晓梅
责任编辑　锁晓梅
封面设计　管军伟

书　　名　20 世纪美国南方文学
作　　者　高红霞　张同俊　编著
出版发行　兰州大学出版社　(地址：兰州市天水南路 222 号　730000)
电　　话　0931-8912613(总编办公室)　0931-8617156(营销中心)
　　　　　0931-8914298(读者服务部)
网　　址　http://www.onbook.com.cn
电子信箱　press@Lzu.edu.cn
印　　刷　兰州德辉印刷有限责任公司
开　　本　787×1092　1/16
印　　张　17.5
字　　数　415 千
版　　次　2011 年 3 月第 1 版
印　　次　2011 年 3 月第 1 次印刷
书　　号　ISBN 978-7-311-03638-6
定　　价　34.50 元

前　言

新时期以来，随着福克纳等美国"南方文艺复兴"作家、作品的译介和研究，我国读者对南方文学的兴趣与日俱增，南方文学瑰丽的地域特色令他们心醉神迷。各大专院校的外国文学专业或英语系专门开设美国南方经典作品欣赏、美国南方文学研究等类型的必修或选修课程。但国内有关美国南方文学研究的选本大多集中在"南方文艺复兴"时期的作家、作品上，对当代，尤其是对20世纪60年代之后的作品很少涉及，致使对南方文学的研究出现了断裂现象。因此，我们决定单独编写一本20世纪美国南方文学的选读来弥补这一缺憾，供在此方面有兴趣的教师和同学使用。

在本选读的编写过程中我们遵循以下几条原则：

首先，在作家的取舍方面，我们遵守"南方文艺复兴"时期的经典作家和20世纪60年代后新兴作家并举的原则(注：非洲裔南方作家不在本书之列，并非种族歧视，而是编写者认为他们更应该属于非裔作家的分支)。如本书包括格拉斯哥、福克纳、沃尔夫、韦尔蒂、麦卡勒斯等"南方文艺复兴"作家的经典长篇或短篇小说；理查德·福特的《体育记者》(1986年)、安妮·泰勒的《思乡餐厅的晚餐》(1982年)等"晚生代"作家的新作品也入选其中。这种编写理念可以让读者对20世纪美国南方文学的发展变化趋势有所了解和把握，理清"晚生代"南方作家对"南方文艺复兴"先辈的文学主题和写作风格的继承和颠覆之脉理。

其次，在作品的取舍方面，我们主要选取南方文学中最具代表性的作品，长、短篇小说兼顾，力求避免重复选择国内其他选本中常见的作品。例如，所选的福克纳的短篇小说《烧马棚》、韦尔蒂的《我为何住在邮局》、雷诺兹·普莱斯的《守丧》等，不仅体现了作者的写作技巧和语言风格，而且还散发出独特清新的南方气息。

再次，在编写上，我们采用了"作者简介"、"作品导读"和"作品选读"的模式。其中，"作者简介"使用汉语并随文标注作品的英文名称和出版年份，以方便读者对作家的进一步查阅；"作品导读"运用英语编写，重点介绍所选作品的背景知识、故事梗概和作品赏析，为读者理解原文提供指导和帮助。

最后，本书的附录部分对美国南方的地理位置、发展历史、重农思想、文艺复兴、意识形态等进行概括，以期对读者了解和研究南方文学有所裨益。

我们的编写者均对所介绍的作家、作品有深入的研究，他们或从事南方文学的教学科研工作，或正在撰写所选作家的博士或硕士研究论文。具体分工如下：高红霞：前言、绪论、第2、6、11单元、附录和参考文献；张同俊：第4、7、10、14、16单元。另外，兰州大学外国语学院的研究生张军红同学、王晓梅同学、张旭慧同学、李颖娟同学以及于向红同学参编并校对了其他章节。

在本书的编写过程中，得到兰州大学图书馆外文库的老师和兰州大学外国语学院的老师、同学的大力支持，在此对他们表示衷心的感谢。兰州大学出版社的锁晓梅博士对全书进行了校对并提出了许多宝贵意见，在此对她也表示真诚的感谢。

虽然我们已经尽了最大的努力，对所选内容也进行了数次校对，但本书肯定尚未达到完善的水平。我们衷心希望广大读者不吝赐教！

目 录
Contents

绪论:20 世纪美国南方文学概述

美国文学的发展经历过几次意义深远的“复兴”:19 世纪 30 年代的“新英格兰文艺复兴”,孕育了爱默生、梭罗、霍桑、惠特曼、麦尔维尔和迪金森等伟大作家,是美国文学独立的“宣言书”。1910—1920 年间的“二次文艺复兴”,涌现出庞德、桑德堡、弗罗斯特等诗人和刘易斯、海明威及其他“迷惘的一代”小说家。他们的杰出成就让美国“屹立于世界文学之林”。20 世纪 30 年代,南方文学在经历了长期的沉寂、酝酿之后,迎来了文学、艺术创作的巅峰时刻。逃逸派、重农派和“新批评”者登临文学舞台,南方顿时成为美国文学的“歌鸟之巢”[①]。南方文学“复兴”的主要动因来源于美国政治、文化的重大变革。现代化逐渐威胁着南方人的意识形态和价值观念。他们不得不用新的方法去考察现实、认识社会、审视历史。因此,“过去历史的撕扯和现代社会的挤压之间的巨大张力为南方文学复兴提供了土壤”[②],并催生了威廉·福克纳、凯瑟琳·安·波特、埃伦·格拉斯哥、托马斯·沃尔夫、卡罗琳·戈登、约翰·C·兰色姆、罗伯特·佩恩·华伦、艾伦·泰特等第一代以及卡森·麦卡勒斯、弗兰纳里·奥康纳、尤多拉·韦尔蒂、威廉·斯泰伦等第二代“南方文艺复兴”时期的优秀作家。他们对南方沉重的历史意识、瑰丽的地方特色和浓郁的家族观念等主题展开热情饱满的书写,使美国文学焕发出别样的魅力,形成了“南方文艺复兴”的“历史—家族—地域”三位一体的经典文学主题。南方作家在诗歌、小说和文学理论上的辉煌成绩造就了“南方文艺复兴”及其后来南方文学的繁荣局面。

南方人悠闲宁静的田园生活方式和“重农”主义传统、“种植园”家族的“罗曼司”、“宗教文化的地方自立”以及“沉重的历史感和共同的社会记忆”等南方特性培育了南方文艺的独特性和南方人性格中的保守主义。内战失败后,南方被北方“强行”推入现代化,经历了军事、政治、经济、文化、社会、家庭和宗教等多方面的被迫改制,使“视荣誉高于一切”的南方人遭受到前所未有的打击和屈辱。南方人的保守思想让他们本能地反感北方的工商资本主义文明对他们意识形态的重建。原有价值体系和经济模式的逐渐消失使南方人失去了共同的精神家园,这更加剧了他们的“历史围困感”。他们愈加珍惜传统的“历史—家族—地域”主题,集体演绎着“为了忘却的纪念”的悲怆情怀。

①Louis D. Rubin, JR. (ed.) The History of Southern Literature. Louisiana State University Press, 1985:262.

②Richard King. A Southern Renaissance: The Cultural Awakening of the American South 1930-1955. New York: Oxford University Press,1980:5.

但是,20世纪后半期,“南方文艺复兴”文学的三大经典主题面临着“断裂”还是“延续”的危机。现代化的日益深化迫使南方步入了后工业、后现代社会,完成了城市化、经济一体化、文化多元化的转变。在历史、秩序、结构、意义等受到质疑和挑战的后现代社会,人们的信仰和价值观被科学技术和工业文明带来的物质至上和精神空虚所取代。20世纪60年代以来,彼得·泰勒(Peter Taylor)、安·泰勒(Anne Tyler)、理查德·福特(Richard Ford)、鲍比·安·梅森(Bobbie Ann Mason)、考迈克·麦卡锡(Cormac McCarthy)、哈波·李(Harper Lee)、哈瑞·克鲁斯(Harry Crews)、约瑟芬·哈姆佛瑞斯(Josephine Humphreys)、巴瑞·汉纳(Barry Hannah)、雷诺兹·普莱斯(Reynolds Price)、安德鲁·杜巴斯(Andrew Dubus)、约翰·巴斯(John Barth)、爱丽丝·沃克(Alice Walker)、俄内斯特·盖恩斯(Ernest J. Gaines)等新一代作家登上了南方文学的舞台。新生代南方作家在消费资本主义文化、后现代主义价值观念的影响下,逐渐放弃了南方传统的家族、历史、地域等主题。他们的作品也显示出典型的后现代主义特征:“对本质和意义消解的平面无深度化”、“对生存状态临摹再现的错乱零散化”和“对传统质疑否定的碎片拼贴化”。他们似乎用后现代的“含混性”、“间断性”、“多元性”、“随意性”和“反叛性”等方式消解价值体系、淡化南方意识,从而解构“南方文艺复兴”“家族—历史—地域”文学主题的严肃性和凝重感。南方文学在后现代时期似乎呈现出“众声喧哗”、主题“杂陈”的局面。

一、南方文学历史主题的发展演变

内战失败的创伤造成南方人强烈“向后看”的历史意识,也赋予“南方文艺复兴”文学关注“历史”的核心主题。对奴隶制的负罪感和对过去的留恋使“复兴”作家带着负疚、屈辱而又自尊、骄傲的复杂情感去追问、反思和剖析南方的过去,历史占据着他们作品的中心位置。沉思历史对现实的影响,借助集体记忆去恢复、重构历史,期望借此抵制北方工商资本主义现代化的步步进逼。福克纳、华伦、泰特等南方作家从主观情感的角度去处理时间,打破了线性进步论意义上的时间观念,即在“过去—现在—未来”线性系列上的“新/旧—进步/落后—好/坏”的基本时间序列及叙事模式,取消“未来”的终极价值和伦理意义。所以,萨特认为:“福克纳干脆把时间斩了首,去掉了时间的未来。”他们通过对“情感”时间的认同和对“机械”时间的排斥来表达对旧南方历史的依恋和对北方现代化进程的批判。

南方文学巨擘福克纳的“约克纳帕塔法”世系小说弥漫着浓烈的历史意识。他的小说世界分为代表南方传统道德和历史意识的“沙多里斯”和代表北方工商资本主义价值观念的“斯诺普斯”两大世界。“沙多里斯”们是南方最后的贵族,他们沉浸在南方的历史中,旧南方的神话在他们的记忆中复活,旧南方的过去在他们的想象中浮现。而“斯诺普斯”们则试图斩断与历史的联系,他们投机钻营、唯利是图,藐视南方的传统观念。福克纳通过在情感上对沙多里斯的认同和对斯诺普斯的反感表现厚重的历史意识,他不得已地遵循着历史的必然律,无可奈何地把崇尚南方历史、注重南方尊严的康普生-沙多里斯、卡洛瑟斯-麦卡斯林等贵族大家族送上灭亡之路,眼睁睁地看着对金钱念念不忘、对历史不闻不问的斯诺普斯主义在南方蔓延。因此,宿命和怀旧成就了福克纳作品的历史悲剧感。泰特沿袭了福克纳的历史意识,他的《父亲们》认为传统的行为模式、庆祝活动、宗教礼仪等在历史中发挥着重要作用,深刻影响着当今人们的思想和行为。

麦卡勒斯、奥康纳、韦尔蒂等淡化了作品中福克纳、泰特式的历史悲剧性。她们不愿抱残守缺,被历史团团围困,沉湎于南方的过去,对传统历史进行浪漫化的想象,但她们坚持认为南方并不会轻易地被北方同化,从而匆忙地走向资本主义的现代化。与重农派作家相似,她们严厉抨击北方资本主义制度下的都市生活和世俗文化。奥康纳对《暴力得逞》中的雷勃、《持久的寒冷》中的福克斯、《所有上升的东西都必须汇合》中的朱丽安等代表的都市世俗生活进行了无情的讽刺和批判。韦尔蒂的《乐观者的女儿》表现出对母亲代表的"旧"南方历史意识的依恋和对继母代表的"新"历史意识的厌恶,"新"与"旧"的冲突反映出作者的价值观念取向。

进入后现代,新历史主义在美国本土产生了巨大影响,人们对历史的认识发生了极大的改变,开始反思历史的权威性和客观性。历史被抽空了内涵,只降解成各种文档、照片和影视材料,失去了指导意义和价值功能,变成在主观意识驱动下借助语言建立起来的符号体系,历史的功能和本质不断地受到人们的质疑。这种趋势充分反映在20世纪60年代后新一代南方作家的作品中。理查德·福特发表于1986年的《体育记者》和1995年的《独立日》是对"南方文艺复兴"作家历史意识的彻底解构。小说主人公巴斯克姆把离开南方认为是摆脱历史阴影、清扫传统束缚的主要手段。鲍比·安·梅森在《羽冠》(1993年)、约瑟芬·哈姆佛瑞斯在《睡梦》(1984年)中用遗忘、拒斥、揭露的手法消解历史。她们再也不相信历史的真实意义和终极价值,认为南方人要对历史进行理性思考,切断历史的沉重锁链,从令人窒息的历史负担中解脱出来,积极融入美国的现代化,紧抱历史只会将自己更加边缘化、更加自绝于时代。麦卡锡在1979年发表的《萨特里》、汉纳在1980年发表的《瑞》中,更是通过描写狂乱、丑陋、暴力和荒唐等对南方历史、庄园神话予以冷嘲热讽和猛烈颠覆。

二、南方文学家族主题的发展演变

南方"家庭罗曼司"是"南方文艺复兴"的第二个经典主题,构成了南方文学、文化的基石。在"秩序稳定、信仰虔诚、政治保守的南方,家庭、血缘、宗族是南方作家的常见主题"①。奴隶制庄园经济决定了南方人聚族而居的生活习惯和父权制大家庭的主导地位。内战失败后,南方的庄园经济模式遭受重创,庄园主大家庭也随之消亡。对南方大家庭的依恋和对北方工商资本主义家庭观的反感使"复兴"作家对家族主题投入了创造性的激情,并对南方的家族神话展开集中书写,贵族大家族的衰落史构成了当时文学创作的主旋律。南方作家围绕家庭完整、家族荣誉、尊卑秩序、淑女观念等问题进行创作,形成了南方家族小说叙事的母题谱系,主要包括"家族神话与家园追寻母题"、"父权至上与女性从属母题"、"血缘秩序与乱伦母题"、"家族本位与复仇母题"等。这些母题具现在"复兴"时期的家族小说创作中,充当着分辨其思想艺术特征的重要参照系,使它们获得了表现上的丰富性、外延

①Thomas Daniel Young. The Past in the Present: A Thematic Study of Modern Southern Fiction. Louisiana State University Press, 1981:2.

上的广阔性和文化上的独特性。

家族小说是福克纳小说创作的核心，他对自己的家族小说及故事内容进行整体布局和精心规划。《沙多里斯》、《喧哗与骚动》、《我弥留之际》、《没有被征服的》、《押沙龙，押沙龙！》、《去吧，摩西》以及后来的“斯诺普斯三部曲”《村子》、《小镇》和《大宅》等小说中的大家族都分布在神话王国“约克纳帕塔法县”，各家居有定所、相互关联：康普生-沙多里斯世家、斯诺普斯世家、卡洛瑟斯-麦卡斯林世家和拉特里夫-本特伦家族居住在法国人湾的森林深处；萨德本家族居住在约克纳帕塔法县的“萨德本百哩地”。福克纳主要描述这几大家族的盛衰荣辱史：崇尚传统、注重尊严的康普生-沙多里斯世家；无视道德、追求利润的斯诺普斯世家；逃避责任、回归自然的卡洛瑟斯-麦卡斯林世家；专心建造纯白人家族“王朝”的萨德本世家；没有过去、只有“现在”的拉特里夫-本特伦家族。泰特的长篇小说《父亲们》也采用家庭主题，以1860—1861年的弗吉尼亚为背景，巴肯家族的悲剧和南方的社会、文化变革交织在一起，表现作者对南方即将逝去的农耕生活方式和乡村生活习俗可能引发的后果的预测和忧虑。

家庭也是“复兴”时期女作家钟爱的主题，表现南方妇女的女性特质、婚姻观念、家庭关系、社会角色等，对南方传统的家族观念进行修改和补充，强调女性在家庭中的创造力和重要性。安·波特以家族历史为题材表现南方的审美观念、生活方式和风俗习惯。她的《老人》及《马戏团》、《坟》、《旧秩序》等米兰达系列小说从女性视角讲述具有复杂历史背景的家族故事及其对主人公行为规范的影响。韦尔蒂以自己熟悉的南方风土人情为创作素材，运用南方方言及写实手法、以女性经验表现南方人的内心世界，探讨家庭关系、时事变迁、爱恨矛盾和地区历史等。她的《乐观者的女儿》表现了女主人公劳雷尔对家族传统价值的珍视、对继母等代表的新南方价值观的反感；《三角洲婚礼》通过描写费尔查尔德家族中女性的爱情、婚姻等问题，辐射整个三角洲地区，对女性在家庭中的作用、地位以及她们与土地、自然之间的关系展开讨论。佐拉·尼尔·赫斯顿的《他们眼望上苍》中的女主人公珍妮逃脱“玩偶之家”，追求真爱，寻找社会和家庭地位，成为独立自尊的女性。

在当代南方作家的家族小说中，家庭观念的淡化和家庭结构的调整使南方传统的家族主题发生了明显的改变，失去了清晰可辨的母题形态，带有美国后现代家庭小说的共性。旧秩序下稳定、封闭的大家庭向开放、动态的现代化核心家庭过渡。家庭和婚姻复杂多变、危机四伏，充满不稳定性；夫妻之间感情冷漠、情爱关系脆弱。迷惘、彷徨、失望、痛苦、压抑、焦虑、空虚似乎成了后现代南方家庭的主旋律，传统的“家族神话”和家庭观念荡然无存。斯泰伦、考迈克、梅森、福特、普莱斯、安·泰勒等用后现代的颠覆精神改写着南方家庭的传统意义和情感功能，旧南方的“家庭罗曼司”在他们的作品中几乎消失殆尽。

威廉·斯泰伦的长篇小说《在黑暗中躺下》描写女主人公佩登，虽然生活在弗吉尼亚的富裕家庭里，但自私、背叛、嫉妒、仇恨、报复和乱伦倾向等畸形家庭关系使她的性格扭曲、变态，最终自杀身亡。在沃克·珀西的《看电影的人》中，主人公宾克斯是一个滑稽可笑、与社会格格不入、无所事事的“影院常客”。他沉湎于影院，不与家人交流，津津有味地重述电影的虚假情节，逃避家庭责任。雷诺兹·普莱斯的小说三部曲《地衣之表》、《休息的承诺》和

《光明之源》讲述梅菲尔德家族和肯德尔家族四代人近一个世纪的故事,描写家庭生活带来的苦恼,小说中弥漫着过去以及逃离过去对个人和家庭造成的影响。安妮·泰勒彻底改写了家的传统概念,拆除封闭家庭的围栏,打破了人们在家中寻求庇护的希望。在她的代表作《思乡餐厅的晚餐》中,母亲塔尔脾气暴躁,控制欲极强,命令孩子言听计从,导致家庭封闭、压抑,家人之间缺乏温暖和亲情。家俨然已成空壳,再也无法给家庭成员提供身体的港湾和心灵的慰藉,他们纷纷寻求家庭外的解脱和拯救。

三、南方文学地域主题的发展演变

独特的自然、历史因素以及长期的农业传统使南方人深深地眷恋着乡土。土地是他们安身立命、繁衍生息的地方,更是他们的心灵家园和情感归属。家乡的山川、沃土、房屋、居民都令南方人魂牵梦萦,土地凝聚着南方的历史、荣耀、梦想和希望。地域情结升华为某种精神力量,具有神话意义,是作家创作灵感的源泉,浓缩成“南方文艺复兴”文学的又一经典主题。“逃逸派”的主将兰色姆、泰特、戴维森和沃伦等诗人和南方传统文化的维护者发起了“重农派”运动,崇尚自给自足的农业经济和悠闲宁静的田园生活,抵制北方工业资本主义在南方的蔓延。他们认为唯利是图、物欲横流的工业社会扼杀了文学艺术的生命力。在“重农思想”的影响下,“复兴”作家们对“地域”倾注了丰沛的感情。他们的“集体乡愁”造就了南方文学创作的现代神话：内战让南方人失去了伊甸园，北方工商资本主义者是撒旦,诱惑纯洁的南方走向现代化城市的地狱。

“复兴”作家对南方土地的眷恋和对地域情结的思考使他们的作品散发出浓郁的南方气息。“重农思想和庄园神话在斯塔克·杨的《玫瑰如此之红》和玛格丽特·米切尔的《飘》中得到集中体现”[1]。福克纳对“约克纳帕塔法”的激情“图绘”更是把南方的“地域情结”推向顶峰。福克纳发现自己那“邮票般”大小的故乡蕴涵着永远都写不完的故事,那里的山川河流、森林广场、人口密度、家族分布、规模大小、居舍农庄、仆从角色、肤色身份、家庭关系等等,事无巨细、历历在目。那里充满了人性的委靡,却生活着故乡的祖祖辈辈,是福克纳魂牵梦萦的瑰丽故乡。在他眼里,“故乡的土地不仅是美国南方神话的化身,还是普遍人性的缩影”[2]。怪不得他在《熊》中把大森林看做“情人”、“妻子”。韦尔蒂的作品大多以她熟悉的密西西比州小镇为背景,她认为“地方”饱含人生哲理,启迪人生智慧,是南方的生命之源,更是他们的灵魂之源。麦卡勒斯的南方“咖啡馆”虽然令人“伤心”,可它也如“丝”如“歌”,展示着南方地域的“怪诞”和“迷人”。

随着科技的发展、交通的便捷、媒介的普及、人口的流动和经济一体化的加深,重建后的南方逐渐融入美国的现代化。城市的兴起和铁路的畅通很快打破了地域界限,消除了文化差异,蚕食着地域情结。南方人摆脱了对土地和家乡的依恋之情,年轻人选择流向大城市,或到北方城市寻找更好的学习、工作机会,离开南方割断了他们与故土的情感纽带。新

①William J. Cooper, JR., Thomas E. Terrill. The American South: A History [M]. New York: Alfred A. Knopf, INC. 1991: 655.

②John Dennis Anderson. Student Companion to William Faulkner[M]. Westport, Connecticut: Greenwood Press, 2007:1.

生代南方作家作品中的地方特色淡化,地域情结消失,乡土意识淡薄。对现代化的认同使他们尽快地从静态、单一的地方情结中解放出来,他们通过变动不居的场景描写、国际型人物的塑造和普适性的取材来反映他们超越南方界限的视野, 南方再也不是他们情感的牵挂和灵感的源泉。

虽然普莱斯、盖恩斯等少数作家依然坚守南方的地域意识,但地域主题在当代南方文学中的淡出似乎是不争的事实。普莱斯的小说大多以北卡莱罗纳州东部的家乡为背景,他的创作"傲然沿袭"南方小说的地域、家族等主题,在南方文学的沿革中占有非常重要的地位。他重新点亮了南方区域作家逐渐退色的光环,"他可能就是继承南方文艺复兴传统的最后一位伟大的小说家"①。同样,盖恩斯被称为"南方的最后一位地域作家"。他认识到南方的地方特色很快就会被"麦当劳快餐"取而代之,"地方意识和社区主题在当代南方文学中已经濒临灭绝"②,他倔强地坚持社区意识、家庭观念和地方情结的小说创作主题。他的故事大多发生在一个以里弗湖为蓝本的贝欧尼庄园里,演绎南方人,尤其是黑人的悲欢离合,生动再现南方的民间习俗和地方文化,歌颂南方简朴的乡村生活,批判繁复喧闹、人际关系冷漠的大都市生活,强调社区观念的价值和地域情结的重要性。

理查德·福特、威廉·斯泰伦和沃克·珀西却拒绝被贴上"南方作家"的标签,他们认为"自己是作家但不是南方作家"。珀西的作品以南方港口城市新奥尔良为背景,但他争辩说自己用哲学思辨、天主教和存在主义观点去描写爱情、性与个人责任之间的关系,探讨"现代社会中人的普遍困境"和人生意义。斯泰伦竭力摆脱地域情结的影响,在《索菲的选择》中放弃了南方的地域主题,讲述一位波兰妇女在奥斯维辛集中营里的悲惨遭遇。选择"大屠杀"为创作题材、集中营为故事背景,是"斯泰伦等南方作家现在要脱掉地方色彩的襁褓,把注意力要转向其他方面的创作观的充分体现"③。福特的作品大都以蒙大拿州、怀俄明州、墨西哥或巴黎为背景,主人公居无定所,或被家族驱逐,他们与某个地方之间建立起来的是一种临时短暂、无法永恒的关系。他们的主人公出生在南方,但没有生活在某一个固定的地方。《独立日》的主人公巴斯克姆认为"地方毫无意义,从不配合你并为你提供尊严",失去了精神寄托的功能。"西部在南方当代文学中频繁出现,挑战地域意识在南方人心理上的旧有观念"④,考迈克·麦卡锡、福特、巴瑞·汉纳等把作品的背景移向"希望之地"——西部,这种"地域的西部化"似乎代表着当代南方文学的一个发展趋势。现代南方作家地域情结的逐渐淡化以及他们对旧南方文学地域主题的颠覆,表现出后现代人精神上的流浪和徘徊。

四、南方文学的发展走向

20世纪60年代以来,新生代南方作家文学主题和写作风格的变化引发了评论界的广泛关注和激烈争论:当代南方作家是否延续了"南方文艺复兴"的"历史—家族—地域"主

①萨克文·伯科维奇主编,孙宏主译.剑桥美国文学史(第七卷)[M].北京:中央编译出版社,2005:423.

②Rose Anne Brister. The Last Regionalist?: An Interview with Ernest J. Gains. Callaloo, Vol.26, No. 3 [M]. The Johns Hopkins University Press, 2003: 549.

③杨仁敬.20世纪美国文学史.青岛:青岛出版社,1999:544.

④Joseph M. Flora. Relocating Southerners in the West[M]. The Southern Literary Journal, Vol. 33, No.2, (Spring, 2001) 150-152:150.

题？南方文学是否还能保持风格鲜明的地域特色？如果没有地域特色，南方文学还有存在的必要和价值吗？围绕这些辩论产生了南方文学的“延续说”和“断裂说”两种截然不同的观点。南方著名学者布鲁克斯(Cleanth Brooks)、鲁宾(Louis Rubin)、霍曼(Hugh Holman)、伍德沃德(C. Van Woodward)等支持南方文学的“延续说”。他们认为在后现代美国的价值观念和欣赏趣味的影响下，南方文学发生了很大的变化，其中也不乏对传统主题的颠覆因素，但在对待家庭、宗教、地域、历史的态度上当代作家继承了南方传统，他们清醒地认识到这些“精髓”关系到南方文学的存亡。南方杰出作家彼得·泰勒 1986 年在长篇小说《孟菲斯的召唤》中也对南方文学面临的断裂与延续表现出极其矛盾的态度。没有历史，没有罪愆，没有家庭，甚至没有生活：人们无法想象摆脱令人“烦恼”的南方重负以后的局面，至少对于南方作家来说是如此。小说用隐喻的手法表明南方作家在文学上所处的困境：与“南方文艺复兴”那代作家断绝“那耗尽其才能的关系，但是如果他们真的中断了这种关系，他们还得冒着失去小说创作活力的风险”。

但同样是南方著名评论家的沃尔特·苏里文(Walter Sullivan)和奎因(Matthew Quinn)却斩断了这种延续的可能性。他们认为南方小说是否保持南方特色必须基于它们是否关注南方的历史文化、宗教信仰、风俗习惯、地域特色等。在他们看来，支撑传统南方文学的文化已不复存在，文化的消亡定会导致相应的文学的消亡。对当代南方文学的解读应该建立在寻找区域之外和主要潮流影响之下南方作家的最佳创作主题和写作模式。关于南方文学的延续与断裂，两个阵营各执一词，彼此无法说服对方，因为他们都在当代南方文学里为自己的观点找到了强有力的证据。彼得·泰勒、普莱斯、富莱德·恰贝尔、文代尔·贝瑞、欧内斯特·盖恩斯、爱丽丝·沃克等遵循了传统的南方文学主题，他们是续写旧南方文学模式的代表；而理查德·福特、沃克·珀西、斯泰伦、梅森、巴瑞·汉纳、考迈克·麦卡锡、哈瑞·克鲁斯等的长篇小说则是背离“南方文艺复兴”主题和写作模式的有力证据[1]。这种辩论正好说明了当代南方文学的矛盾处境：延续中存在断裂，断裂中又存在延续。“南方文艺复兴”的主题就在延续和断裂的辩证关系中发展变化着。

---

①李杨.美国南方文学后现代时期的嬗变[M].济南：山东大学出版社，2006：14.

Unit 1
Ellen Glasgow (1873–1945)
埃伦·格拉斯哥

作者简介

埃伦·格拉斯哥，美国小说家，"南方文艺复兴"的先驱，1873年出生于弗吉尼亚州里士满(Richmond)，父亲是西弗吉尼亚地区的苏格兰与爱尔兰混血后裔，信奉加尔文教。母亲出身于信仰新教圣公会的贵族家庭。格拉斯哥16岁时听力受损，后来完全失聪。孤僻的性格使她喜好阅读，这为她以后的文学创作奠定了基础。她少年时便开始尝试写作，1897年第一部小说《子孙》(*The Descendant*)匿名出版。该作品鲜明的反叛意识立刻吸引了批评界的注意。此后十年，她内心充满对父亲的憎恶和对母亲的同情，这形成了她内省的文学倾向和叛逆的性格。20岁时，随着母亲的去世和姐夫(她的精神导师)的自杀，她变得更加沮丧，更加孤独，并终生未嫁。她以现实主义的手法描写家乡弗吉尼亚州的社会历史。1900年发表的《人民之声》(*The Voice of the People*)确立了她知名小说家的地位。在《战场》(*The Battle- Ground*, 1902)中，尽管她没有完全摆脱浪漫主义文学的影响，但她对内战的处理要比其他作家现实得多。20世纪初，她创作了一些既立足于现实主义又不乏复杂心理描写的短篇小说。从1913年发表《弗吉尼亚》(*Virginia*)开始，她的创作基调发生变化，表现出敏锐的讽刺性和对南方女性社会地位的深刻认识。1925年她创作的《不毛之地》(*Barren Ground*)得到了评论界的好评。接着她发表了带有讽刺性的三部曲：《浪漫的喜剧演员》(*The Romantic Comedians*, 1926)，《他们不惜干蠢事》(*They Stooped to Folly*, 1929)，《受庇护的生活》(*The Sheltered Life*, 1932)，其中《受庇护的生活》与《不毛之地》尤佳。在这三部作品中，她把批评的锋芒直接指向了弗吉尼亚的上层社会。在最后写的一部重要小说《钢铁筋骨》(*Vein of Iron*, 1935)中，她的创作背景又回到了早期作品中所描写的乡村世界。小说《我们的这一生》(*In This Our Life*, 1941)荣获1942年的"普利策"奖。另一部自传性作品——《女人的内心世界》(*The Woman Within*)在她去世9年后才出版。这部自传为她赢得了社会现实主义者、社会历史学家、讽刺家以及礼仪和道德编年史家的美誉。她在作品中表现的对南方狭隘虚伪的社会形态及道德意识的讽刺、对南方等级制度和男性霸权主义的谴责正是南方文学迈向20世纪时所迫切需要的。

作品导读

Jordan's End, published in 1923, is a story grounded both in realism and in the sort of psychological complexity. It is a dark tale of the demise of a once prominent Virginia planter's family in the years following the end of the Civil War. In this sad tale, Glasgow makes every effort to set a tone of hopelessness and despair, painting a depressing picture of an unsustainable life style fallen into ruin. In this shorter fiction, the physician-narrator recounts two house calls made thirty years ago when he began his medical practice in a remote part of Virginia. The doctor is asked to see Alan Jordan at the request of his wife, Judith. They live with their son and three elderly female relatives in a deteriorating house on a secluded estate known as Jordan's End. The Jordan clan is notorious for marrying their own relatives, but Alan wedded someone else outside his family. Judith is beautiful, and in the doctor's eyes, ethereal. Alan's infirmity began three years ago with brooding and melancholy but has now progressed to episodes of withdrawal alternating with agitation. A renowned psychiatrist from Baltimore evaluates Alan, and deems his condition incurable, and thus recommends institutionalization. Mental illness and insanity – the result of heredity and inbreeding – seem to affect all the Jordan men. Alan's grandfather and two uncles are in an asylum. After the narrator examines Alan, he gives Judith a bottle of opiate medication to help ease her husband's restlessness. Several days later, the doctor is soon called back to Jordan's End. He finds Alan's dead body in bed covered by a linen sheet and notices that the full bottle of medicine he left is now empty. The doctor can neither decide whether Judith has killed her husband nor does he really want to know. The story ends with the doctor's leaving. By delineating a tale of family insularity and madness, *Jordan's End* calls to mind another literary work – *The Fall of the House of Usher* by Edgar Allan Poe. As with many of her novels and short stories, Ellen Glasgow appears to be expressing her views on the Southern social class structure of the pre-Civil War and post-Civil War South. It appears that within her body of work Glasgow was writing about a lifestyle she both knew and understood, and later came to scorn. It seems she took every opportunity through her writing to challenge the status quo of Southern elitist culture. In *Jordan's End*, Glasgow seems to be making a pointed social comment on the consequences of an elite Southern social system based primarily on heredity, specifically primogenitureship.

作品选读

Jordan's End

At the fork of the road there was the dead tree where buzzards were roosting, and through its boughs I saw the last flare of the sunset. On either side the November woods were flung in broken masses against the sky. When I stopped they appeared to move closer and surround me with vague, glimmering shapes. It seemed to me that I had been driving for hours; yet the ancient negro who brought the message had told me to follow the Old Stage Road till I came to Buzzard's Tree at the fork. "F'om dar on hit's moughty nigh ter Marse Jur'dn's place," the old man had assured me, adding tremulously, "en young Miss she sez you mus'come jes'ez quick ez you kin." I was young then (that was more than thirty years ago), and I was just beginning the practice of medicine in one of the more remote countries of Virginia.

My mare stopped, and leaning out, I gazed down each winding road, where it branched off, under half bared boughs, into the autumnal haze of the distance. In a little while the red would fade from the sky, and the chill night would find me still hesitating between those dubious ways which seemed to stretch into an immense solitude. While I waited uncertainly there was a stir in the boughs overhead, and a buzzard's feather floated down and settled slowly on the robe over my knees. In the effort to drive off depression, I laughed aloud and addressed my mare in a jocular tone:

"We'll choose the most God-forsaken of the two, and see where it leads us."

To my surprise the words brought an answer from the trees at my back. "If you're goin'to Isham's store, keep on the Old Stage Road," piped a voice from the underbrush.

Turning quickly, I saw the dwarfed figure of a very old man, with a hunched back, who was dragging a load of pine knots out of the woods. Though he was so stopped that his head reached scarcely higher than my wheel, he appeared to possess unusual vigour for one of his age and infirmities. He was dressed in a rough overcoat of some wood brown shade, beneath which I could see his overalls of blue jeans. Under a thatch of grizzled hair his shrewd little eyes twinkled cunningly, and his bristly chin jutted so far forward that it barely escaped the descending curve of his nose. I remembered thinking that he could not be far from a hundred; his skin was so wrinkled and weather-beaten that, at a distance, I had mistaken him for a negro.

I bowed politely. "Thank you, but I am going to Jordan's End," I replied.

He cackled softly. "Then you take the bad road. Thar's Jur'dn's turnout." He pointed to the sunken trail, deep in mud, on the right. "An'if you ain't objectin' to a little comp'ny, I'd be obleeged if you'd give me a lift. I'm bound thar on my own o'count, an'it's a long ways to tote these here lightwood knots."

While I drew back my robe and made room for him, I watched him heave the load of resinous pine into the buggy, and then scramble with agility to his place at my side.

"My name is Peterkin," he remarked by way of introduction. "They call me Father Peterkin along o'the gran'child'en." He was a garrulous soul, I suspected, and would not be averse to imparting the information I wanted.

"There's not much travel this way, " I began, as we turned out of the cleared space into the deep tunnel of the trees. Immediately the twilight enveloped us, though now and then the dusky glow in the sky was still visible. The air was sharp with the tang of autumn; with the effluvium of rotting leaves, the drift of wood smoke, the ripe flavour of crushed apples.

"Thar's nary a stranger, thoughten he was a doctor, been to Jur'dn's End as fur back as I kin recollect. Ain't you the new doctor?"

"Yes, I am the doctor." I glanced down at the gnomelike shape in the wood brown overcoat. "Is it much farther?"

"Naw, suh, we're all but thar jest as soon as we come out of Whitten woods."

"If the road is so little traveled, how do you happen to be going there?"

Without turning his head, the old man wagged his crescent shaped profile. "Oh, I live on the place. My son Tony works a slice of the farm on shares, and I manage to lend a hand at the harvest or corn shuckin', and, now-and-agen, with the cider. The old gentleman used to run the place that away afore he went deranged, an' now that the young one is laid up, thar ain't nobody to look arter the farm but Miss Judith. Them old ladies don't count. Thar's three of'em, but they're all addle-brained an' look as if the buzzards had picked 'em. I reckon that comes from bein' shut up with crazy folks in that thar old tumbledown house. The roof ain't been patched fur so long that the shingles have most rotted away, an' thar's times, Tony says, when you kin skearcely hear yo' years fur the rumpus the wrens an' rats are makin' over-head."

"What is the trouble with them – the Jordans, I mean?"

"Jest run to seed, suh, I reckon."

"Is there no man of the family left?"

For a minute Father Peterkin made no reply. Then he shifted the bundle of pine knots, and responded warily. "Young Alan, he's still livin' on the old place, but I hear he's been took now, an' is goin' the way of all the rest of 'em. 'Tis a hard trial for Miss Judith, po' young thing, an' with a boy nine year old that's the very spit an' image of his pa. Wall, wall, I kin recollect away back yonder when old Mr. Timothy Jur'dn was the proudest man anywhar aroun' in these parts; but arter the War things sorter begun to go down hill with him, and he was obleeged to draw in his horns."

"Is he still living?"

The old man shook his head. "Mebbe he is, an' mebbe he ain't. Nobody knows but the Jur'dn's, an' they ain't tellin' fur the axin'."

"I suppose it was this Miss Judith who sent for me?"

"'Twould most likely be she, suh. She was one of the Yardlys that lived over yonder at Yardly's Field; an' when young Mr. Alan begun to take notice of her, 'twas the first time sence way back that one of the Jur'dn's had gone courtin' outside the family. That's the reason the blood went bad like it did, I reckon. Thar's a sayin' down aroun' here that Jur'dn an' Jur'dn won't mix." The name was invariably called Jurdin by all classes; but I had already discovered that names are rarely pronounced as they are spelled in Virginia.

"Have they been married long?"

"Ten year or so, suh. I remember as well as if 'twas yestiddy the day young Alan brought her home as a bride, an' thar warn't a soul besides the three daft old ladies to welcome her. They drove over in my son Tony's old buggy, though 'twas spick an' span then. I was goin' to the house on an arrant, an' I was standin' right down thar at the ice pond when they come by. She hadn't been much in these parts, an' none of us had ever seed her afore. When she looked up at young Alan her face was pink all over and her eyes war shinin' bright as the moon. Then the front do' opened an' them old ladies, as black as crows, flocked out on the po'ch. Thar never was anybody as peart-lokin' as Miss Judith was when she come here; but soon arterwards she begun to peak an' pine, though she never lost her sperits an' went mopin' roun' like all the other women folks at Jur'dn's End. They married sudden, an' folks do say she didn't know nothin' about the family, an' young Alan didn't know much mo'than she did. The old ladies had kep' the secret away from him, sorter believin' that what you don't know cyarn' hurt you. Anyways they never let it leak out tell arter his chile was born. Thar ain't never been but that one, an' old Aunt Jerusly declars he was born with a caul over his face, so mebbe things will be all right fur him in the long run."

"But who are the old ladies? Are their husbands living?"

When Father Peterkin answered the question he had dropped his voice to a hoarse murmur. "Deranged. All gone deranged," he replied.

I shivered, for a chill depression seemed to emanate from the November woods. As we drove on, I remembered grim tales of enchanted forests filled with evil faces and whispering voices. The scents of wood earth and rotting leaves invaded my brain like a magic spell. On either side the forest was as still as death. Not a leaf quivered, not a bird moved, not a small wild creature stirred in the underbrush. Only the glossy leaves and the scarlet berries of the holly appeared alive amid the bare interlacing branches of the trees. I began to long for an autumn clearing and the red light of the afterglow.

"Are they living or dead?" I asked presently.

"I've hearn strange tattle," answered the old man nervously, "but nobody kin tell. Folks do say as young Alan's pa is shut up in a padded place, and that his gran'pa died thar arter thirty years. His uncles went crazy too, an' the daftness is beginnin' to crop out in the women. Up tell now it has been mostly the men. One time I remember old Mr. Peter Jur'dn tryin' to burn down the place in the dead of the night. Thar's the end of the wood, suh. If you'll jest let me down here, I'll be gittin' along home across the old-field, an' thanky too."

At last the woods ended abruptly on the edge of an abandoned field which was thickly sown with scrub pine and broomsedge. The glow in the sky had faded now to a thin yellow-green, and a melancholy twilight pervaded the landscape. In this twilight I looked over the few sheep huddled together on the ragged lawn, and saw the old brick house crumbling beneath its rank growth of ivy. As I drew nearer I had the feeling that the surrounding desolation brooded there like some sinister influence.

Forlorn as it appeared at this first approach, I surmised that Jordan's End must have possessed once charm as well as distinction. The proportions of the Georgian front were impressive, and there was beauty of design in the quaint doorway, and in the steps of rounded stone which were brocaded now with a pattern of emerald moss. But the whole place was badly in need of repair. Looking up, as I stopped, I saw that the eaves were falling away, that crumbled shutters were sagging from loosened hinges, that odd scraps of hemp sacking or oil cloth were stuffed into windows where panes were missing. When I stepped on the floor of the porch, I felt the rotting boards give way under my feet.

After thundering vainly on the door, I descended the steps, and followed the beaten path that led round the west wing of the house. When I had passed an old boxwood tree at the corner, I saw a woman and a boy of nine years or so come out of a shed, which I took to be the smokehouse, and begin to gather chips from the woodpile. The woman carried a basket made of splits on her arm, and while she stooped to fill this, she talked to the child in a soft musical voice. Then, at a sound that I made, she put the basket aside, and rising to her feet, faced me in the pallid light from the sky. Her head was thrown back, and over her dress of some dark calico, a tattered gray shawl clung to her figure. That was thirty years ago; I am not young any longer; I have been in many countries since then, and looked on many women; but her face, with that wan light on it, is the last one I shall forget in my life. Beauty! Why, that woman will be beautiful when she is a skeleton, was the thought that flashed into my mind.

She was very tall, and so thin that her flesh seemed faintly luminous, as if an inward light pierced the transparent substance. It was the beauty, not of earth, but of triumphant spirit. Perfection, I suppose, is the rarest thing we achieve in this world of incessant compromise with inferior forms; yet the woman who stoop there in that ruined place appeared to me to have stepped straight out of legend or allegory. The contour of her face was Italian in its pure oval; her hair swept in wings of dusk above her clear forehead; and, from the faintly shadowed hollows beneath her brows, the eyes that looked at me were purple-black, like dark pansies.

"I had given you up," she began in a low voice, as if she were afraid of being overheard. "You are the doctor?"

"Yes, I am the doctor. I took the wrong road and lost my way. Are you Mrs. Jordan?"

She bowed her head. "Mrs. Alan Jordan. There are three Mrs. Jordans besides myself. My husband's grandmother and the wives of his two uncles."

"And it is your husband who is ill?"

"My husband, yes. I wrote a few days ago to Doctor Carstairs." (Thirty years ago Carstairs, of Baltimore, was the leading alienist in the country.) "He is coming tomorrow morning; but last night my husband was so restless that I sent for you today." Her rich voice, vibrating with suppressed feeling, made me think of stained glass windows and low organ music.

"Before we go in," I asked, "will you tell me as much as you can?"

Instead of replying to my request, she turned and laid her hand on the boy's shoulder. "Take the chips to Aunt Agatha, Benjamin," she said, "and tell her that the doctor has come."

While the child picked up the basket and ran up the sunken steps to the door, she watched him with breathless anxiety. Not until he had disappeared into the hall did she lift her eyes to my face again. Then, without answering my question, she murmured, with a sigh which was like the voice of that autumn evening, "We were once happy here." She was trying, I realized, to steel her heart against the despair that threatened it.

My gaze swept the obscure horizon, and returned to the mouldering woodpile where we were standing. The yellow - green had faded from the sky, and the only light came from the house where a few scattered lamps were burning. Through the open door I could see the hall, as bare as if the house were empty, and the spiral staircase which crawled to the upper story. A fine old place once, but repulsive now in its abject decay, like some young blood of former days who has grown senile.

"Have you managed to wring a living out of the land?" I asked, because I could think of no words that were less compassionate.

"At first a poor one," she answered slowly. "We worked hard, harder than any negro in the fields, to keep things together, but we were happy. Then three years ago this illness came, and after that everything went against us. In the beginning it was simply brooding, a kind of melancholy, and we tried to ward it off by pretending that it was not real, that we imagined it. Only of late, when it became so much worse, have we admitted the truth, have we faced the reality—"

This passionate murmur, which had almost the effect of a chant rising out of the loneliness, was addressed, not to me, but to some abstract and implacable power. While she uttered it her composure was like the tranquility of the dead. She did not lift her hand to hold her shawl, which was slipping unnoticed from her shoulders, and her eyes, so like dark flowers in their softness, did not leave my face.

"If you will tell me all, perhaps I may be able to help you," I said.

"But you know our story," she responded. " You must have heard it."

"Then it is true? Heredity, intermarriage, insanity?"

She did not wince at the bluntness of my speech. "My husband's grandfather is in an asylum, still living after almost thirty years. His father – my husband's, I mean – died there a few years ago. Two of his uncles are there. When it began I don't know, or how far back it reaches. We have never talked of it. We have tried always to forget it – Even now I cannot put the thing into words – My husband's mother died of a broken heart, but the grandmother and the two others are still living. You will see them when you go into the house. They are old women now, and they feel nothing."

"And there have been other cases?"

"I do not know. Are not four enough?"

"Do you know if it has assumed always the same form?" I was trying to be as brief as I could.

She flinched, and I saw that her unnatural calm was shaken at last. "The same, I believe. In the beginning there is melancholy, moping, Grandmother calls it, and then–" She flung out her arms with a despairing gesture, and I was reminded again of some tragic figure of legend.

"I know, I know," I was young, and in spite of my pride, my voice trembled. "Has there been in any case partial recovery, recurring at intervals?"

"In his grandfather's case, yes. In the others none. With them it has been hopeless from the beginning."

"And Carstairs is coming?"

"In the morning. I should have waited, but last night—" Her voice broke, and she drew the tattered shawl about her with a shiver. "Last night something happened. Something happened," she repeated, and could not go on. Then, collecting her strength with an effort which made her tremble like a blade of grass in the wind, she continued more quickly, "Today he has been better. For the first time he has slept, and I have been able to leave him. Two of the hands from the fields are in the room." Her tone changed suddenly, and a note of energy passed into it. Some obscure resolution brought a tinge of color to her pale cheek. "I must know," she added, "if this is as hopeless as all the others."

I took a step toward the house. "Carstairs's opinion is worth as much as that of any man living," I answered.

"But will he tell me the truth?"

I shook my head. "He will tell you what he thinks. No man's judgment is infallible."

Turning away from me, she moved with an energetic step to the house. As I followed her into the hall the threshold creaked under my tread, and I was visited by an apprehension, or, if you prefer, by a superstitious dread of the floor above. Oh, I got over that kind of thing before I was many years older; though in the end I gave up medicine, you know, and turned to literature as a safer outlet for a suppressed imagination.

But the dread was there at that moment, and it was not lessened by the glimpse I caught, at the foot of the spiral staircase, of a scantily furnished room, where three lean black-robed figures, as impassive as the Fates, were grouped in front of a wood fire. They were doing something with their hands. Knitting, crocheting, or plaiting straw?

At the head of the stairs the woman stopped and looked back at me. The light from the kerosene lamp on the wall fell over her, and I was struck afresh not only by the alien splendour of her beauty, but even more by the look of consecration, of impassioned fidelity that illumined her face.

"He is very strong," she said in a whisper. "Until this trouble came on him he had never had a day's illness in his life. We hoped that hard work, not having time to brood, might save us; but it has only brought the thing we feared sooner."

There was a question in her eyes, and I responded in the same subdued tone. "His health, you say, is good?" What else was there for me to ask when I understood everything?

A shudder ran through her frame. "We used to think that a blessing, but now—" She broke off and then added in a lifeless voice, "We keep two field hands in the room day and night, lest one should forget to watch the fire, or fall asleep."

A sound came from a room at the end of the hall, and, without finishing her sentence, she moved swiftly toward the closed door. The apprehension, the dread, or whatever you choose to call it, was so strong upon me, that I was seized by an impulse to turn and retreat down the spiral staircase. Yes, I know why some men turn cowards in battle.

"I have come back, Alan," she said in a voice that wrung my heartstrings.

The room was dimly lighted; and for a minute after I entered, I could see nothing clearly except the ruddy glow of the wood fire in front of which two negroes were seated on low wooden stools. They had kindly faces, these men; there was a primitive humanity in their features, which might have been modeled out of the dark earth of the fields.

Looking round the next minute, I saw that a young man was sitting away from the fire, huddled over in a ctretonne-covered chair with a high back and deep wings. At our entrance the negroes glanced up with surprise; but the man in the winged chair neither lifted his head nor turned his eyes in our direction. He sat there, lost within the impenetrable wilderness of the insane, as remote from us and from the sound of our voices as if he were the inhabitant of an invisible world. His head was sunk forward; his eyes were staring fixedly at some image we could not see; his fingers, moving restlessly, were plaiting and unplaiting the fringe of a plaid shawl. Distraught as he was, he still possessed the dignity of mere physical perfection. At his full height he must have measured not under six feet three; his hair was the color of ripe wheat, and his eyes, in spite of their fixed gaze, were as blue as the sky after rain. And this was only the beginning, I realized. With that constitution, that physical frame, he might live to be ninety.

"Alan!" breathed his wife again in her pleading murmur.

If he heard her voice, he gave no sign of it. Only when she crossed the room and bent over his chair, he put out his hand, with a gesture of irritation, and pushed her away, as if she were a veil of smoke which came between him and the object at which he was looking. Then his hand fell back to its old place, and he resumed his mechanical plaiting of the fringe.

The woman lifted her eyes to mine. "His father did that for twenty years," she said in a whisper that was scarcely more than a sigh of anguish.

When I had made my brief examination, we left the room as we had come, and descended the stairs together. The three old women were still sitting in front of the wood fire. I do not think they had moved since we went upstairs; but, as we reached the hall below, one of them, the youngest, I imagine, rose from her chair, and came out to join us. She was crocheting something soft and small, an infant's sacque, I perceived as she approached, of pink wool. The ball had rolled from her lap as she stood up, and it trailed after her now, like a woolen rose, on the bare floor. When the skein pulled at her, she turned back and stooped to pick up the ball, which she rewound with caressing fingers. Good God, an infant's sacque in that house!

"Is it the same thing?" she asked.

"Hush!" responded the younger woman kindly. Turning to me she added, "We cannot talk here," and opening the door, passed out on the porch. Not until we had reached the lawn, and walked in silence to where my buggy stood beneath an old locust tree, did she speak again.

Then she said only, "You know now?"

"Yes, I know," I replied, averting my eyes from her face while I gave my directions as briefly as I could. "I will leave an opiate," I said. "Tomorrow, if Carstairs should not come, send for me again. If he does come," I added, "I will talk to him and see you afterward."

"Thank you," she answered gently; and taking the bottle from my hand, she turned away and walked quickly back to the house.

I watched her as long as I could; and then getting into my buggy, I turned my mare's head toward the woods, and drove by moonlight, past Buzzard's Tree and over the Old Stage Road, to my home. "I will see Carstairs tomorrow," was my last thought that night before I slept.

But, after all, I saw Carstairs only for a minute as he was taking the train. Life at its beginning and its end had filled my morning; and when at last I reached the little station, Carstairs had paid his visit, and was waiting on the platform for the approaching express. At first he showed a disposition to question me about the shooting, but as soon as I was able to make my errand clear, his jovial face clouded.

"So you've been there?" he said. "They didn't tell me. An interesting case, if it were not for that poor woman. Incurable, I'm afraid, when you consider the predisposing causes. The race is pretty well deteriorated, I suppose. God! what isolation! I've advised her to send him away. There are three others, they tell me, at Staunton."

The train came; he jumped on it, and was whisked away while I gazed after him. After all, I was none the wiser because of the great reputation of Carstairs.

All that day I heard nothing more from Jordan's End; and then, early next morning, the same decrepit negro brought me a message.

"Young Miss, she tole me ter ax you ter come along wid me jes'ez soon ez you kin git ready."

"I'll start at once, Uncle, and I'll take you with me."

My mare and buggy stood at the door. All I needed to do was to put on my overcoat, pick up my hat, and leave word, for a possible patient, that I should return before noon. I knew the road now, and I told myself, as I set out, that I would make as quick a trip as I could. For two nights I had been haunted by the memory of that man in the armchair, plaiting and unplaiting the fringe of the plaid shawl. And his father had done that, the woman had told me, for twenty years!

It was a brown autumn morning, raw, windless, with an overcast sky and a peculiar illusion of nearness about the distance. A high wind had blown all night, but at dawn it had dropped suddenly, and now there was not so much as a ripple in the broomsedge. Over the fields, when we came out of the woods, the thin trails of blue smoke were as motionless as cobwebs. The lawn surrounding the house looked smaller than it had appeared to me in the twilight, as if the barren fields had drawn closer since my last visit. Under the trees, where the few sheep were browsing, the piles of leaves lay in windrifts along the sunken walk and against

the wings of the house.

When I knocked the door was opened immediately by one of the old women, who held a streamer of black cloth or rusty crape in her hands.

"You may go straight upstairs," she croaked; and, without waiting for an explanation, I entered the hall quickly, and ran up the stairs.

The door of the room was closed, and I opened it noiselessly, and stepped over the threshold. My first sensation, as I entered, was one of cold. Then I saw that the windows were wide open, and that the room seemed to be full of people, though, as I made out presently, there was no one there except Alan Jordan's wife, her little son, the two old aunts, and an aged crone of a negress. On the bed there was something under a yellowed sheet of fine linen (what the negress call "a burial sheet," I suppose), which had been handed down from some more affluent generation.

When I went over, after a minute, and turned down one corner of the covering, I saw that my patient of the other evening was dead. Not a line of pain marred his features, not a thread of gray dimmed the wheaten gold of his hair. So he must have looked, I thought, when she first loved him. He had gone from life, not old, enfeebled and repulsive, but enveloped still in the romantic illusion of their passion.

As I entered, the two old women, who had been fussing about the bed, drew back to make way for me, but the witch of a negress did not pause in the weird chant, an incantation of some sort, which she was mumbling. From the rag carpet in front of the empty fireplace, the boy, with his father's hair and his mother's eyes, gazed at me silently, broodingly, as if I were trespassing; and by the open window, with her eyes on the ashen November day, the young wife stood as motionless as a statue. While I looked at her a redbird flew out of the boughs of a cedar, and she followed it with her eyes.

"You sent for me?" I said to her.

She did not turn. She was beyond the reach of my voice, of any voice, I imagine; but one of the palsied old women answered my question.

"He was like this when we found him this morning," she said. "He had a bad night, and Judith and the two hands were up with him until daybreak. Then he seemed to fall asleep, and Judith sent the hands, turn about, to get their breakfast."

While she spoke my eyes were on the bottle I had left there. Two nights ago it had been full, and now it stood empty, without a cork, on the mantelpiece. They had not even thrown it away. It was typical of the pervading inertia of the place that the bottle should still be standing there awaiting my visit.

For an instant the shock held me speechless; when at last I found my voice it was to ask mechanically.

"When did it happen?"

The old woman who had spoken took up the story. "Nobody knows. We have not touched him. No one but Judith has gone near him." Her words trailed off into unintelligible muttering.

If she had ever had her wits about her, I dare say fifty years at Jordan's End had unsettled them completely.

I turned to the woman at the window. Against the gray sky and the black intersecting branches of the cedar, her head, with its austere perfection, was surrounded by that visionary air of legend. So Antigone might have looked on the day of her sacrifice, I reflected. I had never seen a creature who appeared so withdrawn, so detached, from all human associations. It was as if some spiritual isolation divided her from her kind.

"I can do nothing," I said.

For the first time she looked at me, and her eyes were unfathomable. "No, you can do nothing," she answered. "He is safely dead."

The negress was still crooning on; the other old women were fussing helplessly. It was impossible in their presence, I felt, to put in words the thing I had to say.

"Will you come downstairs with me?" I asked. "Outside of this house?"

Turning quietly, she spoke to the boy. "Run out and play, dear. He would have wished it."

Then, without a glance toward the bed, or the old women gathered about it, she followed me over the threshold, down the stairs, and out on the deserted lawn. The ashen day could not touch her, I saw then. She was either so remote from it, or so completely a part of it, that she was impervious to its sadness. Her white face did not become more pallid as the light struck it; her tragic eyes did not grow deeper; her frail figure under the thin shawl did not shiver in the raw air. She felt nothing, I realized suddenly.

Wrapped in that silence as in a cloak, she walked across the windrifts of leaves to where my mare was waiting. Her step was so slow, so unhurried, that I remember thinking she moved like one who had all eternity before her. Oh, one has strange impressions, you know, at such moments!

In the middle of the lawn, where the trees had been stripped bare in the night, and the leaves were piled in long mounds like double graves, she stopped and looked in my face. The air was so still that the whole place might have been in a trance or asleep. Not a branch moved, not a leaf rustled on the ground, not a sparrow twittered in the ivy; and even the few sheep stood motionless, as if they were under a spell. Farther away, beyond the sea of broomsedge, where no wind stirred, I saw the flat desolation of the landscape. Nothing moved on the earth, but high above, under the leaden clouds, a buzzard was sailing.

I moistened my lips before I spoke. "God knows I want to help you!" At the back of my brain a hideous question was drumming. How had it happened? Could she have killed him? Had that delicate creature nerved her will to the unspeakable act? It was incredible. It was inconceivable. And yet...

"The worst is over," she answered quietly, with that tearless agony which is so much more terrible than any outburst of grief. "Whatever happens, I can never go through the worst again. Once in the beginning he wanted to die. His great fear was that he might live too long, until it was too late to save himself. I made him wait then. I held him back by a promise."

So she had killed him, I thought. Then she went on steadily, after a minute, and I doubted again.

"Thank God, it was easier for him than he feared it would be," she murmured.

No, it was not conceivable. He must have bribed one of the negroes. But who had stood by and watched without intercepting? Who had been in the room? Well, either way! "I will do all I can to help you," I said.

Her gaze did not waver. "There is so little that any one can do now," she responded, as if she had not understood what I meant. Suddenly, without the warning of a sob, a cry of despair went out of her, as if it were torn from her breast. "He was my life," she cried, "and I must go on! "

So full of agony was the sound that it seemed to pass like a gust of wind over the broomsedge. I waited until the emptiness had opened and closed over it. Then I asked as quietly as I could:

"What will you do now?"

She collected herself with a shudder of pain. "As long as the old people live, I am tied here. I must bear it out to the end. When they die, I shall go away and find work. I am sending my boy to school. Doctor Carstairs will look after him, and he will help me when the time comes. While my boy needs me, there is no release."

While I listened to her, I knew that the question on my lips would never be uttered. I should always remain ignorant of the truth. The thing I feared most, standing there alone with her, was that some accident might solve the mystery before I could escape. My eyes left her face and wandered over the dead leaves at our feet. No, I had nothing to ask her.

"Shall I come again?" That was all.

She shook her head. "Not unless I send for you. If I need you, I will send for you," she answered; but in my heart I knew that she would never send for me.

I held out my hand, but she did not take it; and I felt that she meant me to understand, by her refusal, that she was beyond all consolation and all companionship. She was nearer to the bleak sky and the deserted fields than she was to her kind.

As she turned away, the shawl slipped from her shoulders to the dead leaves over which she was walking; but she did not stoop to recover it, nor did I make a movement to follow her. Long after she had entered the house I stood there, gazing down on the garment that she had dropped. Then climbing into my buggy, I drove slowly across the field and into the woods.

Unit 2
William Faulkner (1897–1962)
威廉·福克纳

作者简介

威廉·福克纳，美国“南方文学”的代表作家，生于密西西比州新奥尔巴尼(New Albany)的一个没落贵族家庭，后随家迁居奥克斯福(Oxford)。10岁时他就开始阅读莎士比亚、巴尔扎克和康拉德。福克纳在中学时代就迷上诗歌，并在就读于耶鲁大学的好友斯通(Phil Stone)的帮助和指导下，开始系统阅读。他认真研究了19世纪英国浪漫主义诗人和法国象征主义诗歌，这不仅对他的诗歌而且对他的小说创作裨益匪浅。1918年他加入加拿大皇家飞行队，但训练还未结束就签订了停战协议。退伍回乡后，他作为“特殊学生”进入密西西比大学，不到一年又退学。1924年，福克纳发表第一部诗集《大理石牧神》(*The Marble Faun*)后，动身去欧洲旅行，途经新奥尔良时结识了安德森(Sherwood Anderson)并在他的帮助下发表了第一部小说《士兵的报酬》(*Soldier's Pay*, 1926)。这部典型的“迷惘的一代”型作品并不成功。在安德森的影响下，他从诗歌转向小说，而且还把注意力和创作热情集中在他最熟悉的美国南方。出版《蚊群》(*Mosquitoes*, 1927)之后，福克纳以“邮票般大小的故乡”为蓝图，虚构了著名的“约克纳帕塔法县”(Yoknapatawpha County)，开始了规模宏大、人物众多、时代漫长的“约克纳帕塔法”世系小说创作，其焦点是反映南方庄园文学传统以及现代文化和种族思想撞击下的家族问题，再现了美国南方两百多年社会变迁和家族盛衰的历史文化进程，提供了研究旧南方家庭生活、社会制度及家族文化的史诗。他的主要作品有《萨多里斯》(*Sartoris*, 1929)、《喧哗与骚动》(*The Sound and the Fury*, 1929)、《我弥留之际》(*As I Lay Dying*, 1930)、《八月之光》(*Light in August*, 1932)、《押沙龙！押沙龙！》(*Absalom, Absalom!* 1936)和《去吧，摩西》(*Go Down, Moses*, 1942)等。福克纳还在艺术手法上进行革新，运用“意识流”、“多角度叙述”、“时序倒错”、“叠错重复结构”、“象征隐喻”和“神话暗指”等手法，通过晦涩、朦胧、冗长、生硬的语言来达到特殊的诗学效果。他荣获1949年“诺贝尔文学奖”、1954年和1962年的“普利策奖”等。他的作品还包括《没有被征服的》(*The Unvanquished*, 1938)、《坟墓的闯入者》(*Intruder in the Dust*, 1948)、《修女安魂曲》(*Requiem For a Nun*, 1951)、《寓言》(*A Fable*,1954)、《掠夺者》(*The Reivers*, 1962)和被称为“斯诺普斯”三部曲(*Snopes Trilogy*)的《村子》(*The Hamlet*, 1940)、《小镇》(*The Town*, 1957)和《大宅》(*The Mansion*, 1959)。福克纳创作了19部长篇小说、一百多篇短篇小说、7部诗集。他在叙事内容和叙事策略方面的大胆创新为他赢得了世界文学巨匠的美誉。

作品导读

Barn Burning, published in 1938, is a story of the Snopeses, a poor white family who appears in a number of Faulkner's narratives of fictional Yoknapatawpha County. In this particular story, the boy named Colonel Sartoris (Sarty) Snopes struggles to revolt against his father Abner, a corrupt and violent man who avenges himself on socially established whites by burning their barns and carrying out other acts of contempt. The story opens with Abner being driven out of town after burning down a neighboring farmer's barn. The neighbor is able to save his animals but not the barn. No palpable proof can point to Abner as the culprit, which allows him to evade the usually severe punishment for such a grave crime. The Snopes family is ordered to move to begin life anew, but Abner cannot seem to control his pyromania and hatred for society. After his expulsion, Abner finds work as a tenant farmer in the employ of Major de Spain and his wife Lula. Shortly after arriving at his new house, Abner visits Major de Spain's house and tracks horse droppings on a blond rug. Major de Spain orders Abner to clean the rug, which he in turn directs his daughters to do, and they clean it so incompetently that it is damaged beyond repair. Major de Spain levies on Abner a fine of 20 bushels of corn against the price of the rug. At court, a Justice of the Peace reduces the fine to 10 bushels of corn. Feeling once again wronged, Abner makes preparations to light fire to Major de Spain's barn. Sarty warns Major de Spain of his father's intentions to burn down his barn and then flees. He is soon overtaken by Major de Spain on his horse and jumps into the ditch to get out of the way. The young Sartoris then hears the sound of three gun shots, perhaps indicating his father's murder and potentially that of his older brother, who was his father's accomplice. (However, as Faulkner often does, he makes references to the characters in a later work, revealing that neither the father nor the brother was killed.) Profoundly affected by his father's legacy, the boy does not return to his family but continues on with his life alone. The conflict of the story, centered on the boy's consciousness, is between his natural allegiance to the father and his aspiration toward standards of truth and justice. This novelette comes from the mid-point of William Faulkner's career and finds its creator in consummate control of the modernist devices that he had brought to American prose: stream-of-consciousness narration, decadent and even culturally degenerate settings, extended sentences – interrupted by qualifying clauses – that give the effect of continuously suspended or deferred resolution of the action, and images of extreme violence.

作品选读

Barn Burning

The Store in which the Justice of the Peace's court was sitting smelled of cheese. The boy, crouched on his nail keg at the back of the crowded room, knew he smelled cheese, and more: from where he sat he could see the ranked shelves close-packed with the solid, squat, dynamic shapes of tin cans whose labels his stomach read, not from the lettering which meant nothing to his mind but from the scarlet devils and the silver curve of fish – this, the cheese which he knew he smelled and the hermetic meat which his intestines believes he smelled coming in intermittent gusts momentary and brief between the other constant one, the smell and sense just a little of fear because mostly of despair and grief, the old fierce pull of blood. He could not see the table where the Justice sat and before which his father and his father's enemy (*our enemy he thought in that despair; ourn! mine and hisn both! He's my father*!) stood, but he could hear them, the two of them that is, because his father had said no word yet:

"But what proof have you, Mr. Harris?"

"I told you. The hog got into my corn. I caught it up and sent it back to him. He had no fence that would hold it. I told him so, warned him. The next time I put the hog in my pen. When he came to get it I gave him enough wire to patch up his pen. The next time I put the hog up and kept it. I rode down to his house and saw the wire I gave him still rolled on to the spool in his yard. I told him he could have the hog when he paid me a dollar pound fee. That evening a nigger came with the dollar and got the hog. He was a strange nigger. He said, 'He say to tell you wood and hay kin burn.' I said, 'What?' 'That whut he say to tell you,' the nigger said. 'Wood and hay kin burn.' That night my barn burned. I got the stock out but I lost the barn."

"Where is the nigger? Have you got him?"

"He was a strange nigger, I tell you. I don't know what became of him."

"But that's not proof. Don't you see that's not proof?"

"Get that boy up here. He knows." For a moment the boy thought too that the man meant his older brother until Harris said, "Not him. The little one. The boy," and, crouching, small for his age, small and wiry like his father, in patched and faded jeans even too small for him, with straight, uncombed, brown hair and eyes gray and wild as storm scud, he saw the men between himself and the table part and become a lane of grim faces, at the end of which he saw the Justice, a shabby, collarless, graying man in spectacles, beckoning him. He felt no floor under his bare feet; he seemed to walk beneath the palpable weight of the grim turning faces. His father, stiff in his black Sunday coat donned not for the trial but for the moving, did not even look at him. *He aims for me to lie*, he thought, again with that frantic grief and despair. *And I will have to do hit*.

"What's your name, boy?" the Justice said.

"Colonel Sartoris Snopes," the boy whispered.

"Hey?" the Justice said. "Talk louder. Colonel Sartoris? I reckon anybody named for Colonel Sartoris in this country can't help but tell the truth, can they?" The boy said nothing. *Enemy! Enemy!* he thought; for a moment he could not even see, could not see that the Justice's face was kindly nor discern that his voice was troubled when he spoke to the man named Harris: "Do you want me to question the boy?" But he could hear, and during those subsequent long seconds while there was absolutely no sound in the crowded little room save that of quiet and intent breathing it was as if he had swung outward at the end of a grape vine, over a ravine, and at the top of the swing had been caught in a prolonged instant of mesmerized gravity, weightless in time.

"No!" Harris said violently, explosively. "Damnation! Send him out of here!" Now time, the fluid world, rushed beneath him again, the voices coming to him again through the smell of cheese and sealed meat, the fear and despair and the old grief of blood:

"This case is closed. I can't find against you, Snopes, but I can give you advice. Leave this country and don't come back to it."

His father spoke for the first time, his voice cold and harsh, level, without emphasis: "I aim to. I don't figure to stay in a country among people who..." he said something unprintable and vile, addressed to no one.

"That'll do," the Justice said, "Take your wagon and get out of this country before dark. Case dismissed."

His father turned, and he followed the stiff black coat, the wiry figure walking a little stiffly from where a Confederate provost's man's musket ball had taken him in the heel on a stolen horse thirty years ago, followed the two backs now, since his older brother had appeared from somewhere in the crowd, no taller than the father but thicker, chewing tobacco steadily, between the two lines of grim-faced men and out of the store and across the worn gallery and down the sagging steps and among the dogs and half-grown boys in the mild May dust, where as he passed a voice hissed:

"Barn burner!"

Again he could not see, whirling: there was a face in a red haze, moonlike, bigger than the full moon, the owner of it half again his size, he leaping in the red haze toward the face, feeling no blow, feeling no shock when his head struck the earth, scrabbling up and leaping again, feeling no blow this time either and tasting no blood, scrabbling up to see the other boy in full flight and himself already leaping into pursuit as his father's hand jerked him back, the harsh, cold voice speaking above him: "Go get in the wagon."

It stood in a grove of locusts and mulberries across the road. His two hulking sisters in their Sunday dresses and his mother and her sister in calico and sunbonnets were already in it, sitting on and among the sorry residue of the dozen and more movings which even the boy could remember – the battered stove, the broken beds and chairs, the clock inlaid with mother-

of-pearl, which would not run, stopped at some fourteen minutes past two o'clock of a dead and forgotten day and time, which had been his mother's dowry. She was crying, though when she saw him she drew her sleeve across her face and began to descend from the wagon. "Get back," the father said.

"He's hurt. I got to get some water and wash his..."

"Get back in the wagon," his father said. He got in too, over the tail-gate. His father mounted to the seat where the older brother already sat and struck the gaunt mules two savage blows with the peeled willow, but without heat. It was not even sadistic; it was exactly that same quality which in later years would cause his descendants to over-run the engine before putting a motor car into motion, striking and reining back in the same movement. The wagon went on, the store with its quiet crowd of grimly watching men dropped behind; a curve in the road hid it. *Forever* he thought. *Maybe he's done satisfied now, now that he has*...stopping himself, not to say it aloud even to himself. His mother's hand touched his shoulder.

"Does hit hurt?" she said.

"Naw," he said. "Hit don't hurt. Lemme be."

"Can't you wipe some of the blood off before hit dries?"

"I'll wash tonight," he said. "Lemme be, I tell you."

The wagon went on. He did not know where they were going. None of them ever did or ever asked, because it was always somewhere, always a house of sorts waiting for them a day or two days or even three days away. Likely his father had already arranged to make a crop on another farm before he...Again he had to stop himself. He (the father) always did. There was something about his wolflike independence and even courage when the advantage was at least neutral which impressed strangers, as if they got from his latent ravening ferocity not so much a sense of dependability as a feeling that his ferocious conviction in the rightness of his own actions would be of advantage to all whose interest lay with his.

That night they camped, in a grove of oaks and beeches where a spring ran. The nights were still cool and they had a fire against it, of a rail lifted from a nearby fence and cut into lengths – a small fire, neat, niggard almost, a shrewd fire; such fires were his father's habit and custom always, even in freezing weather. Older, the boy might have remarked this and wondered why not a big one; why should not a man who had not only seen the waste and extravagance of war, but who had in his blood an inherent voracious prodigality with material not his own, have burned everything in sight? Then he might have gone a step farther and thought that that was the reason: that niggard blaze was the living fruit of nights passed during those four years in the woods hiding from all men, blue or gray, with his strings of horses (captured horses, he called them). And older still, he might have divined the true reason: that the element of fire spoke to some deep mainspring of his father's being, as the element of steel or of powder spoke to other men, as the one weapon for the preservation of integrity, else breath were not worth the breathing, and hence to be regarded with respect and used with discretion.

But he did not think this now and he had seen those same niggard blazes all his life. He merely ate his supper beside it and was already half asleep over his iron plate when his father called him, and once more he followed the stiff back, the stiff and ruthless limp, up the slope and on to the starlit road where, turning, he could see his father against the stars but without face or depth – a shape black, flat, and bloodless as though cut from tin in the iron folds of the frockcoat which had not been made for him, the voice harsh like tin and without heat like tin:

"You were fixing to tell them. You would have told him." He didn't answer. His father struck him with the flat of his hand on the side of the head, hard but without heat, exactly as he had struck the two mules at the store, exactly as he would strike either of them with any stick in order to kill a horse fly, his voice still without heat or anger: "You're getting to be a man. You got to learn. You got to learn to stick to your own blood or you ain't going to have any blood to stick to you. Do you think either of them, any man there this morning, would? Don't you know all they wanted was a chance to get at me because they knew I had them beat? Eh?" Later, twenty years later, he was to tell himself, "If I had said they wanted only truth, justice, he would have hit me again." But now he said nothing. He was not crying. He just stood there. "Answer me," his father said.

"Yes," he whispered. His father turned.

"Get on to bed. We'll be there tomorrow."

Tomorrow they were there. In the early afternoon the wagon stopped before a paintless two-room house identical almost with the dozen others it had stopped before even in the boy's ten years, and again, as on the other dozen occasions, his mother and aunt got down and began to unload the wagon, although his two sisters and his father and brother had not moved.

"Likely hit ain't fitten for hawgs," one of the sisters said.

"Nevertheless, fit it will and you'll hog it and like it," his father said. "Get out of them chairs and help your Ma unload."

The two sisters got down, big, bovine, in a flutter of cheap ribbons; one of them drew from the jumbled wagon bed a battered lantern, the other a worn broom. His father handed the reins to the older son and began to climb stiffly over the wheel. "When they get unloaded, take the team to the barn and feed them." Then he said, and at first the boy thought he was still speaking to his brother: "Come with me."

"Me?" he said.

"Yes," his father said. "You."

"Abner," his mother said. His father paused and looked back – the harsh level stare beneath the shaggy, graying, irascible brows.

"I reckon I'll have a word with the man that aims to begin tomorrow owning me body and soul for the next eight months."

They went back up the road. A week ago – or before last night, that is – he would have asked where they were going, but not now. His father had struck him before last night but never before had he paused afterward to explain why; it was as if the blow and the following calm, outrageous voice still rang, repercussed, divulging nothing to him save the terrible handicap of being young, the light weight of his few years, just heavy enough to prevent his soaring free of the world as it seemed to be ordered but not heavy enough to keep him footed solid in it, to resist it and try to change the course of its events.

Presently he could see the grove of oaks and cedars and the other flowering trees and shrubs where the house would be, though not the house yet. They walked beside a fence massed with honeysuckle and Cherokee roses and came to a gate swinging open between two brick pillars, and now, beyond a sweep of drive, he saw the house for the first time and at that instant he forgot his father and the terror and despair both, and even when he remembered his father again (who had not stopped) the terror and despair did not return. Because, for all the twelve movings, they had sojourned until now in a poor country, a land of small farms and fields and houses, and he had never seen a house like this before. *Hit's big as a courthouse* he thought quietly, with a surge of peace and joy whose reason he could not have thought into words, being too young for that: *They are safe from him. People whose lives are a part of this peace and dignity are beyond his touch, he no more to them than a buzzing wasp: capable of stinging for a little moment but that's all; the spell of this peace and dignity rendering even the barns and stable and cribs which belong to it impervious to the puny flames he might contrive*...this, the peace and joy, ebbing for an instant as he looked again at the stiff black back, the stiff and implacable limp of the figure which was not dwarfed by the house, for the reason that it had never looked big anywhere and which now, against the serene columned backdrop, had more than ever that impervious quality of something cut ruthlessly from tin, depthless, as though, sidewise to the sun, it would cast no shadow. Watching him, the boy remarked the absolutely undeviating course which his father held and saw the stiff foot come squarely down in a pile of fresh droppings where a horse had stood in the drive and which his father could have avoided by a simple change of stride. But it ebbed only for a moment, though he could not have thought this into words either, walking on in the spell of the house, which he could even want but without envy, without sorrow, certainly never with that ravening and jealous rage which unknown to him walked in the ironlike black coat before him: *Maybe he will feel it too. Maybe it will even change him now from what maybe he couldn't help but be.*

They crossed the portico. Now he could hear his father's stiff foot as it came down on the boards with clocklike finality, a sound out of all proportion to the displacement of the body it bore and which was not dwarfed either by the white door before it, as though it had attained to a sort of vicious and ravening minimum not to be dwarfed by anything – the flat, wide, black hat, the formal coat of broadcloth which had once been black but which had now that friction-glazed greenish cast of the bodies of old house flies, the lifted sleeve which was too large, the lifted hand like a curled claw. The door opened so promptly that the boy knew the Negro must have been watching them all the time, an old man with neat grizzled hair, in a linen jacket, who stood barring the door with his body, saying, "Wipe yo foots, white man, fo you come in here. Major ain't home nohow."

"Get out of my way, nigger," his father said, without heat too, flinging the door back and the Negro also and entering, his hat still on his head. And now the boy saw the prints of the stiff foot on the doorsill and saw them appear on the pale rug behind the machinelike deliberation of the foot which seemed to bear(or transmit) twice the weight which the body compassed. The Negro was shouting "Miss Lula! Miss Lula! " somewhere behind them, then the boy, deluged as though by a warm wave by a suave turn of carpeted stair and a pendant glitter of chandeliers and a mute gleam of gold frames, heard the swift feet and saw her too, a lady – perhaps he had never seen her like before either – in a gray, smooth gown with lace at the throat and an apron tied at the waist and the sleeves turned back, wiping cake or biscuit dough from her hands with a towel as she came up the hall, looking not at his father at all but at the tracks on the blond rug with an expression of incredulous amazement.

"I tried," the Negro cried. "I tole him to..."

"Will you please go away?" she said in a shaking voice. "Major de Spain is not at home. Will you please go away?"

His father had not spoken again. He did not speak again. He did not even look at her. He just stood stiff in the center of the rug, in his hat, the shaggy iron-gray brows twitching slightly above the pebble-colored eyes as he appeared to examine the house with brief deliberation. Then with the same deliberation he turned; the boy watched him pivot on the good leg and saw the stiff foot drag round the arc of the turning, leaving a final long and fading smear. His father never looked at it, he never once looked down at the rug. The Negro held the door. It closed behind them, upon the hysteric and indistinguishable woman-wail. His father stopped at the top of the steps and scraped his boot clean on the edge of it. At the gate he stopped again. He stood for a moment, planted stiffly on the stiff foot, looking back at the house. "Pretty and white, ain't it?" he said. "That's sweat. Nigger sweat. Maybe it ain't white enough yet to suit him. Maybe he wants to mix some white sweat with it."

Two hours later the boy was chopping wood behind the house within which his mother and aunt and the two sisters (the mother and aunt, not the two girls, he knew that; even at this distance and muffled by walls the flat loud voices of the two girls emanated an incorrigible idle inertia) were setting up the stove to prepare a meal, when he heard the hooves and saw the linen-clad man on a fine sorrel mare, whom he recognized even before he saw the rolled rug in front of the Negro youth following on a fat bay carriage horse – a suffused, angry face vanishing, still at full gallop, beyond the corner of the house where his father and brother were sitting in the two tilted chairs; and a moment later, almost before he could have put the axe down, he heard the hooves again and watched the sorrel mare go back out of the yard, already galloping again. Then his father began to shout one of the sisters' names, who presently emerged backward from the kitchen door dragging the rolled rug along the ground by one end while the other sister walked behind it.

"If you ain't going to tote, go on and set up the wash pot," the father said.

"You, Sarty! " the second shouted. "Set up the wash pot! " His father appeared at the door, framed against that shabbiness, as he had been against that other bland perfection, impervious to either, the mother's anxious face at his shoulder.

"Go on," the father said, "Pick it up." The two sisters stooped, broad, lethargic; stooping, they presented an incredible expanse of pale cloth and a flutter of tawdry ribbons.

"If I thought enough of a rug to have to git hit all the way from France I wouldn't keep hit where folks coming in would have to tromp on hit," the first said. They raised the rug.

"Abner," the mother said, "Let me do it."

"You go back and git dinner," his father said, "I'll tend to this."

From the woodpile through the rest of the afternoon the boy watched them, the rug spread flat in the dust beside the bubbling wash pot, the two sisters stooping over it with that profound and lethargic reluctance, while the father stood over them in turn, implacable and grim, driving them though never raising his voice again. He could smell the harsh homemade lye they were using; he saw his mother come to the door once and look toward them with an expression not anxious now but very like despair; he saw his father turn, and he fell to with the axe and saw from the corner of his eye his father raise from the ground a flattish fragment of field stone and examine it and return to the pot, and this time his mother actually spoke: "Abner, Abner, Please don't. Please, Abner."

Then he was done too. It was dusk; the whippoorwills had already begun. He could smell coffee from the room where they would presently eat the cold food remaining from the mid-afternoon meal, though when he entered the house he realized they were having coffee again probably because there was a fire on the hearth, before which the rug now lay spread over the backs of the two chairs. The tracks of his father's foot were gone. Where they had been were now long, water-cloudy scoriations resembling the sporadic course of a Lilliputian mowing machine.

It still hung there while they ate the cold food and then went to bed, scattered without order or claim up and down the two rooms, his mother in one bed, where his father would later lie, the older brother in the other, himself, the aunt, and the two sisters on pallets on the floor. But his father was not in bed yet. The last thing the boy remembered was the depthless, harsh silhouette of the hat and coat bending over the rug and it seemed to him that he had not even closed his eyes when the silhouette was standing over him, the fire almost dead behind it, the stiff foot prodding him awake. "Catch up the mule," his father said.

When he returned with the mule, his father was standing in the black door, the rolled rug over his shoulder. "Ain't you going to ride?" he said.

"No. Give me your foot."

He bent his knee into his father's hand, the wiry, surprising power flowed smoothly, rising, he rising with it, on to the mule's bare back (they had owned a saddle once; the boy could remember it though not when or where) and with the same effortlessness his father swung the rug up in front of him. Now in the starlight they retraced the afternoon's path, up the dusty road rife with honeysuckle, through the gate and up the black tunnel of the drive to the lightless house, where he sat on the mule and felt the rough warp of the rug drag across his thighs and vanish.

"Don't you want me to help?" he whispered. His father did not answer and now he heard again that stiff foot striking the hollow portico with that wooden and clocklike deliberation, that outrageous overstatement of the weight it carried. The rug, hunched, not flung (the boy could tell that even in the darkness) from his father's shoulder, struck the angle of wall and floor with a sound unbelievably loud, thunderous, then the foot again, unhurried and enormous; a light came on in the house and the boy sat, tense, breathing steadily and quietly and just a little fast, though the foot itself did not increase its beat at all, descending the steps now; now the boy could see him.

"Don't you want to ride now?" he whispered. "We kin both ride now," the light within the house altering now, flaring up and sinking. He's coming down the stairs now, he thought. He had already ridden the mule up beside the horse block; presently his father was up behind him and he doubled the reins over and slashed the mule across the neck, but before the animal could begin to trot the hard, thin arm came round him, the hard, knotted hand jerking the mule back to a walk.

In the first red rays of the sun they were in the lot, putting plow gear on the mules. This time the sorrel mare was in the lot before he heard it at all, the rider collarless and even bareheaded, trembling, speaking in a shaking voice as the woman in the house had done, his father merely looking up once before stooping again to the hame he was buckling, so that the man on the mare spoke to his stooping back:

"You must realize you have ruined that rug. Wasn't there anybody here, any of your women..." He ceased, shaking, the boy watching him, the older brother leaning now in the stable door, chewing, blinking slowly and steadily at nothing apparently. "It cost a hundred dollars. But you never had a hundred dollars. You never will. So I'm going to charge you twenty bushels of corn against your crop. I'll add it in your contract and when you come to the commissary you can sign it. That won't keep Mrs. de Spain quiet but maybe it will teach you to wipe your feet off before you enter house again."

Then he was gone. The boy looked at his father, who still had not spoken or even looked up again, who was now adjusting the logger-head in the hame.

"Pap," he said. His father looked at him – the inscrutable face, the shaggy brows beneath which the gray eyes glinted coldly. Suddenly the boy went toward him, fast, stopping as suddenly. "You done the best you could! " he cried. "If he wanted hit done different why didn't he wait and tell you how? He won't git no twenty bushels! He won't git none! We'll get hit and hide hit! I kin watch..."

"Did you put the cutter back in that straight stock like I told you?"

"No, sir," he said.

"Then go do it."

That was Wednesday. During the rest of that week he worked steadily, at what was within his scope and some which was beyond it, with an industry that did not need to be driven nor even commanded twice; he had this from his mother, with the difference that some at least of what he did he liked to do, such as splitting wood with the half-size axe which his mother and aunt had earned, or saved money somehow, to present him with at Christmas. In company with the two older women(and on one afternoon, even one of the sisters), he built pens for the shoat and the cow which were a part of his father's contract with the landlord, and one afternoon, his father being absent, gone somewhere on one of the mules, he went to the field.

They were running a middle buster now, his brother holding the plow straight while he handled the reins, and walking beside the straining mule, the rich black soil shearing cool and damp against his bare ankles, he thought *Maybe this is the end of it. Maybe even that twenty bushels that seems hard to have to pay for just a rug will be a cheap price for him to stop forever and always from being what he used to be; thinking, dreaming now, so that his brother had to speak sharply to him to mind the mule: Maybe he even won't collect the twenty bushels. Maybe it will all add up and balance and vanish – corn, rug, fire; the terror and grief, the being pulled two ways like between two teams of horses – gone, done with for ever and ever.*

Then it was Saturday; he looked up from beneath the mule he was harnessing and saw his father in the black coat and hat. "Not that," his father said, "That wagon gear." And then, two hours later, sitting in the wagon bed behind his father and brother on the seat, the wagon accomplished a final curve, and he saw the weathered paintless store with its tattered tobacco- and patent-medicine posters and the tethered wagons and saddle animals below the gallery. He mounted the gnawed steps behind his father and brother, and there again was the lane of quiet, watching faces for the three of them to walk through. He saw the man in spectacles sitting at the plank table and he did not need to be told this was a Justice of the Peace; he sent one glare of fierce, exultant, partisan defiance at the man in collar and cravat now, whom he had seen but twice before in his life, and that on a galloping horse, who now wore on his face an expression not of rage but of amazed unbelief which the boy could not have known was at the incredible circumstance of being sued by one of his own tenants, and came and stood against his father and cried at the Justice: "He ain't done it! He ain't burnt..."

"Go back to the wagon," his father said.

"Burnt?" the Justice said. "Do I understand this rug was burned too?"

"Does anybody here claim it was?" his father said, "Go back to the wagon." But he did not, he merely retreated to the rear of the room, crowded as that other had been, but not to sit down this time, instead, to stand pressing among the motionless bodies, listening to the voices:

"And you claim twenty bushels of corn is too high for the damage you did to the rug?"

"He brought the rug to me and said he wanted the tracks washed out of it. I washed the tracks out and took the rug back to him."

"But you didn't carry the rug back to him in the same condition it was in before you made the tracks on it."

His father did not answer, and now for perhaps half a minute there was no sound at all save that of breathing, the faint, steady suspiration of complete and intent listening.

"You decline to answer that, Mr. Snopes?" Again his father did not answer. "I'm going to find against you, Mr. Snopes. I'm going to find that you were responsible for the injury to Major de Spain's rug and hold you liable for it. But twenty bushels of corn seems a little high for a man in your circumstances to have to pay. Major de Spain claims it cost a hundred dollars. October corn will be worth about fifty cents. I figure that if Major de Spain can stand a ninety-five-dollar loss on something he paid cash for, you can stand a five-dollar loss you haven't earned yet. I hold you in damages to Major de Spain to the amount of ten bushels of corn over and above your contract with him, to be paid to him out of your crop at gathering time. Court adjourned."

It had taken no time hardly, the morning was but half begun. He thought they would return home and perhaps back to the field, since they were late, far behind all other farmers. But instead his father passed on behind the wagon, merely indicating with his hand for the older brother to follow with it, and crossed the road toward the blacksmith shop opposite, pressing on after his father, overtaking him, speaking, whispering up at the harsh, calm face beneath the weathered hat: "He won't git no ten bushels neither. He won't git one. We'll..." until his father glanced for an instant down at him, the face absolutely calm, the grizzled eyebrows tangled above the cold eyes, the voice almost pleasant, almost gentle:

"You think so? Well, we'll wait till October anyway."

The matter of the wagon – the setting of a spoke or two and the tightening of the tires – did not take long either, the business of the tires accomplished by driving the wagon into the spring branch behind the shop and letting it stand there, the mules nuzzling into the water from time to time, and the boy on the seat with the idle reins, looking up the slope and through the sooty tunnel of the shed where the slow hammer rang and where his father sat on an upended cypress bolt, easily, either talking or listening, still sitting there when the boy brought the dripping wagon up out of the branch and halted it before the door.

"Take them on to the shade and hitch," his father said. He did so and returned. His father and the smith and a third man squatting on his heels inside the door were talking, about crops and animals; the boy, squatting too in the ammoniac dust and hoof-parings and scales of rust, heard his father tell a long and unhurried story out of the time before the birth of the older brother even when he had been a professional horsetrader. And then his father came up beside him where he stood before a tattered last year's circus poster on the other side of the store, gazing rapt and quiet at the scarlet horses, the incredible poisings and convolutions of tulle and tights and the painted leers of comedians, and said, "It's time to eat."

But not at home. Squatting beside his brother against the front wall, he watched his father emerge from the store and produce from a paper sack a segment of cheese and divide it carefully and deliberately into three with his pocket knife and produce crackers from the same sack. They all three squatted on the gallery and ate, slowly, without talking; then in the store again, they drank from a tin dipper tepid water smelling of the cedar bucket and of living beech trees. And still they did not go home. It was a horse lot this time, a tall rail fence upon and along which men stood and sat and out of which one by one horses were led, to be walked and trotted and then cantered back and forth along the road while the slow swapping and buying went on and the sun began to slant westward, they – the three of them – watching and listening, the older brother with his muddy eyes and his steady, inevitable tobacco, the father commenting now and then on certain of the animals, to no one in particular.

It was after sundown when they reached home. They ate supper by lamplight, then, sitting on the doorstep, the boy watched the night fully accomplish, listening to the whippoorwills and the frogs, when he heard his mother's voice: "Abner! No! No! Oh, God. Oh, God. Abner!" and he rose, whirled, and saw the altered light through the door where a candle stub now burned in a bottle neck on the table and his father, still in the hat and coat, at once formal and burlesque as though dressed carefully for some shabby and ceremonial violence, emptying the reservoir of the lamp back into the five-gallon kerosene can from which it had been filled, while the mother tugged at his arm until he shifted the lamp to the other hand and flung her back, not savagely or viciously, just hard, into the wall, her hands flung out against the wall for balance, her mouth open and in her face the same quality of hopeless despair as had been in her voice. Then his father saw him standing in the door.

"Go to the barn and get that can of oil we were oiling the wagon with," he said. The boy did not move. Then he could speak.

"What..." he cried. "What are you..."

"Go get that oil," his father said. "Go."

Then he was moving, running, outside the house, toward the stable: this the old habit, the old blood which he had not been permitted to choose for himself, which had been bequeathed him willy nilly and which had run for so long (and who knew where, battening on what of outrage and savagery and lust) before it came to him. *I could keep on, he thought. I could run on and on and never look back, never need to see his face again. Only I can't. I can't,* the rusted can in his hand now, the liquid sploshing in it as he ran back to the house and into it, into the sound of his mother's weeping in the next room, and handed the can to his father.

"Ain't you going to even send a nigger?" he cried. "At least you sent a nigger before!"

This time his father didn't strike him. The hand came even faster than the blow had, the same hand which had set the can on the table with almost excruciating care flashing from the can toward him too quick for him to follow it, gripping him by the back of his shirt and on to tiptoe before he had seen it quit the can, the face stooping at him in breathless and frozen ferocity, the cold, dead voice speaking over him to the older brother who leaned against the table, chewing with that steady, curious, sidewise motion of cows:

"Empty the can into the big one and go on. I'll catch up with you."

"Better tie him up to the bedpost," the brother said.

"Do like I told you," the father said. Then the boy was moving, his bunched shirt and the

hard, bony hand between his shoulder-blades, his toes just touching the floor, across the room and into the other one, past the sisters sitting with spread heavy thighs in the two chairs over the cold hearth, and to where his mother and aunt sat side by side on the bed, the aunt's arms about his mother's shoulders.

"Hold him," the father said. The aunt made a startled movement. "Not you," the father said. "Lennie. Take hold of him. I want to see you do it." His mother took him by the wrist. "You'll hold him better than that. If he gets loose don't you know what he is going to do? He will go up yonder." He jerked his head toward the road. "Maybe I'd better tie him."

"I'll hold him," his mother whispered.

"See you do then." Then his father was gone, the stiff foot heavy and measured upon the boards, ceasing at last.

Then he began to struggle. His mother caught him in both arms, he jerking and wrenching at them. He would be stronger in the end, he knew that. But he had no time to wait for it. "Lemme go! " he cried. "I don't want to have to hit you."

"Let him go! " the aunt said. "If he don't go, before God, I am going up there myself! "

"Don't you see I can't?" his mother cried. "Sarty! Sarty! No! No! Help me, Lizzie! "

Then he was free. His aunt grasped at him but it was too late. He whirled, running, his mother stumbled forward on to her knees behind him, crying to the nearer sister: "Catch him, Net! Catch him! " But that was too late too, the sister (the sisters were twins, born at the same time, yet either of them now gave the impression of being, encompassing as much living meat and volume and weight as any other two of the family) not yet having begun to rise from the chair, her head, face, alone merely turned, presenting to him in the flying instant an astonishing expanse of young female features untroubled by any surprise even, wearing only an expression of bovine interest. Then he was out of the room, out of the house, in the mild dust of the starlit road and the heavy rifeness of honeysuckle, the pale ribbon unspooling with terrific slowness under his running feet, reaching the gate at last and turning in, running, his heart and lungs drumming, on up the drive toward the lighted house, the lighted door. He did not knock, he burst in, sobbing for breath, incapable for the moment of speech; he saw the astonished face of the Negro in the linen jacket without knowing when the Negro had appeared.

"De Spain! " he cried, panted. "Where's..." Then he saw the white man too emerging from a white door down the hall. "Barn! " he cried. "Barn! "

"What?" the white man said. "Barn?"

"Yes! " the boy cried. "Barn! "

"Catch him! " the white man shouted.

But it was too late this time too. The Negro grasped his shirt, but the entire sleeve, rotten with washing, carried away, and he was out that door too and in the drive again, and had actually never ceased to run even while he was screaming into the white man's face.

Behind him the white man was shouting, "My horse! Fetch my horse! " and he thought for an instant of cutting across the park and climbing the fence into the road, but he did not know the park nor how high the vine-massed fence might be and he dared not risk it. So he ran on down the drive, blood and breath roaring; presently he was in the road again though he could not see it. He could not hear either: the galloping mare was almost upon him before he heard her, and even then he held his course, as if the very urgency of his wild grief and need must in a moment more find him wings, waiting until the ultimate instant to hurl himself aside and into the weed-choked roadside ditch as the horse thundered past and on, for an instant in furious silhouette against the stars, the tranquil early summer night sky which, even before the shape of the horse and rider vanished, strained abruptly and violently upward: a long, swirling roar incredible and soundless, blotting the stars, and he springing up and into the road again, running again, knowing it was too late yet still running even after he heard the shot and, an instant later, two shots, pausing now without knowing he had ceased to run, crying "Pap! Pap!", running again before he knew he had begun to run, stumbling, tripping over something and scrabbling up again without ceasing to run, looking backward over his shoulder at the glare as he got up, running on among the invisible trees, panting, sobbing, "Father! Father!"

At midnight he was sitting on the crest of a hill. He did not know it was midnight and he did not know how far he had come. But there was no glare behind him now and he sat now, his back toward what he had called home for four days anyhow, his face toward the dark woods which he would enter when breath was strong again, small, shaking steadily in the chill darkness, hugging himself into the remainder of his thin, rotten shirt, the grief and despair now no longer terror and fear but just grief and despair. *Father. My father*, he thought. "He was brave!" he cried suddenly, aloud but not loud, no more than a whisper: "He was! He was in the war! He was in Colonel Sartoris' cav'ry!" not knowing that his father had gone to that war a private in the fine old European sense, wearing no uniform, admitting the authority of and giving fidelity to no man or army or flag, going to war as Malbrouck himself did: for booty – it meant nothing and less than nothing to him if it were enemy booty or his own.

The slow constellations wheeled on. It would be dawn and then sun-up after a while and he would be hungry. But that would be tomorrow and now he was only cold, and walking would cure that. His breathing was easier now and he decided to get up and go on, and then he found that he had been asleep because he knew it was almost dawn, the night almost over. He could tell that from the whippoorwills. They were everywhere now among the dark trees below him, constant and inflectioned and ceaseless, so that, as the instant for giving over to the day birds drew nearer and nearer, there was no interval at all between them. He got up. He was a little stiff, but walking would cure that too as it would the cold, and soon there would be the sun. He went on down the hill, toward the dark woods within which the liquid silver voices of the birds called unceasing – the rapid and urgent beating of the urgent and quiring heart of the late spring night. He did not look back.

Unit 3
Allen Tate (1899–1979)
艾伦·泰特

作者简介

艾伦·泰特，诗人、小说家、文艺批评家。1899年11月19日出生于肯塔基州(Kentucky)。1923年毕业于范德比尔特大学(Vanderbilt University)，与“新批评”主将兰色姆(Ransom)一起创办了《逃逸者》(*The Fugitive*)，并在该刊物上发表诗作。1925年以后，他在明尼苏达大学执教。从20世纪40年代开始，泰特在几所学院及大学教授英语，1951年他成为明尼苏达大学的英语教授，1968年退休。泰特是南方文学团体“重农派”或“逃逸者派”的重要成员，他赞成南方回归昔日的农业经济、保持传统的文化理念，抗议把所谓的工业化等同于社会的文明进步。他认为拯救南方的出路在于人们摒弃工业化、恢复传统价值观，尤其是南方自己的文化传统和宗教信仰。他也是《我将表明我的立场》(*I'll Take My Stand*)(1930年)的重要执笔者之一。他的作品深深地植根于南方的社会和文化背景中，注重形式和结构，文字的含糊和句子的断裂所造成的阅读紧张正是其作品的活力所在。他获得“博林根奖”(1956)、“布兰代斯奖”(1961)、“佛伦萨斯但丁学会金质奖”(1962)、“美国诗人学会奖”(1963)等多种奖励。泰特的主要作品包括：传记《石墙杰克逊：一位好军人》(*Stonewall Jackson: The Good Soldier*, 1928)、《杰弗逊·戴维斯兴衰记》(*Jefferson Davis: His Rise and Fall*, 1929)；诗集《蒲柏先生及其他诗歌》(*Mr. Pope and Other Poems*, 1928)、《地中海及其他诗歌》(*The Mediterranean and Other Poems*, 1936)、《诗歌精选》(*Selected Poems*, 1937)等，他的诗歌技巧完美、意象新颖。他的评论作品有《有关诗歌及思想的保守散文》(*Reactionary Essays on Poetry and Ideas, 1928–1948*,1948)、《疯狂的理性》(*Reason in Madness*,1941)、《现代社会中的学者》(*The Man of Letters in the Modern World*,1955)，这几本书中的有些文章在美国各个大学中颇具影响力。《父辈》(*The Fathers*,1938)是泰特唯一的一部长篇小说。小说以1860—1861年的弗吉尼亚为背景，表现了作者对南方即将逝去的农耕生活方式和乡野生活习俗所引起的后果的预测和忧虑。《父辈》采用南方小说常见的主题，即一个南方白人有一个没有得到公开承认的同父异母的黑人兄弟，他屡次出卖这个混血兄弟。在小说的最后，主人公莱西·巴肯选择了他的精神之父乔治·波西而背弃了他的生身之父巴肯少校，原因是莱西选择了放弃旧南方而接受现代社会的同化，这一点正是泰特相信又害怕南方也会作出的选择。小说中巴肯家族的悲剧和南方的社会、文化变革交织在一起，不仅富于历史的真实性，而且具有探究人类灵魂的深度。

作品导读

Setting just before and during the American Civil War (1861 - 1865), *The Fathers* (1938) details the tragic fall of two families joined by marriage – the Buchans, of Fairfax County and the Poseys, of Georgetown in the District of Columbia. Their violent and psychologically complex story, narrated by the elderly doctor Lacy Buchan, is intended to mirror the decline of "Old Virginia" and the rise of a new society unbound to traditional, agrarian codes.

The novel, which spans fourteen months from 1860 until 1861, is divided into three parts: "Pleasant Hill", "The Crisis", and "The Abyss". The first is set at the Fairfax County plantation of the Buchan family, modeled after the childhood home of Tate's mother. As *The Fathers* opens, sixty-five-year-old Lacy Buchan recalls his mother's death fifty years earlier, as well as the occasion of George Posey's engagement to Lacy's sister, Susan. Major Lewis Buchan, Lacy's aristocratic father, opposes the match, and here Tate establishes the story's most important conflict – between the old order, represented by the Major, and the new, represented by George Posey.

Informed by a traditional code that exists outside of himself, the Major resists change. Not so is George, who acts according to personal whims that are incomprehensible to almost everyone around him. Change does come, of course, and like a whirlwind it blows the House of Buchan down. "Why cannot life change without tangling the lives of innocent persons?" Lacy wonders. "Why do innocent persons cease their innocence and become violent and evil in themselves that such great changes may take place?"

In the second section, "The Crisis", the action shifts to Washington, D.C. Amid the capital's preparations for war, the families must choose sides. Semmes and later Lacy both join Virginia brigades, and again the Major's protests are useless. "Your pa is still living before he was born – in 1789," one of Lacy's cousins tells him. "He thinks the government is a group of high-minded gentlemen who are trying to yield everything to one another. Damn it, Lacy, it's just men like your pa who are the glory of the Old Dominion, and the surest proof of her greatness, that are going to ruin us." Disenchanted and defeated ideologically, the Major returns to Pleasant Hill without his sons. Lacy, meanwhile, relocates to the Poseys' Georgetown home. So begins the novel's final section, "The Abyss".

Drawing on the macabre world of Edgar Allan Poe, *The Fathers* descends into darkness. Lacy compares George Posey's "Mad Uncle Jarman" to Poe's haunted artist Roderick Usher, but the rot of madness has spread throughout the family. Posey's mother and aunt have sealed themselves in their rooms while George's wife, Susan Buchan – overwhelmed by a world floating free from the rigid codes of her youth – slowly loses control. The end comes when both Lacy and Semmes fall in love with George's sister, Jane. Susan, aghast that anyone else should come under the Poseys' spell, conspires to have George's former slave and half-brother, Yellow Jim, rape Jane. Semmes shoots Jim, and George – for reasons that strike those involved as mysterious – shoots his old friend Semmes.

In a state of shock, Lacy returns to Pleasant Hill, where Union troops surround the plantation. When Posey impulsively strikes their captain, the man burns Pleasant Hill to the ground – but not before the Major, who has refused to vacate the premises, hangs himself. With "a wisp of smoke hanging in the air", the novel's devastation is finally complete.

The following excerpt is from the beginning part: *Pleasant Hill*.

作品选读

Pleasant Hill

It was ONLY TODAY as I was walking down Fayette Street towards the river that I got a whiff of salt fish, and I remembered the day I stood at Pleasant Hill. It was late April and the blossoms shot into the air like spray. My mother was dead. Crowds of the connection had arrived the night before; and I had come, a boy of fifteen, after breakfast, out into the yard. Under the tree I could still taste the salt of the roe herring that Aunt Myra Parrish had kept serving to the kin and friends from Washington and Alexandria. There was old Uncle Armistead, my father's brother and twenty years his elder, born at the end of the Revolution and older than even his eighty years: who deaf and half blind said only "Hanh?" to remarks directed to him, and he never asked a question. My mind now echoes "Hanh?" to the smell of the herring and I can see the black coffin of my mother lying in the hush of the front parlor, a white, long room.

My name is Lacy Gore Buchan, the third son and the last child of my parents. My father was the late Major Lewis Buchan, a native of Spotsylvania Country, Virginia, who died as I shall relate, at the beginning of the war, in Fairfax Country at Pleasant Hill, a "place" that came to us through his mother, who was a Lewis of Spotsylvania. My father, through his father Dr. John Buchan, was the grandson of the "immigrant," Benjamin Buchan, a Scots adventurer who ordinarily must have followed his compatriots west of the Blue Ridge had he not won the hand of Mary Armistead the very year of his landing, I think 1741; Mary Armistead thus became my great-grandmother, and by means of certain dower properties to which she fell heir – after her father's displeasure with the adventurer had been conquered by the grave – the name of Buchan, obscure in origin, became assimilated to that unique order of society known latterly as the Virginian aristocracy. Of my mother's people I know, first-hand, much less. She was Sarah Semmes Gore of the Valley of Virginia; on the Gore side, Scotch-Irish; on the

Semmes, of Maryland stock that had migrated to the Valley around 1800. My mother might have said of my father,"Thy people are my people," for she became a pure Buchan – in all but religion; she could not have added, "and thy God my God." She remained a Presbyterian.

The death of my mother is a suitable beginning for my story. There, for the last time, I saw my whole family assembled from that region, down to the fifth and sixth degree of kin, besides three or four of the Poseys, the family of my remarkable brother-in-law, George Posey from Georgetown, who had the year before married my lovely sister Susan. A year later came the war; we were uprooted from Pleasant Hill, and were never together again.

Of the Poseys I shall have a good deal to say hereafter. They were a respectable family of Anne Arundel County, Maryland, quiet, presentable, and at one time, in the day of old Samuel Posey, George's grandfather, possessed of considerable landed property and servants; but otherwise, like, the Buchans, undistinguished. Mr. Rozier Posey, George's father, moved down to Charles County, and in George's boyhood the family left the land and settled permanently in Georgetown, in a tall red brick house on Vista Avenue, overlooking the Potomac. The family, I say, was unexceptional. I cannot understand why they came out, in the old phrase, "at the little end of the horn," as they grievously did.

That, perhaps more than anything else, is the reason why an unmarried old man, having nothing else to do, with a competence saved from the practice of medicine, thinks he has a story to tell. Is it not something to tell, when a score of people whom I knew and loved, people beyond whose lives I could imagine no other life, either out of violence in themselves or the times, or out of some misery or shame, scattered into the new life of the modern age where they cannot even find themselves? Why cannot life change without tangling the lives of innocent persons? Why do innocent persons cease their innocence and become violent and evil in themselves that such great changes may take place?

These questions must go unanswered. I have a story to tell but I cannot explain the story. I cannot say: if Susan had not married George Posey then Susan could not have known Jane Posey and influenced her. But of course I might not have known Jane either. Could I have known her without Susan, I might have married her, for I loved her. That no doubt was the life I wanted. But what I wanted and did not get would not have changed the events by which all these people were tortured. It would have all happened in some other way.

I see figures on the lawn that morning at Pleasant Hill, I hear voices. Of that large company I remember the ordinary tone of the conversation, the hospitable anxiety of the nearer connection for the comfort of the more distant kin and friends; it was like a family infare but that my sister sat in the back parlor with my poor father and the kindly smiles never broke into laughter. Only Uncle Armistead sat all day in the front parlor by the coffin. Aunt Myra – his sister and my father's – went in to him, or took the kin in to the presence of the dead: a small decisive woman, Aunt Myra, with deep eyes and a long straight eyes: she would say to Uncle Armistead: "Brother, go into the chamber and lie down." The "chamber" was my own mother's bedroom where the family sat informally. But Uncle Armistead only replied, "Hanh?" and took another toddy from Sam, the little colored boy he had brought with him from Falls Church.

But as I went aimlessly about the lawn, a mysterious exile from the other children, I seemed to see the home of my childhood with new eyes. I could feel that people were waiting, waiting; but it was different from our waiting for my mother, over many days, to die. The waiting was hurried; there was hurried deliberation in Aunt Myra's managing everything. Out of this changed tempo trivial incidents emerged, and were fixed in my memory: and changed even was the air of the place.

I remember George Posey coming out into the yard, not restlessly but inquiringly, swinging a riding crop and looking from tree to tree and off into the slanting fields. How big and mature he was! He was actually only eleven years older than I was – a man of twenty-six, married a year to my sister and the father of a baby girl in whom I took no interest. He was a good six feet three, and standing he always rested squarely though easily on both feet, his head back, his arms limp at his sides: he seemed taller than he was because he looked at you from the angle of his backward tilted head. He stood looking at the long gallery, two stories, on slender square posts, across the whole front of the house; and his lips moved. I thought he had spoken to me. I ran nearer.

"Brother George!" I cried.

He mentioned me to him, put his hand on my head, and smiled down at me.

"You are my friend, Lacy boy."

He resumed his gaze. I too looked up at the gallery sagging at one end, at the cracked paint on the weatherboarding, at the wisps of smoke struggling out of the big red end-chimneys, then off up the ridge towards the Negro cabins, a pink brick row, and towards the stables and, back of them, near the woods, the big unpainted tobacco barn. I looked at Brother George but he was as fixed as a marble in Mr. Corcoran's gallery. A phrase of my father's comes to mind, for at that moment Brother George's face was a "study." His eyes roved to my mother's garden, down towards the lower end of the ridge by the side of the house: the garden was a big square bordered by box, the inside a tangle of shrubs from which now I saw the first shoots of April green. And on the hither side of the garden I saw the horseblock, and old millstone standing on edge and half buried in the ground: there began the long line of gnarled cedars winding with the muddy lane along the side of the ridge, the half-mile to the old Ox Road, the "big road" that led into the great world – Fairfax, Occoquan, Pohick, Alexandria, then down the Potomac by salt water to the cities beyond the main!

Then for the first time in the wonder of death I saw the whole place all together. Looking back through the cloud of George Posey's life and my sister Susan's, I think that he too saw as a world, as a strange place, the home of his wife's family, as if he had never seen it before. How handsome he was! His hand on my head, I glanced from the gray homespun of my trousers and jacket to the rich broadcloth of his black double-breasted coat with the big square lapels. It fitted him like a glove, and the silver buttons glistened in the sunlight. He turned my head and looked down into my eyes.

"Son, I've got to go." Putting on his black silk hat, he glanced at the front door where people were still going in and out. "Go tell Coriolanus to saddle my horse!"

I was off like a shot towards the side of the house to the path that led to the stable; then I slowed to a walk, in doubt that a boy should be running on the day his mother was dead. Round the corner of the house, out of sight of the porch, there was little Jane Posey, Brother George's sister, just my age, stooping in a bed of new violets. She looked stiffly dressed up, in poke bonnet, blue velvet jacket, with the pantalettes showing white at the hem of her dress. She looked up with doe-like eyes and said, "Hello!" I paused, but she picked violets as if I had passed on. I suppose it was out of the wonderful loneliness of that day that I wished to say something later, at some certain moment, in a world in which nothing could be counted on, it was so quietly bustling and strange, I said, "Wait for me."

I ran again, as if being out of sight made it proper, and vaulted the rail fence into the stable lot. I shouted, "Uncle Lanus!" Then I saw him, his white wool first, and the faded-brushed broadcloth above the tallow-grease on his boots. He sat on a stool, his hands folded; he raised his eyes gently, with the polite attention of an old gentleman whom nothing can surprise.

"Brother George says saddle his horse." Then, as if I suddenly knew something important: "Quick!"

The old man placed his hands on his knees and rose. He vanished into the stalls, and I looked at the back of the house. One of the Negro girls was hanging a red quilt over the rail of the upper back gallery: it had come from my mother's bed. Over to the right beyond the out-kitchen, by the smokehouse, Henry Jackson, the yard boy, now that the severe old Coriolanus was out of sight, was whistling; one of the young wenches passed and he laughed and slapped her; she giggled. I felt an almost uncontrollable desire to laugh. I looked down at the pawed earth. There was a piece of old strap. If I wanted it I knew I had better get it into my pocket before the old Negro came out again. With one motion I had it and it was in my pants pocket. I looked again towards the smokehouse. The Negroes had gone. I lifted my gaze beyond the smokehouse to the rear of my mother's garden down the ridge towards the three big chestnut trees. By a low wall I could see Mr. Higgins, the overseer, squatting on his heels and smoking; just below him two Negro men with shovels were scarring the red earth with the new grave.

Coriolanus was talking to the big bay mare, and now he led her out. But he did not lead her to the gate; he stopped. There was anxiety in his weathered face, as if he did not know what he was expected to do. "Come here, Lacy," he said, and when he said it, his anxiety left him. I came nearer. He handed me the bridle and turned away as if he would have nothing to do with this business. He sat down on his stool, folded his hands, and looked me calmly in the eyes.

"I knowed he'd do it," he said.

He couldn't have known anything of the kind, but there it was; I actually got a little comfort out of the fact that someone imagined he had predicted Brother George's impulse, which had surprised and excited me. And I was more excited than ever now that I was leading

Queen Susie, the fine mare Brother George had bought from Colonel Tayloe the day before he had become engaged to my sister; I led her through the stable-lot gate, down the short lane by the side of the house and into the front yard. There was Brother George on the far side by the horseblock, one foot on the block, holding his elbow on his knee, his chin in his hand. I pressed right on, but all the way I admired him all over again: the frank, open face, the careless, cold blue eyes, the cheerful mouth with the corners curving upward in a kindly smile. He never looked any other way – only even more that way sometimes, when he broke into a sudden laugh that startled you at first; yet in the end you laughed too, without reason, and you felt you were only waiting for him to tell you what to do. I had heard my father say that George could make anybody do anything. In my boyish delight I would have anyday followed him over a precipice, just for his bidding. I know distinctly that I thought of him always boldly riding somewhere, and because I couldn't see where, I suppose I thought of a precipice. Yet I am sure he had never done anything crudely bold that would arrest the attention of a boy.

I was at the block, the mare whinnied, and Brother George noticed me. I held the bridle out to him, but he ignored it. He took his foot off the block and stood erect. I followed his eyes to the front gallery, where Sister Susan was coming rapidly down the steps. He advanced to meet her, pausing to flick a spot of mud off his knee with his whip, for the world as if he were walking towards some natural object, like a gnarled tree, that had engaged his curiosity. The permanent smile was on his face. They met about fifty feet from where I stood holding the mare, halfway between the block and the steps.

My sister was not beautiful, but she was lovely; the hazel eyes, set deep in their sockets under a wide low brow, dominated her face. Her hair was like an acorn, her skin fair almost to monotony, not pale but without trace of color; she was like pear blossoms against a lingering winter landscape. Her face was all structure, with just enough smooth surface to bring all the strong lines together into design. I know now, what I could not have known or cared about then, that she had got that face from papa, who had got it through his mother Margaret Lewis from his people, the Washburns, a family greatly distinguished in the Revolution, whom recent members of our own family are proud of being descended from: in the old days the Washburns were unlike other people for their saying so. Some of them over in the Valley of Virginia had always said that if only Mr. Jefferson had not been so perversely democratic they would be the royal family. Well, papa – who had been a fine horseman in his youth – used to say that perhaps he could have qualified as Master of the Horse; but he was not sure, he was perversely democratic too: he was only Major Lewis Buchan by grace of the country militia that had not fought since 1812.

George was taking off his beaver hat, smiling, while Susan, speaking in a low tone, looked him gravely in the eye. For an instant Brother George hung his head as if he were impressed by her earnest words, whatever they were, and she smiled at him and placed the tips of her fingers on his forearm. Standing so, she raised her voice and I heard the one word – "Papa." That must have been too much for Brother George. He said – raising his head, the permanent smile a little tighter on his lips – he said:

"No, damn it."

Her fingers lingered on his sleeve. She withdrew them, clenched them at her side, and turned so quickly that I heard her hoops swish under the heavy black silk of her skirt. Ladies did not run in those days, but she very nearly ran, with the rigid plunging and dipping of the hoops, until she sailed up the steps and with the same motion went through the front door. Not until the door had closed behind her did I see Brother George. He was smiling, not after the vanished figure of his wife, but at Mr. Higgins, who had slid noiselessly into the scene, and was squatting on his heels (he never stood up, he only walked or squatted) not ten feet away from Brother George, a little to one side. He was a hatchet-faced, impassive young man, quite honest – said my father – of the small-farming class for generations: if he never entered our front door, we never entered his simply because we were not wanted. Mr. Higgins, squatting there in his black store clothes, did not smile. Brother George turned on his heel and approached Queen Susie. He looked a little surprised when he saw me; he had forgotten that I was there. He must have forgotten Mr. Higgins, who shifted his balance a little, took his pipe out of his mouth, and said:

"I like the mar' better ever' time I see her."

Brother George had heard no words but only a voice. He looked off over my head as he took the bridle from my hand.

"No, God damn it! " he said. He put his foot into the stirrup as he threw the bridle over the mare's head, and he was off before he was well seated, down the lane under the broken cedars.

Mr. Higgins' expression had not changed, nor did it change when he spoke to me.

"Boy," he said, "hit ain't right fer a man to gallivant off on a day like this."

I remember, of the minutes before he spoke, a suspicion that I should not have been present, that I did not want to be there in the midst of things that I could not understand; perhaps I went far enough with Mr. Higgins to appreciate the correct sentiment that he had expressed. But now that he had expressed it I resented it.

"You can't say nothin' against Brother George." I burst into tears.

The next thing I knew I was running to the house by way of the dogwood tree, towards the crape myrtles under the windows of mother's bedroom. Then I was around the side of the house. There was Jane Posey, a large bunch of sweet violets in her hand, sitting on a root of the big sugar maple that went up the side of the house and canopied the roof. She was not "little Jane" any longer since the birth of Susan's and George's even smaller Jane: both were named for Brother George's mother whom I knew later as Aunt Jane Anne, after the families became intimate. So the Jane there under the tree I had never thought of as little, only as Jane, a large child for her fifteen years, with mournful brown eyes and, as I look back, a docility of nature that made her a joy to her family. I suppose my face was wet, but before I could feel my shame Jane said, "Hello," exactly as she had said it before. "I waited," she said. Now I felt

ashamed; so I said, "Let's go around back and play." The meek round eyes fixed me in wonder. "We can't play," she said.

I was blushing as I heard: "Mercy, child, where you been all this time?" It was Aunt Myra, severe but kind, looking round the end of the house from the upper gallery. "I've looked for you high and low," she said. Jane got up and walked slowly round the house towards the steps, and when Aunt Myra disappeared I knew that she had not been looking for me. I looked about me; the yard was deserted, I could hear only the plunk of an ax in the distance and a calf bawling over the hill in the cuppen. I was alone in a world that had been created by George Posey, out of the dead world of my mother: an emotion that the years alone can enlighten, for a child, expecting nothing of people, is shocked only when what happens has not happened before. It was the first time anything could happen at my mother's death! Yet the savage sense of propriety so acute in children told me that I had witnessed an event extraordinary and violent, more violent even than the death which had not happened to me till now but which could always happen in the world in which I lived. I thought: Suppose papa should die? I could understand it, and I went round to the back gallery and up the gallery stairs, thinking that George Posey could never have anything to do with death.

Unit 4
Robert Penn Warren (1905–1989)
罗伯特·潘·沃伦

作者简介

罗伯特·潘·沃伦，小说家、诗人、文学评论家和教育家。1905 年 4 月 24 日出生于肯塔基州(Kentucky)。1925 年范德比尔特大学毕业后，沃伦进入加利福尼亚大学学习，1927 年获得硕士学位。从 1930 年起他在范德比尔特大学和明尼苏达大学执教。他的作品，无论是诗歌、小说还是散文、戏剧都充满了美国南方的历史氛围。1939 年出版的第一部小说《夜骑者》(*Night Rider*)描写了肯塔基州农民和烟草公司之间的斗争，以讽刺的笔调描绘南方田园生活结束后人们的精神困境。这部小说也使沃伦闻名美国。之后他与克林斯·布鲁克斯等人合作创办了《南方评论》(*The Southern Review*)杂志。在他们担任主编的七年时间内，《南方评论》成为美国文坛最有影响力的文学期刊之一。他们合著的《理解诗歌》(*Understanding Poetry*, 1938)对传播“新批评”文学流派发挥了重要作用。“新批评”主张对具体作品进行独立、细致的研究。他们提倡的文本“细读”批评方法在 20 世纪五六十年代曾风靡一时，支配着美国的批评界和大学的文学教学。1946 年，沃伦的长篇小说《全是国王的臣民》(*All the King's Men*)奠定了他在美国文坛的重要地位，并获得普利策奖。后来他又以诗集《承诺》(*Promise: Poems*: 1954–1956)和《此时与彼时》(*Now and Then: Poems*: 1976–1978)两次获得普利策诗歌奖。他是迄今为止唯一一位在小说和诗歌两个领域都获得普利策奖的作家。在 1986 年，他荣膺美国第一任桂冠诗人。评论界称沃伦为“最杰出的文学家”以及“20 世纪后半叶最重要的美国诗人”。在长达 68 年的文学生涯中，沃伦共推出 10 部长篇小说，17 本诗集，16 篇短篇小说，7 部戏剧和电视剧本，5 本文学教材，8 本散文集，两本儿童故事集和 100 多篇杂文。沃伦的其他作品还包括：小说《天堂门口》(*At Heaven's Gate*, 1943)、《足够的空间和时间》(*World Enough and Time*, 1950)、《一群天使》(*Band of Angels*, 1955)、《山洞》(*The Cave*, 1959) 和《荒野》(*Wilderness: A Tale of the Civil War*, 1961) 等；诗集《龙兄弟》(*Brother to Dragon: A Tale in Verse and Voices*, 1953)、《化身》(*Incarnations: Poems* 1966–1968)、《诗选》(*Selected Poems*, 1923–1943)以及文学教材《理解小说》(*Understanding Fiction*, 1943)等。沃伦前期的诗歌在形式、风格和观点等方面受艾略特的影响，约束了诗人的个性发挥；他后期的诗风有了明显的改变，形成了“硬朗的、如谜的、真实的”个性化新风格。他还著有短篇小说集《阁楼上的马戏团》(*The Circus in the Attic*, 1948)，其中的《草莓之冬》(*Blackberry Winter*)是沃伦最出色的短篇小说之一。

作品导读

The novelette, *Blackberry Winter*, is a recollection of one memorable day in the childhood of Seth, the narrator, then nine years old. It is told as a first-person narrative, more than thirty-five years later. The title refers to the weather phenomenon of a period of cool temperatures in June. The story takes place in middle Tennessee.

On this unseasonably cold day Seth's mother forbids him to go outside barefoot, but he disobeys her, wanting to "rub [his] feet over the wet shivery grass and make the perfect mark of [his] foot in the smooth, creamy, red mud." But before getting out the door, Seth notices something unusual: out of the window a man is coming along by the path of the woods. The boy watches the man follow a path where the family's fence meets the woods. From a distance he can tell that the man is a stranger and that he is approaching the house. After Seth's mother calls off the dogs the man is near enough for closer inspection, and the boy sees that he is carrying a paper parcel in one hand and a switch-blade knife in the other. According to the narrator's assessment of the stranger, "Everything was wrong about what he wore." His worn khaki pants and dark wool coat and hat, his tie stuffed in a pocket and his city shoes mark him as both strange and menacing. Despite premonitions of danger, however, the boy is fascinated and drawn to the man who has come looking for a handout or work.

Seth watches while the tramp washed his dirty hands before eating. Finally the man makes the boy feel so uncomfortable that he leaves, suddenly remembering that "the creek was in flood over the bridge, and that people were down there watching it." Seth and the men watch as the swollen creek carries debris along its course, and they are fascinated by the sight of a dead cow. Uncomprehending, Seth listens as the men discuss whose cow it likely was and whether a man could get hungry enough to eat a drowned cow.

Although his father takes him to the gate of their farm, Seth does not go home immediately. Instead he decides to stop off at a sharecropper family's cabin, where his playmate Jebb lives with his parents Dellie and Old Jebb. He expects to be welcomed by the usual cheer in the cabin, but instead encounters Dellie sick in bed and Old Jebb forecasting that the cold weather is a sign of the end of the world as we've known it, evidence that the earth is tired of "sinful folks." Although Seth tells Old Jebb about the man at the house with a knife, the news barely penetrates the gloom of the cabin and the preoccupation of the family.

The story reaches a climax when the stranger comes head to head with the father. Seth's father tells the tramp that he won't be hiring him for another day's work and pays him a half dollar for a half day's work. Then the man curses the farm, mocks Seth's father, and spits on the ground. Seth's father stares the man down and he retreats. Seth, however, still cannot resist the man's horrible appeal and follows him. Seth asks where he came from and the man rebuffs him, but the boy keeps following. Finally, the tramp threatens: "Stop following me. You don't stop following me and I cut yore throat, you little son-of-a-bitch".

The story ends with the older Seth explaining that both his parents are now dead, Dellie's dead, but Old Jebb is still alive and well over a hundred years of age. The narrator also confesses that although the tramp had threatened to kill him for following him, that he "did follow him, all the years".

作品选读

Blackberry Winter

It was getting into June and past eight o'clock in the morning, but there was a fire – even if it wasn't a big fire, just a fire of chunks – on the hearth, of the big stone fireplace in the living room. I was standing on the hearth, almost into the chimney, hunched over the fire, working my bare toes slowly on the warm stone. I relished the heat which made the skin of my bare legs warp and creep and tingle, even as I called to my mother, who was somewhere back in the dining room or kitchen, and said: "But it's June, I don't have to put them on!"

"You put them on if you are going out," she called.

I tried to assess the degree of authority and conviction in the tone, but at that distance it was hard to decide. I tried to analyze the tone, and then I thought what a fool I had been to start out the back door and let her see that I was barefoot. If I had gone out the front door or the side door she would never have known, not till dinner time anyway, and by then the day would have been half gone and I would have been all over the farm to see what the storm had done and down to the creek to see the flood. But it had never crossed my mind that they would try to stop you from going barefoot in June, no matter if there had been a gully-washer and a cold spell.

Nobody had ever tried to stop me in June as long as I could remember, and when you are nine years old, what you remember seems forever; for you remember everything and everything is important and stands big and full and fills up Time and is so solid that you can walk around and around it like a tree and look at it. You are aware that time passes, that there is a movement in time, but that is not what Time is. Time is not a movement, a flowing, a wind then, but is, rather, a kind of climate in which things are, and when a thing happens it begins to live and keeps on living and stands solid in Time like the tree that you can walk around. And if there is a movement, the movement is not Time itself, any more than a breeze is climate, and all the breeze does it to shake a little the leaves on the tree which is alive and solid. When you are ninc, you know that there are things that you don't know, but you know that when you know something you know it. You know how a thing has been and you know that you can go barefoot in June. You don not understand that voice from back in the kitchen which says that you cannot go barefoot outdoors and run to see what has happened and rub your feet over the wet shivery grass and make the perfect mark of your foot in the smooth, creamy, red mud and then muse upon it as though you had suddenly come upon that single mark on the glistening auroral beach of the world. You have never seen a beach, but you have read the book and how the footprint was there.

The voice had said what it had said, and I looked savagely at the black stockings and the strong, scuffed brown shoes which I had brought from my closet as far as the hearth rug. I called once more, "But it's June," and waited.

"It's June," the voice replied from far away, "but it's blackberry winter."

I had lifted my head to reply to that, to make one more test of what was in that tone, when I happened to see the man.

The fireplace in the living was at the end; for the stone chimney was built, as in so many of the farmhouses in Tennessee, at the end of a gable, and there was a window on each side of the chimney. Out of the window on the north side of the fireplace I could see the man. When I saw the man I did not call out what I had intended, but, engrossed by the strangeness of the sight, watched him, still far off, come along the path by the edge of the woods.

What was strange was that there should be a man there at all. That path went along the yard fence, between the fence and the woods which came right down to the yard, and then on back past the chicken runs and on by the woods until it was lost to sight where the woods bulged out and cut off the back field. There the path disappeared into the woods. It led on back, I knew, through the woods and to the swamp, skirted the swamp where the big trees gave way to sycamores and water oaks and willows and tangled cane, and then led on to the river. Nobody ever went back there except people who wanted to gig frogs in the swamp or to fish in the river or to hunt in the woods, and those people, if they didn't have a standing permission from my father, always stopped to ask permission to cross the farm. But the man whom I now saw wasn't, I could tell even at that distance, a sportsman. And what would a sportsman have been doing down there after a storm? Besides, he was coming from the river, and nobody had gone down there that morning. I knew that for a fact, because if anybody had passed, certainly if a stranger had passed, the dogs would have made a racket and would have been out on him. But this man was coming up from the river and had come up through the woods. I suddenly had a vision of him moving up the grassy path in the woods, in the green twilight under the big trees, not making any sound on the path, while now and then, like drops off the eaves, a big drop of water would fall from a leaf or bough and strike s stiff oak leaf lower down with a small, hollow sound like a drop of water hitting tin. That sound, in the silence of woods, would be very significant.

When you are a boy and stand in the stillness of woods, which can be so still that your heart almost stops beating and makes you want to stand there in the green twilight until you feel your very feet sinking into and clutching the earth like roots and your body breathing slow through its pores like the leaves – when you stand there and wait for the next drop to drop with its small, flat sound to a lower leaf, that sound seems to measure out something, to put an end to something, to begin something, and you cannot wait for it to happen and are afraid it will not happen, and then when it has happened, you are waiting again, almost afraid.

But the man whom I saw coming through the woods in my mind's eye did not pause and wait, growing into the ground and breathing with the enormous, soundless breathing of the leaves. Instead, I saw him moving in the green twilight inside my head as he was moving at that very moment along the path by the edge of the woods, coming toward the house. He was moving steadily, but not fast, with his shoulders hunched a little and his head thrust forward, like a man who has come a long way and has a long way to go. I shut my eyes for a couple of seconds, thinking that when I opened them he would not be there at all. There was no place for him to have come from, and there was no reason for him to come where he was coming, toward our house. But I opened my eyes, and there he was, and he was coming steadily along the side of the woods. He was not yet even with the back chicken yard.

"Mama," I called.

"You put them on," the voice said.

"There's a man coming." I called, "out back."

She did not reply to that, and I guessed that she had gone to the kitchen window to look. She would be looking at the man and wondering who he was and what he wanted, the way you always do in the country, and if I went back there now she would not notice right off whether or not I was barefoot. So I went back to the kitchen.

She was standing by the window. "I don't recognize him," she said, not looking around at me.

"Where could he be coming from?" I asked.

"I don't know," she said.

"What would he be doing down at the river? At night? In the storm?"

She studied the figure out the window, then said, "Oh, I reckon maybe he cut across from the Dunbar place."

That was, I realized, a perfectly rational explanation. He had not been down at the river in the storm, at night. He had come over this morning. You could cut across from the Dunbar place if you didn't mind breaking through a lot of elder and sassafras and blackberry bushes which had about taken over the old cross path, which nobody ever used any more. That satisfied me for a moment, but only for a moment. "Mama," I asked, "what would he be doing over at the Dunbar place last night?"

Then she looked at me, and I knew I had made a mistake, for she was looking at my barefoot. "You haven't got your shoes on," she said.

But I was saved by the dogs. That instant there was a bark which I recognized as Sam, the collie, and then a heavier, churning kind of bark which was Bully, and I saw a streak of white as Bully tore round the corner of the back porch and headed out for the man. Bully was a big,

bone-white bull dog, the kind of dog that they used to call a farm bull dog but that you don't see any more, heavy chested and heavy headed, but with pretty long legs. He could take a fence as light as a hound. He had just cleared the white paling fence toward the woods when my mother ran out to the back porch and began calling, "Here you, Bully! Here you!"

Bully stopped in the path, waiting for the man, but he gave a few more of those deep, gargling, savage barks that reminded you of something down a stone-lined well. The red clay mud, I saw, was splashed up over his white chest and looked exciting, like blood.

The man, however, had not stopped walking even when Bully took the fence and started at him. He had kept right on coming. All he had done was to switch a little paper parcel which he carried from the right hand to the left, and then reach into his pants pocket to get something. Then I saw the glitter and knew that he had a knife in his hand, probably the kind of mean knife just made for devilment and nothing else, with a blade as long as the blade of a frog-sticker, which will snap out ready when you press a button in the handle. That knife must have had a button in the handle, or else how could he have had the blade out glittering so quick and with just one hand?

Pulling his knife against the dogs was a funny thing to do, for Bully was a big, powerful brute and fast, and Sam was all right. If those dogs had meant business, they might have knocked him down and ripped him before he got a stroke in. He ought to have picked up a heavy stick, something to take a swipe at them with and something which they could see and respect when they came at him. But he apparently did not know much about dogs. He just held the knife blade close against the right leg, low down, and kept on moving down the path.

Then my mother had called, and Bully had stopped. So the man let blade of the knife snap back into the handle, and dropped it into his pocket, and kept on coming. Many women would have been afraid with the strange man who they knew had that knife in his pocket. That is, if they were alone in the house with nobody but a nine-year-old boy. And mother was alone, for my father had gone off, and Dellie, the cook, was down at her cabin because she wasn't feeling well. But my mother wasn't afraid. She wasn't a big woman, but she was clear and brisk about everything she did and looked everybody and everything right in the eye from her own blue eyes in her tanned face. She had been the first woman in the country to ride a horse astride (that was back when she was a girl and long before I was born), and I have seen her snatch up a pump gun and go out and knock a chicken hawk out of the air like a busted skeet when he came over her chicken yard. She was a steady and self-reliant woman, and when I think of her now after all the years she has been dead, I think of her brown hands, not big, but somewhat square for a woman's hands, with square-cut nails. They looked, as a matter of fact, more like a young boy's hands than a grown woman's. But back then it never crossed my mind that she would ever be dead.

She stood on the back porch and watched the man enter the back gate, where the dogs (Bully had leaped back into the yard) were dancing and muttering and giving sidelong glances back to my mother to see if she meant what she had said. The man walked right by the dogs, almost brushing them, and didn't pay them any attention. I could see now that he wore old khaki pants, and a dark wool coat with stripes in it, and a gray felt hat. He had on a gray shirt with blue stripes in it, and no tie. But I could see a tie, blue and reddish, sticking in his side coat-pocket. Everything was wrong about what he wore. He ought to have been wearing blue jeans or overalls, and a straw hat or an old black felt hat, and the coat, granting that he might have been wearing a wool coat and not a jumper, ought not to have had those stripes. Those clothes, despite the fact that they were old enough and dirty enough for any tramp, didn't belong there in our back yard, coming down the path, in Middle Tennessee, miles away from any big town, and even a mile off the pike.

When he got almost to the steps, without having said anything, my mother, very matter-of-factly, said, "Good morning."

"Good morning," he said, and stopped and looked her over. He did not take off his hat, and under the brim you could see the perfectly unmemorable face, which wasn't old and wasn't young, or thick or thin. It was grayish and covered with about three days of stubble. The eyes were a kind of nondescript, muddy hazel, or something like that, rather bloodshot. His teeth, when he opened his mouth, showed yellow and uneven. A couple of them had been knocked out. You knew that they had been knocked out, because there was a scar, not very old, there on the lower lip just beneath the gap.

"Are you hunting work?" my mother asked him.

"Yes," he said – not "Yes, mam" – and still did not take off his hat.

"I don't know about my husband, for he isn't here," she said, and didn't mind a bit telling the tramp, or whoever he was, with the mean knife in his pocket, that no man was around, "but I can give you a few things to do. The storm has drowned a lot of my chicks. Three coops of them. You can gather them up and bury them. Bury them deep so the dogs won't get at them. In the woods. And fix the coops the wind blew over. And down yonder beyond that pen by the edge of the woods are some drowned poults. They got out and I couldn't get them in. Even after it started to rain hard. Poults haven't got any sense."

"What are them things – poults?" he demanded, and spat on the brick wall. He rubbed his foot over the spot, and I saw that he wore a black, pointed-toe low shoe, all cracked and broken. It was a crazy kind of shoe to be wearing in the country.

"Oh, they're young turkeys," my mother was saying. "And they haven't got any sense. I oughtn't to try to raise them around here with so many chickens, anyway. They don't thrive near chickens, even in separate pens. And I won't give up my chickens." Then she stopped herself and resumed briskly on the note of business. "When you finish that, you can fix my flower beds. A lot of trash and mud and gravel has washed down. Maybe you can save some of my flowers if you are careful."

"Flowers," the man said, in a low, impersonal voice which seemed to have a wealth of meaning, but a meaning which I could not fathom. As I think back on it, it probably was not pure contempt. Rather, it was a kind of impersonal and distant marveling that he should be on the verge of grubbing in a flower bed. He said the word, and then looked off across the yard.

"Yes, flowers," my mother replied with some asperity, as though she would have nothing said or implied against flowers. "And they were very fine this year." Then she stopped and looked at the man. "Are you hungry?" she demanded.

"Yeah," he said.

"I'll fix you something," she said, "before you get started." She turned to me. "Show him where he can wash up," she commanded, and went into the house.

I took the man to the end of the porch where a pump was and where a couple of wash pans sat on a low shelf for people to use before they went into the house. I stood there while he laid down his little parcel wrapped in newspaper and took off his hat and looked around for a nail to hang it on. He poured the water and plunged his hands into it. They were big hands, and strong looking, but they did not have the creases and the earthblack dirt ground into the skin and under the nails. After he had washed his hands, he poured another basin of water and washed his face. He dried his face, and with the towel still dangling in his grasp, stepped over to the mirror on the house wall. He rubbed one hand over the stubble on his face. Then he carefully inspected his face, turning first one side and then the other, and stepped back and settled his striped coat down on his shoulders. He had the movements of a man who has just dressed up to go to church or a party – the way he settled his coat and smoothed it and scanned himself in the mirror.

Then he caught my glance on him. He glared at me for an instant out of the bloodshot eyes, then demanded in a low, harsh voice, "What you looking at?"

"Nothing," I managed to say, and stepped back a step from him.

He flung the towel down, crumpled, on the shelf, and went toward the kitchen door and entered without knocking.

My mother said something to him which I could not catch. I started to go in again, then thought about my bare feet, and decided to go back of the chicken yard, where the man would have to come to pick up the dead chicks. I hung around behind the chicken house until he came out.

He moved across the chicken yard with a fastidious, not quite finicking motion, looking down at the curdled mud flecked with bits of chicken-droppings. The mud curled up over the soles of his black shoes. I stood back from him some six feet and watched him pick up the first of the drowned chicks. He held it up by one foot and inspected it.

There is nothing deader looking than a drowned chick. The feet curl in that feeble, empty way which back when I was a boy, even if I was a country boy who did not mind hog-killing or frog-gigging, made me feel hollow in the stomach. Instead of looking plump and fluffy, the body is stringy and limp with the fluff plastered to it, and the neck is long and loose like a little string of rag. And the eyes have that bluish membrane over them which makes you think of a very old man who is sick about to die.

The man stood there and inspected the chick. Then he looked all around as though he didn't know what to do with it.

"There's a great big old basket in the shed," I said, and pointed to the shed attached to the chickenhouse.

He inspected me as though he had just discovered my presence, and moved toward the shed.

"There's a spade there, too," I added.

He got the basket and began to pick up the other chicks, picking each one up slowly by a foot and then flinging it into the basket with a nasty, snapping motion. Now and then he would look at me out of the bloodshed eyes. Every time he seemed on the verge of saying something, but he did not. Perhaps he was building up to say something to me, but I did not wait that long. His way of looking at me made me so uncomfortable that I left the chicken yard.

Besides, I had just remembered that the creek was in flood, over the bridge, and that people were down there watching it. So I cut across the farm toward the creek. When I got to the big tobacco field I saw that it had not suffered much. The land lay right and not many tobacco plants had washed out of the ground. But I knew that a lot of tobacco round the country had been washed right out. My father said so at breakfast.

My father was down at the bridge. When I came out of the gap in the osage hedge into the road, I saw him sitting on his mare over the heads of the other man who were standing around, admiring the flood. The creek was big here, even in low water; for only a couple of miles away it ran into the river, and when a real flood came, the red water got over the pike where it dipped down to the bridge, which was an iron bridge, and high over the floor and even the side railings of the bridge. Only the upper iron work would show, with the water boiling and frothing red and white around it. That creek rose so fast and so heavy because a few miles back it came down out of the hills, where the gorges filled up with water in no time when a rain came. The creek ran in a deep bed with limestone bluffs along both sides until it got within three quarters of a mile of the bridge, and when it came out from between those bluffs in flood it was boiling and hissing and steaming like water from a fire hose.

Whenever there was a flood, people from half the country would come down to see the sight. After a gully-washer there would not be any work to do anyway. If it didn't ruin your crop, you couldn't plow and you felt like taking a holiday to celebrate. If it did ruin your crop, there wasn't anything to do except to try to take your mind off the mortgage, if you were rich enough to have a mortgage, and if you couldn't afford a mortgage you needed something to take your mind off how hungry you would be by Christmas. So people would come down to the bridge and look at the flood. It made something different from the run days.

There would not be much talking after the first few minutes of trying to guess how high the water was this time. The men and kids just stood around, or sat their horses or mules, as the case might be, or stood up in the wagon beds. They looked at the strangeness of the flood for an hour or two, and then somebody would say that he had better be getting on home to dinner and would start walking down the gray, puddled limestone pike, or would touch heel to his mount and start off. Everybody always knew what it would be like when he got down to the bridge, but people always came. It was like church or a funeral. They always came, that is, if it was summer and the flood unexpected. Nobody ever came down in winter to see high water.

When I came out of the gap in the bodock hedge, I saw the crowd, perhaps fifteen or twenty men and a lot of kids, and saw my father sitting his mare, Nellie Gray. He was a tall, limber man and carried himself well. I was always proud to see him sit a horse, he was so quiet and straight, and when I stepped through the gap of the hedge that morning, the first thing that happened was, I remember, the warm feeling I always had when I saw him up on a horse, just sitting. I did not go toward him, but skirted the crowd on the far side, to get a look at the creek. For one thing, I was not sure what he would say about the fact that I was barefoot. But the first thing I knew, I heard his voice calling, "Seth! "

I went toward him, moving apologetically past the men, who bent their large, red or thin, sallow faces above me. I knew some of the men, and knew their names, but because those I knew were there in a crowd, mixed with the strange faces, they seemed foreign to me, and not friendly. I did not look up at my father until I was almost within touching distance of his heel. Then I looked up and tried to read his face, to see if he was angry about my being barefoot. Before I could decide anything from that impassive, high-boned face, he had learned over and reached a hand to me. "Grab on," he commanded.

"I grabbed on and gave a little jump," and he said, "Up-see-daisy! " and whisked me, light as a feather, up to the pommel of his McClellan saddle.

"You can see better up here," he said, slid back on the cantle a little to make me more comfortable, and then, looking over my head at the swollen, tumbling water, seemed to forget all about me. But his right hand was laid on my side, just above my thigh, to steady me.

I was sitting there as quiet as I could, feeling the faint stir of my father's chest against my shoulders as it rose and fell with his breath, when I saw the cow. At first, looking up the creek, I thought it was just another big piece of driftwood steaming down the creek in the ruck of water, but all at once a pretty good-size boy who had climbed part way up a telephone pole by the pike so that he could see better yelled out, "Golly-damn, look at that-air cow! "

Everybody looked. It was a cow all right, but it might just as well have been driftwood; for it was dead as a chunk, rolling and roiling down the creek, appearing and disappearing, feet up or head up, it didn't matter which.

The cow started up the talk again. Somebody wondered whether it would hit one of the clear places under the top girder of the bridge and get through or whether it would get tangled in the drift and trash that had piled against the upright girders and braces. Somebody remembered how about ten years before so much driftwood had piled up on the bridge that it was knocked off its foundations. Then the cow hit. It hit the edge of the drift against one of the girders, and hung there. For a few seconds it seemed as though it might tear loose, but then we saw that it was really caught. It bobbed and heaved on its side there in a slow, grinding, uneasy fashion. It had a yoke around its neck, the kind made out of a forked limb to keep a

jumper behind fence.

"She shore jumped one fence," one of the men said.

And another: "Well, she done jumped her last one, fer a fack."

Then they began to wonder about whose cow it might be. They decided it must belong to Milt Alley. They said that he had a cow that was a jumper, and kept her in a fenced-in piece of ground up the creek. I had never seen Milt Alley, but I knew who he was. He was a squatter and lived up the hills a way, on a shirt-tail patch of set-on-edge land, in a cabin. He was pore white trash. He had lots of children. I had seen the children at school, when they came. They were thin-faced, with straight, sticky-looking, dough-colored hair, and they smelled something like old sour buttermilk, not because they drank so much buttermilk but because that is the sort of smell which children out of those cabins tend to have. The big Alley boy drew dirty pictures and showed them to the little boys at school.

That was Milt Alley's cow. It looked like the kind of cow he would have, a scrawny, old, sway-backed cow, with a yoke around her neck. I wondered if Milt Alley had another cow.

"Poppa," I said, "do you think Milt Alley has got another cow?"

"You say 'Mr. Alley.'" My father said quietly.

"Do you think he has?"

"No telling," my father said.

Then a big gangly boy, about fifteen, who was sitting on a scraggly little old mule with a piece of croker sack thrown across the saw-tooth spine, and who had been staring at the cow, suddenly said to nobody in particular, "Reckin anybody ever et drownt cow?"

He was the kind of boy who might just as well as not have been the son of Milt Alley, with his faded and patched overalls ragged at the bottom of the pants and the mud-stiff brogans hanging off his skinny, bare ankles at the level of the mule's belly. He had said what he did, and then looked embarrassed and sullen when all the eyes swung at him. He hadn't meant to say it, I am pretty sure now. He would have been too proud to say it, just as Milt Alley would have been too proud. He had just been thinking out loud, and the words had popped out.

There was an old man standing there on the pike, and old man with a white beard. "Son," he said to the embarrassed and sullen boy on the mule, "you live long enough and you'll find a man will eat anything when the time comes."

"Time gonna come fer some folks this year," another man said.

"Son," the old man said, "in my time I et things a man don't like to think on. I was a sojer and I rode with Gin'l Forrest, and them things we et when the time come. I tell you. I et meat what got up and run when you taken out yore knife to cut a slice to put on the fire. You had to knock it down with a carbeen butt, it was so active. That-air meat would jump like a bullfrog, it was so full of skippers."

But nobody was listening to the old man. The boy on the mule turned his sullen sharp face from him, dug a heel into the side of the mule and went off up the pike with a motion which made you think that any second you would hear mule bones clashing inside that lank and scrofulous hide.

"Cy Dundee's boy," a man said, and nodded toward the figure going up the pike on the mule.

"Reckin Cy Dunbee's younguns seen times they'd settle fer drownt cow," another man said.

The old man with the beard peered at them both from his weak, slow eyes, first at one and then at the other. "Live long enough," he said, "and a man will settle fer what he kin git."

Then there was silence again, with the people looking at the red, foam-flecked water.

My father lifted the bridle rein in his left hand, and the mare turned and walked around the group and up the pike. We rode on up to our big gate, where my father dismounted to open it and let me myself ride Nellie Gray through. When he got to the lane that led off from the drive about two hundred yards from our house, my father said, "Grab on." I grabbed on, and he let me down to the ground. "I'm going to ride down and look at my corn," he said. "You go on." He took the lane, and I stood there on the drive and watched him ride off. He was wearing cowhide boots and an old hunting coat, and I thought that that made him look very military, like a picture. That and the way he rode.

I did not go to the house. Instead, I went by the vegetable garden and crossed behind the stables, and headed down for Dellie's cabin. I wanted to go down and play with Jebb, who was Dellie's little boy about two years older than I was. Besides, I was cold. I shivered as I walked, and I had goose-flesh. The mud which crawled up between my toes with every step I took was like ice. Dellie would have a fire, but she wouldn't make me put on shoes and stockings.

Dellie's cabin was of logs, with one side, because it was on a slope, set on limestone chunks, with a little porch attached to it, and had a little white-washed fence around it and a gate with plow-points on a wire to clink when somebody came in, and had two big white oaks in the yard and some flowers and a nice privy in the back with some honeysuckle growing over it. Dellie and Old Jebb, who was Jebb's father and who lived with Dellie and had lived with her for twenty-five years even if they never had got married, were careful to keep everything nice around their cabin. They had the name all over the community for being clean and clever Negroes. Dellie and Jebb were what they used to call "white-folks' niggers." There was a big difference between their cabin and the other two cabins weatherproof, but he couldn't undertake to go down and pick up after the litter they strewed. They didn't take the trouble to have a vegetable patch like Dellie and Jebb or to make preservers from wild plum, and jelly from crab apple the way Dellie did. They were shiftless, and my father was always threatening to get shed of them. But he never did. When they finally left, they just up and left on their own, for no reason, to go and be shiftless somewhere else. Then some more came. But meanwhile they lived down there, Matt Rawson and his family, and Sid Turner and his, and I played with their children all over the farm when they weren't working. But when I wasn't around they were mean sometimes to Little Jebb. That was because the other tenants down there were jealous of Dellie and Jebb.

I was so cold that I ran the last fifty yards to Dellie's gate. As soon as I had entered the yard, I saw that the storm had been hard on Dellie's flowers. The yard was, as I have said, on a slight slope, and the water running across had gutted the flower beds and washed out all the good black woods-earth which Dellie had brought in. What little grass there was in the yard was plastered sparsely down on the ground, the way the drainage water had left it. It reminded me of the way the fluff was plastered down on the skin of the drowned chicks that the strange man had been picking up, up in my mother's chicken yard.

I took a few steps up the path to the cabin, and then I saw that the drainage water had washed a lot of trash and filth out from under Dellie's house. Up toward the porch, the ground was not clean any more. Old pieces of rag, two or three rusted cans, pieces of rotten rope, some hunks of old dog dung, broken glass, old paper, and all sorts of things like that had washed out from under Dellie's house to foul her clean yard. It looked just as bad as the yards of the other cabins, or worse. It was worse, as a matter of fact, because it was a surprise. I had never thought of all that filth being under Dellie's house. It was not anything against Dellie that the stuff had been under the cabin. Trash will get under any house. But I did not think of that when I saw the foulness which had washed out on the ground which Dellie sometimes used to sweep with a twig broom to make nice and clean.

I picked my way past the filth, being careful not to get my bare feet on it, and mounted to Dellie's door. When I knocked, I heard her voice telling me to come in.

It was dark inside the cabin, after the daylight, but I could make out Dellie piled up in bed under a quilt, and Little Jebb crouched by the hearth, where a low fire simmered. "Howdy," I said to Dellie, "How you feeling?"

Her big eyes, the whites surprising and glaring in the black face, fixed on me as I stood there, but she did not reply. It did not look like Dellie, or act like Dellie, who would grumble and bustle around our kitchen, talking to herself, scolding me or Little Jebb, clanking pans, making all sorts of unnecessary noises and mutterings like an old-fashioned black steam thrasher engine when it has got up an extra head of steam and keeps popping the governor and rumbling and shaking on its wheels. But now Dellie just lay up there on the bed, under the patch-work quilt, and turned the black face, which I scarcely recognized, and the glaring white eyes to me.

"How you feeling?" I repeated.

"I'se sick," the voice said croakingly out of the strange black face which was not attached to Dellie's big, squat body, but stuck out from under a pile of tangled bedclothes. Then the voice added: "Mighty sick."

"I'm sorry," I managed to say.

The eyes remained fixed on me for a moment, then they left me and the head rolled back on the pillow. "Sorry," the voice said, in a flat way which wasn't question or statement of anything. It was just the empty word put into the air with no meaning or expression, to float off like a feather or a puff of smoke, while the big eyes, with the whites like the peeled white of hard-boiled eggs, stared at the ceiling.

"Dellie," I said after a minute, "there's a tramp up at the house. He's got a knife."

She was not listening. She closed her eyes.

I tiptoed over to the hearth where Jebb was and crouched beside him. We began to talk in low voices. I was asking him to get out his train and play train. Old Jebb had put spool wheels on three cigar boxes and put wire links between the boxes to make a train for Jebb. The box that was the locomotive had the top closed and a length of broom stick for a smoke stack. Jebb didn't want to get the train out, but I told him I would go home if he didn't. So he got out the train, and the colored rocks, and fossils of crinoid stems, and other junk he used for the load, and we began to push it around, talking the way we thought trainmen talked, making a chuck-chucking sound under the breath for the noise of the locomotive and now and then uttering low, cautious toots for the whistle. We got so interested in playing train that the toots got louder. Then, before he thought, Jebb gave a good, loud *toot-toot*, blowing for a crossing.

"Come here," the voice said from the bed.

Jebb got up slow from his hands and knees, giving me a sudden, naked, inimical look.

"Come here!" the voice said.

Jebb went to the bed. Dellie propped herself weakly up on one arm, muttering, "Come closer."

Jebb stood closer.

"Last thing I do, I'm gonna do it," Dellie said. "Donne tole you to be quiet."

Then she slapped him. It was an awful slap, more awful for the kind of weakness which it came from and brought to focus. I had seen her slap Jebb before, but the slapping had always been the kind of easy slap you would expect from a good-natured, grumbling Negro woman like Dellie. But this was different. It was so awful that Jebb didn't make a sound. The tears just popped out and ran down his face, and his breath came sharp, like gasps.

Dellie fell back. "Cain't even be sick," she said to the ceiling. "Git sick and they won't even let you lay. They tromp all over you. Cain't even be sick." Then she closed her eyes.

I went out of the room. I almost ran getting to the door, and I did run across the porch and down the steps and across the yard, not caring whether or not I stepped on the filth which had washed out from under the cabin. I ran almost all the way home. Then I thought about my mother catching me with the bare feet. So I went down to the stables.

I heard a noise in the crib, and opened the door. There was Big Jebb, sitting on an old nail keg, shelling corn into a bushel basket. I went in, pulling the door shut behind me, and crouched on the floor near him. I crouched there for a couple of minutes before either of us spoke, and watched him shelling the corn.

He had very big hands, knotted and grayish at the joints, with calloused palms which seemed to be streaked, with the rust coming up between the fingers to show from the back. His hands were so strong and tough that he could take a big ear of corn and rip the grains right off the cob with the palm of his hands, all in one motion, like a machine. "Work long as me," he would say, "and the good Lawd'll give you a hand lak cassion won't nuthin' hurt." And his hands did look like cast iron, old cast iron streaked with rust.

He was an old man, up in his seventies, thirty years or more older than Dellie, but he was strong as a bull. He was a squat sort of man, heavy in the shoulders, with remarkably long arms, the kind of build they say the river natives have on the Congo from paddling so much in their boats. He had a round bullet-head, set on powerful shoulders. His skin was very black, and the thin hair on his head was now grizzled like tufts of old cotton batting. He had small eyes and a flat nose, not big, and the kindest and wisest old face in the world, the blunt, sad, wise face of an old animal peering tolerantly out on the goings-on of the merely human creatures before him. He was a good man, and I loved him next to my mother and father. I crouched there on the floor of the crib and watched him shell corn with the rusty cast-iron hands, while he looked down at me out of the little eyes set in the blunt face.

"Dellie says she's might sick," I said.

"Yeah," he said.

"What's she sick from?"

"Woman-mizry," he said.

"What's woman-mizry?"

"Hit comes on'em," he said. "Hit just comes on'em when the time comes."

"What is it?"

"Hit is the change," he said. "Hit is the change of life and time."

"What changes?"

"You too young to know."

"Tell me."

"Time come and you find out everything."

I knew that there was no use in asking him any more. When I asked him things and he said that, I always knew that he would not tell me. So I continued to crouch there and watch him. Now that I had sat there a little while, I was cold again.

"What you shiver fer?" he asked me.

"I'm cold. I'm cold because it's blackberry winter," I said.

"My mother says it is."

"Ain't sayen Miss Sallie doan know and ain't sayen she do. But folks doan know everything."

"Why isn't it blackberry winter?"

"Too late fer blackberry winter. Blackberries done bloomed."

"She said it was."

"Blackberry winter just a leetle cold spell. Hit come and then hit go away, and hit is growed summer of a sudden lak a gunshot. Ain't no tellen hit will go way this time."

"It's June," I said.

"June," he replied with great contempt. "That what folks say. What June mean? Maybe hit is coming cold to stay."

"Why?"

"Cause this-here old yearth is tahrd. Hit is tahrd and ain't gonna perduce. Lawd let hit come rain one time forty days and forty nights,' cause He was tahrd of sinful folks. Maybe this-here old yearth say to the Lawd, I done plum tahrd, Lawd, lemme rest. And Lawd say, Yearth, you done yore best, you give'em cawn and you give'em taters, and all they think on is they gut, and, Yearth, you kin take a rest."

"What will happen?"

"Folks will eat up everything. The yearth won't perduce no more. Folks cut down all the trees and burn' em cause they cold, and the yearth won't grow no more. I been tellen folks. Sayen, maybe this year, hit is the time. But they doan listen to me, how the tearth is tahrd. Maybe this year they find out."

"Will everything die?"

"Everything and everybody, hit will be so."

"This year?"

"Ain't no tellen. Maybe this year."

"My mother said it is blackberry winter," I said confidently, and got up.

"Ain't sayen nuthin' agin Miss Sallie," he said.

I went to the door of the crib. I was really cold now. Running, I had got up a sweat and now I was worse.

I hung on the door, looking at Jebb, who was shelling corn again.

"There's a tramp came to the house," I said. I had almost forgotten the tramp.

"Yeah."

"He came by the back way. What was he doing down there in the storm?"

"They comes and they goes," he said, "and ain't no tellen."

"He had a mean knife."

"The good ones and the bad ones, they comes and they goes. Storm or sun, light or dark. They is folks and they goes lak folks."

I hung on the door, shivering.

He studied me a moment, then said, "You git on to the house. You ketch yore death. Then what yore mammy say?"

I hesitated.

"You git," he said.

When I came to the back yard, I saw that my father was standing by the back porch and the tramp was walking toward him. They began talking before I reached them, but I got there just as my father was saying, "I'm sorry, but I haven't got any work. I got all the hands on the place I need now. I won't need any extra until wheat thrashing."

The stranger made no reply, just looked at my father.

My father took out his leather coin purse, and got out a half-dollar. He held it toward the man. "This is for half a day," he said.

The man looked at the coin, and then at my father, making no motion to take the money. But that was the right amount. A dollar a day was what you paid them back in 1910. And the man hadn't even worked half a day.

Then the man reached out and took the coin. He dropped it into the right side pocket of his coat. Then he said, very slowly and without feeling: "I didn't want to work on your – farm."

He used the word which they would have frailed me to death for using.

I looked at my father's face and it was streaked white under the sunburn. Then he said, "Get off this place. Get off this place or I won't be responsible."

The man dropped his right hand into his pants pocket. It was the pocket where he kept the knife. I was just about to yell to my father about the knife when the hand came back out with nothing in it. The man gave a kind of twisted grin, showing where the teeth had been knocked out above the new scar. I thought that instant how maybe he had tried before to pull a knife on somebody else and had got his teeth knocked out.

So now he just gave that twisted, sickish grin out of the unmemorable, grayish face, and then spat on the brick path. The glob landed just about six inches from the toe of my father's right boot. My father looked down at it, and so did I. I thought that if the glob had hit my father's boot something would have happened. I looked down and saw the bright glob, and on one side of it my father's strong cowhide boots, with the brass eyelets and the leather thongs, heavy boots splashed with good red mud and set solid on the bricks, and on the other side the pointed-toe, broken, black shoes, on which the mud looked so sad and out of place. Then I saw one of the black shoes move a little, just a twitch first, then a real step backward.

The man moved in a quarter circle to the end of the porch, with my father's steady gaze upon him all the while. At the end of the porch, the man reached up to the shelf where the wash pans were to get his little newspaper-wrapped parcel. Then he disappeared around the corner of the house and my father mounted the porch and went into the kitchen without a word.

I followed around the house to see what the man would do. I wasn't afraid of him now, no matter if he did have the knife. When I got around in front, I saw him going out the yard gate and starting up the drive toward the pike. So I ran to catch up with him. He was sixty yards or so up the drive before I caught up.

I did not walk right up even with him at first, but trailed him, the way a kid will, about seven or eight feet behind, now and then running two or three steps in order to hold my place against his longer stride. When I first came up behind him, he turned to give me a look, just a meaningless look, and then fixed his eyes up the drive and kept on walking.

When we had got around the bend in the drive which cut the house from sight, and were going along by the edge of the woods, I decided to come up even with him. I ran a few steps, and was by his side, or almost, but some feet off to the right. I walked along in this position for a while, and he never noticed me. I walked along until we got within sight of the big gate that let on the pike.

Then I said: "Where did you come from?"

He looked at me then with a look which seemed almost surprised that I was there. Then he said, "It ain't none of yore business."

We went on another fifty feet.

Then I said, "Where are you going?"

He stopped, studied me dispassionately for a moment, then suddenly took a step toward me and leaned his face down at me. The lips jerked back, but not in any grin, to show where the teeth were knocked out and to make the scar on the lower lip come white with the tension.

He said: "Stop following me. You don't stop following me and I cut yore throat, you little son-of-a-bitch."

Then he went on to the gate, and up the pike.

That was thirty-five years ago. Since that time my father and mother have died. I was still a boy, but a big boy, when my father got cut on the blade of a mowing machine and died of lockjaw. My mother sold the place and went to the town to live with her sister. But she never took hold after my father's death, and she died within three years, right in middle life. My aunt always said, "Sallie just died of a broken heart, she was so devoted." Dellie is dead, too, but she died, I heard, quite a long time after we sold the farm.

As for Little Jebb, he grew up to be a mean and ficey Negro. He killed another Negro in a fight and got sent to the penitentiary, where he is yet, the last I heard tell. He probably grew up to be mean and ficey from just being picked on so much by the children of the other tenants, who were jealous of Jebb and Dellie for being thrifty and clever and being white-folks' niggers.

Old Jebb lived forever. I saw him ten years ago and he was about a hundred then, and not looking much different. He was living in town then, on relief – that was back in the Depression – when I went to see him. He said to me: "Too strong to die. When I was a young feller just comen on and seen how things wuz, I prayed the Lawd. I said, Oh, Lawd, gimme strength and meke me strong fer to do and to in-dure. The Lawd hearkened to my prayer. He give me strength. I was in-duren proud fer being strong and me much man. The Lawd give me my prayer and my strength. But now He done gone off and fergot me and left me alone with my strength. A man doan know what to pray fer, and him mortal."

Jebb is probably living yet, as far as I know.

That is what has happened since the morning when the tramp leaned his face down at me and showed his teeth and said: "Stop following me. You don't stop following me and I cut yore throat, you little son-of-a-bitch." That was what he said, for me not to follow him. But I did follow him, all the years.

Unit 5
Thomas Wolfe(1900–1938)
托马斯·沃尔夫

作者简介

托马斯·沃尔夫,美国南方小说家,生于北卡罗莱纳州(North Carolina)山区小城阿什维尔(Asheville)。父亲是雕刻墓碑的石匠,母亲当过书籍推销员和教师。他家的八个孩子中仅有六个存活,他是最小的一个。所以,死亡、孤独和成长是沃尔夫一直关注的主题。1916年沃尔夫进入北卡罗来纳大学学习,爱好喜剧。1920年大学毕业后,他参加了哈佛大学教授贝克主办的著名戏剧实验班,创作了独幕剧《巴克·戈文的归来》(*The Return of Buck Gavin*)和《第三个夜晚》(*The Third Night*)等。1924年他在纽约大学教授英语。1929年发表第一部长篇小说《天使,望故乡》(*Look Homeward, Angel*),并一举成名。这部小说的创作开始于1925年,经过四年的努力,沃尔夫终于完成了这部风格清新、笔调细腻、形象感人、富有乡土气息的作品。此后,他辞去大学教师的工作,专心从事写作,相继出版长篇小说《关于时间和河流》(*Of Time and the River*,1935)和短篇小说集《从死亡到早晨》(*From Death to Morning*,1935)。1938年9月15日沃尔夫因患脑炎死于马里兰州的巴尔的摩。他留下的大量遗稿由爱德华·阿什维尔(Edward Ashville)编辑成两部长篇小说《蛛网与岩石》(*The Web and the Rock*,1939)和《不能再回家》(*You Can't Go Home Again*,1940)出版。沃尔夫的其他主要作品还包括短篇小说集《远山》(*The Hills Beyond*,1941)、《短篇小说集》(*The Collected Stories*,1987)、《书信集》(*The Letters of Thomas Wolfe*,1956)和散文集《群山》(*The Mountains*,1971)等,都由后人从沃尔夫的遗稿中整理出版。他的文学创作观主要收于《一部小说的故事》(*The Story of a Novel*,1936)中。

托马斯·沃尔夫是一位精力充沛、想象力丰富的作家。他以年轻人成长的迷惘、失落与孤寂为主题,却始终不忘留下一丝希望,暗示"美国梦"仍具有现实意义。他的家人和他自己后来都成为他小说人物的原型,小说主人公尤金·甘特和后来的乔治·韦伯都是托马斯·沃尔夫的化身,沃尔夫的作品实际上是他个人生活小说化的编年史。因此他被认为是20世纪自传色彩最浓的美国小说家。沃尔夫的作品感情奔放、文笔流畅、气势磅礴,以浓郁的抒情魅力以及暗示和象征等手法有力地感染着读者。1938年沃尔夫去世后,威廉·福克纳将他列为他们那一代最好的作家。"垮掉派"作家杰克·凯鲁亚克也将沃尔夫视为自己的文学偶像。

作品导读

Look Homeward, Angel is a novel with a strong sense of autobiography, which comprehensively displays the life in the American South from 1900 to 1920. The novel is mainly about a young man's burning desire to leave his small town and tumultuous family in search of a better life. It is divided into three parts with a total of forty chapters and follows the trajectory of Eugene Gant, the protagonist who is generally believed to be a depiction of Wolfe himself, a brilliant and restless young man whose wanderlust and passion shape his adolescent years in rural North Carolina. The first 90 pages of the book deal with an early biography of Gant's parents, very closely based on the actual history of Wolfe's own mother and father. It begins with his father, Oliver's decision to become a stone cutter after seeing a statue of a stone angel. The novel covers the span of time from Gant's birth to the age of 19. The setting is the fictional town and state of Altamont, Catawba, which is considered to be a not-so-subtle mirror of his hometown, Asheville, North Carolina. Eugene Gant is a moonstruck, sensitive youth who lives in the boardinghouse run by his domineering mother Eliza. His father, W. O. Gant, is a blustering, frequently drunken dreamer and his elder brother Ben is too frail to live in the real world he longs for. Eugene's own world seems shattered when Ben dies and when his affair with the Gants' boarder, Laura James, ends. As he goes off to college he can only hope to overcome his past and make something of himself. This autobiographical story about the quest for a greater intellectual life has resonated with and influenced generations of readers, including some of today's most important novelists. Rich with lyrical prose and vivid characterizations, this twentieth-century American classic will capture the hearts and imaginations of every reader.

Look Homeward, Angel is a novel of growth. The protagonist is born into a Southern family and community, experiences childhood and youth, goes away to college, and at the end is preparing to leave for the North. Along with the developing personality of Eugene Gant there are characterizations of his mother, his father, his brothers Ben, Steve, and Luke, and his sister Helen. The process chronicled is that of estrangement and loss in time. The death of Ben severs the last tie that fastens Eugene to Altamont and the family. Yet at the same time the story being told by a remembering narrator whose recreation of his earlier experiences invests family and setting, people and place with dignity and vitality, so that if at the close Eugene Gant is ready to put Altamont behind him forever, clearly the autobiographical author has taken the community right along with him.

In the following excerption, near the conclusion of the novel, Wolfe's protagonist, Eugene Gant, has been called home from college to the bedside of his older brother, Ben, who is dying of pneumonia. Eugene encounters his mother and father, his brother Luke and his sister, Helen, as they all gather in the Gant home.

作品选读

Look Homeward, Angel

Chapter 35

[Ben]

There was no train until the next day. Heston quieted him during the evening with a stiff drink of gin manufactured from alcohol taken from the medical laboratory. Eugene was silent and babbled incoherently by starts: he asked the medical student a hundred questions about the progress and action of the disease.

"If it were double pneumonia she would have said so. Doesn't it seem that way to you? Hey?" he demanded feverishly.

"I should think so," said Heston. He was a kind and quiet boy.

Eugene went to Exeter the next morning to catch the train. All through a dreary gray afternoon it pounded across the sodden State. Then, there was a change and a terrible wait of several hours at a junction. Finally, as dark came, he was being borne again toward the hills.

Within his berth he lay with hot sleepless eyes, staring out at the black mass of the earth, the bulk of the hills. Finally, in the hours after midnight, he dropped into a nervous doze. He was wakened by the clatter of the trucks as they began to enter the Altamont yards. Dazed, half-dressed, he was roused by the grinding halt, and a moment later was looking out through the curtains into the grave faces of Luke and Hugh Barton.

"Ben's very sick," said Hugh Barton.

Eugene pulled on his shoes and dropped to the floor, stuffing his collar and tie into a coat pocket.

"Let's go," he said. "I'm ready."

They went softly down the aisle, amid the long dark snores of the sleepers. As they walked through the empty station toward Hugh Barton's car, Eugene said to the sailor:

"When did you get home, Luke?"

"I came in last night," he said. "I've been here only a few hours."

It was half-past three in the morning. The ugly station settlement lay fixed and horrible, like something in a dream. His strange and sudden return to it heightened his feeling of unreality. In one of the cars lined at the station curbing, the driver lay huddled below his blanket. In the Greek's lunchroom a man sat sprawled faced downward on the counter. The lights were dull and weary: a few burned with slow lust in the cheap station-hotels.

Hugh Barton, who had always been a cautious driver, shot away with a savage grinding of gears. They roared townward through the rickety slums at fifty miles an hour.

"I'm afraid B-B-B-Ben is one sick boy," Luke began.

"How did it happen?" Eugene asked. "Tell me."

He had taken influenza, they told Eugene, from one of Daisy's children. He had moped about, ill and feverish, for a day or two, without going to bed.

"In that G-g-g-god dam cold barn," Luke burst out. "If that boy dies it's because he c-c-c-couldn't keep warm."

"Never mind about that now," Eugene cried irritably, "go on."

Finally he had gone to bed, and Mrs. Pert had nursed him for a day or two.

"She was the only one who d-d-d-did a damn thing for him," said the sailor. Eliza, at length, had called in Cardiac.

"The d-d-damned old quack," Luke stuttered.

"Never mind! Never mind!" Eugene yelled. "Why dig it up now? Get on with it!"

After a day or two, he had grown apparently convalescent, and Cardiac told him he might get up if he liked. He got up and moped about the house for a day, in a cursing rage, but the next day he lay a-bed, with a high fever. Coker at length had been called in, two days before –

"That's what they should have done at the start," growled Hugh Barton over his wheel.

"Never mind!" screamed Eugene. "Get on with it."

And Ben had been desperately ill, with pneumonia in both lungs, for over a day. The sad prophetic story, a brief and terrible summary of the waste, the tardiness, and the ruin of their lives, silenced them for a moment with its inexorable sense of tragedy. They had nothing to say.

The powerful car roared up into the chill dead Square. The feeling of unreality grew upon the boy. He sought for his life, for the bright lost years, in this mean cramped huddle of brick and stone. Ben and I, here by the City Hall, the Bank, the grocery-store (he thought). Why here? In Gath or Ispahan. In Corinth or Byzantium. Not here. It is not real.

A moment later, the big car sloped to a halt at the curb, in front of Dixieland. A light burned dimly in the hall, evoking for him chill memories of damp and gloom. A warmer light burned in the parlor, painting the lowered shade of the tall window a warm and mellow orange.

"Ben's in that room upstairs," Luke whispered, "where the light is."

Eugene looked up with cold dry lips to the bleak front room upstairs, with its ugly Victorian bay-window. It was next to the sleeping-porch where, but three weeks before, Ben had hurled into the darkness his savage curse at life. The light in the sickroom burned grayly, bringing to him its grim vision of struggle and naked terror.

The three men went softly up the walk and entered the house. There was a faint clatter from the kitchen, and voices.

"Papa's in here," said Luke.

Eugene entered the parlor and found Gant seated alone before a bright coal-fire. He looked up dully and vaguely as his son entered.

"Hello, papa," said Eugene, going to him.

"Hello, son," said Gant. He kissed the boy with his bristling cropped mustache. His thin lip began to tremble petulantly.

"Have you heard about your brother?" he snuffled. "To think that this should be put upon me, old and sick as I am. O Jesus, it's fearful–"

Helen came in from the kitchen.

"Hello, Slats," she said, heartily embracing him. "How are you, honey? He's grown four inches more since he went away," she jeered, sniggering. "Well, 'Gene, cheer up! Don't look so blue. While there's life there's hope. He's not gone yet, you know." She burst into tears, hoarse, unstrung, hysterical.

"To think that this must come upon me," Gant sniffled, responding mechanically to her grief, as he rocked back and forth on his cane and stared into the fire. "O boo-hoo-hoo! What have I done that God should–"

"You shut up! " she cried, turning upon him in a blaze of fury. "Shut your mouth this minute. I don't want to hear any more from you! I've given my life to you! Everything's been done for you, and you'll be here when we're all gone. You're not the one who's sick." Her feeling toward him had, for the moment, gone rancorous and bitter.

"Where's mama?" Eugene asked.

"She's back in the kitchen," Helen said. "I'd go back and say hello before you see Ben if I were you." In a low brooding tone, she continued: "Well, forget about it. It can't be helped now."

He found Eliza busy over several bright bubbling pots of water on the gas-stove. She bustled awkwardly about, and looked surprised and confused when she saw him.

"Why, what on earth, boy! When'd you get in?"

He embraced her. But beneath her matter-of-factness, he saw the terror in her heart: her dull black eyes glinted with bright knives of fear.

"How's Ben, mama?" he asked quietly.

"Why-y," she pursed her lips reflectively, "I was just saying to Doctor Coker before you came in. 'Look here,' I said. 'I tell you what, I don't believe he's half as bad off as he looks. Now, if only we can hold on till morning. I believe there's going to be a change for the better.'"

"Mama, in heaven's name! " Helen burst out furiously. "How can you bear to talk like that? Don't you know that Ben's condition is critical? Are you never going to wake up?"

Her voice had its old cracked note of hysteria.

"Now, I tell you, son," said Eliza, with a white tremulous smile, "when you go in there to see him, don't make out as if you knew he was sick. If I were you, I'd make a big joke of it all. I'd laugh just as big as you please and say, 'See here, I thought I was coming to see a sick man. Why, pshaw! ' (I'd say) 'there's nothing wrong with you. Half of it's only imagination! '"

"O mama! for Christ's sake! " said Eugene frantically. "For Christ's sake! "

He turned away, sick at heart, and caught at his throat with his fingers.

Then he went softly upstairs with Luke and Helen, approaching the sick-room with a shriveled heart and limbs which had gone cold and bloodless. They paused for a moment, whispering, before he entered. The wretched conspiracy in the face of death filled him with horror.

"N-n-n-now, I wouldn't stay but a m-m-m-minute," whispered Luke. "It m-m-might make him nervous."

Eugene, bracing himself, followed Helen blindly into the room.

"Look who's come to see you," her voice came heartily. "It's Highpockets."

For a moment Eugene could see nothing, for dizziness and fear. Then, in the gray shaded light of the room, he descried Bessie Gant, the nurse, and the long yellow skull's-head of Coker, smiling wearily at him, with big stained teeth, over a long chewed cigar. Then, under the terrible light which fell directly and brutally upon the bed alone, he saw Ben. And in that moment of searing recognition he saw, what they had all seen, that Ben was dying.

Ben's long thin body lay three-quarters covered by the bedding; its gaunt outline was bitterly twisted below the covers, in an attitude of struggle and torture. It seemed not to belong to him, it was somehow distorted and detached as if it belonged to a beheaded criminal. And the sallow yellow of his face had turned gray; out of this granite tint of death, lit by two red flags of fever, the stiff black furze of a three-day beard was growing. The beard was somehow horrible; it recalled the corrupt vitality of hair, which can grow from a rotting corpse. And Ben's thin lips were lifted, in a constant grimace of torture and strangulation, about his white somehow dead-looking teeth, as inch by inch he gasped a thread of air into his lungs.

And the sound of this gasping – loud, hoarse, rapid, unbelievable, filling the room, and orchestrating every moment in it – gave to the scene its final note of horror.

Ben lay upon the bed below them, drenched in light, like some enormous insect on a naturalist's table, fighting, while they looked at him, to save with his poor wasted body the life that no one could save for him. It was monstrous, brutal.

As Eugene approached, Ben's fear-bright eyes rested upon the younger brother for the first time and bodilessly, without support, he lifted his tortured lungs from the pillow, seizing the boy's wrists fiercely in the hot white circle of his hands, and gasping in strong terror like a child: "Why have you come? Why have you come home, 'Gene?"

The boy stood white and dumb for a moment, while swarming pity and horror rose in him.

"They gave us a vacation, Ben," he said presently. "They had to close down on account of the flu."

Then he turned away suddenly into the black murk, sick with his poor lie, and unable to face the fear in Ben's gray eyes.

"All right, 'Gene," said Bessie Gant, with an air of authority. "Get out of here – you and Helen both. I've got one crazy Gant to look after already. I don't want two more in here." She spoke harshly, with an unpleasant laugh.

She was a thin woman of thirty-eight years, the wife of Gant's nephew, Gilbert. She was of mountain stock: she was coarse, hard, and vulgar, with little pity in her, and a cold lust for the miseries of sickness and death. These inhumanities she cloaked with her professionalism, saying:

"If I gave way to my feelings, where would the patient be?"

When they got out into the hall again, Eugene said angrily to Helen: "Why have you got that death's-head here? How can he get well with her around? I don't like her! "

"Say what you like – she's a good nurse." Then, in a low voice, she said: "What do you think?"

He turned away, with a convulsive gesture. She burst into tears, and seized his hand.

Luke was teetering about restlessly, breathing stentorously and smoking a cigarette, and Eliza, working her lips, stood with an attentive ear cocked to the door of the sick-room. She was holding a useless kettle of hot water.

"Huh? Hah? What say?" asked Eliza, before any one had said anything. "How is he?" Her eyes darted about at them.

"Get away! Get away! Get away! " Eugene muttered savagely. His voice rose. "Can't you get away?"

He was infuriated by the sailor's loud nervous breathing, his large awkward feet. He was angered still more by Eliza's useless kettle, her futile hovering, her "huh?" and "hah?"

"Can't you see he's fighting for his breath? Do you want to strangle him? It's messy! Messy! Do you hear?" His voice rose again.

The ugliness and discomfort of the death choked him; and the swarming family, whispering outside the door, pottering uselessly around, feeding with its terrible hunger for death on Ben's strangulation, made him mad with alternate fits of rage and pity.

Indecisively, after a moment, they went downstairs, still listening for sounds in the sick-room.

"Well, I tell you," Eliza began hopefully. "I have a feeling, I don't know what you'd call it–" She looked about awkwardly and found herself deserted. Then she went back to her boiling pots and pans.

Helen, with contorted face, drew him aside, and spoke to him in whispered hysteria, in the front hall.

"Did you see that sweater she's wearing? Did you see it? It's filthy! " Her voice sank to a brooding whisper. "Did you know that he can't bear to look at her? She came into the room yesterday, and he grew perfectly sick. He turned his head away and said 'O Helen, for God's sake, take her out of here.' You hear that, don't you. Do you hear? He can't stand to have her come near him. He doesn't want her in the room."

"Stop! Stop! For God's sake, stop! " Eugene said, clawing at his throat.

The girl was for the moment insane with hatred and hysteria.

"It may be a terrible thing to say, but if he dies I shall hate her. Do you think I can forget the way she's acted? Do you?" Her voice rose almost to a scream. "She's let him die here before her very eyes. Why, only day before yesterday, when his temperature was 104, she was

talking to Old Doctor Doak about a lot. Did you know that?"

"Forget about it! " he said frantically. "She'll always be like that! It's not her fault. Can't you see that? O God, how horrible! How horrible! "

"Poor old mama! " said Helen, beginning to weep. "She'll never get over this. She's scared to death! Did you see her eyes? She knows, of course she knows! "

Then suddenly, with mad brooding face, she said: "Sometimes I think I hate her! I really think I hate her." She plucked at her large chin, absently. "Well, we mustn't talk like this," she said. "It's not right. Cheer up. We're all tired and nervous. I believe he's going to get all right yet."

Day came gray and chill, with a drear reek of murk and fog. Eliza bustled about eagerly, pathetically busy, preparing breakfast. Once she hurried awkwardly upstairs with a kettle of water, and stood for a second at the door as Bessie Gant opened it, peering in at the terrible bed, with her white puckered face. Bessie Gant blocked her further entrance, and closed the door rudely. Eliza went away making flustered apologies.

For, what the girl had said was true, and Eliza knew it. She was not wanted in the sick-room; the dying boy did not want to see her. She had seen him turn his head wearily away when she had gone in. Behind her white face dwelt this horror, but she made no confession, no complaint. She bustled around doing useless things with an eager matter-of-factness. And Eugene, choked with exasperation at one moment, because of her heavy optimism, was blind with pity the next when he saw the terrible fear and pain in her dull black eyes. He rushed toward her suddenly, as she stood above the hot stove, and seized her rough worn hand, kissing it and babbling helplessly.

"O mama! Mama! It's all right! It's all right! It's all right."

And Eliza, stripped suddenly of her pretenses, clung to him, burying her white face in his coat sleeve, weeping bitterly, helplessly, grievously, for the sad waste of the irrevocable years – the immortal hours of love that might never be relived, the great evil of forgetfulness and indifference that could never be righted now. Like a child she was grateful for his caress, and his heart twisted in him like a wild and broken thing, and he kept mumbling:

"It's all right! It's all right! It's all right! " – knowing that it was not, could never be, all right.

"If I had known. Child, if I had known," she wept, as she had wept long before at Grover's death.

"Brace up! " he said. "He'll pull through yet. The worst is over."

"Well, I tell you," said Eliza, drying her eyes at once, "I believe it is. I believe he passed the turning-point last night. I was saying to Bessie –"

The light grew. Day came, bringing hope. They sat down to breakfast in the kitchen, drawing encouragement from every scrap of cheer doctor or nurse would give them. Coker departed, non-committally optimistic. Bessie Gant came down to breakfast and was professionally encouraging.

"If I can keep his damn family out of the room, he may have some chance of getting well."

They laughed hysterically, gratefully, pleased with the woman's abuse.

"How is he this morning?" said Eliza. "Do you notice any improvement?"

"His temperature is lower, if that's what you mean."

They knew that a lower temperature in the morning was a fact of no great significance, but they took nourishment from it: their diseased emotion fed upon it – they had soared in a moment to a peak of hopefulness.

"And he's got a good heart," said Bessie Gant. "If that holds out, and he keeps fighting, he'll pull through."

"D-d-don't worry about his f-f-fighting," said Luke, in a rush of eulogy. "That b-b-boy'll fight as long as he's g-g-got a breath left in him."

"Why, yes," Eliza began, "I remember when he was a child of seven – I know I was standing on the porch one day – the reason I remember is Old Mr. Buckner had just come by with some butter and eggs your papa had –"

"O my God!" groaned Helen, with a loose grin. "Now we'll get it."

"Whah – whah!" Luke chortled crazily, prodding Eliza in the ribs.

"I'll vow, boy!" said Eliza angrily. "You act like an idiot. I'd be ashamed!"

"Whah – whah – whah!"

Helen sniggered, nudging Eugene.

"Isn't he crazy, though? Tuh-tuh-tuh-tuh-tuh." Then, with wet eyes, she drew Eugene roughly into her big bony embrace.

"Poor old 'Gene. You always got on together, didn't you? You'll feel it more than any of us."

"He's not b-b-buried yet," Luke cried heartily. "That boy may be here when the rest of us are pushing d-d-daisies."

"Where's Mrs. Pert?" said Eugene. "Is she in the house?"

A strained and bitter silence fell upon them.

"I ordered her out," said Eliza grimly, after a moment. "I told her exactly what she was – a whore." She spoke with the old stern judiciousness, but in a moment her face began to work and she burst into tears. "If it hadn't been for that woman I believe he'd be well and strong today. I'll vow I do!"

"Mama, in heaven's name!" Helen burst out furiously. "How dare you say a thing like that? She was the only friend he had: when he was taken sick she nursed him hand and foot. Why, the idea! The idea!" she panted in her indignation. "If it hadn't been for Mrs. Pert he'd have been dead by now. Nobody else did anything for him. You were willing enough, I notice, to keep her here and take her money until he got sick. No, sir!" she declared with emphasis. "Personally, I like her. I'm not going to cut her now."

"It's a d-d-d-damn shame!" said Luke, staunch to his goddess. "If it hadn't been for

Mrs. P–P–P–Pert and you, Ben would be S. O. L. Nobody else around here gave a damn. If he d–d–d–dies, it's because he didn't get the proper care when it would have done him some good. There's always been too d–d–damn much thought of saving a nickel, and too d–d–damn little about flesh and blood! "

"Well, forget about it! " said Helen wearily. "There's one thing sure: I've done everything I could. I haven't been to bed for two days. Whatever happens, I'll have no regrets on that score." Her voice was filled with a brooding ugly satisfaction.

"I know you haven't! I know that! " The sailor turned to Eugene in his excitement, gesticulating. "That g–g–girl's worked her fingers to the bone. If it hadn't been for her – " His eyes got wet; he turned his head away and blew his nose.

"Oh, for Christ's sake! " Eugene yelled, springing up from the table. "Stop it, won't you! Let's wait till later."

In this way, the terrible hours of the morning lengthened out, while they spent themselves trying to escape from the tragic net of frustration and loss in which they were caught. Their spirits soared to brief moments of insane joy and exultancy, and plunged into black pits of despair and hysteria. Eliza alone seemed consistently hopeful. Trembling with exacerbated nerves, the sailor and Eugene paced the lower hall, smoking incessant cigarettes, bristling as they approached each other, ironically polite when their bodies touched. Gant dozed in the parlor or in his own room, waking and sleeping by starts, moaning petulantly, detached, vaguely aware only of the meaning of events, and resentful because of the sudden indifference to him. Helen went in and out of the sick-room constantly, dominating the dying boy by the power of her vitality, infusing him with moments of hope and confidence. But when she came out, her hearty cheerfulness was supplanted by the strained blur of hysteria; she wept, laughed, brooded, loved, and hated by turns.

Eliza went only once into the room. She intruded with a hotwater bag, timidly, awkwardly, like a child, devouring Ben's face with her dull black eyes. But when above the loud labor of his breath his bright eyes rested on her, his clawed white fingers tightened their grip in the sheets, and he gasped strongly, as if in terror:

"Get out! Out! Don't want you."

Eliza left the room. As she walked she stumbled a little, as if her feet were numb and dead. Her white face had an ashen tinge, and her dull eyes had grown bright and staring. As the door closed behind her, she leaned against the wall and put one hand across her face. Then, in a moment, she went down to her pots again.

Frantically, angrily, with twitching limbs they demanded calm and steady nerves from one another; they insisted that they keep away from the sick-room – but, as if drawn by some terrible magnet, they found themselves again and again outside the door, listening, on tiptoe, with caught breath, with an insatiate thirst for horror, to the hoarse noise of his gasping as he strove to force air down into his strangled and cemented lungs. And eagerly, jealously, they sought entrance to the room, waiting their turn for carrying water, towels, supplies.

Mrs. Pert, from her refuge in the boarding-house across the street, called Helen on the phone each half-hour, and the girl talked to her while Eliza came from the kitchen into the hall, and stood, hands folded, lips pursed, with eyes that sparkled with her hate.

The girl cried and laughed as she talked.

"Well ...that's all right, Fatty... You know how I feel about it... I've always said that if he had one true friend in the world, it's you...and don't think we're ALL ungrateful for what you've done..."

During the pauses, Eugene could hear the voice of the other woman across the wires, sobbing.

And Eliza said, grimly: "If she calls up again you let me talk to her. I'll fix her! "

"Good heavens, mama! " Helen cried angrily. "You've done enough already. You drove her out of the house when she'd done more for him than all his family put together." Her big strained features worked convulsively. "Why, it's ridiculous! "

Within Eugene, as he paced restlessly up and down the hall or prowled through the house a-search for some entrance he had never found, a bright and stricken thing kept twisting about like a trapped bird. This bright thing, the core of him, his Stranger, kept twisting its head about, unable to look at horror, until at length it gazed steadfastly, as if under a dreadful hypnosis, into the eyes of death and darkness. And his soul plunged downward, drowning in that deep pit: he felt that he could never again escape from this smothering flood of pain and ugliness, from the eclipsing horror and pity of it all. And as he walked, he twisted his own neck about, and beat the air with his arm like a wing, as if he had received a blow in his kidneys. He felt that he might be clean and free if he could only escape into a single burning passion – hard, and hot, and glittering – of love, hatred, terror, or disgust. But he was caught, he was strangling, in the web of futility – there was no moment of hate that was not touched by a dozen shafts of pity: impotently, he wanted to seize them, cuff them, shake them, as one might a trying brat, and at the same time to caress them, love them, comfort them.

As he thought of the dying boy upstairs, the messy ugliness of it – as they stood whimpering by while he strangled – choked him with fury and horror. The old fantasy of his childhood came back to him: he remembered his hatred of the semi-private bathroom, his messy discomfort while he sat at stool and stared at the tub filled with dirty wash, sloppily puffed and ballooned by cold gray soapy water. He thought of this as Ben lay dying.

Their hopes revived strongly in the forenoon when word came to them that the patient's temperature was lower, his pulse stronger, the congestion of the lungs slightly relieved. But at one o'clock, after a fit of coughing, he grew delirious, his temperature mounted, he had increasing difficulty in getting his breath. Eugene and Luke raced to Wood's pharmacy in Hugh Barton's car, for an oxygen tank. When they returned, Ben had almost choked to death. Quickly they carried the tank into the room, and placed it near his head. Bessie Gant seized the cone, and started to put it over Ben's mouth, commanding him to breathe it in. He fought it away tigerishly: curtly the nurse commanded Eugene to seize his hands.

Eugene gripped Ben's hot wrists: his heart turned rotten. Ben rose wildly from his pillows, wrenching like a child to get his hands free, gasping horribly, his eyes wild with terror:

"No! No! Gene! Gene! No! No! "

Eugene caved in, releasing him and turning way, white-faced, from the accusing fear of the bright dying eyes. Others held him. He was given temporary relief. Then he became delirious again.

By four o'clock it was apparent that death was near. Ben had brief periods of consciousness, unconsciousness, and delirium – but most of the time he was delirious. His breathing was easier, he hummed snatches of popular songs, some old and forgotten, called up now from the lost and secret adyts of his childhood; but always he returned, in his quiet humming voice, to a popular song of war-time – cheap, sentimental, but now tragically moving: "Just a Baby's Prayer at Twilight,"

...when lights are low.

Poor baby's years

Helen entered the darkening room.

Are filled with tears.

The fear had gone out of his eyes: above his gasping he looked gravely at her, scowling, with the old puzzled child's stare. Then, in a moment of fluttering consciousness, he recognized her. He grinned beautifully, with the thin swift flicker of his mouth.

"Hello, Helen! It's Helen! " he cried eagerly.

She came from the room with a writhen and contorted face, holding the sobs that shook her until she was half-way down the stairs.

As darkness came upon the gray wet day, the family gathered in the parlor, in the last terrible congress before death, silent, waiting. Gant rocked petulantly, spitting into the fire, making a weak whining moan from time to time. One by one, at intervals, they left the room, mounting the stairs softly, and listening outside the door of the sick-room. And they heard Ben, as, with incessant humming repetition, like a child, he sang his song,

There's a mother there at twilight

Who's glad to know –

Eliza sat stolidly, hands folded, before the parlor fire. Her dead white face had a curious carven look; the inflexible solidity of madness.

"Well," she said at length, slowly, "you never know. Perhaps this is the crisis. Perhaps –" her face hardened into granite again. She said no more.

Coker came in and went at once, without speaking, to the sick-room. Shortly before nine o'clock Bessie Gant came down.

"All right," she said quietly. "You had all better come up now. This is the end."

Eliza got up and marched out of the room with a stolid face. Helen followed her: she was panting with hysteria, and had begun to wring her big hands.

"Now, get hold of yourself, Helen," said Bessie Gant warningly. "This is no time to let yourself go."

Eliza went steadily upstairs, making no noise. But, as she neared the room, she paused, as if listening for sounds within. Faintly, in the silence, they heard Ben's song. And suddenly, casting away all pretense, Eliza staggered, and fell against the wall, turning her face into her hand, with a terrible wrenched cry:

"O God! If I had known! If I had known! "

Then, weeping with bitter unrestraint, with the contorted and ugly grimace of sorrow, mother and daughter embraced each other. In a moment they composed themselves, and quietly entered the room.

Eugene and Luke pulled Gant to his feet and supported him up the stairs. He sprawled upon them, moaning in long quivering exhalations.

"Mer-ci-ful God! That I should have to bear this in my old age. That I should – "

"Papa! For God's sake! " Eugene cried sharply. "Pull yourself together! It's Ben who's dying – not us! Let's try to behave decently to him for once."

This served to quiet Gant for a moment. But as he entered the room, and saw Ben lying in the semi-conscious coma that precedes death, the fear of his own death overcame him, and he began to moan again. They seated him in a chair, at the foot of the bed, and he rocked back and forth, weeping:

"O Jesus! I can't bear it! Why must you put this upon me? I'm old and sick, and I don't know where the money's to come from. How are we ever going to face this fearful and croo-el winter? It'll cost a thousand dollars before we're through burying him, and I don't know where the money's to come from." He wept affectedly with sniffling sobs.

"Hush! hush! " cried Helen, rushing at him. In her furious anger, she seized him and shook him. "You damned old man, you, I could kill you! How dare you talk like that when your son's dying? I've wasted six years of my life nursing you, and you'll be the last one to go! " In her blazing anger, she turned accusingly on Eliza:

"You've done this to him. You're the one that's responsible. If you hadn't pinched every penny he'd never have been like this. Yes, and Ben would be here, too! " She panted for breath for a moment. Eliza made no answer. She did not hear her.

"After this, I'm through! I've been looking for you to die – and Ben's the one who has to go." Her voice rose to a scream of exasperation. She shook Gant again. "Never again! Do you hear that, you selfish old man? You've had everything – Ben's had nothing. And now he's the one to go. I hate you! "

"Helen! Helen! " said Bessie Gant quietly. "Remember where you are."

"Yes, that means a lot to us," Eugene muttered bitterly.

Then, over the ugly clamor of their dissension, over the rasp and snarl of their nerves, they heard the low mutter of Ben's expiring breath. The light had been re-shaded: he lay, like his own shadow, in all his fierce gray lonely beauty. And as they looked and saw his bright eyes already blurred with death, and saw the feeble beating flutter of his poor thin breast, the

strange wonder, the dark rich miracle of his life surged over them its enormous loveliness. They grew quiet and calm, they plunged below all the splintered wreckage of their lives, they drew together in a superb communion of love and valiance, beyond horror and confusion, beyond death.

And Eugene's eyes grew blind with love and wonder: an enormous organ-music sounded in his heart, he possessed them for a moment, he was a part of their loveliness, his life soared magnificently out of the slough and pain and ugliness. He thought:

"That was not all! That really was not all!"

Helen turned quietly to Coker, who was standing in shadow by the window, chewing upon his long unlighted cigar.

"Is there nothing more you can do? Have you tried everything? I mean – EVERYTHING?"

Her voice was prayerful and low. Coker turned toward her slowly, taking the cigar between his big stained fingers. Then, gently, with his weary yellow smile, he answered: "Everything. Not all the king's horses, not all the doctors and nurses in the world, can help him now."

"How long have you known this?" she said.

"For two days," he answered. "From the beginning." He was silent for a moment. "For ten years!" he went on with growing energy. "Since I first saw him, at three in the morning, in the Greasy Spoon, with a doughnut in one hand and a cigarette in the other. My dear, dear girl," he said gently as she tried to speak, "we can't turn back the days that have gone. We can't turn life back to the hours when our lungs were sound, our blood hot, our bodies young. We are a flash of fire – a brain, a heart, a spirit. And we are three-cents-worth of lime and iron – which we cannot get back."

He picked up his greasy black slouch hat, and jammed it carelessly upon his head. Then he fumbled for a match and lit the chewed cigar.

"Has everything been done?" she said again. "I want to know! Is there anything left worth trying?"

He made a weary gesture of his arms.

"My dear girl!" he said. "He's drowning! Drowning!"

She stood frozen with the horror of his pronouncement.

Coker looked for a moment at the gray twisted shadow on the bed. Then, quietly, sadly, with tenderness and tired wonder, he said: "Old Ben. When shall we see HIS like again?"

Then he went quietly out, the long cigar clamped firmly in his mouth.

In a moment, Bessie Gant, breaking harshly in upon their silence with ugly and triumphant matter-of-factness, said: "Well, it will be a relief to get this over. I'd rather be called into forty outside cases than one in which any of these damn relations are concerned. I'm dead for sleep."

Helen turned quietly upon her.

"Leave the room!" she said. "This is our affair now. We have the right to be left alone."

Surprised, Bessie Gant stared at her for a moment with an angry, resentful face. Then she left the room.

The only sound in the room now was the low rattling mutter of Ben's breath. He no longer gasped; he no longer gave signs of consciousness or struggle. His eyes were almost closed; their gray flicker was dulled, coated with the sheen of insensibility and death. He lay quietly upon his back, very straight, without sign of pain, and with a curious upturned thrust of his sharp thin face. His mouth was firmly shut. Already, save for the feeble mutter of his breath, he seemed to be dead – he seemed detached, no part of the ugly mechanism of that sound which came to remind them of the terrible chemistry of flesh, to mock at illusion, at all belief in the strange passage and continuance of life.

He was dead, save for the slow running down of the worn-out machine, save for that dreadful mutter within him of which he was no part. He was dead.

But in their enormous silence wonder grew. They remembered the strange flitting loneliness of his life, they thought of a thousand forgotten acts and moments – and always there was something that now seemed unearthly and strange: he walked through their lives like a shadow – they looked now upon his gray deserted shell with a thrill of awful recognition, as one who remembers a forgotten and enchanted word, or as men who look upon a corpse and see for the first time a departed god.

Luke, who had been standing at the foot of the bed, now turned to Eugene nervously, stammering in an unreal whisper of wonder and disbelief:

"I g–g–g–guess Ben's gone."

Gant had grown very quiet: he sat in the darkness at the foot of the bed, leaning forward upon his cane, escaped from the revery of his own approaching death, into the waste land of the past, blazing back sadly and poignantly the trail across the lost years that led to the birth of his strange son.

Helen sat facing the bed, in the darkness near the windows. Her eyes rested not on Ben but on her mother's face. All by unspoken consent stood back in the shadows and let Eliza repossess the flesh to which she had given life.

And Eliza, now that he could deny her no longer, now that his fierce bright eyes could no longer turn from her in pain and aversion, sat near his head beside him, clutching his cold hand between her rough worn palms.

She did not seem conscious of the life around her. She seemed under a powerful hypnosis: she sat very stiff and erect in her chair, her white face set stonily, her dull black eyes fixed upon the gray cold face.

They sat waiting. Midnight came. A cock crew. Eugene went quietly to a window and stood looking out. The great beast of night prowled softly about the house. The walls, the windows seemed to bend inward from the thrusting pressure of the dark. The low noise in the wasted body seemed almost to have stopped. It came infrequently, almost inaudibly, with a faint fluttering respiration.

Helen made a sign to Gant and Luke. They rose and went quietly out. At the door she paused, and beckoned to Eugene. He went to her.

"You stay here with her," she said. "You're her youngest. When it's over, come and tell us."

He nodded, and closed the door behind her. When they had gone, he waited, listening for a moment. Then he went to where Eliza was sitting. He bent over her.

"Mama! " he whispered. "Mama! "

She gave no sign that she had heard him. Her face did not move; she did not turn her eyes from their fixed stare.

"Mama! " he said more loudly. "Mama! "

He touched her. She made no response.

"Mama! Mama! "

She sat there stiffly and primly like a little child.

Swarming pity rose in him. Gently, desperately, he tried to detach her fingers from Ben's hand. Her rough clasp on the cold hand tightened. Then, slowly, stonily, from right to left, without expression, she shook her head.

He fell back, beaten, weeping, before that implacable gesture. Suddenly, with horror, he saw that she was watching her own death, that the unloosening grip of her hand on Ben's hand was an act of union with her own flesh, that, for her, Ben was not dying – but that a part of HER, of HER life, HER blood, HER body, was dying. Part of her, the younger, the lovelier, the better part, coined in her flesh, borne and nourished and begun with so much pain there twenty-six years before, and forgotten since, was dying.

Eugene stumbled to the other side of the bed and fell upon his knees. He began to pray. He did not believe in God, nor in Heaven or Hell, but he was afraid they might be true. He did not believe in angels with soft faces and bright wings, but he believed in the dark spirits that hovered above the heads of lonely men. He did not believe in devils or angels, but he believed in Ben's bright demon to whom he had seen him speak so many times.

Eugene did not believe in these things, but he was afraid they might be true. He was afraid that Ben would get lost again. He felt that no one but he could pray for Ben now: that the dark union of their spirits made only HIS prayers valid. All that he had read in books, all the tranquil wisdom he had professed so glibly in his philosophy course, and the great names of Plato and Plotinus, of Spinoza and Immanuel Kant, of Hegel and Descartes, left him now, under the mastering surge of his wild Celtic superstition. He felt that he must pray frantically as long as the little ebbing flicker of breath remained in his brother's body.

So, with insane sing-song repetition, he began to mutter over and over again: "Whoever You Are, be good to Ben to – night. Show him the way... Whoever You Are, be good to Ben to–night. Show him the way..." He lost count of the minutes, the hours: he heard only the feeble rattle of dying breath, and his wild synchronic prayer.

Light faded from his brain, and consciousness. Fatigue and powerful nervous depletion conquered him. He sprawled out on the floor, with his arms pillowed on the bed, muttering drowsily. Eliza, unmoving, sat across the bed, holding Ben's hand. Eugene, mumbling, sank into an uneasy sleep.

He awoke suddenly, conscious that he had slept, with a sharp quickening of horror. He was afraid that the little fluttering breath had now ceased entirely, that the effect of his prayer was lost. The body on the bed was almost rigid: there was no sound. Then, unevenly, without rhythm, there was a faint mutter of breath. He knew it was the end. He rose quickly and ran to the door. Across the hall, in a cold bedroom, on two wide beds, Gant, Luke, and Helen lay exhausted.

"Come," cried Eugene. "He's going now."

They came quickly into the room. Eliza sat unmoving, oblivious of them. As they entered the room, they heard, like a faint expiring sigh, the final movement of breath.

The rattling in the wasted body, which seemed for hours to have given over to death all of life that is worth saving, had now ceased. The body appeared to grow rigid before them. Slowly, after a moment, Eliza withdrew her hands. But suddenly, marvelously, as if his resurrection and rebirth had come upon him, Ben drew upon the air in a long and powerful respiration; his gray eyes opened. Filled with a terrible vision of all, Life in the one monent, he seemed to rise forward bodilessly without support – a flame, a light, a glory – joined at length in death to the dark spirit who had brooded upon each footstep of his lonely adventure on earth; and, casting the fierce sword of his glance with utter and final comprehension upon the room haunted with its gray pageantry of cheap loves and dull consciences and on all those uncertain mummers of waste and confusion fading now from the bright window of his eyes, he passed instantly, scornful and unafraid, as he had lived, into the shades of death.

We can believe in the nothingness of life, we can believe in the nothingness of death and of life after death – but who can believe in the nothingness of Ben? Like Apollo, who did his penance to the high god in the sad house of King Admetus, he came, a god with broken feet, into the gray hovel of this world. And he lived here a stranger, trying to recapture the music of the lost world, trying to recall the great forgotten language, the lost faces, the stone, the leaf, the door.

O Artemidorus, farewell!

Unit 6
Katherine Anne Porter(1890–1980)
凯瑟琳·安妮·波特

作者简介

凯瑟琳·安妮·波特，美国南方重要的短篇小说女作家，1890 年 5 月 15 日出生于得克萨斯州印第安克里克(Indian Creek, Texas)的一个天主教家庭。她童年时接受修道院教育，后抛弃信仰出走。波特曾任《评论家》(*Fort Worth Critic*) 周刊编辑，《落基山新闻》(*Rocky Mountain News*)记者和艺术专栏评论员。20 世纪 20 年代初期，波特侨居墨西哥、德国、法国等，寻找写作题材，并在墨西哥参与了左翼政治活动。她晚年曾在多所大学任教。1958 年她继福克纳之后在美国弗吉尼亚大学担任驻校作家；她还担任过国会图书馆诗学顾问和全国文学艺术协会副主席。她的小说创作开始于 20 世纪 20 年代初期，她的作品多次获奖。1922 年 12 月，她的第一篇短篇小说《玛丽亚·孔塞普西翁》(*Maria Concepcion*) 问世。1930 年，她的第一个短篇小说集《开花的犹大树》(*Flowering Judas and Other Stories*)使她名噪一时，其中《弃妇》(*The Jilting of Granny Weatherall*)和以墨西哥为背景的《开花的犹大树》最为成功。该短篇小说集使她获得了 1931 年美国古根海姆研究基金会提供的资助。后来出版的短篇小说集有《中午酒》(*Noon Wine*,1937)、《灰白马、灰白骑士》(*Pale Horse, Pale Rider*,1939)、《斜塔》(*The Leaning Tower*,1944)等。1965 年推出的《波特小说集》(*Collected Stories*)为她赢得全国"图书奖"和"普利策奖"。

1962 年出版的《愚人船》(*Ship of Fools*) 是波特唯一的一部长篇小说，描写了一艘从墨西哥开往德国的客轮在海上航行 27 天中所发生的故事。小说人物众多，没有连贯的故事情节，作者凭借她敏锐的观察力和想象力，采用象征手法刻画了一幅现实主义的世态画卷，具有深刻的道德寓意和哲理性。波特的其他作品有杂文集《过去的日子》(*The Days Before*,1952)、短篇小说《圣诞故事》(*A Christmas Story*,1967)和非小说类作品《千古奇冤》(*The Never-Ending Wrong*,1977)等。她的作品多以精美而充满活力的散文、精微的心理洞察和准确的表达而著称，很有思想深度。她的短篇小说更是受人欢迎，它们结构丰满、人物刻画复杂、描写细腻、文字讲究、风格优美。批评家认为她善于探寻幻想与现实、背叛与内疚、邪恶与灾难以及人的孤独、苦闷、失意与隔阂等问题，结合白描、象征和意识流等手法，形成了含蓄、细腻和多彩的文风，被推崇为小说家中的文体家。

作品导读

Flowering Judas is a short story based in part on the real-life experiences of the author, Katherine Anne Porter. She lived for a time in early 20th Century in Mexico, studying art and working as a teacher and journalist. Persons she encountered during her stay in Mexico served as models for the characters in the story. She infuses some of herself into her protagonist, Laura, a beautiful American woman, who takes up residence in Mexico to help the downtrodden. She teaches English to children and delivers messages, cigarettes, money, and narcotics to the jailed or fugitive revolutionaries. However, Laura avoids committing herself to anything or anyone. Her students love her, but she stands aloof from them. Men court her, but she rejects them. She sometimes sneaks into a Catholic church to practice the religion of her youth, but she fails to embrace the church as an essential part of her life. Nothing gains her full attention.

In this story, the character of Laura is set against that of Braggioni, a corrupt revolutionary leader who is courting her. To Laura's dismay, he frequently visits her at home, hoping to seduce her. During an evening they spend together, Braggioni's singing and conversation mirrors Laura's growing disenchantment with the revolutionary ideal that brought her to Mexico. When Braggioni returns to his wife one evening, Laura falls asleep, dreaming of Eugenio, another revolutionary leader, whom Laura visits and gives narcotics in prison. He commits suicide with sleeping pills she had brought him. In the dream he asks her to eat the flowers of the Judas tree so as to travel with him to the land of death, but when he accuses her of being a murder, she awakens herself, crying aloud "No!" in negation of the nameless disaster that she has long feared.

Gradually, the reader recognizes Laura as a character whose spiritual betrayal is far more profound than the revolutionary leader's corruption. The ending of this story does not provide a simple resolution. It is only in Laura's dream at the end of the story, a dream brought on by her recognition that by betraying Eugenio she has betrayed herself, and that she comes to a horrifying understanding of her condition: her fear of love, of life. Porter ends the story here; we do not know if Laura's realization will save her from what she has become. Her dream, which as Robert Penn Warren wrote, "embodies but does not resolve the question," tantalizes us with its implications.

Flowering Judas

Braggioni sits heaped upon the edge of a straight-backed chair much too small for him, and sings to Laura in a furry, mournful voice. Laura has begun to find reasons for avoiding her own house until the latest possible moment, for Braggioni is there almost every night. No matter how late she is, he will be sitting there with a surly, waiting expression, pulling at his kinky yellow hair, thumbing the strings of his guitar, snarling a tune under his breath. Lupe the Indian maid meets Laura at the door, and says with a flicker of a glance towards the upper room, "He waits."

Laura wishes to lie down, she is tired of her hairpins and the feel other long tight sleeves, but she says to him, "Have you a new song for me this evening?" If he says yes, she asks him to sing it. If he says no, she remembers his favorite one, and asks him to sing it again. Lupe brings her a cup of chocolate and a plate of rice, and Laura eats at the small table under the lamp, first inviting Braggioni, whose answer is always the same: "I have eaten, and besides, chocolate thickens the voice."

Laura says, "Sing, then," and Braggioni heaves himself into song. He scratches the guitar familiarly as though it were a pet animal, and sings passionately off key, taking the high notes in a prolonged painful squeal. Laura, who haunts the markets listening to the ballad singers, and stops every day to hear the blind boy playing his reed-flute in Sixteenth of September Street, listens to Braggioni with pitiless courtesy, because she dares not smile at his miserable performance. Nobody dares to smile at him. Braggioni is cruel to everyone, with a kind of specialized insolence, but he is so vain of his talents, and so sensitive to slights, it would require a cruelty and vanity greater than his own to lay a finger on the vast cureless wound of his self-esteem. It would require courage, too, for it is dangerous to offend him, and nobody has this courage.

Braggioni loves himself with such tenderness and amplitude and eternal charity that his followers – for he is a leader of men, a skilled revolutionist, and his skin has been punctured in honorable warfare-warm themselves in the reflected glow, and say to each other: "He has a real nobility, a love of humanity raised above mere personal affections." The excess of this self-love has flowed out, inconveniently for her, over Laura, who, with so many others, owes her comfortable situation and her salary to him. When he is in a very good humor, he tells her, "I am tempted to forgive you for being a gringa, gringita! "and Laura, burning, imagines herself leaning forward suddenly, and with a sound backhanded slap wiping the suety smile from his face. If he notices her eyes at these moments he gives no sign.

She knows what Braggioni would offer her, and she must resist tenaciously without appearing to resist, and if she could avoid it she would not admit even to herself the slow drift of his intention. During these long evenings which have spoiled a long month for her, she sits in her deep chair with an open book on her knees, resting her eyes on the consoling rigidity of the printed page when the sight and sound of Braggioni singing threaten to identify themselves with all her remembered afflictions and to add their weight to her uneasy premonitions of the future. The gluttonous bulk of Braggioni has become a symbol of her many disillusions, for a revolutionist should be lean, animated by heroic faith, a vessel of abstract virtues. This is nonsense, she knows it now and is ashamed of it. Revolution must have leaders, and leadership is a career for energetic men. She is, her comrades tell her, full of romantic error, for what she defines as cynicism in them is merely "a developed sense of reality." She is almost too willing to say, "I am wrong, I suppose I don't really understand the principles," and afterward she makes a secret truce with herself, determined not to surrender her will to such expedient logic. But she cannot help feeling that she has been betrayed irreparably by the disunion between her way of living and her feeling of what life should be, and at times she is almost contented to rest in this sense of grievance as a private store of consolation. Sometimes she wishes to run away, but she stays. Now she longs to fly out of this room, down the narrow stairs, and into the street where the houses lean together like conspirators under a single mottled lamp, and leave Braggioni singing to himself.

Instead she looks at Braggioni, frankly and clearly, like a good child who understands the rules of behavior. Her knees cling together under sound blue serge, and her round white collar is not purposely nun-like. She wears the uniform of an idea, and has renounced vanities. She was born Roman Catholic, and in spite of her fear of being seen by someone who might make a scandal of it, she slips now and again into some crumbling little church, kneels on the chilly stone, and says a Hail Mary on the gold rosary she bought in Tehuantepec. It is no good and she ends by examining the altar with its tinsel flowers and ragged brocades, and feels tender about the battered doll-shape of some male saint whose white, lace-trimmed drawers hang limply around his ankles below the hieratic dignity of his velvet robe. She has encased herself in a set of principles derived from her early training, leaving no detail of gesture or of personal taste untouched, and for this reason she will not wear lace made on machines. This is her private heresy, for in her special group the machine is sacred, and will be the salvation of the workers. She loves fine lace, and there is a tiny edge of fluted cobweb on this collar, which is one of twenty precisely alike, folded in blue tissue paper in the upper drawer of her clothes chest.

Braggioni catches her glance solidly as if he had been waiting for it, leans forward, balancing his paunch between his spread knees, and sings with tremendous emphasis, weighing his words. He has, the song relates, no father and no mother, nor even a friend to console him; lonely as a wave of the sea he comes and goes, lonely as a wave. His mouth opens round and yearns sideways, his balloon cheeks grow oily with the labor of song. He bulges marvelously in his expensive garments. Over his lavender collar, crushed upon a purple necktie, held by a diamond hoop: over his ammunition belt of tooled leather worked in silver, buckled cruelly around his gasping middle: over the tops of his glossy yellow shoes Braggioni swells with ominous ripeness, his mauve silk hose stretched taut, his ankles bound with the stout leather thongs of his shoes.

When he stretches his eyelids at Laura she notes again that his eyes are the true tawny yellow cat's eyes. He is rich, not in money, he tells her, but in power, and this power brings with it the blameless ownership of things, and the right to indulge his love of small luxuries. "I have a taste for the elegant refinements," he said once, flourishing a yellow silk handkerchief before her nose. "Smell that? It is Jockey Club, imported from New York." Nonetheless he is wounded by life. He will say so presently. "It is true everything turns to dust in the hand, to gall on the tongue." He sighs and his leather belt creaks like a saddle girth. "I am disappointed in everything as it comes. Everything." He shakes his head. "You, poor thing, you will be disappointed too. You are born for it. We are more alike than you realize in some things. Wait and see. Some day you will remember what I have told you, you will know that Braggioni was your friend."

Laura feels a slow chill, a purely physical sense of danger, a warning in her blood that violence, mutilation, a shocking death, wait for her with lessening patience. She has translated this fear into something homely, immediate, and sometimes hesitates before crossing the street. "My personal fate is nothing, except as the testimony of a mental attitude," she reminds herself, quoting from some forgotten philosophic primer, and is sensible enough to add, "Anyhow, I shall not be killed by an automobile if I can help it."

"It may be true I am as corrupt, in another way, as Braggioni," she thinks in spite of herself, "as callous, as incomplete," and if this is so, any kind of death seems preferable. Still she sits quietly, she does not run. Where could she go? Uninvited she has promised herself to this place; she can no longer imagine herself as living in another country, and there is no pleasure in remembering her life before she came here.

Precisely what is the nature of this devotion, its true motives, and what are its obligations? Laura cannot say. She spends part of her days in Xochimilco, near by, teaching Indian children to say in English, "The cat is on the mat." When she appears in the classroom they crowd about her with smiles on their wise, innocent, clay-colored faces, crying, "Good morning, my titcher! " in immaculate voices, and they make of her desk a fresh garden of flowers every day.

During her leisure she goes to union meetings and listens to busy important voices quarreling over tactics, methods, internal politics. She visits the prisoners of her own political faith in their cells, where they entertain themselves with counting cockroaches, repenting of their indiscretions, composing their memoirs, writing out manifestoes and plans for their comrades who are still walking about free, hands in pockets, sniffing fresh air. Laura brings them food and cigarettes and a little money, and she brings messages disguised in equivocal phrases from the men outside who dare not set foot in the prison for fear of disappearing into the cells kept empty for them. If the prisoners confuse night and day, and complain, "Dear little Laura, time doesn't pass in this infernal hole, and I won't know when it is time to sleep unless I have a reminder," she brings them their favorite narcotics, and says in a tone that does not wound them with pity, "Tonight will really be night for you," and though her Spanish amuses them, they find her comforting, useful. If they lose patience and all faith, and curse the slowness of their friends in coming to their rescue with money and influence, they trust her not to repeat everything, and if she inquires, "Where do you think we can find money, or influence?" they are certain to answer, "Well, there is Braggioni, why doesn't he do something?"

She smuggles letters from headquarters to men hiding from firing squads in back streets in mildewed houses, where they sit in tumbled beds and talk bitterly as if all Mexico were at their heels, when Laura knows positively they might appear at the band concert in the Alameda on Sunday morning, and no one would notice them. But Braggioni says, "Let them sweat a little. The next time they may be careful. It is very restful to have them out of the way for a while." She is not afraid to knock on any door in any street after midnight, and enter in the darkness, and say to one of these men who is really in danger: "They will be looking for you – seriously – tomorrow morning after six. Here is some money from Vicente. Go to Vera Cruz and wait."

She borrows money from the Roumanian agitator to give to his bitter enemy the Polish agitator. The favor of Braggioni is their disputed territory, and Braggioni holds the balance nicely, for he can use them both. The Polish agitator talks love to her over cafe tables, hoping to exploit what he believes is her secret sentimental preference for him, and he gives her misinformation which he begs her to repeat as the solemn truth to certain persons. The Roumanian is more adroit. He is generous with his money in all good causes, and lies to her with an air of ingenuous candor, as if he were her good friend and confidant. She never repeats anything they may say. Braggioni never asks questions. He has other ways to discover all that he wishes to know about them.

Nobody touches her, but all praise her gray eyes, and the soft, round under lip which promises gayety, yet is always grave, nearly always firmly closed: and they cannot understand why she is in Mexico. She walks back and forth on her errands, with puzzled eyebrows, carrying her little folder of drawings and music and school papers. No dancer dances more beautifully than Laura walks, and she inspires some amusing, unexpected ardors, which cause little gossip, because nothing comes of them. A young captain who had been a soldier in Zapata's army attempted, during a horseback ride near Cuernavaca, to express his desire for her with the noble simplicity befitting a rude folk-hero: but gently, because he was gentle. This gentleness was his defeat, for when he alighted, and removed her foot from the stirrup, and essayed to draw her down into his arms, her horse, ordinarily a tame one, shied fiercely, reared and plunged away. The young hero's horse careened blindly after his stablemate, and the hero did not return to the hotel until rather late that evening. At breakfast he came to her table in full charro dress, gray buck-skin jacket and trousers with strings of silver buttons down the leg, and he was in a humorous, careless mood. "May I sit with you?" and "You are a wonderful rider. I was terrified that you might be thrown and dragged. I should never have forgiven myself. But I cannot admire you enough for your riding."

"I learned to ride in Arizona," said Laura.

"If you will ride with me again this morning, I promise you a horse that will not shy with you," he said. But Laura remembered that she must return to Mexico City at noon.

Next morning the children made a celebration and spent their playtime writing on the blackboard, "We lov ar ticher," and with tinted chalks they drew wreaths of flowers around the words. The young hero wrote her a letter: "I am a very foolish, wasteful, impulsive man. I should have first said I love you, and then you would not have run away. But you shall see me again." Laura thought, "I must send him a book of colored crayons," but she was trying to forgive herself for having spurred her horse at the wrong moment.

A brown, shock-haired youth came and stood in her patio one night and sang like a lost soul for two hours, but Laura could think of nothing to do about it. The moonlight spread a wash of gauzy silver over the clear spaces of the garden, and the shadows were cobalt blue. The scarlet blossoms of the Judas tree were dull purple, and the names of the colors repeated themselves automatically in her mind, while she watched not the boy, but his shadow, fallen like a dark garment across the fountain rim, trailing in the water. Lupe came silently and whispered expert counsel in her ear: "If you will throw him one little flower, he will sing another song or two and go away." Laura threw the flower, and he sang a last song and went away with the flower tucked in the band of his hat, Lupe said, "He is one of the organizers of the Typographers Union, and before that he sold corridos in the Merced market, and before that, he came from Guanajuato, where I was born. I would not trust any man, but I trust least those from Guanajuato."

She did not tell Laura that he would be back again the next night, and the next, nor that he would follow her at a certain fixed distance around the Merced market, through the Zocolo, up Francisco I. Madero Avenue, and so along the Paseo de la Reforma to Chapultepec Park, and into the Philosopher's Footpath, still with that flower withering in his hat, and an indivisible attention in his eyes.

Now Laura is accustomed to him, it means nothing except that he is nineteen years old and is observing a convention with all propriety, as though it were founded on a law of nature, which in the end it might well prove to be. He is beginning to write poems which he prints on a wooden press, and he leaves them stuck like handbills in her door. She is pleasantly disturbed by the abstract, unhurried watchfulness of his black eyes which will in time turn easily towards another object. She tells herself that throwing the flower was a mistake, for she is twenty-two years old and knows better; but she refuses to regret it, and persuades herself that her negation of all external events as they occur is a sign that she is gradually perfecting herself in the stoicism she strives to cultivate against that disaster she fears, though she cannot name it.

She is not at home in the world. Every day she teaches children who remain strangers to her, though she loves their tender round hands and their charming opportunist savagery. She knocks at unfamiliar doors not knowing whether a friend or a stranger shall answer, and even if a known face emerges from the sour gloom of that unknown interior, still it is the face of a stranger. No matter what this stranger says to her, nor what her message to him, the very cells of her flesh reject knowledge and kinship in one monotonous word. No. No. No. She draws her strength from this one holy talismanic word which does not suffer her to be led into evil. Denying everything, she may walk anywhere in safety, she looks at everything without amazement.

No, repeats this firm unchanging voice of her blood; and she looks at Braggioni without amazement. He is a great man, he wishes to impress this simple girl who covers her great round breasts with thick dark cloth, and who hides long, invaluably beautiful legs under a heavy skirt. She is almost thin except for the incomprehensible fullness of her breasts, like a nursing mother's, and Braggioni, who considers himself a judge of women, speculates again on the puzzle of her notorious virginity, and takes the liberty of speech which she permits without a sign of modesty, indeed, without any sort of sign, which is disconcerting.

"You think you are so cold, gringita! Wait and see. You will surprise yourself some day! May I be there to advise you?" He stretches his eyelids at her, and his ill-humored cat's eyes waver in a separate glance for the two points of light marking the opposite ends of a smoothly drawing path between the swollen curve of her breasts. He is not put off by that blue serge, nor by her resolutely fixed gaze. There is all the time in the world. His cheeks are bellying with the wind of song. "O girl with the dark eyes," he sings, and reconsiders. "But yours are not dark. I can change all that. O girl with the green eyes, you have stolen my heart away!" Then his mind wanders to the song, and Laura feels the weight of his attention being shifted elsewhere. Singing thus, he seems harmless, he is quite harmless, there is nothing to do but sit patiently and say "No," when the moment comes. She draws a full breath, and her mind wanders also, but not far. She dares not wander too far.

Not for nothing has Braggioni taken pains to be a good revolutionist and a professional lover of humanity. He will never die of it. He has the malice, the cleverness, the wickedness, the sharpness of wit, the hardness of heart, stipulated for loving the world profitably. He will never die of it. He will live to see himself kicked out from his feeding trough by other hungry world-saviors. Traditionally he must sing in spite of his life which drives him to bloodshed, he tells Laura, for his father was a Tuscany peasant who drifted to Yucatan and married a Maya woman: a woman of race, an aristocrat. They gave him the love and knowledge of music, thus: and under the rip of his thumbnail, the strings of the instrument complain like exposed nerves.

Once he was called Delgadito by all the girls and married women who ran after him; he was so scrawny all his bones showed under his thin cotton clothing, and he could squeeze his emptiness to the very backbone with his two hands. He was a poet and the revolution was only a dream then: too many women loved him and sapped away his youth, and he could never find enough to eat anywhere, anywhere! Now he is a leader of men, crafty men who whisper in his ear, hungry men who wait for hours outside his office for a word with him, emaciated men with wild faces who waylay him at the street gate with a timid, "Comrade, let me tell you..." and they blow the foul breath from their empty stomachs in his face.

He is always sympathetic. He gives them handfuls of small coins from his own pockets, he promises them work, there will be demonstrations, they must join the unions and attend the meetings, above all they must be on the watch for spies. They are closer to him than his own brothers, without them he can do nothing – until tomorrow, comrade!

Until tomorrow. "They are stupid, they are lazy, they are treacherous, they would cut my throat for nothing," he says to Laura. He has good food and abundant drink, he hires an automobile and drives in the Paseo on Sunday morning, and enjoys plenty of sleep in a soft bed beside a wife who dares not disturb him; and he sits pampering his bones in easy billows of fat, singing to Laura, who knows and thinks these things about him. When he was fifteen, he tried to drown himself because he loved a girl, his first love, and she laughed at him. "A thousand women have paid for that," and his tight little mouth turns down at the corners. Now he perfumes his hair with Jockey Club, and confides to Laura: "One woman is really as good as another for me, in the dark. I prefer them all."

His wife organizes unions among the girls in the cigarette factories, and walks in picket lines, and even speaks at meetings in the evening. But she cannot be brought to acknowledge the benefits of true liberty. "I tell her I must have my freedom. She does not understand my point of view." Laura has heard this many times. Bragoloni scratches the guitar and meditates. "She is an instinctively virtuous woman, pure gold, no doubt of that. If she were not, I should lock her up, and she knows it."

His wife, who works so hard for the good of the factory girls, employs part of her leisure lying on the floor weeping because there are so many women in the world, and only one husband for her, and she never knows where nor when to look for him. He told her: "Unless you can learn to cry when I am not here, I must go away for good." That day he went away and took a room at the Hotel Madrid.

It is this month of separation for the sake of higher principles that has been spoiled not only for Mrs. Braggioni, whose sense of reality is beyond criticism, but for Laura, who feels herself bogged in a nightmare. Tonight Laura envies Mrs. Braggioni, who is alone, and free to weep as much as she pleases about a concrete wrong. Laura has just come from a visit to the prison, and she is waiting for tomorrow with a bitter anxiety as if tomorrow may not come, but time may be caught immovably in this hour, with herself transfixed, Braggioni singing on forever, and Eugenio's body not yet discovered by the guard.

Braggioni says: "Are you going to sleep?" Almost before she can shake her head, he begins telling her about the May-day disturbances coming on in Morelia, for the Catholics hold a festival in honor of the Blessed Virgin, and the Socialists celebrate their martyrs on that day. "There will be two independent processions, starting from either end of town, and they will march until they meet, and the rest depends..." He asks her to oil and load his pistols. Standing up, he unbuckles his ammunition belt, and spreads it laden across her knees. Laura sits with the shells slipping through the cleaning cloth dipped in oil, and he says again he cannot understand why she works so hard for the revolutionary idea unless she loves some man who is in it. "Are you not in love with someone?" "No," says Laura. "And no one is in love with you?" "No." "Then it is your own fault. No woman need go begging. Why, what is the matter with you? The legless beggar woman in the Alameda has a perfectly faithful lover. Did you know that?"

Laura peers down the pistol barrel and says nothing, but a long, slow faintness rises and subsides in her; Braggioni curves his swollen fingers around the throat of the guitar and softly smothers the music out of it, and when she hears him again he seems to have forgotten her, and is speaking in the hypnotic voice he uses when talking in small rooms to a listening, close-gathered crowd. Some day this world, now seemingly so composed and eternal, to the edges of every sea shall be merely a tangle of gaping trenches, of crashing walls and broken bodies. Everything must be torn from its accustomed place where it has rotted for centuries, buried skyward and distributed, cast down again clean as rain, without separate identity. Nothing shall survive that the stiffened hands of poverty have created for the rich and no one shall be left alive except the elect spirits destined to procreate a new world cleansed of cruelty and injustice, ruled by benevolent anarchy: "Pistols are good, I love them, cannon are even better, but in the end I pin my faith to good dynamite," he concludes, and strokes the pistol lying in her hands. "Once I dreamed of destroying this city, in case it offered resistance to General Ortiz, but it fell into his hands like an over-ripe pear."

He is made restless by his own words, rises and stands waiting. Laura holds up the belt to him: "Put that on, and go kill somebody in Morelia, and you will be happier," she says softly. The presence of death in the room makes her bold. "Today, I found Eugenio going into a stupor. He refused to allow me to call the prison doctor. He had taken all the tablets I brought him yesterday. He said he took them because he was bored."

"He is a fool, and his death is his own business," says Braggioni, fastening his belt carefully.

"I told him if he had waited only a little while longer, you would have got him set free," says Laura. "He said he did not want to wait."

"He is a fool and we are well rid of him," says Braggioni, reaching for his hat.

He goes away. Laura knows his mood has changed, she will not see him any more for a while. He will send word when he needs her to go on errands into strange streets, to speak to the strange faces that will appear, like clay masks with the power of human speech, to mutter their thanks to Braggioni for his help. Now she is free, and she thinks, I must run while there is time. But she does not go.

Braggioni enters his own house where for a month his wife has spent many hours every night weeping and tangling her hair upon her pillow. She is weeping now, and she weeps more at the sight of him, the cause of all her sorrows. He looks about the room. Nothing is changed, the smells are good and familiar, he is well acquainted with the woman who comes toward him with no reproach except grief on her face. He says to her tenderly: "You are so good, please don't cry any more, you dear good creature." She says, "Are you tired, my angel? Sit here and

I will wash your feet." She brings a bowl of water, and kneeling, unlaces his shoes, and when from her knees she raises her sad eyes under her blackened lids, he is sorry for everything, and bursts into tears. "Ah, yes, I am hungry, I am tired, let us eat something together," he says, between sobs. His wife leans her head on his arm and says, "Forgive me! " and this time he is refreshed by the solemn, endless rain of her tears.

Laura takes off her serge dress and puts on a white linen nightgown and goes to bed. She turns her head a little to one side, and lying still, reminds herself that it is time to sleep. Numbers tick in her brain like little clocks, soundless doors close of themselves around her. If you would sleep, you must not remember anything, the children will say tomorrow, good morning, my teacher, the poor prisoners who come every day bringing flowers to their jailor. 1–2–3–4–5–it is monstrous to confuse love with revolution, night with day, life with death – ah, Eugenio!

The tolling of the midnight bell is a signal, but what does it mean? Get up, Laura, and follow me: come out of your sleep, out of your bed out of this strange house. What are you doing in this house? Without a word, without fear she rose and reached for Eugenio's hand, but he eluded her with a sharp, sly smile and drifted away. This is not all, you shall see–Murderer, he said, follow me, I will show you a new country but it is far away and we must hurry. No, said Laura, not unless you take my hand, no; and she clung first to the stair rail, and then to the topmost branch of the Judas tree that bent down slowly and set her upon the earth, and then to the rocky ledge of a cliff, and then to the jagged wave of a sea that was not water but a desert of crumbling stone. Where are you taking me, she asked in wonder but without fear. To death, and it is a long way off, and we must hurry, said Eugenio. No, said Laura, not unless you take my hand. Then eat these flowers, poor prisoner, said Eugenio in a voice of pity, take and eat: and from the Judas tree he stripped the warm bleeding flowers, and held them to her lips. She saw that his hand was fleshless, a cluster of small white petrified branches, and his eye sockets were without light, but she ate the flowers greedily for they satisfied both hunger and thirst. Murderer! said Eugenio, and Cannibal! This is my body and my blood. Laura cried No! and at the sound of her own voice, she awoke trembling, and was afraid to sleep again.

Unit 7
Eudora Welty(1909–2001)
尤多拉·韦尔蒂

作者简介

尤多拉·韦尔蒂，美国南方著名女作家，短篇小说家，评论家，出生于密西西比州的杰克逊(Jackson)。她的父亲是一家保险公司的经理，母亲是一名教师，家境富裕。韦尔蒂自幼喜爱阅读并尝试小说写作，表现出不俗的文学天赋。1925 年中学毕业后考入密西西比州立女子学院学习，两年后进入威斯康星大学主修英国文学，期间阅读了大量西方名著，之后于 1929 年考入哥伦比亚商学院攻读广告学硕士学位。1931 年毕业时恰逢美国经济大萧条，加上父亲去世的双重打击迫使韦尔蒂返回故乡，在报社担任记者，从事采访和摄影。后来她担任公共关系协调员，经常到密西西比州各地走访，这段经历为她后来的创作提供了大量素材。韦尔蒂终身未嫁，2001 年在家乡与世长辞，享年 92 岁。

韦尔蒂一生笔耕不辍，在小说、摄影等多个领域都有建树。她在短篇小说方面的成就尤为突出，她成功地把南方的哥特风格和乡土色彩融合在作品中，作品颇受读者青睐。她著有 5 部短篇小说集：《绿色的帷幕》(*A Curtain of Green*，1941)、《宽网》(*The Wide Net*，1943)、《金苹果》(*The Golden Apples*，1949)、《英尼斯法轮号上的新娘及其他故事》(*The Bride of Innisfallen*，1955)以及《月亮湖》(*Moon Lake*, 1980)。她的 5 部长篇小说包括《强盗新郎》(*The Robber Bridegroom*，1942)、《三角洲的婚礼》(*Delta Wedding*，1946)、《沉思的心》(*The Ponder Heart*，1954)、《败局》(*Losing Battles*，1970) 和《乐观者的女儿》(*The Optimist's Daughter*，1972)。她的成就不仅体现在小说方面，还著有文学评论《小说中的地点》(*Place in Fiction*, 1957)、儿童文学《鞋鸟》(*The Shoe Bird*，1964)、摄影作品集《某时，某地》(*One Time, One Place*，1971)和自传《一位作家的开端》(*One Writer's Beginnings*，1984)。

韦尔蒂是“南方文学”流派中继福克纳之后最优秀的作家之一。韦尔蒂深谙南方的风土人情，她的作品大多以她熟悉的密西西比州小镇为背景，常常使用写实的手法来描绘普通人的生活悲喜剧。她也能充分运用南方方言来表现南方人的内心世界，探讨家庭关系、时事变迁、爱恨矛盾和地区历史等。韦尔蒂于 1952 年被推选为美国文学艺术院院士。她一生获得过多项奖励：1955 年获“威廉·迪恩·豪威尔斯奖”；1972 年获“普利策奖”；先后 6次获“欧·亨利短篇小说奖”。她的家乡密西西比州在 1973 年把每年的 5 月 2 日定为该州的“尤多拉·韦尔蒂日”。1980 年她获得美国总统卡特授予的自由勋章。此外，1988 年，代表美国文学最高成就的《美国文学巨人作品》系列收录了她的作品，打破了多年只收录已故作家作品的传统，在美国文学界引起轰动。

作品导读

Being collected in Welty's short story collection *A Curtain of Green* (1941), "Why I live at the P.O." is set in a large family in which most families don't have exact names, for example, Sister, Mama, Papa-Daddy. The story depicts the wildly loquacious Sister and her ongoing arguments with her sister Stella-Rondo. Welty's fiction cultivates the "heart's field" and invites us to observe what grows there. According to Welty said, "The truth is fiction depends for its life on place." At the beginning of the story, the narrator, Sister, tells us that she has lived a peaceful life with her families in the town China Grove, Mississippi until her sister Stella-Rondo has returned home. Sister develops a competitive and contentious relationship with Stella, thus Stella's returning arouses a series of arguments, which could be used to explain why Sister has to move out and lives at the local post office.

To be specific, Stella returns home with a little girl named Shirley-T and explains that the girl is adopted by her. Everyone in the family believes that except Sister. Stella is very angry and decides to turn others against Sister. At first, Stella makes Papa-Daddy (their maternal grandfather) believe that Sister is ungraceful to him because she uses Papa's influence in community to find a position at the local post office and she even wants Papa to cut off his beard that he loves so much. Therefore, Papa-Daddy is very angry with Sister. Next, Uncle Rondo (their uncle) appears wearing a kimono, that's a gift for Stella, Sister considers him as her ally in the family but at last Stella wins his favor by serving him at table and telling him that Sister has laughed at him because he eats up ketchup while wearing kimono. Sister fails again. What's more, Sister goes to kitchen and has a conversation about Stella's situation with Mama, Sister insists that the girl Shirley-T is not adopted while Mama doesn't agree with her and slaps her as response. In the end, it seems that everyone in the family turns against Sister, so Sister decides to leave home and tells them they have to come to the post office if they want to see her again, but such threat doesn't work. Five days later, Sister hasn't seen any family members in the post office, because the post office is in the charge of her family and many residents in that town also support her family. However, Sister sets up a nice home at the P.O. and claims she will never want to know the truth about Stella and Mr. Whitaker even if she gets such a chance!

Why I Live at the P.O.

I was getting along fine with Mama, Papa-Daddy and Uncle Rondo until my sister Stella-Rondo just separated from her husband and came back home again. Mr. Whitaker! Of course I went with Mr. Whitaker first, when he first appeared here in China Grove, taking "Pose Yourself" photos, and Stella-Rondo broke us up. Told him I was one-sided. Bigger on one side than the other, which is a deliberate, calculated falsehood: I'm the same. Stella-Rondo is exactly twelve months to the day younger than I am and for that reason she's spoiled.

She's always had anything in the world she wanted and then she'd throw it away. Papa-Daddy gave her this gorgeous Add-a-Pearl necklace when she was eight years old and she threw it away playing baseball when she was nine, with only two pearls.

So as soon as she got married and moved away from home the first thing she did was separate! From Mr. Whitaker! This photographer with the popeyes she said she trusted. Came homé from one of those towns up in Illinois and to our complete surprise brought this child of two.

Mama said she like to make her drop dead for a second. "Here you had this marvelous blonde child and never so much as wrote your mother a word about it," says Mama. "I'm thoroughly ashamed of you." But of course she wasn't.

Stella-Rondo just calmly takes off this hat, I wish you could see it. She says, "Why, Mama, Shirley-T.'s adopted, I can prove it."

"How?" says Mama, but all I says was, "H'm! " There I was over the hot stove, trying to stretch two chickens over five people and a completely unexpected child into the bargain, without one moment's notice.

"What do you mean – 'H'm! '?" says Stella-Rondo, and Mama says, "I heard that, Sister."

I said that oh, I didn't mean a thing, only that whoever Shirley-T. was, she was the spit-image of Papa-Daddy if he'd cut off his beard, which of course he'd never do in the world. Papa-Daddy's Mama's papa and sulks.

Stella–Rondo got furious! She said, "Sister, I don't need to tell you you got a lot of nerve and always did have and I'll thank you to make no future reference to my adopted child whatsoever."

"Very well," I said. "Very well, very well. Of course I noticed at once she looks like Mr. Whitaker's side too. That frown. She looks like a cross between Mr. Whitaker and Papa-Daddy."

"Well, all I can say is she isn't."

"She looks exactly like Shirley Temple to me," says Mama, but Shirley-T. just ran away

from her.

So the first thing Stella-Rondo did at the table was turn Papa-Daddy against me.

"Papa-Daddy," she says. He was trying to cut up his meat. "Papa-Daddy!" I was taken completely by surprise. Papa-Daddy is about a million years old and's got this long-long beard. "Papa-Daddy, Sister says she fails to understand why you don't cut off your beard."

So Papa-Daddy l-a-y-s down his knife and fork! He's real rich. Mama says he is, he says he isn't. So he says, "Have I heard correctly? You don't understand why I don't cut off my beard?"

"Why," I says, "Papa-Daddy, of course I understand, I did not say any such of a thing, the idea!"

He says, "Hussy!"

I says, "Papa-Daddy, you know I wouldn't any more want you to cut off your beard than the man in the moon. It was the farthest thing from my mind! Stella-Rondo sat there and made that up while she was eating breast of chicken."

But he says, "So the postmistress fails to understand why I don't cut off my beard. Which job I got you through my influence with the government. 'Bird's nest' – is that what you call it?"

Not that it isn't the next to smallest P.O. in the entire state of Mississippi.

I says, "Oh, Papa-Daddy," I says, "I didn't say any such of a thing, I never dreamed it was a bird's nest, I have always been grateful though this is the next to smallest P.O. in the state of Mississippi, and I do not enjoy being referred to as a hussy by my own grandfather."

But Stella-Rondo says, "Yes, you did say it too. Anybody in the world could of heard you, that had ears."

"Stop right there," says Mama, looking at me.

So I pulled my napkin straight back through the napkin ring and left the table.

As soon as I was out of the room Mama says, "Call her back, or she'll starve to death," but Papa-Daddy says, "This is the beard I started growing on the Coast when I was fifteen years old." He would of gone on till nightfall if Shirley-T. hadn't lost the Milky Way she ate in Cairo.

So Papa-Daddy says, "I am going out and lie in the hammock, and you can all sit here and remember my words: I'll never cut off my beard as long as I live, even one inch, and I don't appreciate it in you at all." Passed right by me in the hall and went straight out and got in the hammock.

It would be a holiday. It wasn't five minutes before Uncle Rondo suddenly appeared in the hall in one of Stella-Rondo's flesh-colored kimonos, all cut on the bias, like something Mr. Whitaker probably thought was gorgeous.

"Uncle Rondo!" I says. "I didn't know who that was! Where are you going?"

"Sister," he says, "get out of my way, I'm poisoned."

"If you're poisoned stay away from Papa-Daddy," I says. "Keep out of the hammock,

Papa-Daddy will certainly beat you on the head if you come within forty miles of him. He thinks I deliberately said he ought to cut off his beard after he got me the P.O., and I've told him and told him and told him, and he acts like he just don't hear me. Papa-Daddy must of gone stone deaf."

"He picked a fine day to do it then," says Uncle Rondo, and before you could say "Jack Robinson" flew out in the yard.

What he'd really done, he'd drunk another bottle of that prescription. He does it every single Fourth of July as sure as shooting, and it's horribly expensive. Then he falls over in the hammock and snores. So he insisted on zigzagging right on out to the hammock, looking like a half-wit.

Papa-Daddy woke up with this horrible yell and right there without moving an inch he tried to turn Uncle Rondo against me. I heard every word he said. Oh, he told Uncle Rondo I didn't learn to read till I was eight years old and he didn't see how in the world I ever got the mail put up at the P.O., much less read it all, and he said if Uncle Rondo could only fathom the lengths he had gone to get me that job! And he said on the other hand he thought Stella-Rondo had a brilliant mind and deserved credit for getting out of town. All the time he was just lying there swinging as pretty as you please and looping out his beard, and poor Uncle Rondo was *pleading* with him to slow down the hammock, it was making him as dizzy as a witch to watch it. But that's what Papa-Daddy likes about a hammock. So Uncle Rondo was too dizzy to get turned against me for the time being. He's Mama's only brother and is a good case of a one-track mind. Ask anybody. A certified pharmacist.

Just then I heard Stella-Rondo raising the upstairs window. While she was married she got this peculiar idea that it's cooler with the windows shut and locked. So she has to raise the window before she can make a soul hear her outdoors.

So she raises the window and says, "Oh!" You would have thought she was mortally wounded.

Uncle Rondo and Papa-Daddy didn't even look up, but kept right on with what they were doing. I had to laugh.

I flew up the stairs and threw the door open! I says, "What in the wide world's the matter, Stella-Rondo? You mortally wounded?"

"No," she says, "I am not mortally wounded but I wish you would do me the favor of looking out that window there and telling me what you see."

So I shade my eyes and look out the window.

"I see the front yard," I says.

"Don't you see any human beings?" she says.

"I see Uncle Rondo trying to run Papa-Daddy out of the hammock," I says. "Nothing more. Naturally, it's so suffocating-hot in the house, with all the windows shut and locked, everybody who cares to stay in their right mind will have to go out and get in the hammock before the Fourth of July is over."

"Don't you notice anything different about Uncle Rondo?" asks Stella-Rondo.

"Why, no, except he's got on some terrible-looking flesh-colored contraption I wouldn't be found dead in, is all I can see," I says.

"Never mind, you won't be found dead in it, because it happens to be part of my trousseau, and Mr. Whitaker took several dozen photographs of me in it," says Stella-Rondo. "What on earth could Uncle Rondo mean by wearing part of my trousseau out in the broad open daylight without saying so much as 'Kiss my foot,' knowing?I only got home this morning after my separation and hung my negligee up on the bathroom door, just as nervous as I could be?"

"I'm sure I don't know, and what do you expect me to do about it?" I says. "Jump out the window?"

"No, I expect nothing of the kind. I simply declare that Uncle Rondo looks like a fool in it, that's all," she says. "It makes me sick to my stomach."

"Well, he looks as good as he can," I says. "As good as anybody in reason could." I stood up for Uncle Rondo, please remember. And I said to Stella-Rondo, "I think I would do well not to criticize so freely if I were you and came home with a two-year-old child I had never said a word about, and no explanation whatever about my separation."

"I asked you the instant I entered this house not to refer one more time to my adopted child, and you gave me your word of honor you would not," was all Stella-Rondo would say, and started pulling out every one of her eyebrows with some cheap Kress tweezers.

So I merely slammed the door behind me and went down and made some green-tomato pickle. Somebody had to do it. Of course Mama had turned both the Negroes loose; she always said no earthly power could hold one anyway on the Fourth of July, so she wouldn't even try. It turned out that Jaypan fell in the lake and came within a very narrow limit of drowning.

So Mama trots in. Lifts up the lid and says, "H'm! Not very good for your Uncle Rondo in his precarious condition, I must say. Or poor little adopted Shirley-T. Shame on you!"

That made me tired. I says, "Well, Stella-Rondo had better thank her lucky stars it was her instead of me came trotting in with that very peculiar-looking child. Now if it had been me that trotted in from Illinois and brought a peculiar-looking child of two, I shudder to think of the reception I'd of got, much less controlled the diet of an entire family."

"But you must remember, Sister, that you were never married to Mr. Whitaker in the first place and didn't go up to Illinois to live," says Mama, shaking a spoon in my face. "If you had I would of been just as overjoyed to see you and your little adopted girl as I was to see Stella-Rondo, when you wound up with your separation and came on back home."

"You would not," I says.

"Don't contradict me, I would," says Mama.

But I said she couldn't convince me though she talked till she was blue in the face. Then I said, "Besides, you know as well as I do that that child is not adopted."

"She most certainly is adopted," says Mama, stiff as a poker.

I says, "Why, Mama, Stella-Rondo had her just as sure as anything in this world, and just too stuck up to admit it."

"Why, Sister," said Mama. "Here I thought we were going to have a pleasant Fourth of July, and you start right out not believing a word your own baby sister tells you!"

"Just like Cousin Annie Flo. Went to her grave denying the facts of life," I remind Mama.

"I told you if you ever mentioned Annie Flo's name I'd slap your face," says Mama, and slaps my face.

"All right, you wait and see," I says.

"I," says Mama, "I prefer to take my children's word for anything when it's humanly possible." You ought to see Mama, she weighs two hundred pounds and has real tiny feet.

Just then something perfectly horrible occurred to me.

"Mama," I says, "can that child talk?" I simply had to whisper! "Mama, I wonder if that child can be – you know – in any way? Do you realize," I says, "that she hasn't spoken one single, solitary word to a human being up to this minute? This is the way she looks," I says, and I looked like this.

Well, Mama and I just stood there and stared at each other. It was horrible!

"I remember well that Joe Whitaker frequently drank like a fish," says Mama. "I believed to my soul he drank chemicals." And without another word she marches to the foot of the stairs and calls Stella-Rondo.

"Stella-Rondo? O–o–o–o–o! Stella-Rondo!"

"What?" says Stella-Rondo from upstairs. Not even the grace to get up off the bed.

"Can that child of yours talk?" asks Mama.

Stella-Rondo says, "Can she what?"

"Talk! Talk!" says Mama. "Burdyburdyburdyburdy!"

So Stella-Rondo yells back, "Who says she can't talk?"

"Sister says so," says Mama.

"You didn't have to tell me, I know whose word of honor don't mean a thing in this house," says Stella-Rondo.

And in a minute the loudest Yankee voice I ever heard in my life yells out, "OE'm Pop–OE the Sailor–r–r–r Ma–a–an!" and then somebody jumps up and down in the upstairs hall. In another second the house would of fallen down.

"Not only talks, she can tap-dance!" calls Stella-Rondo. "Which is more than some people I won't name can do."

"Why, the little precious darling thing!" Mama says, so surprised. "Just as smart as she can be!" Starts talking baby talk right there. Then she turns on me. "Sister, you ought to be thoroughly ashamed! Run upstairs this instant and apologize to Stella-Rondo and Shirley-T."

"Apologize for what?" I says. "I merely wondered if the child was normal, that's all. Now that she's proved she is, why, I have nothing further to say."

But Mama just turned on her heel and flew out, furious. She ran right upstairs and hugged

the baby. She believed it was adopted. Stella-Rondo hadn't done a thing but turn her against me from upstairs while I stood there helpless over the hot stove. So that made Mama, Papa-Daddy and the baby all on Stella-Rondo's side.

Next, Uncle Rondo.

I must say that Uncle Rondo has been marvelous to me at various times in the past and I was completely unprepared to be made to jump out of my skin, the way it turned out. Once Stella-Rondo did something perfectly horrible to him – broke a chain letter from Flanders Field – and he took the radio back he had given her and gave it to me. Stella-Rondo was furious! For six months we all had to call her Stella instead of Stella-Rondo, or she wouldn't answer. I always thought Uncle Rondo had all the brains of the entire family. Another time he sent me to Mammoth Cave, with all expenses paid.

But this would be the day he was drinking that prescription, the Fourth of July.

So at supper Stella-Rondo speaks up and says she thinks Uncle Rondo ought to try to eat a little something. So finally Uncle Rondo said he would try a little cold biscuits and ketchup, but that was all. So she brought it to him.

"Do you think it wise to disport with ketchup in Stella-Rondo's flesh-colored kimono?" I says. Trying to be considerate! If Stella-Rondo couldn't watch out for her trousseau, somebody had to.

"Any objections?" asks Uncle Rondo, just about to pour out all the ketchup.

"Don't mind what she says, Uncle Rondo," says Stella-Rondo. "Sister has been devoting this solid afternoon to sneering out my bedroom window at the way you look."

"What's that?" says Uncle Rondo. Uncle Rondo has got the most terrible temper in the world. Anything is liable to make him tear the house down if it comes at the wrong time.

So Stella-Rondo says, "Sister says, 'Uncle Rondo certainly does look like a fool in that pink kimono!'"

Do you remember who it was really said that?

Uncle Rondo spills out all the ketchup and jumps out of his chair and tears off the kimono and throws it down on the dirty floor and puts his foot on it. It had to be sent all the way to Jackson to the cleaners and re-pleated.

"So that's your opinion of your Uncle Rondo, is it?" he says. "I look like a fool, do I? Well, that's the last straw. A whole day in this house with nothing to do, and then to hear you come out with a remark like that behind my back!"

"I didn't say any such of a thing, Uncle Rondo," I says, "and I'm not saying who did, either. Why, I think you look all right. Just try to take care of yourself, and not talk and eat at the same time," I says. "I think you better go lie down."

"Lie down my foot," says Uncle Rondo. I ought to of known by that he was fixing to do something perfectly horrible.

So he didn't do anything that night in the precarious state he was in – just played Casino with Mama and Stella-Rondo and Shirley-T. and gave Shirley-T. a nickel with a head on both sides. It tickled her nearly to death, and she called him "Papa." But at 6:30 A.M. the next morning, he threw a whole five-cent package of some unsold one-inch firecrackers from the store as hard as he could into my bedroom and they every one went off. Not one bad one in the string. Anybody else, there'd be one that wouldn't go off.

Well, I'm just terribly susceptible to noise of any kind, the doctor has always told me I was the most sensitive person he had ever seen in his whole life, and I was simply prostrated. I couldn't eat! People tell me they heard it as far as the cemetery, and old Aunt Jep Patterson, that had been holding her own so good, thought it was Judgment Day and she was going to meet her whole family. It's usually so quiet here.

And I'll tell you it didn't take me any longer than a minute to make up my mind what to do. There I was with the whole entire house on Stella-Rondo's side and turned against me. If I have anything at all I have pride.

So I just decided I'd go straight down to the P.O. There's plenty of room there in the back, I says to myself.

Well! I made no bones about letting the family catch on to what I was up to. I didn't try to conceal it.

The first thing they knew, I marched in where they were all playing Old Maid and pulled the electric oscillating fan out by the plug, and everything got real hot. Next I snatched the pillow I'd done the needlepoint on right off the davenport from behind Papa-Daddy. He went "Ugh!" I beat Stella-Rondo up the stairs and finally found my charm bracelet in her bureau drawer under a picture of Nelson Eddy.

"So that's the way the land lies," says Uncle Rondo. There he was, piecing on the ham. "Well, Sister, I'll be glad to donate my army cot if you got any place to set it up, providing you'll leave right this minute and let me get some peace." Uncle Rondo was in France.

"Thank you kindly for the cot and 'peace' is hardly the word I would select if I had to resort to firecrackers at 6:30 A.M. in a young girl's bedroom," I says back to him. "And as to where I intend to go, you seem to forget my position as postmistress of China Grove, Mississippi," I says. "I've always got the P.O."

Well, that made them all sit up and take notice.

I went out front and started digging up some four-o'clocks to plant around the P.O.

"Ah-ah-ah!" says Mama, raising the window. "Those happen to be my four-o'clocks. Everything planted in that star is mine. I've never known you to make anything grow in your life."

"Very well," I says. "But I take the fern. Even you, Mama, can't stand there and deny that I'm the one watered that fern. And I happen to know where I can send in a box top and get a packet of one thousand mixed seeds, no two the same kind, free."

"Oh, where?" Mama wants to know.

But I says, "Too late. You 'tend to your house, and I'll 'tend to mine. You hear things like that all the time if you know how to listen to the radio. Perfectly marvelous offers. Get anything you want free."

So I hope to tell you I marched in and got that radio, and they could of all bit a nail in two, especially Stella-Rondo, that it used to belong to, and she well knew she couldn't get it back, I'd sue for it like a shot. And I very politely took the sewing-machine motor I helped pay the most on to give Mama for Christmas back in 1929, and a good big calendar, with the first-aid remedies on it. The thermometer and the Hawaiian ukulele certainly were rightfully mine, and I stood on the step-ladder and got all my watermelon rind preserves and every fruit and vegetable I'd put up, every jar. Then I began to pull the tacks out of the bluebird wall vases on the archway to the dining room.

"Who told you you could have those, Miss Priss?" says Mama, fanning as hard as she could.

"I bought 'em and I'll keep track of 'em," I says. "I'll tack 'em up one on each side the post-office window, and you can see 'em when you come to ask me for your mail, if you're so dead to see 'em."

"Not I! I'll never darken the door to that post office again if I live to be a hundred," Mama says. "Ungrateful child! After all the money we spent on you at the Normal."

"Me either," says Stella-Rondo. "You can just let my mail lie there and *rot*, for all I care. I'll never come and relieve you of a single, solitary piece."

"I should worry," I says. "And who you think's going to sit down and write you all those big fat letters and postcards, by the way? Mr. Whitaker? Just because he was the only man ever dropped down in China Grove and you got him – unfairly – is he going to sit down and write you a lengthy correspondence after you come home giving no rhyme nor reason whatsoever for your separation and no explanation for the presence of that child? I may not have your brilliant mind, but I fail to see it."

So Mama says, "Sister, I've told you a thousand times that Stella-Rondo simply got homesick, and this child is far too big to be hers," and she says, "Now, why don't you all just sit down and play Casino?"

Then Shirley-T. sticks out her tongue at me in this perfectly horrible way. She has no more manners than the man in the moon. I told her she was going to cross her eyes like that some day and they'd stick.

"It's too late to stop me now," I says. "You should have tried that yesterday. I'm going to the P.O. and the only way you can possibly see me is to visit me there."

So Papa-Daddy says, "You'll never catch me setting foot in that post office, even if I should take a notion into my head to write a letter some place." He says, "I won't have you reachin' out of that little old window with a pair of shears and cuttin' off any beard of mine. I'm too smart for you!"

"We all are," says Stella-Rondo.

But I said, "If you're so smart, where's Mr. Whitaker?"

So then Uncle Rondo says, "I'll thank you from now on to stop reading all the orders I get on postcards and telling everybody in China Grove what you think is the matter with them," but I says, "I draw my own conclusions and will continue in the future to draw them." I says, "If people want to write their inmost secrets on penny postcards, there's nothing in the wide world you can do about it, Uncle Rondo."

"And if you think we'll ever write another postcard you're sadly mistaken," says Mama.

"Cutting off your nose to spite your face then," I says. "But if you're all determined to have no more to do with the U.S. mail, think of this: What will Stella-Rondo do now, if she wants to tell Mr. Whitaker to come after her?"

"Wah!" says Stella-Rondo. I knew she'd cry. She had a conniption fit right there in the kitchen.

"It will be interesting to see how long she holds out," I says. "And now – I am leaving."

"Good-bye," says Uncle Rondo.

"Oh, I declare," says Mama, "to think that a family of mine should quarrel on the Fourth of July, or the day after, over Stella-Rondo leaving old Mr. Whitaker and having the sweetest little adopted child! It looks like we'd all be glad!"

"Wah!" says Stella-Rondo, and has a fresh conniption fit.

"He left her – you mark my words," I says. "That's Mr. Whitaker. I know Mr. Whitaker. After all, I knew him first. I said from the beginning he'd up and leave her. I foretold every single thing that's happened."

"Where did he go?" asks Mama.

"Probably to the North Pole, if he knows what's good for him," I says.

But Stella-Rondo just bawled and wouldn't say another word. She flew to her room and slammed the door.

"Now look what you've gone and done, Sister," says Mama. "You go apologize."

"I haven't got time, I'm leaving," I says.

"Well, what are you waiting around for?" asks Uncle Rondo.

So I just picked up the kitchen clock and marched off, without saying "Kiss my foot" or anything, and never did tell Stella-Rondo good-bye.

There was a nigger girl going along on a little wagon right in front.

"Nigger girl," I says, "come help me haul these things down the hill, I'm going to live in the post office."

Took her nine trips in her express wagon. Uncle Rondo came out on the porch and threw her a nickel.

And that's the last I've laid eyes on any of my family or my family laid eyes on me for five solid days and nights. Stella-Rondo may be telling the most horrible tales in the world about Mr. Whitaker, but I haven't heard them. As I tell everybody, I draw my own conclusions.

But oh, I like it here. It's ideal, as I've been saying. You see, I've got everything catercornered, the way I like it. Hear the radio? All the war news. Radio, sewing machine, book ends, ironing board and that great big piano lamp – peace, that's what I like. Butter-bean vines planted all along the front where the strings are.

Of course, there's not much mail. My family are naturally the main people in China Grove, and if they prefer to vanish from the face of the earth, for all the mail they get or the mail they write, why, I'm not going to open my mouth. Some of the folks here in town are taking up for me and some turned against me. I know which is which. There are always people who will quit buying stamps just to get on the right side of Papa-Daddy.

But here I am, and here I'll stay. I want the world to know I'm happy.

And if Stella-Rondo should come to me this minute, on bended knees, and attempt to explain the incidents of her life with Mr. Whitaker, I'd simply put my fingers in both my ears and refuse to listen.

Unit 8
Walker Percy (1916–1990)
沃克·珀西

作者简介

沃克·珀西，小说家，1916年5月28日出生于阿拉巴马州的伯明翰(Birmingham)，家境富裕。珀西13岁那年，他身为律师的父亲自杀(12年前他的祖父自杀)，两年后母亲也遇车祸身亡。亲人的死亡构成了珀西文学创作的“追寻”，尤其是“寻父”的重要主题。后来是他的叔父威廉·帕西(William Alexander Percy)收养了珀西和他的两个弟弟。这位热爱文学的叔父对珀西的文学创作产生了至关重要的影响。他高中毕业后考入北卡罗来纳州立大学，主攻化学，之后进入哥伦比亚大学医学院深造，毕业后在一所医院任实习医师，不慎感染肺结核。在养病期间他阅读了大量文学作品，尤其对存在主义哲学产生了浓厚的兴趣。珀西发现相对于肉体上的病症研究，自己更喜欢探索人类精神上的缺陷，最终弃医从文。1946年结婚，婚后住在新奥尔良，夫妻双双皈依天主教。帕西把天主教和存在主义哲学相结合，形成了独特的天主教—存在主义世界观。

20世纪50年代初，珀西开始从事文学创作。他早期发表的作品主要是有关哲学和符号学的文章，反应平平。50年代末，珀西开始了小说创作。第一部小说《看电影的人》(*The Moviegoer*, 1961)的主人公是一个滑稽可笑、与社会格格不入、无所事事的“影院常客”，反映出个人生活观念与斯文社会传统之间的冲突，这种冲突只有通过树立道德感和建立融洽的人际关系才能得到解决。该作于1962年获得美国国家图书奖，不仅被视为珀西的代表作，也被认为是存在主义与南方文学完美结合的经典作品。《最后的绅士》(*The Last Gentleman*, 1966)描写了主人公雷特在体验了各种生活方式之后的绝望。《废墟里的爱情》(*Love in the Ruins*, 1971)是一部带有科幻色彩的小说。此后发表的《兰斯洛特》(*Lancelot*, 1977)、《基督再临》(*The Second Coming*, 1980)和《自我毁灭综合征》(*The Thanatos Syndrome*, 1987)从正面或反面证明了一个真理：爱和善是人类生存的根本动力。同时，他还著有两部非小说类散文集《瓶子里的信息》(*The Message in the Bottle*, 1975)和《迷失在宇宙中》(*Lost in the Cosmos*, 1983)。此外，珀西还常在各种杂志上发表或内容严肃或格调轻松的文章。

珀西的文学成就以小说为主，其作品大多以新奥尔良为背景，带有明显的哲学思辨色彩。同时运用天主教和存在主义的观点，描写爱情、性与个人责任之间的关系，以此探讨人生意义和“现代社会中人的普遍困境”之主题。此外，其作品中的人物往往具有一种危机意识，不断地寻求精神上的支柱，珀西也因此被认为是一位道德作家、宗教作家和风俗作家。

作品导读

The Moviegoer is written by Percy under the heavy influence of the existentialism. This novel is considered as one of the best works of the American Southern Literature in the 20th century. It won the National Book Award in 1962 and is accepted as Percy's most popular and most widely read book as well. The main character in this story is John Bolling who is a young stockbroker living in New Orleans after World War II. John has many nicknames given by his friends, families and colleagues, such as Binx. The protagonist records the week of his life prior to his thirtieth birthday. As a stockbroker, he tiptoes through life in bad faith, secretly sickened by the Cartesian world that he seems to support, unable to accept either the stoic/Gnostic course cherished by his aunt Emily or the Christian way lived by his half-brother, Lonnie. For the most part, he self-consciously views the world as a moviegoer, a Platonic spectator, though there are times when he risks pain by searching for an explanation of his father's need to escape "everydayness", a need so acute that he gambled his life in World War II but lost.

Because of his family's problem and his traumatic experiences in the Korean War, John feels disappointed and alienates himself from his actual life. Having difficulty in getting along well with his girlfriend and others, he turns to books and movies, instead of actual life, for comfort and communication. He always goes to the movies and regards himself as a moviegoer and is proud of his social role as a stockbroker. In this story, John is always in a state of searching and is always wandering in many places, such as New Orleans, Chicago and so forth. At the beginning of the story, John receives a letter from his aunt Emily saying that they are in urgent need of a talk with regard to John's cousin Kate, who has been nearly mad since her fiancé's death. Although John's own mother is still alive and has several children now after her remarriage, as a matter of fact, Aunt Emily is the mother figure in John's life. Emily worries about Kate and wants John to accompany her and make her happy. On his way there, John has been on search but the purposes of his search are unclear. He doesn't know and doesn't want to know his purposes of search because he fears to be regarded as ignorant. His search continues ...

The Moviegoer

ONE

1

This morning I got a note from my aunt asking me to come for lunch. I know what this means. Since I go there every Sunday for dinner and today is Wednesday, it can mean only one thing: she wants to have one of her serious talks. It will be extremely grave, either a piece of bad news about her stepdaughter Kate or else a serious talk about me, about the future and what I ought to do. It is enough to scare the wits out of anyone, yet I confess I do not find the prospect altogether unpleasant.

I remember when my older brother Scott died of pneumonia. I was eight years old. My aunt had charge of me and she took me for a walk behind the hospital. It was an interesting street. On one - side were the power plant and blowers and incinerator of the hospital, all humming and blowing out a hot meaty smell. On the other side was a row of Negro houses. Children and old folks and dogs sat on the porches watching us. I noticed with pleasure that Aunt Emily seemed to have all the time in the world and was willing to talk about anything I wanted to talk about. Something extraordinary had happened all right. We walked slowly in step. "Jack," she said, squeezing me tight and smiling at the Negro shacks, "you and I have always been good buddies, haven't we?" "Yes, ma'am." My heart gave a big pump and the back of my neck prickled like a dog's. "I've got bad news for you, son." She squeezed me tighter than ever. "Scotty is dead. Now it's all up to you. It's going to be difficult for you but I know you're going to act like a soldier." This was true. I could easily act like a soldier. Was that all I had to do?

It reminds me of a movie I saw last month out by Lake Pontchartrain. Linda and I went out to a theater in a new suburb. It was evident somebody had miscalculated, for the suburb had quit growing and here was the theater, a pink stucco cube, sitting out in a field all by itself. A strong wind whipped the waves against the seawall; even inside you could hear the racket. The movie was about a man who lost his memory in an accident and as a result lost everything: his family, his friends, his money. He found himself a stranger in a strange city. Here he had to make a fresh start, find a new place to live, a new job, a new girl. It was supposed to be a tragedy, his losing all this, and he seemed to suffer a great deal. On the other hand, things were not so bad after all. In no time he found a very picturesque place to live, a houseboat on the river, and a very handsome girl, the local librarian.

After the movie Linda and I stood under the marquee and talked to the manager, or rather listened to him tell his troubles: the theater was almost empty, which was pleasant for me but not for him. It was a fine night and I felt very good. Overhead was the blackest sky I ever saw;

a black wind pushed the lake toward us. The waves jumped over the seawall and spattered the street. The manager had to yell to be heard while from the sidewalk speaker directly over his head came the twittering conversation of the amnesiac and the librarian. It was the part where they are going through the newspaper files in search of some clue to his identity (he has a vague recollection of an accident). Linda stood by unhappily. She was unhappy for the same reason I was happy – because here we were at a neighborhood theater out in the sticks and without a car (I have a car but I prefer to ride buses and streetcars). Her idea of happiness is to drive downtown and have supper at the Blue Room of the Roosevelt Hotel. This I am obliged to do from time to time. It is worth it, however. On these occasions Linda becomes as exalted as I am now. Her eyes glow, her lips become moist, and when we dance she brushes her fine long legs against mine. She actually loves me at these times – and not as a reward for being taken to the Blue Room. She loves me because she feels exalted in this romantic place and not in a movie out in the sticks.

But all this is history. Linda and I have parted company. I have a new secretary, a girl named Sharon Kincaid.

* * *

For the past four years now I have been living uneventfully in Gentilly, a middle-class suburb of New Orleans. Except for the banana plants in the patios and the curlicues of iron on the Walgreen drugstore one would never guess it was part of New Orleans. Most of the houses are either old-style California bungalows or new-style Daytona cottages. But this is what I like about it. I can't stand the old-world atmosphere of the French Quarter or the genteel charm of the Garden District. I lived in the Quarter for two years, but in the end I got tired of Birmingham businessmen smirking around Bourbon Street and the homosexuals and patio connoisseurs on Royal Street. My uncle and aunt live in a gracious house in the Garden District and are very kind to me. But whenever I try to live there, I find myself first in a rage during which I develop strong opinions on a variety of subjects and write letters to editors, then in a depression during which I lie rigid as a stick for hours staring straight up at the plaster medallion in the ceiling of my bedroom.

Life in Gentilly is very peaceful. I manage a small branch office of my uncle's brokerage firm. My home is the basement apartment of a raised bungalow belonging to Mrs. Schexnaydre, the widow of a fireman. I am a model tenant and a model citizen and take pleasure in doing all that is expected of me. My wallet is full of identity cards, library cards, credit cards. Last year I purchased a flat olive-drab strongbox, very smooth and heavily built with double walls for fire protection, in which I placed my birth certificate, college diploma, honorable discharge, G. I. insurance, a few stock certificates, and my inheritance: a deed to ten acres of a defunct duck club down in St. Bernard Parish, the only relic of my father's many enthusiasms. It is a pleasure to carry out the duties of a citizen and to receive in return a receipt or a neat styrene card with one's name on it certifying, so to speak, one's right to exist. What satisfaction I take in appearing the first day to get my auto tag and brake sticker! I subscribe to *Consumer Reports*

and as a consequence I own a first-class television set, an all but silent air conditioner and a very long lasting deodorant. My armpits never stink. I pay attention to all spot announcements on the radio about mental health, the seven signs of cancer, and safe driving – though, as I say, I usually prefer to ride the bus. Yesterday a favorite of mine, William Holden, delivered a radio announcement on litterbugs. "Let's face it," said Holden. "Nobody can do anything about it – but you and me." This is true. I have been careful ever since.

In the evenings I usually watch television or go to the movies. Week-ends I often spend on the Gulf Coast. Our neighborhood theater in Gentilly has permanent lettering on the front of the marquee reading: Where Happiness Costs So Little. The fact is I am quite happy in a movie, even a bad movie. Other people, so I have read, treasure memorable moments in their lives: the time one climbed the Parthenon at sunrise, the summer night one met a lonely girl in Central Park and achieved with her a sweet and natural relationship, as they say in books. I too once met a girl in Central Park, but it is not much to remember. What I remember is the time John Wayne killed three men with a carbine as he was falling to the dusty street in *Stagecoach*, and the time the kitten found Orson Welles in the doorway in *The Third Man*.

My companion on these evening outings and week-end trips is usually my secretary. I have had three secretaries, girls named Marcia, Linda, and now Sharon. Twenty years ago, practically every other girl born in Gentilly must have been named Marcia. A year or so later it was Linda. Then Sharon. In recent years I have noticed that the name Stephanie has come into fashion. Three of my acquaintances in Gentilly have daughters named Stephanie. Last night I saw a TV play about a nuclear test explosion. Keenan Wynn played a troubled physicist who had many a bad moment with his conscience. He took solitary walks in the desert. But you could tell that in his heart of hearts he was having a very good time with his soul-searching. "What right have we to do what we are doing?" he would ask his colleagues in a bitter voice. "It's my four-year-old daughter I'm really thinking of," he told another colleague and took out a snapshot. "What kind of future are we building for her?" "What is your daughter's name?" asked the colleague, looking at the picture. "Stephanie," said Keenan Wynn in a gruff voice. Hearing the name produced a sharp tingling sensation on the back of my neck. Twenty years from now I shall perhaps have a rosy young Stephanie perched at my typewriter.

Naturally I would like to say that I had made conquests of these splendid girls, my secretaries, casting them off one after the other like old gloves, but it would not be strictly true. They could be called love affairs, I suppose. They started off as love-affairs anyway, fine careless raptures in which Marcia or Linda (but not yet Sharon) and I would go spinning along the Gulf Coast, lie embracing in a deserted cove of Ship Island, and hardly believe our good fortune, hardly believe that the world could contain such happiness. Yet in the case of Marcia and Linda the affair ended just when I thought our relationship was coming into its best phase. The air in the office would begin to grow thick with silent reproaches. It would become impossible to exchange a single word or glance that was not freighted with a thousand hidden meanings. Telephone conversations would take place at all hours of the night, conversations made up mostly of long silences during which I would rack my brain for something to say while on the other end you could hear little else but breathing and sighs. When these long telephone silences come, it is a sure sign that love is over. No, they were not conquests. For in the end my Lindas and I were so sick of each other that we were delighted to say good-by.

I am a stock and bond broker. It is true that my family was somewhat disappointed in my choice of a profession. Once I thought of going into law or medicine or even pure science. I even dreamed of doing something great. But there is much to be said for giving up such grand ambitions and living the most ordinary life imaginable, a life without the old longings; selling stocks and bonds and mutual funds; quitting work at five o'clock like everyone else; having a girl and perhaps one day settling down and raising a flock of Marcias and Sandras and Lindas of my own. Nor is the brokerage business as uninteresting as you might think. It is not a bad life at all.

We live, Mrs. Schexnaydre and I, on Elysian Fields, the main thoroughfare of Faubourg Marigny. Though it was planned to be, like its namesake, the grandest boulevard of the city, something went amiss, and now it runs an undistinguished course from river to lake through shopping centers and blocks of duplexes and bungalows and raised cottages. But it is very spacious and airy and seems truly to stretch out like a field under the sky. Next door to Mrs. Schexnaydre is a brand new school. It is my custom on summer evenings after work to take a shower, put on shirt and pants and stroll over to the deserted playground and there sit on the ocean wave, spread out the movie page of the Times-Picayune on one side, phone book on the other, and a city map in my lap. After I have made my choice, plotted a route – often to some remote neighborhood like Algiers or St. Bernard – I stroll around the schoolyard in the last golden light of day and admire the building. Everything is so spick-and-span: the aluminum sashes fitted into the brick wall and gilded in the sunset, the pretty terrazzo floors and the desks molded like wings. Suspended by wires above the door is a schematic sort of bird, the Holy Ghost I suppose. It gives me a pleasant sense of the goodness of creation to think of the brick and the glass and the aluminum being extracted from common dirt – though no doubt it is less a religious sentiment than a financial one, since I own a few shares of Alcoa. How smooth and well-fitted and thrifty the aluminum feels!

But things have suddenly changed. My peaceful existence in Gentilly has been complicated. This morning, for the first time in years, there occurred to me the possibility of a search. I dreamed of the war, no, not quite dreamed but woke with the taste of it in my mouth, the queasy-quince taste of 1951 and the Orient. I remembered the first time the search occurred to me. I came to myself under a chindolea bush. Everything is upside-down for me, as I shall explain later. What are generally considered to be the best times are for me the worst times, and that worst of times was one of the best. My shoulder didn't hurt but it was pressed hard against the ground as if somebody sat on me. Six inches from my nose a dung beetle was scratching around under the leaves. As I watched, there awoke in me an immense curiosity. I was onto something. I vowed that if I ever got out of this fix, I would pursue the search. Naturally, as soon as I recovered and got home, I forgot all about it. But this morning when I got up, I dressed as usual and began as usual to put my belongings into my pockets: wallet, notebook (for writing down occasional thoughts), pencil, keys, handkerchief, pocket slide rule(for calculating percentage returns on principal). They looked both unfamiliar and at the same time full of clues. I stood in the center of the room and gazed at the little pile, sighting through a hole made by thumb and forefinger. What was unfamiliar about them was that I could see them. They might have belonged to someone else. A man can look at this little pile on his bureau for thirty years and never once see it. It is as invisible as his own hand. Once I saw it, however, the search became possible. I bathed, shaved, dressed carefully, and sat at my desk and poked through the little pile in search of a clue just as the detective on television pokes through the dead man's possessions, using his pencil as a poker.

The idea of a search comes to me again as I am on my way to my aunt's house, riding the Gentilly bus down Elysian Fields. The truth is I dislike cars. Whenever I drive a car, I have the feeling I have become invisible. People on the street cannot see you; they only watch your rear fender until it is out of their way. Elysian Fields is not the shortest route to my aunt's house. But I have my reasons for going through the Quarter. William Holden, I read in the paper this morning, is in New Orleans shooting a few scenes in the Place d'Armes. It would be interesting to catch a glimpse of him.

It is a gloomy March day. The swamps are still burning at Chef Menteur and the sky over Gentilly is the color of ashes. The bus is crowded with shoppers, nearly all women. The windows are steamed. I sit on the lengthwise seat in front. Women sit beside me and stand above me. On the long back seat are five Negresses so black that the whole rear of the bus seems darkened. Directly next to me, on the first cross seat, is a very fine-looking girl. She is a strapping girl but by no means too big, done up head to toe in cellophane, the hood pushed back to show a helmet of glossy black hair. She is magnificent with her split tooth and her Prince Val bangs split on her forehead. Gray eyes and wide black brows, a good arm and a fine swell of calf above her cellophane boot. One of those solitary Amazons one sees on Fifty-seventh Street in New York or in Nieman Marcus in Dallas. Our eyes meet. Am I mistaken or does the corner of her mouth tuck in ever so slightly and the petal of her lower lip curl out ever so richly? She is smiling – at me! My mind hits upon half a dozen schemes to circumvent the terrible moment of separation. No doubt she is a Texan. They are nearly always bad judges of men, these splendid Amazons. Most men are afraid of them and so they fall victim to the first little Mickey Rooney that comes along. In a better world I should be able to speak to her: come, darling, you can see that I love you. If you are planning to meet some little Mickey, think better of it. What a tragedy it is that I do not know her, will probably never see her again. What good times we could have! This very afternoon we could go spinning along the Gulf Coast. What consideration and tenderness I could show her! If it were a movie, I would have only to wait. The bus would get lost or the city would be bombed and she and I would tend the wounded. As it is, I may as well stop thinking about her.

Then it is that the idea of the search occurs to me. I become absorbed and for a minute or so forget about the girl.

"What is the nature of the search?" you ask.

Really it is very simple, at least for a fellow like me; so simple that it is easily overlooked.

The search is what anyone would undertake if he were not sunk in the everydayness of his own life. This morning, for example, I felt as if I had come to myself on a strange island. And what does such a castaway do? Why, he pokes around the neighborhood and he doesn't miss a trick.

To become aware of the possibility of the search is to be onto something. Not to be onto something is to be in despair.

The movies are onto the search, but they screw it up. The search always ends in despair. They like to show a fellow coming to himself in a strange place – but what does he do? He takes up with the local librarian, sets about proving to the local children what a nice fellow he is, and settles down with a vengeance. In two weeks' time he is so sunk in everydayness that he might just as well be dead.

"What do you seek – God?" you ask with a smile.

I hesitate to answer, since all other Americans have settled the matter for themselves and to give such an answer would amount to setting myself a goal which everyone else has reached – and therefore raising a question in which no one has the slightest interest. Who wants to be dead last among one hundred and eighty million Americans? For, as everyone knows, the polls report that 98% of Americans believe in God and the remaining 2% are atheists and agnostics – which leaves not a single percentage point for a seeker. For myself, I enjoy answering polls as much as anyone and take pleasure in giving intelligent replies to all questions.

Truthfully, it is the fear of exposing my own ignorance which constrains me from mentioning the object of my search. For, to begin with, I cannot even answer this, the simplest and most basic of all questions: Am I, in my search, a hundred miles ahead of my fellow Americans or a hundred miles behind them? That is to say: Have 98% of Americans already found what I seek or are they so sunk in everydayness that not even the possibility of a search has occurred to them?

On my honor, I do not know the answer.

As the bus ascends the overpass, a concrete hill which affords a fine view of New Orleans, I discover that I am frowning and gazing at a noble young calf clad in gun-metal nylon. Now beyond question she is aware of me: she gives her raincoat a sharp tug and gives me a look of annoyance – or do I imagine this? I must make sure, so I lift my hat and smile at her as much as to say that we might still become friends. But it is no use. I have lost her forever. She flounces out of the bus in a loud rustle of cellophane.

I alight at Esplanade in a smell of roasting coffee and creosote and walk up Royal Street. The lower Quarter is the best part. The ironwork on the balconies sags like rotten lace. Little French cottages hide behind high walls. Through deep sweating carriageways one catches glimpses of courtyards gone to jungle.

Today I am in luck. Who should come out of Pirate's Alley half a block ahead of me but William Holden!

Holden crosses Royal and turns toward Canal. As yet he is unnoticed. The tourists are either browsing along antique shops or snapping pictures of balconies. No doubt he is on his way to Galatoire's for lunch. He is an attractive fellow with his ordinary good looks, very suntanned, walking along hands in pockets, raincoat slung over one shoulder. Presently he passes a young couple, who are now between me and him. Now we go along, the four of us, not twenty feet apart. It takes two seconds to size up the couple. They are twenty, twenty-one, and on their honeymoon. Not Southern. Probably Northeast. He wears a jacket with leather elbow patches, pipestem pants, dirty white shoes, and affects the kind of rolling seafaring gait you see in Northern college boys. Both are plain. He has thick lips, cropped reddish hair and skin to match. She is mousy. They are not really happy. He is afraid their honeymoon is too conventional, that they are just another honeymoon couple. No doubt he figured it would be fun to drive down the Shenandoah Valley to New Orleans and escape the honeymooners at Niagara Falls and Saratoga. Now fifteen hundred miles from home they find themselves surrounded by couples from Memphis and Chicago. He is anxious; he is threatened from every side. Each stranger he passes is a reproach to him, every doorway a threat. What is wrong? he wonders. She is unhappy but for a different reason, because he is unhappy and she knows it but doesn't know why.

Now they spot Holden. The girl nudges her companion. The boy perks up for a second, but seeing Holden doesn't really help him. On the contrary. He can only contrast Holden's resplendent reality with his own shadowy and precarious existence. Obviously he is more miserable than ever. What a deal, he must be thinking, trailing along behind a movie star – we might just as well be rubbernecking in Hollywood.

Holden slaps his pockets for a match. He has stopped behind some ladies looking at iron furniture on the sidewalk. They look like housewives from Hattiesburg come down for a day of shopping. He asks for a match; they shake their heads and then recognize him. There follows much blushing and confusion. But nobody can find a match for Holden. By now the couple have caught up with him. The boy holds out a light, nods briefly to Holden's thanks, then passes on without a flicker of recognition. Holden walks along between them for a second; he and the boy talk briefly, look up at the sky, shake their heads. Holden gives them a pat on the shoulder and moves on ahead.

The boy has done it! He has won title to his own existence, as plenary an existence now as Holden's, by refusing to be stampeded like the ladies from Hattiesburg. He is a citizen like Holden; two men of the world they are. All at once the world is open to him. Nobody threatens from patio and alley. His girl is open to him too. He puts his arm around her neck, noodles her head. She feels the difference too. She had not known what was wrong nor how it was righted but she knows now that all is well.

Holden has turned down Toulouse shedding light as he goes. An aura of heightened reality moves with him and all who fall within it feel it. Now everyone is aware of him. He creates a regular eddy among the tourists and barkeeps and B-girls who come running to the doors of the joints.

I am attracted to movie stars but not for the usual reasons. I have no desire to speak to Holden or get his autograph. It is their peculiar reality which astounds me. The Yankee boy is well aware of it, even though he pretends to ignore Holden. Clearly he would like nothing better than to take Holden over to his fraternity house in the most casual way. "Bill, I want you to meet Phil. Phil, Bill Holden," he would say and go sauntering off in the best seafaring style.

It is lunch hour on Canal Street. A parade is passing, but no one pays much attention. It is still a week before Mardi Gras and this is a new parade, a women's krewe from Gentilly. A krewe is a group of people who get together at carnival time and put on a parade and a ball. Anyone can form a krewe. Of course there are the famous old krewes like Comus and Rex and Twelfth Night, but there are also dozens of others. The other day a group of Syrians from Algiers formed a krewe named Isis. This krewe today, this must be Linda's krewe. I promised to come to see her. Red tractors pulled the floats along; scaffoldings creak, paper and canvas tremble. Linda, I think, is one of half a dozen shepherdesses dressed in short pleated skirts and mercury sandals with thongs criss-crossed up bare calves. But they are masked and I can't be sure. If she is, her legs are not so fine after all. All twelve legs are shivery and goosepimpled. A few businessmen stop to watch the girls and catch trinkets.

A warm wind springs up from the south piling up the clouds and bearing with it a far-off rumble, the first thunderstorm of the year. The street looks tremendous. People on the far side seem tiny and archaic, dwarfed by the great sky and the windy clouds like pedestrians in old prints. Am I mistaken or has a fog of uneasiness, a thin gas of malaise, settled on the street? The businessmen hurry back to their offices, the shoppers to their cars, the tourists to their hotels. Ah, William Holden, we already need you again. Already the fabric is wearing thin without you.

The mystery deepens. For ten minutes I stand talking to Eddie Lovell and at the end of it, when we shake hands and part, it seems to me that I cannot answer the simplest question about what has taken place. As I listen to Eddie speak plausibly and at length of one thing and another - business, his wife Nell, the old house they are redecorating - the fabric pulls together into one bright texture of investments, family projects, lovely old houses, little theater readings and such. It comes over me: this is how one lives! My exile in Gentilly has been the worst kind of self-deception.

Yes! Look at him. As he talks, he slaps a folded newspaper against his pants leg and his eye watches me and at the same time sweeps the terrain behind me, taking note of the slightest movement. A green truck turns down Bourbon Street; the eye sizes it up, flags it down, demands credentials, waves it on. A businessman turns in at the Maison Blanche building; the eye knows him, even knows what he is up to. And all the while he talks very well. His lips move muscularly, molding words into pleasing shapes, marshalling arguments, and during the slight pauses are held poised, attractively everted in a Charles Boyer pout – while a little web of saliva gathers in a corner like the clear oil of a good machine. Now he jingles the coins deep in his pocket. No mystery here! – he is as cogent as a bird dog quartering a field. He understands everything out there and everything out there is something to be understood.

Eddie watches the last float, a doubtful affair with a squashed cornucopia.

"We'd better do better than that."

"We will."

"Are you riding Neptune?"

"No."

I offer Eddie my four call-outs for the Neptune ball. There is always the problem of out-of-town clients, usually Texans, and especially their wives. Eddie thanks me for this and for something else.

"I want to thank you for sending Mr. Quieulle to me. I really appreciate it."

"Who?"

"Old man Quieulle."

"Yes, I remember." Eddie has sunk mysteriously into himself, eyes twinkling from the depths. "Don't tell me –"

Eddie nods.

" – that he has already set up his trust and up and died?"

Eddie nods, still sunk into himself. He watches me carefully, hanging fire until I catch up with him.

"In Mrs. Quieulle's name?"

Again a nod; his jaw is shot out.

"How big?"

The same dancing look, now almost malignant. "Just short of nine hundred and fifty thou." His tongue curves around and seeks the hollow of his cheek.

"A fine old man," I say absently, noticing that Eddie has become as solemn as a bishop.

"I'll tell you one thing, Binx. I count it a great privilege to have known him. I've never known anyone, young or old, who possessed a greater fund of knowledge. That man spoke to me for two hours about the history of the crystallization of sugar and it was pure romance. I was fascinated."

Eddie tells me how much he admires my aunt and my cousin Kate. Several years ago Kate was engaged to marry Eddie's brother Lyell. On the very eve of the wedding Lyell was killed in an accident, the same accident which Kate survived. Now Eddie comes around to face me, his cottony hair flying up in the breeze. "I have never told anybody what I really think of that woman –" Eddie says "woman" as a deliberate liberty to be set right by the compliment to follow. "I think more of Miss Emily – and Kate – than anyone else in the world except my own mother – and wife. The good that woman has done."

"That's mighty nice, Eddie."

He murmurs something about how beautiful Kate is, that next to Nell etc. – and this is a surprise because my cousin Nell Lovell is a plain horsy old girl. "Will you please give them both my love?"

"I certainly will."

The parade is gone. All that is left is the throb of a drum.

"What do you do with yourself?" asks Eddie and slaps his paper against his pants leg.

"Nothing much," I say, noticing that Eddie is not listening.

"Come see us, fellah! I want you to see what Nell has done." Nell has taste. The two of them are forever buying Shotgun cottages in rundown neighborhoods and fixing them up with shutterblinds in the bathroom, saloon doors for the kitchen, old bricks and a sugar kettle for the back yard, and selling in a few months for a big profit.

The cloud is turning blue and pressing down upon us. Now the street seems closeted; the bricks of the buildings glow with a yellow stored-up light. I look at my watch: one is not late at my aunt's house. In an instant Eddie's hand is out.

"Give the bride and groom my best."

"I will."

"Walter is a wonderful fellow."

"He is."

Before letting me go, Eddie comes one inch closer and asks in a special voice about Kate.

"She seems fine now, Eddie. Quite happy and secure."

"I'm so damn glad. Fellah!" A final shake from side to side, like a tiller. "Come see us!"

"I will! "

Unit 9
Carson McCullers (1917–1967)
卡森·麦卡勒斯

作者简介

卡森·麦卡勒斯，美国南方文学现代派的代表女作家之一，擅长描写孤独者或性格奇异怪僻的人物的内心世界。麦卡勒斯出生在佐治亚州(Columbus, Georgia)的一个小镇上，作品也多以南方小镇为背景。她先去纽约学习音乐，后来改行从事写作，并先后在哥伦比亚大学和纽约大学的写作班学习。20 岁时她与瑞夫斯·麦卡勒斯结婚，1941 年离异，四年后复婚，但二人关系时好时坏，这段婚姻以 1953 年丈夫的自杀了结。麦卡勒斯患有严重的风湿性心脏病，后导致半身不遂，卧榻不起。感情生活的纠葛和长期病痛的折磨，对麦卡勒斯的创作主题和创作风格产生了很大影响。1940 年，23 岁的麦卡勒斯因发表第一部作品《心是孤独的猎手》(*The Heart Is a Lonely Hunter*, 1940)而成名，该书奠定了她的创作特色与艺术风格。《心是孤独的猎手》在美国“现代文库”评出的“20 世纪百佳英文小说”中位列第十七。她的第二部小说《金色眼睛的映像》(*Reflections in a Golden Eye*, 1941)描写了和平时期南方军事基地发生的一起私通事件，该作品被认为是“最具哥特式风格的南方小说”。

美国评论界普遍认为，麦卡勒斯的作品虽然不多，反应的社会面也较窄，但她是一位有特殊建树、有独特风格的作家。她的作品主要致力于表现人类“精神隔绝”的主题。小说人物多为肉体或心灵上的“畸形人”，他们纠缠在爱与恨的复杂关系中，竭力摆脱孤独，但并不成功，因此她的作品总是气氛抑郁，充满怪诞、死亡、暴力。麦卡勒斯擅长对人物进行抽象处理，赋予故事高度的寓言性。虽然她的作品背景都设置在南方小镇，但她明确指出，自己创作的不是地域小说，而是人类孤独的寓言。她的主要作品还包括：《婚礼的成员》(*The Member of the Wedding*, 1946)、《伤心咖啡馆之歌》(*The Ballad of the Sad Cafe*, 1951)、《没有指针的钟》(*Clock Without Hands*, 1961) 和剧本《美丽的平方根》(*The Square Root of Wonderful*, 1958)。其中不少作品被改编成戏剧或电影，影响甚广。1967 年 9 月 29 日麦卡勒斯在纽约州去世，时年 50 岁，遗留下未完成的自传《明亮与暗夜之光》(*Illumination and Night Glare*, 1999)。近年来，由于作品中涉及性别心理异常的人物以及同性恋人物，评论界出现了从同性恋文学的角度研究麦卡勒斯作品的新动向，认为她是主流文化排斥的边缘人的代言者。她的创作特色与艺术风格，从著名中篇小说《伤心咖啡馆之歌》中可以窥见。

作品导读

The Ballad of the Sad Café is about a twisted love triangle in southern gothic style. In the small Georgia town, the protagonist, Miss Amelia Evans, is an independent, lonely town eccentric, selling corn liquor and dispensing medicine in the rural South of the early 20th century. She is the hardest working and best business person. Amelia is 30-year-old tall and strong woman, able to outfight any man. She has retired for some time to the rooms upstairs over her café, and yet she still holds considerable sway over the local backwoods folk, thanks to her skill in healing, and the quality of her whisky. She is not quite a spinster and has been married, briefly, for 10 days to Marvin Macy, the town's toughest criminal, who dotes on her. When she refuses to sleep with him and throws him out of her house on their wedding night he goes on a rampage of crime that leads to his imprisonment. In flashback, Marvin pleads for a space in the marital bed, gradually growing angry and vindictive before he leaves town, disgraced. While Amelia harbors in her heart a failed marriage and other mysteries, a hunchbacked dwarf named Lymon hobbles into town, claiming he is her kin. Believing the little man to be her distant relative Amelia befriends Lymon. They develop an unusual relationship. Amelia is attracted by this dwarf and under his spell she opens her store at night as town's café.

A boisterous clown, Lymon urges Amelia to reopen the café on the main floor of her enormous farmhouse, which gives the locals a venue for something sorely lacking in their lives. Through the café, the town develops a sense of community and pride. But after Marvin is released and returns from prison, Lymon becomes fascinated by him at first sight, who arrives on schedule and brings the party to a halt with his laconic manner, his ironic guitar solos, and his history of emotional warfare with Miss Amelia. The dwarf loves Amelia and possibly Marvin as well, though Miss Amelia seems to appraise love as a foreign concept. All three are crazy. The townsfolk, who are astonished, baffled, cheered and depressed on cue, watch hungrily as Miss Amelia and Marvin Macy edge toward an inevitable showdown: a bare-knuckle fight. Amelia is about to win when Lymon jumps on her back and she is downed in defeat. Marvin and Lymon vandalize the store, destroy the still, and leave town, also leaving Amelia a physically and psychologically broken woman, huddling in her closed café.

The novella ends just like it begins, with a portrait of a sad town that has nothing to hope for. Love is really the central theme of the novella. All of the characters have got the experience of being the lover and the beloved. While all of the characters experience love of some sort, the story is really tragic after all because no one actually succeeds in loving or being loved in return. Just as McCullers wrote in this novella, love is simply "a new, strange loneliness". The distancing effect of the balladeer-narrator allows the larger-than-life characters and strange events to be unified in one of the most intriguing short works in modern Southern fiction.

作品选读

The Ballad of the Sad Café

……

So let the slow years pass and come to a Saturday evening six years after the time when Cousin Lymon came first to the town. It was August and the sky had burned above the town like a sheet of flame all day. Now the green twilight was near and there was a feeling of repose. The street was coated an inch deep with dry golden dust and the little children ran about half-naked, sneezed often, sweated, and were fretful. The mill had closed down at noon. People in the houses along the main street sat resting on their steps and the women had palmetto fans. At Miss Amelia's there was a sign at the front of the premises saying CAFE. The back porch was cool with latticed shadows and there cousin Lymon sat turning the ice-cream freezer – often he unpacked the salt and ice and removed the dasher to lick a bit and see how the work was coming on. Jeff cooked in the kitchen. Early that morning Miss Amelia had put a notice on the wall of the front porch reading: Chicken Dinner – Twenty Cents Tonite. The café was already open and Miss Amelia had just finished a period of work in her office. All the eight tables were occupied and from the mechanical piano came a jingling tune.

In a corner near the door and sitting at a table with a child, was Henry Macy. He was drinking a glass of liquor, which was unusual for him, as liquor went easily to his head and made him cry or sing. His face was very pale and his left eye worked constantly in a nervous tic, as it was apt to do when he was agitated. He had come into the café sidewise and silent, and when he was greeted he did not speak. The child next to him belonged to Horace Wells, and he had been left at Miss Amelia's that morning to be doctored.

Miss Amelia came out from her office in good spirits. She attended to a few details in the kitchen and entered the café with the pope's nose of a hen between her fingers, as that was her favorite piece. She looked about the room, saw that in general all was well, and went over to the corner table by Henry Macy. She turned the chair around and sat straddling the back, as she only wanted to pass the time of day and was not yet ready for her supper. There was a bottle of Kroup Kure in the hip pocket of her overalls – a medicine made from whisky, rock candy, and a secret ingredient. Miss Amelia uncorked the bottle and put it to the mouth of the child. Then she turned to Henry Macy and, seeing the nervous winking of his left eye, she asked:

"What ails you?"

Henry Macy seemed on the point of saying something difficult, but, after a long look into the eyes of Miss Amelia, he swallowed and did not speak.

So Miss Amelia returned to her patient. Only the child's head showed above the table top. His face was very red, with the eyelids half-closed and the mouth partly open. He had a large, hard, swollen boil on his thigh, and had been brought to Miss Amelia so that it could be opened. But Miss Amelia used a special method with children; she did not like to see them hurt, struggling, and terrified. So she had kept the child around the premises all day, giving him licorice and frequent doses of the Kroup Kure, and toward evening she tied a napkin around his neck and let him eat his fill of the dinner. Now as he sat at the table his head wobbled slowly from side to side and sometimes as he breathed there came from him a little worn-out grunt.

There was a stir in the café and Miss Amelia looked around quickly. Cousin Lymon had come in. The hunchback strutted into the café as he did every night, and when he reached the exact center of the room he stopped short and looked shrewdly around him, summing up the people and making a quick pattern of the emotional material at hand that night. The hunchback was a great mischief-maker. He enjoyed any kind of to-do, and without saying a word he could set the people at each other in a way that was miraculous. It was due to him that the Rainey twins had quarreled over a jacknife two years past, and had not spoken one word to each other since. He was present at the big fight between Rip Wellborn and Robert Calvert Hale, and every other fight for that matter since he had come into the town. He nosed around everywhere, knew the intimate business of everybody, and trespassed every waking hour. Yet, queerly enough, in spite of this it was the hunchback who was most responsible for the great popularity of the café. Things were never so gay as when he was around. When he walked into the room there was always a quick feeling of tension, because with this busybody about there was never any telling what might descend on you, or what might suddenly be brought to happen in the room. People are never so free with themselves and so recklessly glad as when there is some possibility of commotion or calamity ahead. So when the hunchback marched into the café everyone looked around at him and there was a quick outburst of talking and a drawing of corks.

Lymon waved his hand to Stumpy MacPhail who was sitting with Merlie Ryan and Henry Ford Crimp. "I walked to Rotten Lake today to fish," he said. "And on the way I stepped over what appeared at first to be a big fallen tree. But then as I stepped over I felt something stir and I taken this second look and there I was straddling this here alligator long as from the front door to the kitchen and thicker than a hog."

The hunchback chattered on. Everyone looked at him from time to time, and some kept track of his chattering and others did not. There were times when every word he said was nothing but lying and bragging. Nothing he said tonight was true. He had lain in bed with a summer quinsy all day long, and had only got up in the late afternoon in order to turn the ice-cream freezer. Everybody knew this, yet he stood there in the middle of the café and held forth with such lies and boasting that it was enough to shrivel the ears.

Miss Amelia watched him with her hands in her pockets and her head turned to one side. There was a softness about her gray, queer eyes and she was smiling gently to herself.

Occasionally she glanced from the hunchback to the other people in the café – and then her look was proud, and there was in it the hint of a threat, as though daring anyone to try to hold him to account for all his foolery. Jeff was bringing in the suppers, already served on the plates, and the new electric fans in the café made a pleasant stir of coolness in the air.

"The little youngun is asleep," said Henry Macy finally.

Miss Amelia looked down at the patient beside her, and composed her face for the matter in hand. The child's chin was resting on the table edge and a trickle of spit or Kroup Kure had bubbled from the corner of his mouth. His eyes were quite closed, and a little family of gnats had clustered peacefully in the corners. Miss Amelia put her hand on his head and shook it roughly, but the patient did not awake. So Miss Amelia lifted the child from the table, being careful not to touch the sore part of his leg, and went into the office. Henry Macy followed after her and they closed the office door.

Cousin Lymon was bored that evening. There was not much going on, and in spite of the heat the customers in the café were good-humored. Henry Ford Crimp and Horace Wells sat at the middle table with their arms around each other, sniggering over some long joke – but when he approached them he could make nothing of it as he had missed the beginning of the story. The moonlight brightened the dusty road, and the dwarfed peach trees were black and motionless: there was no breeze. The drowsy buzz of swamp mosquitoes was like an echo of the silent night. The town seemed dark, except far down the road to the right there was the flicker of a lamp. Somewhere in the darkness a woman sang in a high wild voice and the tune had no start and no finish and was made up of only three notes which went on and on and on. The hunchback stood leaning against the banister of the porch, looking down the empty road as though hoping that someone would come along.

There were footsteps behind him, then a voice: "Cousin Lymon, your dinner is set out upon the table."

"My appetite is poor tonight," said the hunchback, who had been eating sweet snuff all the day. "There is a sourness in my mouth."

"Just a pick," said Miss Amelia. "The breast, the liver, and the heart."

Together they went back into the bright café, and sat down with Henry Macy. Their table was the largest one in the café, and on it there was a bouquet of swamp lilies in a Coca Cola bottle. Miss Amelia had finished with her patient and was satisfied with herself. From behind the closed office door there had come only a few sleepy whimpers, and before the patient could wake up and become terrified it was all over. The child was now slung across the shoulder of his father, sleeping deeply, his little arms dangling loose along his father's back, and his puffed-up face very red – they were leaving the café to go home.

Henry Macy was still silent. He ate carefully, making no noise when he swallowed, and was not a third as greedy as Cousin Lymon who had claimed to have no appetite and was now putting down helping after helping of the dinner. Occasionally Henry Macy looked across at Miss Amelia and again held his peace.

It was a typical Saturday night. An old couple who had come in from the country hesitated for a moment at the doorway, holding each other's hand, and finally decided to come inside. They had lived together so long, this old country couple, that they looked as similar as twins. They were brown, shriveled, and like two little walking peanuts. They left early, and by midnight most of the other customers were gone. Rosser Cline and Merlie Ryan still played checkers, and Stumpy MacPhail sat with a liquor bottle on his table (his wife would not allow it in the home) and carried on peaceable conversations with himself. Henry Macy had not yet gone away, and this was unusual, as he almost always went to bed soon after nightfall. Miss Amelia yawned sleepily, but Lymon was restless and she did not suggest that they close up for the night.

Finally, at one o'clock, Henry Macy looked up at the corner of the ceiling and said quietly to Miss Amelia: "I got a letter today."

Miss Amelia was not one to be impressed by this, because all sorts of business letters and catalogues came addressed to her.

"I got a letter from my brother," said Henry Macy.

The hunchback, who had been goose-stepping about the café with his hands clasped behind his head, stopped suddenly. He was quick to sense any change in the atmosphere of a gathering. He glanced at each face in the room and waited.

Miss Amelia scowled and hardened her right fist, "You are welcome to it," she said.

"He is on parole. He is out of the penitentiary."

The face of Miss Amelia was very dark, and she shivered although the night was warm. Stumpy MacPhail and Merlie Ryan pushed aside their checker game. The café was very quiet.

"Who?" asked Cousin Lymon. His large, pale ears seemed to grow on his head and stiffen. "What?"

Miss Amelia slapped her hands palm down on the table. "Because Marvin Macy is a –" But her voice hoarsened and after a few moments she only said: "He belongs to be in that penitentiary the balance of his life."

"What did he do?" asked Cousin Lymon.

There was a long pause, as no one knew exactly how to answer this. "He robbed three filling stations," said Stumpy MacPhail. But his words did not sound complete and there was a feeling of sins left unmentioned.

The hunchback was impatient. He could not bear to be left out of anything, even a great misery. The name Marvin Marcy was unknown to him, but it tantalized him as did any mention of subjects which others knew about and of which he was ignorant – such as any reference to the old sawmill that had been torn down before he came, or a chance word about poor Morris Finestein, or the recollection of any event that had occurred before his time. Aside from this inborn curiosity, the hunchback took a great interest in robbers and crimes of all varieties. As he strutted around the table he was muttering the words "released on parole" and "penitentiary" to himself. But although he questioned insistently, he was unable to find anything, as nobody would dare to talk about Marvin Macy before Miss Amelia in the café.

"The letter did not say very much," said Henry Macy. "He did not say where he was going."

"Humph! " said Amelia, and her face was still hardened and very dark. "He will never set his split hoof on my premises."

She pushed back her chair from the table, and made ready to close the café. Thinking about Marvin Macy may have set her to brooding, for she hauled the cash register back to the kitchen and put it in a private place. Henry Macy went off down the dark road. But Henry Ford Crimp and Merlie Ryan lingered for a time on the front porch. Later Merlie Ryan was to make certain claims, to swear that on that night he had a vision of what was to come. But the town paid no attention, for that was just the sort of thing that Merlie Ryan would claim. Miss Amelia and Cousin Lymon talked for a time in the parlor. And when at last the hunchback thought that he could sleep she arranged the mosquito netting over his bed and waited until he had finished with his prayers. Then she put on her long nightgown, smoked two pipes, and only after a long time went to sleep.

That autumn was a happy time. The crops around the countryside were good, and over at the Forks Falls market the price of tobacco held firm that year. After the long hot summer the first cool days had a clean bright sweetness. Goldenrod grew along the dusty roads, and the sugar cane was ripe and purple. The bus came each day from Cheehaw to carry off a few of the younger children to the consolidated school to get an education. Boys hunted foxes in the pinewoods, winter quilts were aired out on the wash lines, and sweet potatoes bedded in the ground with straw against the colder months to come. In the evening, delicate shreds of smoke rose from the chimneys, and the moon was round and orange in the autumn sky. There is no stillness like the quiet of the first cold nights in the fall. Sometimes, late in the night when there was no wind, there could be heard in the town the thin wild whistle of the train that goes through Society City on its way far off to the North.

For Miss Amelia Evans this was a time of great activity. She was at work from dawn until sundown. She made a new and bigger condenser for her still, and in one week ran off enough liquor to souse the whole county. Her old mule was dizzy from grinding so much sorghum, and she scalded her Mason jars and put away pear preserves. She was looking forward greatly to the first frost, because she had traded for three tremendous hogs, and intended to make much barbecue, chitterlins, and sausage.

During these weeks there was a quality about Miss Amelia that many people noticed. She laughed often, with a deep ringing laugh, and her whistling had a sassy, tuneful trickery. She was forever trying out her strength, lifting up heavy objects, or poking her tough biceps with her finger. One day she sat down to her typewriter and wrote a story – a story in which there were foreigners, trap doors, and millions of dollars. Cousin Lymon was with her always, traipsing along behind her coat – tails, and when she watched him her face had a bright, soft look, and when she spoke his name there lingered in her voice the undertone of love.

The first cold spell came at last. When Miss Amelia awoke one morning there were frost flowers on the windowpanes, and rime had silvered the patches of grass in the yard. Miss Amelia built a roaring fire in the kitchen stove, then went out of doors to judge the day. The air was cold and sharp, the sky pale green and cloudless. Very shortly people began to come in from the country to find out what Miss Amelia thought of the weather; she decided to kill the biggest hog, and word got round the countryside. The hog was slaughtered and a low oak fire started in the barbecue pit. There was the warm smell of pig blood and smoke in the back yard, the stamp of footsteps, the ring of voices in the winter air. Miss Amelia walked around giving orders and soon most of the work was done.

She had some particular business to do in Cheehaw that day, so after making sure that all was going well, she cranked up her car and got ready to leave. She asked Cousin Lymon to come with her, in fact, she asked him seven times, but he was loath to leave the commotion and wanted to remain. This seemed to trouble Miss Amelia, as she always liked to have him near to her, and was prone to be terribly homesick when she had to go any distance away. But after asking him seven times, she did not urge him any further. Before leaving she found a stick and drew a heavy line all around the barbecue pit, about two feet back from the edge, and told him not to trespass beyond that boundary. She left after dinner and intended to be back before dark.

Now, it is not so rare to have a truck or an automobile pass along the road and through the town on the way from Cheehaw to somewhere else. Every year the tax collector comes to argue with rich people such as Miss Amelia. And if somebody in the town, such as Merlie Ryan, takes a notion that he can connive to get a car on credit, or to pay down three dollars and have a fine electric icebox such as they advertise in the store windows of Cheehaw, then a city man will come out asking meddlesome questions, finding out all his troubles, and ruining his chances of buying anything on the installment plan. Sometimes, especially since they are working on the Forks Falls highway, the cars hauling the chain gang come through the town. And frequently people in automobiles get lost and stop to inquire how they can find the right road again. So, late that afternoon it was nothing unusual to have a truck pass the mill and stop in the middle of the road near the café of Miss Amelia. A man jumped down from the back of the truck, and the truck went on its way.

The man stood in the middle of the road and looked about him. He was a tall man, with brown curly hair, and slow-moving, deep-blue eyes. His lips were red and he smiled the lazy, half-mouthed smile of the braggart. The man wore a red shirt, and a wide belt of tooled leather; he carried a tin suitcase and a guitar. The first person in the town to see this newcomer was Cousin Lymon, who had heard the shifting gears and come around to investigate. The hunchback stuck his head around the corner of the porch, but did not step out altogether into full view. He and the man stared at each other, and it was not the look of two strangers meeting for the first time and swiftly summing up each other. It was a peculiar stare they exchanged between them, like the look of two criminals who recognize each other. Then the man in the red shirt shrugged his left shoulder and turned away. The face of the hunchback was very pale as he watched the man go down the road, and after a few moments he began to follow along carefully, keeping many paces away.

It was immediately known throughout the town that Marvin Macy had come back again. First, he went to the mill, propped his elbows lazily on a window sill and looked inside. He liked to watch others hard at work, as do all born loafers. The mill was thrown into a sort of numb confusion. The dyers left the hot vats, the spinners and weavers forgot about their machines, and even Stumpy MacPhail, who was foreman, did not know exactly what to do. Marvin Macy still smiled his wet half-mouthed smiles, and when he saw his brother, his bragging expression did not change. After looking over the mill Marvin Macy went down the road to the house where he had been raised, and left his suitcase and guitar on the front porch. Then he walked around the millpond, looked over the church, the three stores, and the rest of the town. The hunchback trudged along quietly at some distance behind him, his hands in his pockets, and his little face still very pale.

It had grown late. The red winter sun was setting, and to the west the sky was deep gold and crimson. Ragged chimney swifts flew to their nests; lamps were lighted. Now and then there was the smell of smoke, and the warm rich odor of the barbecue slowly cooking in the pit behind the café. After making the rounds of the town Marvin Macy stopped before Miss Amelia's premises and read the sign above the porch. Then, not hesitating to trespass, he walked through the side yard. The mill whistle blew a thin, lonesome blast, and the day's shift was done. Soon there were others in Miss Amelia's back yard beside Marvin Macy – Henry Ford Crimp, Merlie Ryan, Stumpy MacPhail, and any number of children and people who stood around the edges of the property and looked on. Very little was said. Marvin Macy stood by himself on one side of the pit, and the rest of the people clustered together on the other side. Cousin Lymon stood somewhat apart from everyone, and he did not take his eyes from the face of Marvin Macy.

"Did you have a good time in the penitentiary?" asked Merlie Ryan, with a silly giggle.

Marvin Macy did not answer. He took from his hip pocket a large knife, opened it slowly, and honed the blade on the seat of his pants. Merlie Ryan grew suddenly very quiet and went to stand directly behind the broad back of Stumpy MacPhail.

Miss Amelia did not come home until almost dark. They heard the rattle of her automobile while she was still a long distance away, then the slam of the door and a bumping noise as though she were hauling something up the front steps of her premises. The sun had already set, and in the air there was the blue smoky glow of early winter evenings. Miss Amelia came down the back steps slowly, and the group in her yard waited very quietly. Few people in this world could stand up to Miss Amelia, and against Marvin Macy she had this special and bitter hate. Everyone waited to see her burst into a terrible holler, snatch up some dangerous object, and chase him altogether out of town. At first she did not see Marvin Macy, and her face had the relieved and dreamy expression that was natural to her when she reached home after having gone some distance away.

Miss Amelia must have seen Marvin Macy and Cousin Lymon at the same instant. She looked from one to the other, but it was not the wastrel from the penitentiary on whom she finally fixed her gaze of sick amazement. She, and everyone else, was looking at Cousin Lymon, and he was a sight to see.

The hunchback stood at the end of the pit, his pale face lighted by the soft glow from the smoldering oak fire. Cousin Lymon had a very peculiar accomplishment, which he used whenever he wished to ingratiate himself with someone. He would stand very still, and with just a little concentration, he could wiggle his large pale ears with marvelous quickness and ease. This trick he always used when he wanted to get something special out of Miss Amelia, and to her it was irresistible. Now as he stood there the hunchback's ears were wiggling furiously on his head, but it was not Miss Amelia at whom he was looking this time. The hunchback was smiling at Marvin Macy with an entreaty that was near to desperation. At first Marvin Macy paid no attention to him, and when he did finally glance at the hunchback it was without any appreciation whatsoever.

"What ails this Brokeback?" he asked with a rough jerk of his thumb.

No one answered. And Cousin Lymon, seeing that his accomplishment was getting him nowhere, added new efforts of persuasion. He fluttered his eyelids, so that they were like pale, trapped moths in his sockets. He scraped his feet around on the ground, waved his hands about, and finally began doing a little trotlike dance. In the last gloomy light of the winter afternoon he resembled the child of a swamphaunt.

Marvin Macy, alone of all the people in the yard, was unimpressed.

"Is the runt throwing a fit?" he asked, and when no one answered he stepped forward and gave Cousin Lymon a cuff on the side of his head. The hunchback staggered, then fell back on the ground. He sat where he had fallen, still looking up at Marvin Macy, and with great effort his ears managed one last forlorn little flap.

Now everyone turned to Miss Amelia to see what she would do. In all these years no one had so much as touched a hair of Cousin Lymon's head, although many had had the itch to do so. If anyone even spoke crossly to the hunchback, Miss Amelia would cut off this rash mortal's credit and find ways of making things go hard for him a long time afterward. So now if Miss Amelia had split open Marvin Macy's head with the ax on the back porch no one would have been surprised. But she did nothing of the kind.

There were times when Miss Amelia seemed to go into a sort of trance. And the cause of these trances was usually known and understood. For Miss Amelia was a fine doctor, and did not grind up swamp roots and other untried ingredients and give them to the first patient who came along; whenever she invented a new medicine she always tried it out first on herself. She would swallow an enormous dose and spend the following day walking thoughtfully back and forth from the café to the brick privy. Often, when there was a sudden keen gripe, she would stand quite still, her queer eyes staring down at the ground and her fists clenched; she was trying to decide which organ was being worked upon, and what misery the new medicine might be most likely to cure. And now as she watched the hunchback and Marvin Macy, her face wore this same expression, tense with reckoning some inward pain, although she had taken no new medicine that day.

"That will learn you, Brokeback," said Marvin Macy.

Henry Macy pushed back his limp whitish hair from his forehead and coughed nervously. Stumpy MacPhail and Merlie Ryan shuffled their feet, and the children and black people on the outskirts of the property made not a sound. Marvin Macy folded the knife he had been honing, and after looking about him fearlessly he swaggered out of the yard. The embers in the pit were turning to gray feathery ashes and it was now quite dark.

That was the way Marvin Macy came back from the penitentiary. Not a living soul in all the town was glad to see him. Even Mrs. Mary Hale, who was a good woman and had raised him with love and care – at the first sight of him even this old foster mother dropped the skillet she was holding and burst into tears. But nothing could faze that Marvin Macy. He sat on the back steps of the Hale house, lazily picking his guitar, and when the supper was ready, he pushed the children of the household out of the way and served himself a big meal, although there had been barely enough hoecakes and white meat to go round. After eating he settled himself in the best and warmest sleeping place in the front room and was untroubled by dreams.

Miss Amelia did not open the café that night. She locked the doors and all the windows very carefully, nothing was seen of her and Cousin Lymon, and a lamp burned in her room all the night long.

Marvin Macy brought with him bad fortune, right from the first, as could be expected. The next day the weather turned suddenly, and it became hot. Even in the early morning there was a sticky sultriness in the atmosphere, the wind carried the rotten smell of the swamp, and delicate shrill mosquitoes webbed the green millpond. It was unseasonable, worst than August, and much damage was done. For nearly everyone in the county who owned a hog had copied Miss Amelia and slaughtered the day before. And what sausage could keep in such weather as this? After a few days there was everywhere the smell of slowly spoiling meat, and an atmosphere of dreary waste. Worse yet, a family reunion near the Forks Falls highway ate pork roast and died, every one of them. It was plain that their hog had been infected – and who could tell whether the rest of the meat was safe or not? People were torn between the longing for the good taste of pork, and the fear of death. It was a time of waste and confusion.

The cause of all this, Marvin Macy, had no shame in him. He was seen everywhere. During work hours he loafed about the mill, looking in at the windows, and on Sundays he dressed in his red shirt and paraded up and down the road with his guitar. He was still handsome – with his brown hair, his red lips, and his broad strong shoulders; but the evil in him was now too famous for his good looks to get him anywhere. And this evil was not measured only by the actual sins he had committed. True, he had robbed those filling stations. and before that he

had ruined the tenderest girls in the county, and laughed about it Any number of wicked things could be listed against him, but quite apart from these crimes there was about him a secret meanness that clung to him almost like a smell. Another thing – he never sweated, not even in August, and that surely is a sign worth pondering over.

Now it seemed to the town that he was more dangerous than he had ever been before, as in the penitentiary in Atlanta he must have learned the method of laying charms. Otherwise how could his effect on Cousin Lymon be explained? For since first setting eyes on Marvin Macy the hunchback was possessed by an unnatural spirit. Every minute he wanted to be following along behind this jailbird, and he was full of silly schemes to attract attention to himself. Still Marvin Macy either treated him hatefully or failed to notice him at all. Sometimes the hunchback would give up, perch himself on the banister of the front porch much as a sick bird huddles on a telephone wire, and grieve publicly.

"But why?" Miss Amelia would ask, staring at him with her crossed, gray eyes, and her fists closed tight.

"Oh, Marvin Macy," groaned the hunchback, and the sound of the name was enough to upset the rhythm of his sobs so that he hiccuped. "He has been to Atlanta."

Miss Amelia would shake her head and her face was dark and hardened. To begin with she had no patience with any traveling; those who had made the trip to Atlanta or traveled fifty miles from home to see the ocean – those restless people she despised. "Going to Atlanta does no credit to him."

"He has been to the penitentiary," said the hunchback, miserable with longing.

How are you going to argue against such envies as these? In her perplexity Miss Amelia did not herself sound any too sure of what she was saying. "Been to the penitentiary, Cousin Lymon? Why, a trip like that is no travel to brag about."

During these weeks Miss Amelia was closely watched by everyone. She went about absent-mindedly, her face remote as though she had lapsed into one of her gripe trances. For some reason, after the day of Marvin Macy's arrival, she put aside her overalls and wore always the red dress she had before this time reserved for Sundays, funerals, and sessions of the court. Then as the weeks passed she began to take some steps to clear up the situation. But her efforts were hard to understand. If it hurt her to see Cousin Lymon follow Marvin Macy about the town, why did she not make the issues clear once and for all, and tell the hunchback that if he had dealings with Marvin Macy she would turn him off the premises? That would have been simple, and Cousin Lymon would have had to submit to her, or else face the sorry business of finding himself loose in the world. But Miss Amelia seemed to have lost her will; for the first time in her life she hesitated as to just what course to pursue. And, like most people in such a position of uncertainty, she did the worst thing possible – she began following several courses at once, all of them contrary to each other.

The café was opened every night as usual, and, strangely enough, when Marvin Macy came swaggering through the door, with the hunchback at his heels, she did not turn him out.

She even gave him free drinks and smiled at him in a wild, crooked way. At the same time she set a terrible trap for him out in the swamp that surely would have killed him if he had got caught. She let Cousin Lymon invite him to Sunday dinner, and then tried to trip him up as he went down the steps. She began a great campaign of pleasure for Cousin Lymon – making exhausting trips to various spectacles being held in distant places, driving the automobile thirty miles to a Chautauqua, taking him to Forks Falls to watch a parade. All in all it was a distracting time for Miss Amelia. In the opinion of most people she was well on her way in the climb up fools' hill, and everyone waited to see how it would all turn out.

The weather turned cold again, the winter was upon the town, and night came before the last shift in the mill was done. Children kept on all their garments when they slept, and women raised the backs of their skirts to toast themselves dreamily at the fire. After it rained, the mud in the road made hard frozen ruts, there were faint flickers of lamplight from the windows of the houses, the peach trees were scrawny and bare. In the dark, silent nights of winter-time the café was the warm center point of the town, the lights shining so brightly that they could be seen a quarter of a mile away. The great iron stove at the back of the room roared, crackled, and turned red. Miss Amelia had made red curtains for the windows, and from a salesman who passed through the town she bought a great bunch of paper roses that looked very real.

But it was not only the warmth, the decorations, and the brightness, that made the café what it was. There is a deeper reason why the café was so precious to this town. And this deeper reason has to do with a certain pride that had not hitherto been known in these parts. To understand this new pride the cheapness of human life must be kept in mind. There were always plenty of people clustered around a mill – but it was seldom that every family had enough meal, garments, and fat back to go the rounds. Life could become one long dim scramble just to get the things needed to keep alive. And the confusing point is this: All useful things have a price, and are bought only with money, as that is the way the world is run. You know without having to reason about it the price of a bale of cotton, or a quart of molasses. But no value has been put on human life; it is given to us free and taken without being paid for. What is it worth? If you look around, at times the value may seem to be little or nothing at all. Often after you have sweated and tried and things are not better for you, there comes a feeling deep down in the soul that you are not worth much.

But the new pride that the café brought to this town had an effect on almost everyone, even the children. For in order to come to the café you did not have to buy the dinner, or a portion of liquor. There were cold bottled drinks for a nickel. And if you could not even afford that, Miss Amelia had a drink called Cherry Juice which sold for a penny a glass, and was pink-colored and very sweet. Almost everyone, with the exception of Reverend T. M. Willin, came to the café at least once during the week. Children love to sleep in houses other than their own, and to eat at a neighbor's table; on such occasions they behave themselves decently and are proud. The people in the town were likewise proud when sitting at the tables in the café. They washed before coming to Miss Amelia's, and scraped their feet very politely on the

threshold as they entered the café. There, for a few hours at least, the deep bitter knowing that you are not worth much in this world could be laid low.

The café was a special benefit to bachelors, unfortunate people, and consumptives. And here it may be mentioned that there was some reason to suspect that Cousin Lymon was consumptive. The brightness of his gray eyes, his insistence, his talkativeness, and his cough – these were all signs. Besides, there is generally supposed to be some connection between a hunched spine and consumption. But whenever this subject had been mentioned to Miss Amelia she had become furious; she denied these symptoms with bitter vehemence, but on the sly she treated Cousin Lymon with hot chest platters, Kroup Kure, and such. Now this winter the hunchback's cough was worse, and sometimes even on cold days he would break out in a heavy sweat. But this did not prevent him from following along after Marvin Macy.

Early every morning he left the premises and went to the back door of Mrs. Hale's house, and waited and waited – as Marvin Macy was a lazy sleeper. He would stand there and call out softly. His voice was just like the voices of children who squat patiently over those tiny little holes in the ground where doodlebugs are thought to live, poking the hole with a broom straw, and calling plaintively: "Doodlebug, Doodlebug – fly away home. Mrs. Doodlebug, Mrs. Doodlebug. Come out, come out. Your house is on fire and all your children are burning up." In just such a voice – at once sad, luring, and resigned – would the hunchback call Marvin Macy's name each morning. Then when Marvin Macy came out for the day, he would trail him about the town, and sometimes they would be gone for hours together out in the swamp.

And Miss Amelia continued to do the worst thing possible: that is, to try to follow several courses at once. When Cousin Lymon left the house she did not call him back, but only stood in the middle of the road and watched lonesomely until he was out of sight. Nearly every day Marvin Macy turned up with Cousin Lymon at dinnertime, and ate at her table. Miss Amelia opened the pear preserves, and the table was well-set with ham or chicken, great bowls of hominy grits, and winter peas. It is true that on one occasion Miss Amelia tried to poison Marvin Macy – but there was a mistake, the plates were confused, and it was she herself who got the poisoned dish. This she quickly realized by the slight bitterness of the food, and that day she ate no dinner. She sat tilted back in her chair, feeling her muscle, and looking at Marvin Macy.

Every night Marvin Macy came to the café and settled himself at the best and largest table, the one in the center of the room. Cousin Lymon brought him liquor, for which he did not pay a cent. Marvin Macy brushed the hunchback aside as if he were a swamp mosquito, and not only did he show no gratitude for these favors, but if the hunchback got in his way he would cuff him with the back of his hand, or say: "Out of my way, Brokeback – I'll snatch you bald-headed." When this happened Miss Amelia would come out from behind her counter and approach Marvin Macy very slowly, her fists clenched, her peculiar red dress hanging awkwardly around her bony knees. Marvin Macy would also clench his fists and they would walk slowly and meaningfully around each other. But, although everyone watched breathlessly, nothing ever came of it. The time for the fight was not yet ready.

There is one particular reason why this winter is remembered and still talked about. A great thing happened. People woke up on the second of January and found the whole world about them altogether changed. Little ignorant children looked out of the windows, and they were so puzzled that they began to cry. Old people harked back and could remember nothing in these parts to equal the phenomenon. For in the night it had snowed. In the dark hours after midnight the dim flakes started falling softly on the town. By dawn the ground was covered, and the strange snow banked the ruby windows of the church, and whitened the roofs of the houses. The snow gave the town a drawn, bleak look. The two-room houses near the mill were dirty, crooked, and seemed about to collapse, and somehow everything was dark and shrunken. But the snow itself – there was a beauty about it few people around here had ever known before. The snow was not white, as Northerners had pictured it to be; in the snow there were soft colors of blue and silver, the sky was a gentle shining gray. And the dreamy quietness of falling snow – when had the town been so silent?

People reacted to the snowfall in various ways. Miss Amelia, on looking out of her window, thoughtfully wiggled the toes of her bare foot, gathered close to her neck the collar of her nightgown. She stood there for some time, then commenced to draw the shutters and lock every window on the premises. She dosed the place completely, lighted the lamps, and sat solemnly over her bowl of grits. The reason for this was not that Miss Amelia feared the snowfall. It was simply that she was unable to form an immediate opinion of this new event, and unless she knew exactly and definitely what she thought of a matter (which was nearly always the case) she preferred to ignore it. Snow had never fallen in this county in her lifetime, and she had never thought about it one way or the other. But if she admitted this snowfall she would have to come to some decision, and in those days there was enough distraction in her life as it was already. So she poked about the gloomy, lamp lighted house and pretended that nothing had happened. Cousin Lymon, on the contrary, chased around in the wildest excitement, and when Miss Amelia turned her back to dish him some breakfast he slipped out of the door.

Marvin Macy laid claim to the snowfall. He said that he knew snow, had seen it in Atlanta, and from the way he walked about the town that day it was as though he owned every flake. He sneered at the little children who crept timidly out of the houses and scooped up handfuls of snow to taste. Reverend Willin hurried down the road with a furious face, as he was thinking deeply and trying to weave the snow into his Sunday sermon. Most people were humble and glad about this marvel; they spoke in hushed voices and said "thank you" and "please" more than was necessary. A few weak characters, of course, were demoralized and got drunk – but they were not numerous. To everyone this was an occasion and many counted their money and planned to go to the café that night.

Cousin Lymon followed Marvin Macy about all day, seconding his claim to the snow. He marveled that snow did not fall as does rain, and stared up at the dreamy, gently falling flakes until he stumbled from dizziness. And the pride he took on himself, basking in the glory of Marvin Macy – it was such that many people could not resist calling out to him: "'Oho,' said

the fly on the chariot wheel. 'What a dust we do raise.'"

Miss Amelia did not intend to serve dinner. But when, at six o'clock, there was the sound of footsteps on the porch she opened the front door cautiously. It was Henry Ford Crimp, and though there was no food, she let him sit at a table and served him a drink. Others came. The evening was blue, bitter, and though the snow fell no longer there was a wind from the pine trees that swept up delicate flurries from the ground. Cousin Lymon did not come until after dark, with him Marvin Macy, and he carried his tin suitcase and his guitar.

"So you mean to travel?" said Miss Amelia quickly.

Marvin Macy warmed himself at the stove. Then he settled down at his table and carefully sharpened a little stick. He picked his teeth, frequently taking the stick out of his mouth to look at the end and wipe it on the sleeve of his coat. He did not bother to answer.

The hunchback looked at Miss Amelia, who was behind the counter. His face was not in the least beseeching; he seemed quite sure of himself. He folded his hands behind his back and perked up his ears confidently. His cheeks were red, his eyes shining, and his clothes were soggy wet. "Marvin Macy is going to visit a spell with us," he said.

Miss Amelia made no protest. She only came out from behind the counter and hovered over the stove, as though the news had made her suddenly cold. She did not warm her backside modestly, lifting her skirt only an inch or so, as do most women when in public. There was not a grain of modesty about Miss Amelia, and she frequently seemed to forget altogether that there were men in the room. Now as she stood warming herself, her red dress was pulled up quite high in the back so that a piece of her strong, hairy thigh could be seen by anyone who cared to look at it. Her head was turned to one side, and she had begun talking with herself, nodding and wrinkling her forehead, and there was the tone of accusation and reproach in her voice although the words were not plain. Meanwhile, the hunchback and Marvin Macy had gone upstairs – up to the parlor with the pampas grass and the two sewing machines, to the private rooms where Miss Amelia had lived the whole of her life. Down in the café you could hear them bumping around, unpacking Marvin Macy, and getting him settled.

That is the way Marvin Macy crowded into Miss Amelia's home. At first Cousin Lymon, who had given Marvin Macy his own room, slept on the sofa in the parlor. But the snowfall had a bad effect on him; he caught a cold that turned into a winter quinsy, so Miss Amelia gave up her bed to him. The sofa in the parlor was much too short for her, her feet lapped over the edges, and often she rolled off onto the floor. Perhaps it was this lack of sleep that clouded her wits; everything she tried to do against Marvin Macy rebounded on herself. She got caught in her own tricks, and found herself in many pitiful positions. But still she did not put Marvin Macy off the premises, as she was afraid that she would be left alone. Once you have lived with another, it is a great torture to have to live alone. The silence of a firelit room when suddenly the clock stops ticking, the nervous shadows in an empty house – it is better to take in your mortal enemy than face the terror of living alone.

The snow did not last. The sun came out and within two days the town was just as it had always been before. Miss Amelia did not open her house until every flake had melted. Then she had a big house cleaning and aired everything out in the sun. But before that, the very first thing she did on going out again into her yard, was to tie a rope to the largest branch of the chinaberry tree. At the end of the rope she tied a crocus sack tightly stuffed with sand. This was the punching bag she made for herself and from that day on she would box with it out in her yard every morning. Already she was a fine fighter – a little heavy on her feet, but knowing all manner of mean holds and squeezes to make up for this.

Miss Amelia, as has been mentioned, measured six feet two inches in height. Marvin Macy was one inch shorter. In weight they were about even – both of them weighing close to a hundred and sixty pounds. Marvin Macy had the advantage in slyness of movement, and in toughness of chest. In fact from the outward point of view the odds were altogether in his favor. Yet almost everybody in the town was betting on Miss Amelia; scarcely a person would put up money on Marvin Macy. The town remembered the great fight between Miss Amelia and a Fork Falls lawyer who had tried to cheat her. He had been a huge strapping fellow, but he was left three-quarters dead when she had finished with him. And it was not only her talent as a boxer that had impressed everyone – she could demoralize her enemy by making terrifying faces and fierce noises, so that even the spectators were sometimes cowed. She was brave, she practiced faithfully with her punching bag, and in this case she was clearly in the right. So people had confidence in her, and they waited. Of course there was no set date for this fight. There were just the signs that were too plain to be overlooked.

During these times the hunchback strutted around with a pleased little pinched-up face. In many delicate and clever ways he stirred up trouble between them. He was constantly plucking at Marvin Macy's trouser leg to draw attention to himself. Sometimes he followed in Miss Amelia's footsteps – but these days it was only in order to imitate her awkward long-legged walk; he crossed his eyes and aped her gestures in a way that made her appear to be a freak. There was something so terrible about this that even the silliest customers of the café, such as Merlie Ryan, did not laugh. Only Marvin Macy drew up the left corner of his mouth and chuckled. Miss Amelia, when this happened, would be divided between two emotions. She would look at the hunchback with a lost, dismal reproach – then turn toward Marvin Macy with her teeth clamped.

"Bust a gut!" she would say bitterly.

And Marvin Macy, most likely, would pick up the guitar from the floor beside his chair. His voice was wet and slimy, as he always had too much spit in his mouth. And the tunes he sang glided slowly from his throat like eels. His strong fingers picked the strings with dainty skill, and everything he sang both lured and exasperated. This was usually more than Miss Amelia could stand.

"Bust a gut!" she would repeat, in a shout.

But always Marvin Macy had the answer ready for her. He would cover the strings to silence the quivering leftover tones, and reply with slow, sure insolence.

"Everything you holler at me bounces back on yourself. Yah! Yah!"

Miss Amelia would have to stand there helpless, as no one has ever invented a way out of this trap. She could not shout out abuse that would bounce back on herself. He had the best of her, there was nothing she could do.

So things went on like this. What happened between the three of them during the nights in the rooms upstairs nobody knows. But the café became more and more crowded every night. A new table had to be brought in. Even the Hermit, the crazy man named Rainer Smith, who took to the swamps years ago, heard something of the situation and came one night to look in at the window and brood over the gathering in the bright café. And the climax each evening was the time when Miss Amelia and Marvin Macy doubled their fists, squared up, and glared at each other. Usually this did not happen after any especial argument, but it seemed to come about mysteriously, by means of some instinct on the part of both of them. At these times the café would become so quiet that you could hear the bouquet of paper roses rustling in the draft. And each night they held this fighting stance a little longer than the night before.

The fight took place on Ground Hog Day, which is the second of February. The weather was favorable, being neither rainy nor sunny, and with a neutral temperature. There were several signs that this was the appointed day, and by ten o'clock the news spread all over the county. Early in the morning Miss Amelia went out and cut down her punching bag. Marvin Macy sat on the back step with a tin can of hog fat between his knees and carefully greased his arms and his legs. A hawk with a bloody breast flew over the town and circled twice around the property of Miss Amelia. The tables in the café were moved out to the back porch, so that the whole big room was cleared for the fight. There was every sign. Both Miss Amelia and Marvin Macy ate four helpings of half-raw roast for dinner, and then lay down in the afternoon to store up strength. Marvin Macy rested in the big room upstairs, while Miss Amelia stretched herself out on the bench in her office. It was plain from her white stiff face what a torment it was for her to be lying still and doing nothing, but she lay there quiet as a corpse with her eyes closed and her hands crossed on her chest.

Cousin Lymon had a restless day, and his little face was drawn and tightened with excitement. He put himself up a lunch, and set out to find the ground hog – within an hour he returned, the lunch eaten, and said that the ground hog had seen his shadow and there was to be bad weather ahead. Then, as Miss Amelia and Marvin Macy were both resting to gather strength, and he was left to himself, it occurred to him that he might as well paint the front porch. The house had not been painted for years – in fact, God knows if it had ever been painted at all. Cousin Lymon scrambled around, and soon he had painted half the floor of the porch a gay bright green. It was a loblolly job, and he smeared himself all over. Typically enough he did not even finish the floor, but changed over to the walls, painting as high as he could reach and then standing on a crate to get up a foot higher. When the paint ran out, the right side of the floor was bright green and there was a jagged portion of wall that had been painted. Cousin Lymon left it at that.

There was something childish about his satisfaction with his painting. And in this respect a curious fact should be mentioned. No one in the town, not even Miss Amelia, had any idea how old the hunchback was. Some maintained that when he came to town he was about twelve years old, still a child – others were certain that he was well past forty. His eyes were blue and steady as a child's but there were lavender crepy shadows beneath these blue eyes that hinted of age. It was impossible to guess his age by his hunched queer body. And even his teeth gave no clue – they were all still in his head (two were broken from cracking a pecan), but he had stained them with so much sweet snuff that it was impossible to decide whether they were old teeth or young teeth. When questioned directly about his age the hunchback professed to know absolutely nothing – he had no idea how long he had been on the earth, whether for ten years or a hundred! So his age remained a puzzle.

Cousin Lymon finished his painting at five-thirty o'clock in the afternoon. The day had turned colder and there was a wet taste in the air. The wind came up from the pinewoods, rattling windows, blowing an old newspaper down the road until at last it caught upon a thorn tree. People began to come in from the country; packed automobiles that bristled with the poked-out heads of children, wagons drawn by old mules who seemed to smile in a weary, sour way and plodded along with their tired eyes half-closed. Three young boys came from Society City. All three of them wore yellow rayon shirts and caps put on backward – they were as much alike as triplets, and could always be seen at cock fights and camp meetings. At six o'clock the mill whistle sounded the end of the day's shift and the crowd was complete. Naturally, among the newcomers there were some riffraff, unknown characters, and so forth – but even so the gathering was quiet. A hush was on the town and the faces of people were strange in the fading light. Darkness hovered softly; for a moment the sky was a pale clear yellow against which the gables of the church stood out in dark and bare outline, then the sky died slowly and the darkness gathered into night.

Seven is a popular number, and especially it was a favorite with Miss Amelia. Seven swallows of water for hiccups, seven runs around the millpond for cricks in the neck, seven doses of Amelia Miracle Mover as a worm cure – her treatment nearly always hinged on this number. It is a number of mingled possibilities, and all who love mystery and charms set store by it. So the fight was to take place at seven o'clock. This was known to everyone, not by announcement or words, but understood in the unquestioning way that rain is understood, or an evil odor from the swamp. So before seven o'clock everyone gathered gravely around the property of Miss Amelia. The cleverest got into the café itself and stood lining the walls of the room. Others crowded onto the front porch, or took a stand in the yard.

Miss Amelia and Marvin Macy had not yet shown themselves. Miss Amelia, after resting all afternoon on the office bench, had gone upstairs. On the other hand Cousin Lymon was at your elbow every minute, threading his way through the crowd, snapping his fingers nervously, and batting his eyes. At one minute to seven o'clock he squirmed his way into the café and climbed up on the counter. All was very quiet.

It must have been arranged in some manner beforehand. For just at the stroke of seven Miss Amelia showed herself at the head of the stairs. At the same instant Marvin Macy appeared in front of the café and the crowd made way for him silently. They walked toward each other with no haste, their fists already gripped, and their eyes like the eyes of dreamers. Miss Amelia had changed her red dress for her old overalls, and they were rolled up to the knees. She was barefooted and she had an iron strengthband around her right wrist. Marvin Macy had also rolled his trouser legs – he was naked to the waist and heavily greased; he wore the heavy shoes that had been issued him when he left the penitentiary. Stumpy MacPhail stepped forward from the crowd and slapped their hip pockets with the palm of his right hand to make sure there would be no sudden knives. Then they were alone in the cleared center of the bright café.

There was no signal, but they both struck out simultaneously. Both blows landed on the chin, so that the heads of Miss Amelia and Marvin Macy bobbed back and they were left a little groggy. For a few seconds after the first blows they merely shuffled their feet around on the bare floor, experimenting with various positions, and making mock fists. Then, like wildcats, they were suddenly on each other. There was the sound of knocks, panting, and thumpings on the floor. They were so fast that it was hard to take in what was going on – but once Miss Amelia was hurled backward so that she staggered and almost fell, and another time Marvin Macy caught a knock on the shoulder that spun him around like a top. So the fight went on in this wild violent way with no sign of weakening on either side.

During a struggle like this, when the enemies are as quick and strong as these two, it is worth-while to turn from the confusion of the fight itself and observe the spectators. The people had flattened back as close as possible against the walls. Stumpy MacPhail was in a corner, crouched over and with his fists tight in sympathy, making strange noises. Poor Merlie Ryan had his mouth so wide open that a fly buzzed into it, and was swallowed before Merlie realized what had happened. And Cousin Lymon – he was worth watching. The hunchback still stood on the counter, so that he was raised up above everyone else in the café. He had his hands on his hips, his big head thrust forward, and his little legs bent so that the knees jutted outward. The excitement had made him break out in a rash, and his pale mouth shivered.

Perhaps it was half an hour before the course of the fight shifted. Hundreds of blows had been exchanged, and there was still a deadlock. Then suddenly Marvin Macy managed to catch hold of Miss Amelia's left arm and pinion it behind her back. She struggled and got a grasp around his waist; the real fight was now begun. Wrestling is the natural way of fighting in this county – as boxing is too quick and requires much thinking and concentration. And now that Miss Amelia and Marvin were locked in a hold together the crowd came out of its daze and pressed in closer. For a while the fighters grappled muscle to muscle, their hipbones braced against each other. Backward and forward, from side to side, they swayed in this way. Marvin Macy still had not sweated, but Miss Amelia's overalls were drenched and so much sweat had trickled down her legs that she left wet footprints on the floor. Now the test had come, and in these moments of terrible effort, it was Miss Amelia who was the stronger. Marvin Macy was greased and slippery, tricky to grasp, but she was stronger. Gradually she bent him over backward, and inch by inch she forced him to the floor. It was a terrible thing to watch and their deep hoarse breaths were the only sound in the café. At last she had him down, and straddled; her strong big hands were on his throat.

But at that instant, just as the fight was won, a cry sounded in the café that caused a shrill bright shiver to run down the spine. And what took place has been a mystery ever since. The whole town was there to testify what happened, but there were those who doubted their own eyesight. For the counter on which Cousin Lymon stood was at least twelve feet from the fighters in the center of the café. Yet at the instant Miss Amelia grasped the throat of Marvin Macy the hunchback sprang forward and sailed through the air as though he had grown hawk wings. He landed on the broad strong back of Miss Amelia and clutched at her neck with his clawed little fingers.

The rest is confusion. Miss Amelia was beaten before the crowd could come to their senses. Because of the hunchback the fight was won by Marvin Macy, and at the end Miss Amelia lay sprawled on the floor, her arms flung outward and motionless. Marvin Macy stood over her, his face somewhat popeyed, but smiling his old half-mouthed smile. And the hunchback, he had suddenly disappeared. Perhaps he was frightened about what he had done, or maybe he was so delighted that he wanted to glory with himself alone – at any rate he slipped out of the café and crawled under the back steps. Someone poured water on Miss Amelia, and after a time she got up slowly and dragged herself into her office. Through the open door the crowd could see her sitting at her desk, her head in the crook of her arm, and she was sobbing with the last of her grating, winded breath. Once she gathered her right fist together and knock it three times on the top of her office desk, then her hand opened feebly and lay palm upward and still. Stumpy MacPhail stepped forward and closed the door.

The crowd was quiet, and one by one the people left the café. Mules were waked up and untied, automobiles cranked, and the three boys from Society City roamed off down the road on foot. This was not a fight to hash over and talk about afterward; people went home and pulled the covers up over their heads. The town was dark, except for the premises of Miss Amelia, but every room was lighted there the whole night long.

Marvin Macy and the hunchback must have left the town an hour or so before daylight. And before they went away this is what they did:

They unlocked the private cabinet of curios and took everything in it.

They broke the mechanical piano.

They carved terrible words on the café tables.

They found the watch that opened in the back to show a picture of a waterfall and took that also.

They poured a gallon of sorghum syrup all over the kitchen floor and smashed the jars of preserves.

They went out in the swamp and completely wrecked the still, ruining the big new condenser and the cooler, and setting fire to the shack itself.

They fixed a dish of Miss Amelia's favorite food, grits with sausage, seasoned it with enough poison to kill off the county, and placed this dish temptingly on the café counter.

They did everything ruinous they could think of without actually breaking into the office where Miss Amelia stayed the night. Then they went off together, the two of them.

That was how Miss Amelia was left alone in the town. The people would have helped her if they had known how, as people in this town will as often as not be kindly if they have a chance. Several housewives nosed around with brooms and offered to clear up the wreck. But Miss Amelia only looked at them with lost crossed eyes and shook her head. Stumpy MacPhail came in on the third day to buy a plug of Queenie tobacco, and Miss Amelia said the price was one dollar. Everything in the café had suddenly risen in price to be worth one dollar. And what sort of a café is that? Also, she changed very queerly as a doctor. In all the years before she had been much more popular than the Cheehaw doctor. She had never monkeyed with a patient's soul, taking away from him such real necessities as liquor, tobacco, and so forth. Once in a great while she might carefully warn a patient never to eat fried watermelon or some such dish it had never occurred to a person to want in the first place. Now all this wise doctoring was over. She told one-half of her patients that they were going to die outright, and to the remaining half she recommended cures so far-fetched and agonizing that no one in his right mind would consider them for a moment.

Miss Amelia let her hair grow ragged, and it was turning gray. Her face lengthened, and the great muscles of her body shrank until she was thin as old maids are thin when they go crazy. And those gray eyes – slowly day by day they were more crossed, and it was as though they sought each other out to exchange a little glance of grief and lonely recognition. She was not pleasant to listen to; her tongue had sharpened terribly.

When anyone mentioned the hunchback she would say only this: "Ho! if I could lay hand to him I would rip out his gizzard and throw it to the cat!" But it was not so much the words that were terrible, but the voice in which they were said. Her voice had lost its old vigor; there was none of the ring of vengeance it used to have when she would mention "that loom-fixer I was married to," or some other enemy. Her voice was broken, soft, and sad as the wheezy whine of the church pump-organ.

For three years she sat out on the front steps every night, alone and silent, looking down the road and waiting. But the hunchback never returned. There were rumors that Marvin Macy used him to climb into windows and steal, and other rumors that Marvin Macy had sold him into a side show. But both these reports were traced back to Merlie Ryan. Nothing true was ever heard of him. It was in the fourth year that Miss Amelia hired a Cheehaw carpenter and had him board up the premises, and there in those closed rooms she has remained ever since.

Yes, the town is dreary. On August afternoons the road is empty, white with dust, and the sky above is bright as glass. Nothing moves – there are no children's voices, only the hum of the mill. The peach trees seem to grow more crooked every summer, and the leaves are dull gray and of a sickly delicacy. The house of Miss Amelia leans so much to the right that it is now only a question of time when it will collapse completely, and people are careful not to walk around the yard. There is no good liquor to be bought in the town; the nearest still is eight miles away, and the liquor is such that those who drink it grow warts on their livers the size of goobers, and dream themselves into a dangerous inward world. There is absolutely nothing to do in the town. Walk around the millpond, stand kicking at a rotten stump, figure out what you can do with the old wagon wheel by the side of the road near the church. The soul rots with boredom. You might as well go down to the Forks Falls highway and listen to the chain gang.

THE TWELVE MORTAL MEN

The Forks Falls highway is three miles from the town, and it is here the chain gang has been working. The road is of macadam, and the county decided to patch up the rough places and widen it at a certain dangerous place. The gang is made up of twelve men, all wearing black and white striped prison suits, and chained at the ankles. There is a guard, with a gun, his eyes drawn to red slits by the glare. The gang works all the day long, arriving huddled in the prison cart soon after daybreak, and being driven off again in the gray August twilight. All day there is the sound of the picks striking into the clay earth, hard sunlight, the smell of sweat. And every day there is music. One dark voice will start a phrase, half-sung, and like a question. And after a moment another voice will join in, soon the whole gang will be singing. The voices are dark in the golden glare, the music intricately blended, both somber and joyful. The music will swell until at last it seems that the sound does not come from the twelve men on the gang, but from the earth itself, or the wide sky. It is music that causes the heart to broaden and the listener to grow cold with ecstasy and fright. Then slowly the music will sink down until at last there remains one lonely voice, then a great hoarse breath, the sun, the sound of the picks in the silence.

And what kind of gang is this that can make such music? Just twelve mortal men, seven of them black and five of them white boys from this county. Just twelve mortal men who are together.

Unit 10
Peter Taylor (1917–1994)
彼得·泰勒

作者简介

彼得·泰勒，短篇小说作家，1917年1月出生于美国南部田纳西州的一个中产阶级家庭。他曾就读于孟菲斯、纳西维尔和圣路易斯等学校，毕业于范德比尔特大学。泰勒的童年是在母亲凯瑟琳·泰勒所讲的故事伴随下度过的，并把自己的《短篇小说集》(*Collected Stories*,1968)献给母亲。1936年泰勒进入罗德学院，先后师从著名作家艾伦·泰特(Allen Tate)、约翰·克罗·兰瑟姆(John Crowe Ransom)、罗伯特·佩恩·华伦(Robert Penn Warren)和布鲁克斯(Cleanth Brooks)学习写作。泰勒先后在北卡莱罗纳的女子学院、凯尼恩学院、哈佛大学和弗吉尼亚大学任教。他的小说背景大多设定在他童年时待过的南部城市孟菲斯、纳什维尔和圣路易斯，反映南方城市和农村之间的差异。二战后泰勒开始在《纽约客》(*The New Yorker*)、《南方评论》(*The Southern Review*)等著名刊物上发表短篇小说。1948年出版第一部短篇小说集《一个长四度音程及其他》(*The Long Fourth and Others*, 1948年)，随后又出版多部中篇和短篇小说集，包括《女财主》(*A Woman of Means*, 1950)、《桑顿的寡妇们》(*The Widows of Thornton*,1954)、《幸福家庭全一样》(*Happy Families Are All Alike*,1959)、《莉昂诺拉小姐最后一面及其他》(*Miss Leonora When Last Seen and Other Stories*,1963)；《短篇小说集》(*Collected Stories*,1968)、《在米罗地区及其他》(*In the Miro District and Other Stories*, 1977)、《老林故事》(*The Old Forest*, 1985)和《田纳西的乡间》(*In the Tennessee Country*, 1994)等。

这些作品奠定了泰勒杰出短篇小说家的地位，并为他赢得多个奖项。1959年出版的短篇小说《维纳斯、丘比特、佛利和时间》(*Venus, Cupid, Folly and Time*)获得"欧·亨利短篇小说奖"；1979年泰勒获得全国作家协会颁发的"小说金奖"；1986年获"福克纳奖"。泰勒后期的长篇小说及中篇小说也获得一致好评。长篇小说《孟菲斯的召唤》(*A Summons to Memphis*, 1986)获得普利策奖和海明威奖。本部小说用隐喻的手法表明一代落伍的南方作家在文学上所处的困境：与"南方文艺复兴"那代作家断绝关系之后他们面临失去小说创作活力的危险。没有历史，没有罪愆，没有家庭，甚至没有生活：人们无法想象还有比这样的情形能够更好地象征着成功摆脱令人烦恼的南方重负以后的局面，至少对于南方作家来说是如此。《老林故事》是他20世纪80年代初的佳作，曾被选为"1980年美国最佳小说"之一。他善于表现普通人在关键时刻经历了某种内心启示后能够悟出社会秩序的虚安和罪恶。

作品导读

The title of the story is taken from an allegorical painting by the Florentine artist Agnolo Bronzino. Around 1545, Bronzino was commissioned to create a painting which has come to be known as "Venus, Cupid, Folly, and Time". It displays the ambivalence, eroticism and obscure imagery which is characteristic of the Mannerist period. The themes of the painting appear to be lust, deceit, and jealousy. At times it has also been called "A Triumph of Venus". Its meaning, however, remains elusive. The two central figures in the painting are easily identified as Venus and Cupid. Both are nude, illuminated in a radiant white light. Cupid fondles his mother's bare breast and kisses her lips. They are being showered with rose petals by a boy, believed to represent Folly. The bearded, bald figure at the upper right of the scene is believed to be Time. He is being assisted by another, unknown, figure (Truth?). They draw aside a curtain to reveal the incestuous transgressions of Venus and the adolescent Cupid.

The short story by Taylor is also an allegory about incest though it is not explicitly written. The plot is simple, and mainly depicts the brother Alfred Dorset and the sister Louisa Dorset, a bachelor and a spinster. The two are disliked by all the people, and are suspected to have commit incest. Their dresses, car, house and everything related to them are awful, and they are a shame to the neighborhood. The Dorsets make a living by selling figs and paper flowers, which are also unpleasant ones. Every year the Dorsets give a party for young people, and no adults are allowed into the house. Whoever goes to the party will have a nightmare, but no parents try to prevent their children from going to the party. One year a boy Ned and his sister Emily who are invited to the party plan to play a trick on everyone by smuggling a boy named Tom to the party. Tom goes to the party in Ned's clothes with Emily while Ned slips into the party stealthily that night. At the party Tom and Emily kiss each other without being stopped by the Dorsets and Ned is found as an intruder. A chase of Tom and Ned is followed, then Ned is locked in the upstairs and Tom runs away. Ned and Emily's parents come to fetch their children and blame the Dorsets for all these. The Dorsets are hurt and never give a party again. After that they stop selling figs and paper flowers and never go out of their home. Everyone in the town is curious about what happens that night, and the story is still talked about after the children grow up.

作品选读

Venus, Cupid, Folly and Time

Their house alone would not have made you think there was anything so awfully wrong with Mr. Dorset or his old-maid sister. But certain things about the way both of them dressed had, for a long time, annoyed and disturbed everyone. We used to see them together at the grocery store, for instance, or even in one of the big department stores downtown, wearing their bedroom slippers. Looking more closely, we would sometimes see the cuff of a pajama top or the hem of a hitched-up nightgown showing from underneath their ordinary daytime clothes. Such slovenliness in one's neighbors is so unpleasant that even husbands and wives in West Vesey Place, which was the street where the Dorsets lived, had got so they didn't like to joke about it with each other. Were the Dorsets, poor old things, losing their minds? If so, what was to be done about it? Some neighbors got so they would not even admit to themselves what they saw. And a child coming home with an ugly report on the Dorsets was apt to be told that it was time he learned to curb his imagination.

Mr. Dorset wore tweed caps and sleeveless sweaters. Usually he had his sweater stuffed down inside his trousers with his shirt tails. To the women and young girls in West Vesey Place this was extremely distasteful. It made them feel as though Mr. Dorset had just come from the bathroom and had got his sweater inside his trousers by mistake. There was, in fact, nothing about Mr. Dorset that was not offensive to the women. Even the old touring car he drove was regarded by most of them as a disgrace to the neighborhood. Parked out in front of his house, as it usually was, it seemed a worse violation of West Vesey's zoning than the house itself. And worst of all was seeing Mr. Dorset wash the car.

Mr. Dorset washed his own car! He washed it not back in the alley or in his driveway but out there in the street of West Vesey Place. This would usually be on the day of one of the parties which he and his sister liked to give for young people or on a day when they were going to make deliveries of the paper flowers or the home-grown figs which they sold to their friends. Mr. Dorset would appear in the street carrying two buckets of warm water and wearing a pair of skin-tight coveralls. The skin-tight overalls, of khaki material but faded almost to flesh color, were still more offensive to the women and young girls than his way of wearing his sweaters. With sponges and chamois clothes and a large scrub brush (for use on the canvas top) the old fellow would fall to and scrub away, gently at first on the canvas top and more vigorously as he progressed to the hood and body, just as though the car were something alive. Neighbor children felt that he went after the headlights exactly as if he were scrubbing the poor car's ears. There was an element of brutality in the way he did it and yet an element of tenderness too. An old lady visiting in the neighborhood once said that it was like the cleansing of a sacrificial animal. I suppose it was some such feeling as this that made all women want to turn away their eyes whenever the spectacle of Mr. Dorset washing his car presented itself.

As for Mr. Dorset's sister, her behavior was in its way just as offensive as his. To the men and boys in the neighborhood it was she who seemed quite beyond the pale. She would come out on her front terrace at midday clad in a faded flannel bathrobe and with her dyed black hair all undone and hanging down her back like the hair of an Indian squaw. To us whose wives and mothers did not even come downstairs in their negligees, this was very unsettling. It was hard to excuse it even on the grounds that the Dorsets were too old and lonely and hard-pressed to care about appearances any more.

Moreover, there was a boy who had gone to Miss Dorset's house one morning in the early fall to collect for his paper route and saw this very Miss Louisa Dorset pushing a carpet sweeper about one of the downstairs rooms without a stitch of clothes on. He saw her through one of the little lancet windows that opened on the front loggia of the house, and he watched her for quite a long while. She was cleaning the house in preparation for a party they were giving for young people that night, and the boy said that when she finally got hot and tired she dropped down in an easy chair and crossed her spindly, blue-veined, old legs and sat there completely naked, with her legs crossed and shaking one scrawny little foot, just as unconcerned as if she didn't care that somebody was likely to walk in on her at any moment. After a little bit the boy saw her get up again and go and lean across a table to arrange some paper flowers in a vase. Fortunately he was a nice boy, though he lived only on the edge of the West Vesey Place neighborhood, and he went away without ringing the doorbell or collecting for his paper that week. But he could not resist telling his friends about what he had seen. He said it was a sight he would never forget! And she an old lady more than sixty years old who, had she not been so foolish and self-willed, might have had a house full of servants to push that carpet sweeper for her!

This foolish pair of old people had given up almost everything in life for each other's sake. And it was not at all necessary. When they were young they could have come into a decent inheritance, or now that they were old they might have been provided for by a host of rich relatives. It was only a matter of their being a little tolerant – or even civil – toward their kinspeople. But this was something that old Mr. Dorset and his sister could never consent to do. Almost all their lives they had spoken of their father's kin as "Mama's in-laws" and of their mother's kin as "Papa's in-laws." Their family name was Dorset, not on one side but on both sides. Their parents had been distant cousins. As a matter of fact, the Dorset family in the city of Chatham had once been so large and was so long established there that it would have been hard to estimate how distant the kinship might be. But still it was something that the old couple never liked to have mentioned. Most of their mother's close kin had, by the time I am speaking of, moved off to California, and most of their father's people lived somewhere up East. But Miss Dorset and her old bachelor brother found any contact, correspondence, even an exchange of Christmas cards with these in-laws intolerable. It was a case, so they said, of the in-laws respecting the value of the dollar above all else, whereas they, Miss Louisa and Mr.

Alfred Dorset, placed importance on other things.

They lived in a dilapidated and curiously mutilated house on a street which, except for their own house, was the most splendid street in the entire city. Their house was one that you or I would have ashamed to live in – even in the lean years of the early thirties. In order to reduce taxes the Dorsets had had the third story of the house torn away, leaving an ugly, flat-topped effect without any trim or ornamentation. Also, they had had the south wing pulled down and had sealed the scars not with matching brick but with a speckled stucco that looked raw and naked. All this the old couple did in violation of the strict zoning laws of West Vesey Place, and for doing so they would most certainly have been prosecuted except that they were the Dorsets and except that this was during the Depression when zoning laws weren't easy to enforce in a city like Chatham.

To the young people whom she and her brother entertained at their house once each year Miss Louisa Dorset liked to say: "We have given up everything for each other. Our only income is from our paper flowers and our figs." The old lady, though without showing any great skill or talent for it, made paper flowers. During the winter months, her brother took her in that fifteen-year-old touring cars of theirs, with its steering wheel on the wrong side and with isinglass side curtains that were never taken down, to deliver these flowers to her customers. The flowers looked more like sprays of tinted potato chips than like any real flowers. Nobody could possibly have wanted to buy them except that she charged next to nothing for them and except that to people with children it seemed important to be on the Dorsets' list of worthwhile people. Nobody could really have wanted Mr. Dorset's figs either. He cultivated a dozen little bushes along the back wall of their house, covering them in the wintertime with some odd-looking boxes which he had had constructed for the purpose. The bushes were very productive, but the figs they produced were dried up little things without much taste. During the summer months he and his sister went about in their car, with the side curtains still up, delivering the figs to the same customers who bought the paper flowers. The money they made could hardly have paid for the gas it took to run the car. It was a great waste and it was very foolish of them.

And yet, despite everything, this foolish pair of old people, this same Miss Louisa and Mr. Alfred Dorset, had become social arbiters of a kind in our city. They had attained this position entirely through their fondness for giving an annual dancing party for young people. To *young* people – to *very* young people – the Dorsets' hearts went out. I don't mean to suggest that their hearts went out to orphans or to the children of the poor, for they were not foolish in that way. The guests at their little dancing parties were the thirteen- and fourteen-year-olds from families like the one they had long ago set themselves against, young people from the very houses to which, in season, they delivered their figs and their paper flowers. And when the night of one of their parties came round, it was in fact the custom for Mr. Alfred to go in the same old car and fetch all the invited guests to his house. His sister might explain to reluctant parents that this saved the children the embarrassment of being taken to their first dance by Mommy or Daddy. But the parents knew well enough that for twenty years the Dorsets had permitted no adult person, besides themselves, to put foot inside their house.

At those little dancing parties which the Dorsets gave, peculiar things went on – unsettling things to the boys and girls who had been fetched round in the old car. Sensible parents wished to keep their children away. Yet what could they do? For a Chatham girl to have to explain, a few years later, why she never went to a party at the Dorsets' was like having to explain why she had never been a debutante. For a boy it was like having to explain why he had not gone up East to school or even why his father hadn't belonged to Chatham Racquet Club. If when you were thirteen or fourteen you got invited to the Dorsets' house, you went; it was the way of letting people know from the outset who you were. In a bus, modern city like Chatham you cannot afford to let people forget who you are – not for a moment, not at any age. Even the Dorsets knew that.

Many a little girl, after one of those evenings at the Dorsets', was heard to cry out in her sleep. When waked, or half waked, her only explanation might be: "It was just the fragrance from the paper flowers." Or: "I dreamed I could really smell the paper flowers." Many a boy was observed by his parents to seem "different" afterward. He became "secretive." The parents of the generation that had to attend those parties never pretended to understand what went on at the Dorsets' house. And even to those of us who were in that unlucky generation, it seemed we were half a lifetime learning what really took place during our one evening under the Dorsets' roof. Before our turn to go ever came round, we had for years been hearing about what it was like from older boys and girls. Afterward, we continued to hear about it from those who followed us. And, looking back on it, nothing about the one evening when you were actually there ever seemed quite so real as the glimpses and snatches which you got from those people before and after you – the secondhand impressions of the Dorsets' behavior, of things they said, of looks that passed between them.

Since Miss Dorset kept no servants, she always opened her own door. I suspect that for the guests at her parties the sight of her opening her door, in her astonishing attire, came as the most violent shock of the whole evening. On these occasions, she and her brother got themselves up as we had never seen them before and never would again. The old lady invariably wore a modish white evening gown, a garment perfectly fitted to her spare and scrawny figure and cut in such high fashion that it must necessarily have been new that year. And never to be worn but that one night! Her hair, long and thick and newly dyed for the occasion, would be swept upward and forward in a billowy mass which was topped by a corsage of yellow and coral paper flowers. Her cheeks and lips would be darkly rouged. On her long bony arms and her bare shoulders she would have applied some kind of suntan powder. Whatever else you had been led to expect of the evening, no one had ever warned you sufficiently about the radical change to be noted in her appearance – or in that of her brother, either. By the end of the party Miss Louisa might look as dowdy as ever, and Mr. Alfred a little worse than usual. But at the outset, when the party was assembling in their drawing room, even Mr. Alfred appeared resplendent in a nattily tailored tuxedo, with exactly the shirt, the collar, and the tie which fashion prescribed that year. His gray hair was nicely trimmed, his puffy old face freshly shaven. He was powdered with the same dark powder that his sister used. One felt even that his cheeks had been lightly touched with rouge.

A strange perfume pervaded the atmosphere of the house. The moment you set foot inside, this awful fragrance engulfed you. It was like a mixture of spicy incense and sweet attar of roses. And always, too, there was the profusion of paper flowers. The flowers were everywhere – on every cabinet and console, every inlaid table and carved chest, on every high, marble mantelpiece, on the bookshelves. In the entrance hall special tiers must have been set up to hold the flowers, because they were there in overpowering masses. They were in such abundance that it seemed hardly possible that Miss Dorset could have made them all. She must have spent weeks and weeks preparing them, even months, perhaps even the whole year between parties. When she went about delivering them to her customers, in the months following, they were apt to be somewhat faded and dusty; but on the night of the party, the colors of the flowers seemed even more impressive and more unlikely than their number. They were fuchsia, they were chartreuse, they were coral, aquamarine, brown, they were even black.

Everywhere in the Dorsets' house too were certain curious illuminations and lighting effects. The source of the light was usually hidden and its purpose was never obvious at once. The lighting was a subtler element than either the perfume or the paper flowers, and ultimately it was more disconcerting. A shaft of lavender light would catch a young visitor's eye and lead it, seemingly without purpose, in among the flowers. Then just beyond the point where the strength of the light would begin to diminish, the eye would discover something. In a small aperture in the mass of flowers, or sometimes in a larger grotto-like opening, there would be a piece of sculpture – in the hall a plaster replica of Rodin's "The Kiss," in the library an antique plaque of Leda and the Swan. Or just above the flowers would be hung a picture, usually a black and white print but sometimes a reproduction in color. On the landing of the stairway leading down to the basement ballroom was the only picture that one was likely to learn the title of at the time. It was a tiny color print of Bronzino's "Venus, Cupid, Folly and Time." This picture was not even framed. It was simply tacked on the wall, and it had obviously been torn – rather carelessly, perhaps hurriedly – from a book or magazine. The title and the name of the painter were printed in the white margin underneath.

About these works of art most of us had been warned by older boys and girls; and we stood in painful dread of that moment when Miss Dorset or her brother might catch us staring at any one of their pictures or sculptures. We had been warned, time and again, that during the course of the evening moments would come when she or he would reach out and touch the other's elbow and indicate, with a nod or just the trace of a smile, some guest whose glance had strayed among the flowers.

To some extend the dread which all of us felt that evening at the Dorsets' cast a shadow over the whole of our childhood. Yet for nearly twenty years the Dorsets continued to give their annual party. And even the most sensible of parents were not willing to keep their children away.

But a thing happened finally which could almost have been predicated. Young people, even in West Vesey Place, will not submit forever to the prudent counsel of their parents. Or some of them won't. There was a boy named Ned Meriwether and his sister Emily Meriwether, who lived with their parents in West Vesey Place just one block away from the Dorsets' house. In November, Ned and Emily were invited to the Dorsets' party, and because they dreaded it they decided to play a trick on everyone concerned – even on themselves, as it turned out... They got up a plan for smuggling an uninvited guest into the Dorsets' party.

The parents of this Emily and Ned sensed that their children were concealing something from them and suspected that the two were up to mischief of some kind. But they managed to deceive themselves with the thought that it was only natural for young people – "mere children" – to be nervous about going to the Dorsets' house. And so instead of questioning them during the last hour before they left for the party, these sensible parents tried to do everything in their power to calm their two children. The boy and the girl, seeing this was the case, took advantage of it.

"You must not go down to the front door with us when we leave," the daughter insisted to her mother. And she persuaded both Mr. and Mrs. Meriwether that after she and her brother were dressed for the party they should all wait together in the upstairs sitting room until Mr. Dorset came to fetch the two young people in his car.

When, at eight o'clock, the light of the automobile appeared in the street below, the brother and sister were still upstairs – watching from the bay window of the family sitting room. They kissed Mother and Daddy goodbye and then they flew down the stairs and across the wide, carpeted entrance hall to a certain dark recess where a boy named Tom Bascomb was hidden. This boy was the uninvited guest whom Ned and Emily were going to smuggle into the party. They had left the front door unlatched for Tom, and from the upstairs window just a few minutes ago they had watched him come across their front lawn. Now in the little recess of the hall there was a quick exchange of overcoats and hats between Ned Meriwether and Tom Bascomb; for it was a feature of the plan that Tom should attend the party as Ned and that Ned should go as the uninvited guest.

In the darkness of the recess, Ned fidgeted and dropped Tom Bascomb's coat on the floor. But the boy, Tom Bascomb, did not fidget. He stepped out into the light of the hall and began methodically getting into the overcoat which he would wear tonight. He was not a boy who lived in the West Vesey Place neighborhood (he was in fact the very boy who had once watched Miss Dorset cleaning house without any clothes on), and he did not share Emily's and Ned's nervous excitement about the evening. The sound of Mr. Dorset's footsteps outside did not disturb him. When both Ned and Emily stood frozen by that sound, he continued buttoning the unfamiliar coat and even amused himself by stretching forth one arm to observe how high the sleeve came on his wrist.

The doorbell rang, and from his dark corner Ned Meriwether whispered to his sister and to

Tom: "Don't worry. I'll be at the Dorsets' in plenty of time."

Tom Bascomb only shrugged his shoulders at this reassurance. Presently when he looked at Emily's flushed face and saw her batting her eyes like a nervous monkey, a crooked smile played upon his lips. Then, at a sight from Emily, Tom followed her to the entrance door and permitted her to introduce him to old Mr. Dorset as her brother.

From the window of the upstairs sitting room the Meriwether parents watched Mr. Dorset and this boy and this girl walking across the lawn toward Mr. Dorset's peculiar-looking car. A light shone bravely and protectively from above the entrance of the house, and in its rays the parents were able to detect the strange angle at which Brother was carrying his head tonight and how his new fedora already seemed too small for him. They even noticed that he seemed a bit taller tonight.

"I hope it's all right," said the mother.

"What do you mean 'all right'?" the father asked petulantly.

"I mean –" the mother began, and then she hesitated. She did not want to mention that the boy out there did not look like their own Ned. It would have seemed to give away her feelings too much. "I mean that I wonder that if I should have put Sister in that long dress at this age and let her wear my cape. I'm afraid the cape is really inappropriate. She's still young for that sort of thing."

"Oh," said the father, "I thought you meant something else."

"Whatever else did you think I meant, Edwin?" the mother said, suddenly breathless.

"I thought you meant the business we've discussed before," he said, although this was of course not what he had thought she meant. He had thought she meant that the boy out there did not look like their Ned. To him it had seemed even that the boy's step was different from Ned's. "The Dorsets' parties," he said, "are not very nice affairs to be sending your children to, Muriel. That's all I thought you meant."

"But we can't keep them away," the mother said defensively.

"Oh, it's just that they are growing up faster than we realize," said the father, glancing at his wife out of the corner of his eye.

By this time Mr. Dorset's car had pulled out of sight, and from downstairs Muriel Meriwether thought she heard another door closing. "What was that?" she said, putting one hand on her husband's.

"Don't be so jumpy," her husband said irritably, snatching away his hand. "It's the servants closing up in the kitchen."

Both of them knew that the servants had closed up in the kitchen long before this. Both of them had heard quite distinctly the sound of the side door closing as Ned went out. But they went on talking and deceiving themselves in this fashion during most of the evening.

Even before she opened the door to Mr. Dorset, little Emily Meriwether had known that there would be no difficulty about passing Tom Bascomb off as her brother. In the first place, she knew that without his spectacles Mr. Dorset could hardly see his hand before his face and knew that due to some silly pride he had he never put on his spectacles except when he was behind the wheel of his automobile. This much was common knowledge. In the second place, Emily knew from experience that neither he nor his sister ever made any real pretense of knowing one child in their general acquaintance from another. And so, standing in the doorway and speaking almost in a whisper, Emily had merely to introduce first herself and then her pretended brother to Mr. Dorset. After that the three of them walked in silence from her father's house to the waiting car.

Emily was wearing her mother's second-best evening wrap, a white lapin cape which, on Emily, swept the ground. As she walked between the boy and the man, the touch of the cape's soft silk lining on her bare arms and on her shoulders spoke to her silently of a strange girl she had seen in her looking glass upstairs tonight. And with her every step toward the car the skirt of her long taffeta gown whispered her own name to her: Emily...Emily. She heard it distinctly, and yet the name sounded unfamiliar. Once during this unreal walk from house to car she glanced at the mysterious boy, Tom Bascomb, longing to ask him – if only with her eyes – for some reassurance that she was really she. But Tom Bascomb was absorbed in his own irrelevant observations. With his head tilted back he was gazing upward at the nondescript winter sky where, among drifting clouds, a few pale stars were shedding their dull light alike on West Vesey Place and on the rest of the world. Emily drew her wrap tightly about her, and when presently Mr. Dorset held open the door to the back seat of his car she shut her eyes and plunged into the pitch blackness of the car's interior.

Tom Bascomb was a year older than Ned Meriwether and he was nearly two years older than Emily. He had been Ned's friend first. He and Ned had played baseball together on Saturdays before Emily ever set eyes on him. Yet according to Tom Bascomb himself, with whom several of us older boys talked just a few weeks after the night he went to the Dorsets', Emily always insisted that it was she who had known him first. On what she based this false claim Tom could not say. And on the two or three other occasions when we got Tom to talk bout that night, he kept saying that he didn't understand what it was that had made Emily and Ned quarrel over which of them knew him first and knew him better.

We could have told him what it was, I think. But we didn't. It would have been too hard to say to him that at one time or another all of us in West Vesey had had our Tom Bascombs. Tom lived with his parents in an apartment house on a wide thoroughfare known as Division Boulevard, and his only real connection with West Vesey Place was that that street was included in his paper route. During the early morning hours he rode his bicycle along West Vesey and along other quiet streets like it, carefully aiming a neatly rolled paper at the dark loggia, at the colonnaded porch, or at the ornamented doorway of each of the palazzo and chateaux and manor houses that glowered at him in the dawn. He was well thought of as a paper boy. If by mistake one of his papers went astray and lit on an upstairs balcony or on the roof of a porch, Tom would always take more careful aim and throw another. Even if the paper only went into the shrubbery, Tom got off his bicycle and fished it out. He wasn't the kind of boy to whom it would have occurred that the old fogies and the rich kids in West Vesey could very well get out and scramble for their own papers.

Actually, a party at the Dorsets' house was more a grand tour of the house than a real party. There was a half hour spent over very light refreshments (fruit Jello, English tea biscuits, lime punch). There was another half hour ostensibly given to general dancing in the basement ballroom (to the accompaniment of victrola music). But mainly there was the tour. As the party passed through the house, stopping sometimes to sit down in the principal rooms, the host and the hostess provided entertainment in the form of an almost continuous dialogue between themselves. This dialogue was famous and was full of interest, being all about how much the Dorsrts had given up for each other's sake and about how much higher the tone of Chatham society used to be than it was nowadays. They would invariably speak of their parents, who had died within a year of each other when Miss Louisa and Mr. Alfred were still in their teens; they even spoke of their wicked in-laws. When their parents died, the wicked in-laws had first tried to make them sell the house, then had tried to separate them and send them away to boarding schools, and had ended by trying to marry them off to "just anyone." Their two grandfathers had still been alive in those days and each had had a hand in the machinations, after the failure of which each grandfather had disinherited them. Mr. Alfred and Miss Louisa spoke also of how, a few years later, a procession of "young nobodies" had come of their own accord trying to steal the two of them away from each other. Both he and she would scowl at the very recollection of those "just anybodies" and those "nobodies," those "would-be suitors" who always turned out to be misguided fortune hunters and had to be driven away.

The Dorsets' dialogue usually began in the living room the moment Mr. Dorset returned with his last collection of guests. (He sometimes had to make five or six trips in the car.) There, as in other rooms afterward, they were likely to begin with a reference to the room itself or perhaps to some piece of furniture in the room. For instance, the extraordinary length of the drawing room – or reception room, as the Dorsets called it – would lead them to speak of an even longer room which they had had torn away from the house. "It grieved us, we wept," Miss Dorset would say, "to have Mama's French drawing room torn away from us."

"But we tore it away from ourselves," her brother would add, "as we tore away our in-laws – because we could not afford them." Both of them spoke in a fine declamatory style, but they frequently interrupted themselves with a sad little laugh which expressed something quite different from what they were saying and which seemed to serve them as an aside not meant for our ears.

"That was one of our greatest sacrifices," Miss Dorset would say, referring still to her mother's French drawing room.

And her brother would say, "But we knew the day had passed in Chatham for entertainments worthy of that room."

"It was the room which Mama and Papa loved best, but we gave it up because we knew, from our upbringing, which things to give up."

From this they might go on to anecdotes about their childhood. Sometimes their parents had left them for months or even a whole year at a time with only the housekeeper or with trusted servants to see after them. "You could trust servants then," they explained. And: "In those days parents could do that sort of thing, because in those days there was a responsible body of people within which your young people could always find people companionship."

In the library, to which the party always moved from the drawing room, Mr. Dorset was fond of exhibiting snapshots of the house taken before the south wing was pulled down. As the pictures were passed around, the dialogue continued. It was often there that they told the story of how the in-laws had tried to force them to sell the house. "For the sake of economy! " Mr. Dorset would exclaim, adding an ironic "Ha ha! "

"As though money –" he would begin.

"As though money ever took the place," his sister would come in,"of living with your own kind."

"Or of being well born," said Mr. Dorset.

After the billiard room, where everyone who wanted it was permitted one turn with the only cue that there seemed to be in the house, and after the dining room, where it was promised refreshments would be served later, the guests would be taken down to the ballroom – purportedly for dancing. Instead of everyone's being urged to dance, however, once they were assembled in the ballroom, Miss Dorset would announce that she and her brother understood the timidity which young people felt about dancing and that all that she and he intended to do was to set the party a good example...It was only Miss Louisa and Mr. Dorset who danced. For perhaps thirty minutes, in a room without light excepting that from a few weak bulbs concealed among the flowers, the old couple danced; and they danced with such grace and there was such perfect harmony in all their movements that the guests stood about in stunned silence, as if hypnotized. The Dorsets waltzed, they two-stepped, they even fox-trotted, stopping only long enough between dances for Mr. Dorset, amid general applause, to change the victrola record.

But it was when their dance was ended that all the effects of the Dorsets' careful grooming that night would have vanished. And, alas, they made no effort to restore themselves. During the remainder of the evening Mr. Dorset went about with his bow tie hanging limply on his damp shirtfront, a gold collar button shining above it. A strand of gray hair, which normally covered his bald spot on top, now would have fallen on the wrong side of his part and hung like fringe about his ear. On his face and neck the thick layer of powder was streaked with perspiration. Miss Dorset was usually in an even more disheveled state, depending somewhat upon the fashion of her dress that year. But always her powder was streaked, her lipstick entirely gone, her hair falling down on all sides, and her corsage dangling somewhere about the nape of her neck. In this condition they led the party upstairs again, not stopping until they had reached the second floor of the house.

On the second floor we – the guests – were shown the rooms which the Dorsets' parents had once occupied (the Dorsets' own rooms were never shown). We saw, in glass museum

cases along the hallway, the dresses and suits and hats and even the shoes which Miss Louisa and Mr. Alfred had worn to parties when they were very young. And now the dialogue, which had been left off while the Dorsets danced, was resumed. "Ah, the happy time," one of them would say, "was when we were your age! " And then, exhorting us to be happy and gay while we were still safe in the bosom of our own kind and before the world came crowding in on us with its ugly demands, the Dorsets would recall the happiness they had known when they were very young. This was their piéce de résistance. With many a wink and blush and giggle and shake of the forefinger – and of course standing before the whole party – they each would remind the other of his or her naughty behavior in some old - fashioned parlor game or of certain silly little flirtations which they had long ago caught each other in.

They were on their way downstairs again now, and by the time they had finished with this favorite subject they would be downstairs. They would be in the dark, flower-bedecked downstairs hall and just before entering the dining room for the promised refreshments: the fruit Jello, the English tea biscuits, the lime punch.

And now for a moment Mr. Dorset bars the way to the dining room and prevents his sister from opening the closed door. "Now, my good friends," he says, "let us eat, drink, and be merry! "

"For the night is yet young," says his sister.

"Tonight you must be gay and carefree," Mr. Dorset enjoins.

"Because in this house we are all friends," Miss Dorset says. "We are all young, we all love one another."

"And love can make us all young forever," her brother says.

"Remember! "

"Remember this evening always, sweet young people! "

"Remember! "

"Remember what our life is like here! "

And now Miss Dorset, with one hand on the knob of the great door which she is about to throw open, leans a little toward the guests and whispers hoarsely: "This is what it is like to be young forever! "

Ned Meriwether was waiting behind a big japonica shrub near the sidewalk when, about twenty minutes after he had last seen Emily , the queer old touring car drew up in front of the Dorsets' house. During the interval, the car had gone from the Meriwether house to gather a number of other guests, and so it was not only Emily and Tom who alighted on the sidewalk before the Dorsets' house. The group was just large enough to make it easy for Ned to slip out from his dark hiding place and join them without being noticed by Mr. Dorset. And now the group was escorted rather unceremoniously up to the door of the house, and Mr. Dorset departed to fetch more guests.

They were received at the door by Miss Dorset. Her eyesight was no doubt better than her brother's, but still there was really no danger of her detecting an uninvited guest. Those of us who had gone to that house in the years just before Ned and Emily came along could remember that, during a whole evening, when their house was full of young people, the Dorsets made no introductions and made no effort to distinguish which of their guests was which. They did not even make a count of heads. Perhaps they did vaguely recognize some of the faces, because sometimes when they had come delivering figs or paper flowers to a house they had of necessity encountered a young child there, and always they smiled sweetly at it, asked its age, and calculated on their old fingers how many years must pass before the child would be eligible for an invitation. Yet at those moments something in the way they had held up their fingers and in the way they had gazed at the little face instead of into it had revealed their lack of interest in the individual child. And later, when the child was finally old enough to receive their invitation, he found it was still no different with the Dorsets. Even in their own house it was evidently to the young people as a group that the Dorsets' hearts went out; while they had the boys and girls under their roof they herded them about like so many little thoroughbred calves. Even when Miss Dorset opened the front door she did so exactly as though she was opening a gate. She pulled it open very slowly, standing half behind it to keep out of harm's way. And the children, all huddled together, surged in.

How meticulously this Ned and Emily Meriwether must have laid their plans for that evening! And the whole business might have come out all right if only they could have foreseen the effect which one part of their plan – rather a last-minute embellishment of it – would produce upon Ned himself. Barely ten minutes after they entered the house, Ned was watching Tom as he took his seat on the piano bench beside Emily. Ned probably watched Tom closely, because certainly he knew what the next move was going to be. The moment Miss Louisa Dorset's back was turned Tom Bascomb slipped his arm gently about Emily's little waist and commenced kissing her all over her pretty face. It was almost as if he were kissing away tears.

This spectacle on the piano bench, and others like it which followed, had been an inspiration of the last day or so before the party. Or so Ned and Emily maintained afterward when defending themselves to their parents. But no matter when it was conceived, a part of their plan it was, and Ned must have believed himself fully prepared for it. Probably he expected to join in the round of giggling which it produced from the other guests. But now that the time had come – it is easy to imagine – the boy Ned Meriwether found himself not quite able to join in the fun. He watched with the others, but he was not quite infected by their laughter. He stood a little apart, and probably he was hoping that Emily and Tom would not notice his failure to appreciate the success of their comedy. He was no doubt baffled by his own feelings, by the failure of his own enthusiasm, and by a growing desire to withdraw himself from the plot and from the party itself.

It is easy to imagine Ned's uneasiness and confusion that night. And I believe the account which I have given of Emily's impressions and her delicate little sensations while on the way to the party has a ring of truth about it, though actually the account was supplied by girls who knew her only slightly, who were not at the party, who could not possibly have seen her afterward. It may, after all, represent only what other girls imagined she would have felt. As for the account of how Mr. and Miss Meriwether spent the evening, it is their very own. And they did not hesitate to give it to anyone who would listen.

It was a long time, though, before many of us had a clear picture of the main events of the evening. We heard very soon that the parties for young people were to be no more, that there had been a wild scramble and chase through the Dorsets' house, and that it had ended by the Dorsets locking some boy - whether Ned or Tom was not easy to determine at first - in a queer sort of bathroom in which the plumbing had been disconnected, and even the fixtures removed, I believe. (Later I learned that there was nothing literally sinister about the bathroom itself. By having the pipes disconnected to this, and perhaps other bathrooms, the Dorsets had obtained further reductions in their taxes.) But a clear picture of the whole evening wasn't to be had - not without considerable searching. For one thing, the Meriwether parents immediately, within a week after the party, packed their son and daughter off to boarding schools. Accounts from the other children were contradictory and vague - perversely so, it seemed. Parents reported to each other that the little girls had nightmares which were worse even than those which their older sisters had had. And the boys were secretive and elusive, even with us older boys when we questioned them about what had gone on.

One sketchy account of events leading up to the chase, however, did go the rounds almost at once. Ned must have written it back to some older boy in a letter, because it contained information which no one but Ned could have had. The account went like this: When Mr. Dorset returned from his last roundup of guests, he came hurrying into the drawing room where the others were waiting and said in a voice trembling with excitement: "Now, let us all be seated, my young friends, and let us warm ourselves with some good talk."

At that moment everyone who was not already seated made a dash for a place on one of the divans or love seats or even in one of the broad window seats. (There were no individual chairs in the room.) Everyone made a dash, that is, except Ned. Ned did not move. He remained standing beside a little table rubbing his fingers over its polished surface. And from this moment he was clearly an object of suspicion in the eyes of his host and hostess. Soon the party moved from the drawing room to the library, but in whatever room they stopped Ned managed to isolate himself from the rest. He would sit or stand looking down at his hands until once again an explosion of giggles filled the room. Then he would look up just in time to see Tom Bascomb's cheek against Emily's or his arm about her waist.

For nearly two hours Ned didn't speak a word to anyone. He endured the Dorsets' dialogue, the paper flowers, the perfumed air, the works of art. Whenever a burst of giggling forced him to raise his eyes, he would look up at Tom and Emily and then turn his eyes away. Before looking down at his hands again, he would let his eyes travel slowly about the room until they came to rest on the fingers of the two Dorsets. That, it seems, was how he happened to discover that the Dorsets understood, or thought they understood, what the giggles meant. In the great mirror mounted over the library mantle he saw them exchanging half-suppressed smiles. Their smiles lasted precisely as long as the giggling continued, and then, in the mirror, Ned saw their faces change and grow solemn when their eyes – their identical, tiny, dull, amber-colored eyes – focused upon himself.

From the library the party continued on the regular tour of the house. At last when they had been to the ballroom and watched the Dorsets dance, had been upstairs to gaze upon the faded party clothes in the museum cases, they descended into the downstairs hall and were just before being turned into the dining room. The guests had already heard the Dorsets teasing each other about the silly little flirtations and about their naughtiness in parlor games when they were young and had listened to their exhortations to be gay and happy and carefree. Then just when Miss Dorset leaned toward them and whispered, "This is what it is like to be young forever," there rose a chorus of laughter, breathless and shrill, yet loud and intensely penetrating.

Ned Meriwether, standing on the bottom step of the stairway, lifted his eyes and looked over the heads of the party to see Tom and Emily half hidden in a bower of paper flowers and caught directly in a ray of mauve light. The two had squeezed themselves into a little niche there and stood squarely in front of the Rodin statuary. Tom had one arm placed about Emily's shoulders and he was kissing her lightly first on the lobe of one ear and then on the tip of her nose. Emily stood as rigid and pale as the plaster sculpture behind her and with just the faintest smile on her lips. Ned looked at the two of them and then turned his glance at once on the Dorsets.

He found Miss Louisa and Mr. Alfred gazing quite openly at Tom and Emily and frankly grinning at the spectacle. It was more than Ned could endure. "Don't you know?" He wailed, as if in great physical pain. "Can't you tell? Can't you see who they are? They're *brother* and *sister*! "

From the other guests came one concerted gasp. And then an instant later, mistaking Ned's outcry to be something he had planned all along and probably intended – as they imagined – for the very cream of the jest, the whole company burst once again into laughter – not a chorus of laughter this time but a volley of loud guffaws from the boys, and from the girls a cacophony of separately articulated shrieks and trills.

None of the guests present that night could – or would – give a satisfactory account of what happened next. Everyone insisted that he had not even looked at the Dorsets, that he, or she, didn't know how Miss Louisa and Mr. Alfred reacted at first. Yet this was precisely what those of us who had gone there in the past had to know. And when finally we did manage to get an account of it, we knew that it was a very truthful and accurate one. Because we got it, of course, from Tom Bascomb.

Since Ned's outburst came after the dancing exhibition, the Dorsets were in their most disheveled state. Miss Louisa's hair was fallen half over her face, and that long, limp strand of Mr. Alfred's was dangling about his left ear. Like that, they stood at the doorway to the dining room grinning at Tom Bascomb's antics. And when Tom Bascomb, hearing Ned's wail, whirled about, the grins were still on the Dorsets' face even though the guffaws and the shrieks of laughter were now silenced. Tom said that for several moments they continued to wear their grins like masks and that you couldn't really tell how they were taking it all until presently Miss Louisa's face, still wearing the grin, began turning all the queer colors of her paper flowers. Then the grin vanished from her lips and her mouth fell open and every bit of color went out of her face. She took a step backward and leaned against the doorjamb with her mouth still open and her eyes closed. If she hadn't been on her feet, Tom said he would have thought she was dead. Her brother didn't look at her, but his own grin had vanished just as hers did, and his face, all drawn and wrinkled, momentarily turned a dull copperish green.

Presently, though, he too went white, not white in faintness but in anger. His little brown eyes now shone like resin. And he took several steps toward Ned Meriwether. "What we know is that you are not one of us," he croaked. "We have perceived that from the beginning! We don't know how you got here or who you are. But the important question is, 'What are you doing here among these nice children?'"

The question seemed to restore life to Miss Louisa. Her amber eyes popped wide open. She stepped away from the door and began pinning up her hair which had fallen down on her shoulders, and at the same time addressing the guests who were huddled together in the center of the hall.

"Who is he, children? He is an intruder, that we know. If you know who he is, you must tell us."

"Who am I? Why, I am Tom Bascomb!" shouted Ned, still from the bottom step of the stairway. "I am Tom Bascomb, your paper boy!"

Then he turned and fled up the stairs toward the second floor. In a moment Mr. Dorset was after him.

To the real Tom Bascomb it had seemed that Ned honestly believed what he had been saying; and his own first impulse was to shout a denial. But being a level-headed boy and seeing how bad things were, Tom went instead to Miss Dorset and whispered to her that Tom Bascomb was a pretty tough guy and that she had better let him call the police for her. She told him where the telephone was in the side hall, and he started away.

But Miss Dorset changed her mind. She ran after Tom telling him not to call. Some of the guests mistook this for the beginning of another chase. Before the old lady could overtake Tom, however, Ned himself had appeared in the doorway toward which she and Tom were moving. He had come down the back stairway and he was calling out to Emily, "We're going home, Sis!"

A cheer went up from the whole party. Maybe it was this that caused Ned to lose his head, or maybe it was simply the sight of Miss Dorset rushing at him that did it. At any rate, the next moment he was running up the front stairs again, this time with Miss Dorset in pursuit.

When Tom returned from the telephone, all was quiet in the hall. The guests—everybody

except Emily–had moved to the foot of the stairs and they were looking up and listening. From upstairs Tom could hear Ned saying, "All right. All right. All right." The old couple had him cornered.

Emily was still standing in the little niche among the flowers. And it is the image of Emily Meriwether standing among the paper flowers that tantalizes me whenever I think or hear someone speak of that evening. That, more than anything else, can make me wish that I had been there. I shall never cease to wonder what kind of thoughts were in her head to make her seem so oblivious to all that was going on while she stood there, and, for that matter, what had been in her mind all evening while she endured Tom Bascomb's caresses. When, in years since, I have had reason to wonder what some girl or woman is thinking–some Emily grown older–my mind nearly always returns to the image of that girl among the paper flowers. Tom said that when he returned from the telephone she looked very solemn and pale still but that her mind didn't seem to be on any of the present excitement. Immediately he went to her and said, "Your dad is on his way over, Emily." For it was the Meriwether parents he had telephoned, of course, and not the police.

It seemed to Tom that so far as he was concerned the party was now over. There was nothing more he could do. Mr. Dorset was upstairs guarding the door to the strange little room in which Ned was locked up. Miss Dorset was serving lime punch to the other guests in the dining room, all the while listening with one ear for the arrival of the police whom Tom pretended he had called. When the doorbell finally rang and Miss Dorset hurried to answer it, Tom slipped quietly out through the pantry and through the kitchen and left the house by the back door as the Meriwether parents entered by the front.

There was no difficulty in getting Edwin and Muriel Meriwether, the children's parents, to talk about what happened after they arrived that night. Both of them were sensible and clear-headed people, and they were not so conservative as some of our other neighbors in West Vesey. Being fond of gossip of any kind and fond of reasonably funny stories on themselves, they told how their children had deceived them earlier in the evening and how they had deceived themselves later. They tended to blame themselves more than the children for what had happened. They tried to protect the children from any harm or embarrassment that might result from it by sending them off to boarding school. In their talk they never referred directly to Tom's reprehensible conduct or to the possible motives that the children might have had for getting up their plan. They tried to spare their children and they tried to spare Tom, but unfortunately it didn't occur to them to try to spare the poor old Dorsets.

When Miss Louisa opened the door, Mr. Meriwether said, "I'm Edwin Meriwether, Miss Dorset. I've come for my son Ned."

"And for your daughter Emily, I hope," his wife whispered to him.

"And for my daughter Emily."

Before Miss Dorset could answer him, Edwin Meriwether spied Mr. Dorset descending the stairs. With his wife, Muriel, sticking close to his side Edwin now strode over to the foot of the stairs. "Mr. Dorset," he began, "my son Ned – "

From behind them, Edwin and Muriel now heard Miss Dorset saying, "All the invited guests are gathered in the dining room." From where they were standing the two parents could see into the dining room. Suddenly they turned and hurried in there. Mr. Dorset and his sister of course followed them.

Muriel Meriwether went directly to Emily who was standing in a group of girls. "Emily, where is your brother?"

Emily said nothing, but one of the boys answered: "I think they've got him locked up upstairs somewhere."

"Oh, no! " said Miss Louisa, a hairpin in her mouth – for she was still rather absent-mindedly working at her hair. "It's an intruder that my brother has upstairs."

Mr. Dorset began speaking in a confidential tone to Edwin. "My dear neighbor," he said, "our paper boy saw fit to intrude himself upon our company tonight. But we recognized him as an outsider from the start."

Muriel Meriwether asked: "Where is the paper boy? Where is the paper boy, Emily?"

Again one of the boys volunteered: "He went out through the back door, Mrs. Meriwether."

The eyes of Mr. Alfred and Miss Louisa searched the room for Tom. Finally their eyes met and they smiled coyly. "All the children are being mischievous tonight," said Miss Louisa, and it was quite as though she had said, "all we children." Then, still smiling, she said, "Your tie has come undone, Brother. Mr. and Mrs. Meriwether will hardly know what to think."

Mr. Alfred fumbled for a moment with his tie but soon gave it up. Now with a bashful glance at the Meriwether parents, and giving a nod in the direction of the children, he actually said, "I'm afraid we've all decided to play a trick on Mr. and Mrs. Meriwether."

Miss Louisa said to Emily: "We've hidden our brother somewhere, haven't we?"

Emily's mother said firmly: "Emily, tell me where Ned is."

"He's upstairs, Mother," said Emily in a whisper.

Emily's father said: "I wish you to take me to the boy upstairs, Mr. Dorset."

The coy, bashful expressions vanished from the faces of the two Dorsets. Their eyes were little dark pools of incredulity, growing narrower by the second. And both of them were now trying to put their hair in order. "Why, we know nice children when we see them," Miss Louisa said peevishly. There was a pleading quality in her voice, too. "We know from the beginning that that boy upstairs didn't belong amongst us," she said. "Dear neighbors, it isn't just the money, you know, that makes the difference." All at once she sounded like a little girl about to burst into tears.

"It isn't just the money?" Edwin Meriwether repeated.

"Miss Dorset," said Muriel with new gentleness in her tone, as though she had just recognized that it was a little girl she was talking to, "there has been some kind of mistake – a misunderstanding."

Mr. Alfred Dorset said: "Oh, we wouldn't make a mistake of that kind! People are different. It isn't something you can put your finger on, but it isn't the money."

"I don't know what you're talking about," Edwin said, exasperated. "But I'm going upstairs and find that boy." He left the room with Mr. Dorset following him with quick little steps – steps like those of a small boy trying to keep up with a man.

Miss Louisa now sat down in one of the high-backed dining chairs which were lined up along the oak wainscot. She was trembling, and Muriel came and stood beside her. Neither of them spoke, and in almost no time Edwin Meriwether came downstairs again with Ned. Miss Louisa looked at Ned, and tears came into her eyes. "Where is my brother?" she asked accusingly, as though she thought possibly Ned and his father had locked Mr. Dorset in the bathroom.

"I believe he has retired," said Edwin. "He left us and disappeared into one of the rooms upstairs."

"Then I must go up to him," said Miss Louisa. For a moment she seemed unable to rise. At last she pushed herself up from the chair and walked from the room with the slow, steady gait of a somnambulist. Muriel Meriwether followed her into the hall and as she watched the old woman ascending the steps, leaning heavily on the rail, her impulse was to go and offer to assist her. But something made her turn back into the dining room. Perhaps she imagined that her daughter, Emily, might need her now.

The Dorsets did not reappear that night. After Miss Louisa went upstairs, Muriel promptly got on the telephone and called the parents of some of the other boys and girls. Within a quarter of an hour, half a dozen parents had assembled. It was the first time in many years that any adult had set foot inside the Dorset house. It was the first time that any parents had ever inhaled the perfumed air or seen the masses of paper flowers and the illuminations and the statuary. In the guise of holding consultations over whether or not they should put out the lights and lock up the house, the parents lingered much longer than was necessary before taking the people home. Some of them even tasted the lime punch. But in the presence of their children they made no comment on what had happened and gave no indication of what their own impressions were – not even their impressions of the punch. At last it was decided that two of the men should see to putting out the lights everywhere on the first floor and down in the ballroom. They were a long time in finding the switches for the indirect lighting. In most cases, they simply resorted to unscrewing the bulbs. Meanwhile the children went to the large cloak closet behind the stairway and got their wraps. When Ned and Emily Meriwether rejoined their parents at the front door to leave the house, Ned was wearing his own overcoat and held his own fedora in his hand.

Miss Louisa and Mr. Alfred Dorset lived on for nearly ten years after that night, but they gave up selling their figs and paper flowers and of course they never entertained young people again. I often wonder if growing up in Chatham can ever have seemed quite the same since. Some of the terror must have gone out of it. Half the dread of coming of age must have vanished with the dread of the Dorsets' parties.

After that night, their old car would sometimes be observed creeping about town, but it was never parked in front of their house any more. It stood usually at the side entrance where the Dorsets could climb in and out of it without being seen. They began keeping a servant too – mainly to run their errands for them, I imagine. Sometimes it would be a man, sometimes a woman, never the same one for more than a few months at a time. Both the Dorsets died during the Second World War while many of us who had gone to their parties were away from Chatham. But the story went round – and I am inclined to believe it – that after they were dead and the house was sold, Tom Bascomb's coat and hat were found still hanging in the cloak closet behind the stairs.

Tom himself was a pilot in the war and was a considerable hero. He was such a success and made such a name for himself that he never came back to Chatham to live. He found bigger opportunities elsewhere I suppose, and I don't suppose he ever felt the ties to Chatham that people with Ned's kind of upbringing do. Ned was in the war too, of course. He was in the navy and after the war he did return to Chatham to live, though actually it was not until then that he had spent much time here since his parents bundled him off to boarding school. Emily came home and made her debut just two or three years before the war, but she was already engaged to some boy in the East; she never comes back any more except to bring her children to see their grandparents for a few days during Christmas or at Easter.

I understand that Emily and Ned are pretty indifferent to each other's existence nowadays. I have been told this by Ned Meriwether's own wife. Ned's wife maintains that the night Ned and Emily went to the Dorsets' party marked the beginning of this indifference, that it marked the end of their childhood intimacy and the beginning of a shyness, a reserve, even an animosity between them that was destined to be a sorrow forever to the two sensible parents who had sat in the upstairs sitting room that night waiting until the telephone call came from Tom Bascomb.

Ned's wife is a girl he met while he was in the navy. She was a Wave, and her background isn't the same as his. Apparently, she isn't too happy with life in what she refers to as "Chatham proper." She and Ned have recently moved out into a suburban development, which she doesn't like either and which she refers to as "greater Chatham." She asked me at a party one night how Chatham got its name (she was just making conversation and appealing to my interest in such things) and when I told her that it was named for the Earl of Chatham and pointed out that the city is located in Pitt County, she burst out laughing. "How very elegant," she said. "Why has nobody ever told me that before?" But what interests me most about Ned's wife is that after a few drinks she likes to talk about Ned and Emily and Tom Bascomb and the Dorsets. Tom Bascomb has become a kind of hero – and I don't mean a wartime hero – in her eyes, though of course not having grown up in Chatham she has never seen him in her life. But she is a clever girl, and there are times when she will say to me, "Tell me about Chatham. Tell me about the Dorsets." And I try to tell her. I tell her to remember that Chatham looks upon itself as a rather old city. I tell her to remember that it was one of the first English-speaking settlements west of the Alleghenies and that by the end of the American Revolution, when veterans began pouring westward over the Wilderness Road or down the Ohio River, Chatham was often referred to as a thriving village. Then she tells me that I'm being dull, because it is hard for her to concentrate on any aspect of the story that doesn't center around Tom Bascomb and that night at the Dorsets'.

But I make her listen. Or at least one time I did. The Dorset family, I insisted on saying, was in Chatham even in those earliest times right after the Revolution, but they had come here under somewhat different circumstances from those of the other early settlers. How could that really matter, Ned's wife asked, after a hundred and fifty years? How could distinctions between the first settlers matter after the Irish had come to Chatham, after the Germans, after the Italians? Well, in West Vesey Place it could matter. It had to. If the distinction was false, it mattered all the more and it was all the more necessary to make it.

But let me interject here that Chatham is located in a state about whose history most Chatham citizens – not newcomers like Ned's wife, but old-timers – have little interest and less knowledge. Most of us, for instance, are never even quite sure whether during the 1860's our state did secede or didn't secede. As for the city itself, some of us hold that it is geographically Northern and culturally Southern. Others say the reverse is true. We are all apt to want to feel misplaced in Chatham, and so we are not content merely to say that it is a border city. How you stand on this important question is apt to depend entirely on whether your family is one of those with a good Southern name or one that had its origin in New England, because those are the two main categories of old society families in Chatham.

But truly – I told Ned's wife – the Dorset family was never in either of those categories. The first Dorset had come, with his family and his possessions and even a little capital, direct from a city in the English Midlands to Chatham. The Dorsets came not as pioneers, but paying their way all the way. They had not bothered to stop for a generation or two to put down roots in Pennsylvania or Virginia or Massachusetts. And this was the distinction which some people wished always to make. Apparently those early Dorsets had cared no more for putting down roots in the soil of the New World than they had cared for whatever they had left behind in the Old. They were an obscure mercantile family who came to invest in a new Western city. Within two generations the business – no, the industry! – which they established made them rich beyond any dreams they could have had in the beginning. For half a century they were looked upon, if any family ever was, as our first family.

And then the Dorsets left Chatham – practically all of them except the one old bachelor and the one old maid – left it just as they had come, not caring much about what they were leaving or where they were going. They were city people, and they were Americans. They knew that what they had in Chatham they could buy more of in other places. For them Chatham was an investment that had paid off. They went to live in Santa Barbara and Laguna Beach, in Newport and on Long Island. And the truth which it was so hard for the rest of us to admit was that, despite our families of Massachusetts and Virginia, we were all more like the Dorsets – those Dorsets who left Chatham – than we were unlike them. Their spirit was just a little closer to being the very essence of Chatham than ours was. The obvious difference was that we had to stay on here and pretend that our life had a meaning which it did not. And if it was only by a sort of chance that Miss Louisa and Mr. Alfred played the role of social arbiters among the young people for a number of years, still no one could honestly question their divine right to do so.

"It may have been their right," Ned's wife said at this point, "but just think what might have happened."

"It's not a matter of what might have happened," I said, "It is a matter of what did happen. Otherwise, what have you and I been talking about?"

"Otherwise," she said with an irrepressible shudder, "I would not be forever getting you off in a corner at these parties to talk about my husband and my husband's sister and how it is they care so little for each other's company nowadays.

And I could think of nothing to say to that except that probably we had now pretty well covered our subject.

Unit 11
Flannery O' Connor (1925–1964)
弗兰纳里·奥康纳

作者简介

弗兰纳里·奥康纳，美国南方现代女作家，1925年3月出生于佐治亚州萨凡纳(Savanna, Georgia)一个虔诚的天主教家庭。她早年在天主教会学校接受教育，后迁居原教旨主义盛行、传统上被称做“圣经地带”的佐治亚中部地区，先后在佐治亚州女子学院和爱荷华大学学习。在浓厚的宗教氛围中长大的奥康纳笃信天主教，相信宗教的救赎力量，宗教的“堕落、救赎、末日审判”主题构成了她的创作基础，上帝的恩典成为其作品的主要表现内容。她的创作也带有南方文学的显著特征：浓郁的历史意识、细腻的心理描写等。她笔下的人物常常奇零怪异，身心严重扭曲，死亡、暴力、变态行为在作品中屡见不鲜，构成了她创作的典型风格。她与麦卡勒斯、杜鲁门·卡波特等一起被视为“南方哥特流派”的代表人物。奥康纳宣扬上帝的恩典也与她个人的人生不幸密切相关，她在25岁时身患红斑狼疮恶疾，直到1964年8月去世她都备受病痛折磨，上帝成为她与病魔抗争的精神支柱。奥康纳的代表作是两部长篇小说《慧血》(*Wise Blood*,1952)和《暴力得逞》(*The Violent Bears It Away*,1960)。《慧血》塑造了一位“被基督烦扰”的主人公莫兹背离上帝的精神历程，表现了只有上帝才是拯救世界、拯救人类灵魂的宗教救赎主题。《暴力得逞》记述的是一个精神错乱的南方家族三代人因无法摆脱负罪感而陷入暴力之中的家史小说。

奥康纳以短篇小说见长，在她创作的31篇短篇小说中，有19篇分别收录在短篇小说集《好人难寻》(*A Good Man Is Hard to Find*,1955)和《汇合》(*Everything That Rises Must Converge*,1965)中，其中的一些作品被誉为20世界美国最优秀的短篇小说。在她去世之后，她的一些文学随笔与评论被收入《神秘与习俗：散文拾零》(*Mystery and Manners*,1969)，生前的书信被结集成册《生存习惯》(*The Habit of Being*, 1979)。1971年出版的《短篇小说集》(*The Complete Short Stories*)收集了她生前未发表的12篇短篇小说并获全国图书奖。奥康纳独特的宗教主题、怪诞的写作风格和极具震撼力的作品得到社会和评论家的充分肯定，生前曾获“欧·亨利短篇小说奖”、“美国文学艺术院奖”等多种荣誉和奖励。《好人难寻》是她最有名的短篇小说。它的语言朴素，风格幽默，笔调讥讽。小说以黑色幽默与暴力结合的文字讲述了一个虚构的宗教寓言故事，触及资本主义社会的痼疾，其结尾往往令人感到出乎意料。

作品导读

The story begins with the family's planning for a vacation. The Grandmother complains in vain that she prefers Tennessee to Florida and she seizes every chance to persuade his son to change the destination. She packs herself (and secretly her cat, Pitty Sing) in the car with her son Bailey, his wife, and their children June Star, John Wesley, and the baby. The Grandmother puts on her best dress and hat, so that if she were found dead on the highway everyone would recognize her as a lady. During the trip the Grandmother talks incessantly about her youth in the old south to arouse the interest of the children to go to Tennessee. Then the family stops for lunch at Red Sammy Butts' barbecue place. There the Grandmother talks with the owner about the escaped murderer known as the Misfit. They remark that nowadays a good man is hard to find and the society is more dangerous than before. When they back to their car again the Grandmother tells stories about her childhood home and the secret passage which makes the children persuade their father to drive to the house.

When the Grandmother's directiohs lead them down an abandoned dirt road, she realizes that the house is not in Georgia but in Tennessee. So she upsets her cat, and the cat panics and attacks Bailey, causing him to lose control of the car and roll it into a ditch. When they are waiting for passing cars for help, they unfortunately wait for the arrival of the very Misfit who shoots the whole family to death one by one. The Misfit says that he is angry because he does not want to waste his life serving a figure who may not exist, nor does he want to displease an almighty God who may exist; puzzled by this, he believes that "There's no pleasure but meanness." The Grandmother then reaches out to the Misfit, calling him her "child", prompting the Misfit brutally shoot her to death. When one of the gang remarks on the fun murdering the family, the Misfit angrily reproaches him that "It's no real pleasure".

The story is religious allegory with a perfect combination of O'Connor's black humor and violence. It seems that the gossip and self-centered Grandmother is mainly responsible for the family's tragedy. But in the end of the story her surpassing of her self-centeredness and calling the murderer as one of her own children make her soul redeemed by God.

作品选读

A Good Man Is Hard to Find

The grandmother didn't want to go to Florida. She wanted to visit some of her connections in east Tennessee and she was seizing at every chance to change Bailey's mind. Bailey was the son she lived with, her only boy. He was sitting on the edge of his chair at the table, bent over the orange sports section of the *Journal*. "Now look here, Bailey," she said, "see here, read this," and she stood with one hand on her thin hip and the other rattling the newspaper at his bald head. "Here this fellow that calls himself The Misfit is aloose from the Federal Pen and headed toward Florida and you read here what it says he did to these people. Just you read it. I wouldn't take my children in any direction with a criminal like that aloose in it. I couldn't answer to my conscience if I did."

Bailey didn't look up from his reading so she wheeled around then and faced the children's mother, a young woman in slacks, whose face was as broad and innocent as a cabbage and was tied round with a green head-kerchief that had two points on the top like rabbit's ears. She was sitting on the sofa, feeding the baby his apricots out of a jar. "The children have been to Florida before," the old lady said. "You all ought to take them somewhere else for a change so they would see different parts of the world and be broad. They never have been to east Tennessee."

The children's mother didn't seem to hear her but the eight-year-old boy, John Wesley, a stocky child with glasses, said, "If you don't want to go to Florida, why dontcha stay at home?" He and the little girl, June Star, were reading the funny papers on the floor.

"She wouldn't stay at home to be queen for a day," June Star said without raising her yellow head.

"Yes and what would you do if this fellow, The Misfit, caught you?" the grandmother asked.

"I'd smack his face," John Wesley said.

"She wouldn't stay at home for a million bucks," June Star said. "Afraid she'd miss something. She has to go everywhere we go."

"All right, Miss," the grandmother said. "Just remember that the next time you want me to curl your hair."

June Star said her hair was naturally curly.

The next morning the grandmother was the first one in the car, ready to go. She had her big black valise that looked like the head of a hippoptamus in one corner, and underneath it she was hiding a basket with Pitty Sing, the cat, in it. She didn't intend for the cat to be left alone in the house for three days because he would miss her too much and she was afraid he might brush against one of her gas burners and accidentally asphyxiate himself. Her son, Bailey, didn't like to arrive at a motel with a cat.

She sat in the middle of the back seat with John Wesley and June Star on either side of her. Bailey and the children's mother and the baby sat in the front and they left Atlanta at eight forty-five with the mileage on the car at 55,890. The grandmother wrote this down because she thought it would be interesting to say how many miles they had been when they got back. It took them twenty minutes to reach the outskirts of the city.

The old lady settled herself comfortably, removing her white cotton gloves and putting them up with her purse on the shelf in front of the back window. The children's mother still

had on slacks and still had her head tied up in a green kerchief, but the grandmother had on a navy blue straw sailor hat with a bunch of white violets on the brim and a navy blue dress with a small white dot in the print. Her collar and cuffs were white organdy trimmed with lace and at her neckline she had pinned a purple spray of cloth violets containing a sachet. In case of an accident, anyone seeing her dead on the highway would know at once that she was a lady.

She said she thought it was going to be a good day for driving, neither too hot nor too cold, and she cautioned Bailey that the speed limit was fifty-five miles an hour and that the patrolmen hid themselves behind billboards and small clumps of trees and sped out after you before you had a chance to slow down. She pointed out interesting details of the scenery: Stone Mountain; the blue granite that in some places came up to both sides of the highway; the brilliant red clay banks slightly streaked with purple; and the various crops that made rows of green lace-work on the ground. The trees were full of silver-white sunlight and the meanest of them sparkled. The children were reading comic magazines and their mother had gone back to sleep.

"Let's go through Georgia fast so we won't have to look at it much," John Wesley said.

"If I were a little boy," said the grandmother, "I wouldn't talk about my native state that way. Tennessee has the mountains and Georgia has the hills."

"Tennessee is just a hillbilly dumping ground," John Wesley said, "and Georgia is a lousy state too."

"You said it," June Star said.

"In my time," said the grandmother, folding her thin veined fingers, "children were more respectful of their native states and their parents and everything else. People did right then. Oh look at the cute little pickaninny!" she said and pointed to a Negro child standing in the door of a shack. "Wouldn't that make a picture, now?" she asked and they all turned and looked at the little Negro out of the back window. He waved.

"He didn't have any britches on," June Star said.

"He probably didn't have any," the grandmother explained. "Little niggers in the country don't have things like we do. If I could paint, I'd paint that picture," she said.

The children exchanged comic books.

The grandmother offered to hold the baby and the children's mother passed him over the front seat to her. She set him on her knee and bounced him and told him about the things they were passing. She rolled her eyes and screwed up her mouth and stuck her leathery thin face into his smooth bland one. Occasionally he gave her a faraway smile. They passed a large cotton field with five or fix graves fenced in the middle of it, like a small island. "Look at the graveyard!" the grandmother said, pointing it out. "That was the old family burying ground. That belonged to the plantation."

"Where's the plantation?" John Wesley asked.

"Gone With the Wind", said the grandmother. "Ha. Ha."

When the children finished all the comic books they had brought, they opened the lunch and ate it. The grandmother ate a peanut butter sandwich and an olive and would not let the children throw the box and the paper napkins out the window. When there was nothing else to do they played a game by choosing a cloud and making the other two guess what shape it suggested. John Wesley took one the shape of a cow and June Star guessed a cow and John Wesley said, no, an automobile, and June Star said he didn't play fair, and they began to slap each other over the grandmother.

The grandmother said she would tell them a story if they would keep quiet. When she told a story, she rolled her eyes and waved her head and was very dramatic. She said once when she was a maiden lady she had been courted by a Mr. Edgar Atkins Teagarden from Jasper, Georgia. She said he was a very good-looking man and a gentleman and that he brought her a watermelon every Saturday afternoon with his initials cut in it, E. A. T. Well, one Saturday, she said, Mr. Teagarden brought the watermelon and there was nobody at home and he left it on the front porch and returned in his buggy to Jasper, but she never got the watermelon, she said, because a nigger boy ate it when he saw the initials, E. A. T.! This story tickled John Wesley's funny bone and he giggled and giggled but June Star didn't think it was any good. She said she wouldn't marry a man that just brought her a watermelon on Saturday. The grandmother said she would have done well to marry Mr. Teagarden because he was a gentleman and had bought Coca-Cola stock when it first came out and that he had died only a few years ago, a very wealthy man.

They stopped at The Tower for barbecued sandwiches. The Tower was a part stucco and part wood filling station and dance hall set in a clearing outside of Timothy. A fat man named Red Sammy Butts ran it and there were signs stuck here and there on the building and for miles up and down the highway saying, TRY RED SAMMY'S FAMOUS BARBECUE. NONE LIKE FAMOUS RED SAMMY'S! RED SAM! THE FAT BOY WITH THE HAPPY LAUGH. A VETERAN! SAMMY'S YOUR MAN!

Red Sammy was lying on the bare ground outside The Tower with his head under a truck while a gray monkey about a foot high, chained to a small chinaberry tree, chattered nearby. The monkey sprang back into the tree and got on the highest limb as soon as he saw the children jump out of the car and run toward him.

Inside, The Tower was a long dark room with a counter at one end and tables at the other and dancing space in the middle. They all sat down at a board table next to the nickelodeon and Red Sam's wife, a tall burnt-brown woman with hair and eyes lighter than her skin, came and took their order. The children's mother put a dime in the machine and played "The Tennessee Waltz," and the grandmother said that tune always made her want to dance. She asked Bailey if he would like to dance but he only glared at her. He didn't have a naturally sunny disposition like she did and trips made him nervous. The grandmother's brown eyes were very bright. She swayed her head from side to side and pretended she was dancing in her chair. June Star said play something she could tap to so the children's mother put in another dime and played a fast number and June Star stepped out onto the dance floor and did her tap routine.

"Ain't she cute?" Red Sam's wife said, leaning over the counter. "Would you like to come be my little girl?"

"No, I certainly wouldn't," June Star said. "I wouldn't live in a broken-down place like this for a million bucks! " and she ran back to the table.

"Ain't she cute?" the woman repeated, stretching her mouth politely.

"Aren't you ashamed?" hissed the grandmother.

Red Sam came in and told his wife to quit lounging on the counter and hurry with these people's order. His khaki trousers reached just to his hip bones and his stomach hung over them like a sack of meal swaying under his shirt. He came over and sat down at a table nearby and let out a combination sigh and yodel. "You can't win," he said. "You can't win," and he wiped his sweating red face off with a gray handkerchief. "These days you don't know who to trust," he said. "Ain't that the truth?"

"People are certainly not nice like they used to be," said the grandmother.

"Two fellers come in here last week," Red Sammy said, "driving a Chrysler. It was an old beat-up car but it was a good one and these boys looked all right to me. Said they worked at the mill and you know I let them fellers charge the gas they bought. Now why did I do that?"

"Because you're a good man! " the grandmother said at once.

"Yes'm I suppose so," Red Sam said as if he were struck with this answer.

His wife brought the orders, carrying the five plates all at once without a tray, two in each hand and one balanced on her arm. "It isn't a soul in this green world of God's that you can trust," she said. "And I don't count anybody out of that, not nobody," she repeated, looking at Red Sammy.

"Did you read about that criminal, The Misfit, that's escaped?" asked the grandmother.

"I wouldn't be a bit surprised if he didn't attack this place right here," said the woman. "If he hears about it being here, I wouldn't be none surprised to see him. If he hears it's two cent in the cash register, I wouldn't be a tall surprised if he..."

"That'll do," Red Sam said. "Go bring these people their Co'Colas," and the woman went off to get rest of the order.

"A good man is hard to find," Red Sammy said. "Everything is getting terrible. I remember the day you could go off and leave your screen door unlatched. Not no more."

He and the grandmother discussed better times. The old lady said that in her opinion Europe was entirely to blame for the way things were now. She said the way Europe acted you would think we were made of money and Red Sam said it was no use talking about it, she was exactly right. The children ran outside into the white sunlight and looked at the monkey in the lacy chinaberry tree. He was busy catching fleas on himself and biting each one carefully between his teeth as if it were a delicacy.

They drove off again into the hot afternoon. The grandmother took cat naps and woke up every few minutes with her own snoring. Outside of Toombsboro she woke up and recalled an old plantation that she had visited in this neighborhood once when she was a young lady. She said the house had six white columns across the front and that there was an avenue of oaks leading up to it and two little wooden trellis arbors on either side in front where you sat down with your suitor after a stroll in the garden. She recalled exactly which road to turn off to get to it. She knew that Bailey would not be willing to lose any time looking at an old house, but the more she talked about it, the more she wanted to see it once again and find out if the little twin arbors were still standing. "There was a secret panel in this house," she said craftily, not telling the truth but wishing that she were, "and the story went that all the family silver was hidden in it when Sherman came through but it was never found..."

"Hey!" John Wesley said. "Let's go see it! We'll find it! We'll poke all the woodwork and find it! Who lives there? Where do you turn off at? Hey Pop, can't we turn off there?"

"We never have seen a house with a secret panel!" June Star shrieked. "Let's go to the house with the secret panel! Hey, Pop, can't we go see the house with the secret panel!"

"It's not far from here, I know," the grandmother said. "It wouldn't take over twenty minutes."

Bailey was looking straight ahead. His jaw was as rigid as a horseshoe. "No," he said.

The children began to yell and scream that they wanted to see the house with the secret panel. John Wesley kicked the back of the front seat and June Star hung over her mother's shoulder and whined desperately into her ear that they never had any fun even on their vacation, and that they could never do what THEY wanted to do. The baby began to scream and John Wesley kicked the back of the seat so hard that his father could feel the blows in his kidney.

"All right!" he shouted and drew the car to a stop at the side of the road. "Will you all shut up? Will you all just shut up for one second? If you don't shut up, we won't go anywhere."

"It would be very educational for them," the grandmother murmured.

"All right," Bailey said, "but get this: this is the only time we're going to stop for anything like this. This is the one and only time."

"The dirt road that you have to turn down is about a mile back," the grandmother directed. "I marked it when we passed."

"A dirt road," Bailey groaned.

After they had turned around and were headed toward the dirt road, the grandmother recalled other points about the house, the beautiful glass over the front doorway and the candle-lamp in the hall. John Wesley said that the secret panel was probably in the fireplace.

"You can't go inside this house," Bailey said. "You don't know who lives there."

"While you all talk to the people in front, I'll run around behind and get in a window," John Wesley suggested.

"We'll all stay in the car," his mother said.

They turned onto the dirt road and the car raced roughly along in a swirl of pink dust. The grandmother recalled the times when there were no paved roads and thirty miles was a day's journey. The dirt road was hilly and there were sudden washes in it and sharp curves on dangerous embankments. All at once they would be on a hill, looking down over the blue tops of trees for miles around, then the next minute, they would be in a red depression with the dust-coated trees looking down on them.

"This place had better turn up in a minute," Bailey said, "or I'm going to turn around."

The road looked as if no one had traveled on it in months.

"It's not much farther," the grandmother said and just as she said it, a horrible thought came to her. The thought was so embarrassing that she turned red in the face and her eyes dilated and her feet jumped up, upsetting her valise in the corner. The instant the valise moved, the newspaper top she had over the basket under it rose with a snarl and Pitty Sing, the cat, sprang onto Bailey's shoulder.

The children were thrown to the floor and their mother, clutching the baby, was thrown out the door onto the ground, the old lady was thrown into the front seat. The car turned over once and landed right-side-up in a gulch off the side of the road. Bailey remained in the driver's seat with the cat-gray-striped with a broad white face and an orange nose-clinging to his neck like a caterpillar.

As soon as the children saw they could move their arms and legs, they scrambled out of the car, shouting, "We've had an ACCIDENT!" The grandmother was curled up under the dashboard, hoping she was injured so that Bailey's wrath would not come down on her all at once. The horrible thought she had had before the accident was that the house she had remembered so vividly was not in Georgia but in Tennessee.

Bailey removed the cat from his neck with both hands and flung it out the window against the side of a pine tree. Then he got out of the car and started looking for the children's mother. She was sitting against the side of the red gutted ditch, holding the screaming baby, but she only had a cut down her face and a broken shoulder. "We've had an ACCIDENT!" the children screamed in a frenzy of delight.

"But nobody's killed," June Star said with disappointment as the grandmother limped out of the car, her hat still pinned to her head but the broken front brim standing up at a jaunty angle and the violet spray hanging off the side. They all sat down in the ditch, except the children, to recover from the shock. They were all shaking.

"Maybe a car will come along," said the children's mother hoarsely.

"I believe I have injured an organ," said the grandmother, pressing her side, but no one answered her. Bailey's teeth were clattering. He had on a yellow sport shirt with bright blue parrots designed in it and his face was as yellow as the shirt. The grandmother decided that she would not mention that the house was in Tennessee.

The road was about ten feet above and they could see only the tops of the trees on the other side of it. Behind the ditch they were sitting in there were more woods, tall and dark and deep. In a few minutes they saw a car some distance away on top of a hill, coming slowly as if the occupants were watching them. The grandmother stood up and waved both arms dramatically to attract their attention. The car continued to come on slowly, disappeared around a bend and appeared again, moving even slower, on top of the hill they had gone over. It was a big black battered hearse-like automobile. There were three men in it.

It camc to a stop just over them and for some minutes, the driver looked down with a steady expressionless gaze to where they were sitting, and didn't speak. Then he turned his head and muttered something to the other two and they got out. One was a fat boy in black trousers and a red sweat shirt with a silver stallion embossed on the front of it. He moved around on the right side of them and stood staring, his mouth partly open in a kind of loose grin. The other had on khaki pants and a blue striped coat and a gray hat pulled down very low, hiding most of his face. He came around slowly on the left side. Neither spoke.

The driver got out of the car and stood by the side of it, looking down at them. He was an older man than the other two. His hair was just beginning to gray and he wore silver-rimmed spectacles that gave him a scholarly look. He had a long creased face and didn't have on any shirt or undershirt. He had on blue jeans that were too tight for him and was holding a black hat and a gun. The two boys also had guns.

"We've had an ACCIDENT! " the children screamed.

The grandmother had the peculiar feeling that the bespectacled man was someone she knew. His face was as familiar to her as if she had known him all her life but she could not recall who he was. He moved away from the car and began to come down the embankment, placing his feet carefully so that he wouldn't slip. He had on tan and white shoes and no socks, and his ankles were red and thin. "Good afternoon," he said. "I see you all had you a little spill."

"We turned over twice! " said the grandmother.

"Oncet", he corrected. "We seen it happen. Try their car and see will it run, Hiram," he said quietly to the boy with the gray hat.

"What you got that gun for?" John Wesley asked. "Whatcha gonna do with that gun?"

"Lady," the man said to the children's mother, "would you mind calling them children to sit down by you? Children make me nervous. I want all you to sit down right together there where you're at."

"What are you telling us what to do for?" June Star asked.

Behind them the line of woods gaped like a dark open mouth. "Come here," said their mother.

"Look here now," Bailey began suddenly, "we're in a predicament! We're in..."

The grandmother shrieked. She scrambled to her feet and stood staring. "You're The Misfit! " she said. "I recognized you at once! "

"Yes'm," the man said, smiling slightly as if he were pleased in spite of himself to be known, "but it would have been better for all of you, lady, if you hadn't of reckernized me."

Bailey turned his head sharply and said something to his mother that shocked even the children. The old lady began to cry and The Misfit reddened.

"Lady," he said, "don't you get upset. Sometimes a man says things he don't mean. I don't reckon he meant to talk to you thataway."

"You wouldn't shoot a lady, would you?" the grandmother said and removed a clean handkerchief from her cuff and began to slap at her eyes with it.

The Misfit pointed the toe of his shoe into the ground and made a little hole and then covered it up again. "I would hate to have to," he said.

"Listen," the grandmother almost screamed, "I know you're a good man. You don't look a bit like you have common blood. I know you must come from nice people!"

"Yes mam," he said, "finest people in the world." When he smiled he showed a row of strong white teeth. "God never made a finer woman than my mother and my daddy's heart was pure gold," he said. The boy with the red sweat shirt had come around behind them and was standing with his gun at his hip. The Misfit squatted down on the ground. "Watch them children, Bobby Lee," he said. "You know they make me nervous." He looked at the six of them huddled together in front of him and he seemed to be embarrassed as if he couldn't think of anything to say. "Ain't a cloud in the sky," he remarked, looking up at it. "Don't see no sun but don't see no cloud neither."

"Yes, it's a beautiful day," said the grandmother. "Listen," she said, "you shouldn't call yourself The Misfit because I know you're a good man at heart. I can just look at you and tell."

"Hush!" Bailey yelled. "Hush! Everybody shut up and let me handle this!" He was squatting in the position of a runner about to sprint forward but he didn't move.

"I pre-chate that lady," The Misfit said and drew a little circle in the ground with the butt of his gun.

"It'll take a half a hour to fix this here car," Hiram called, looking over the raised hood of it.

"Well, first you and Bobby Lee get him and that little boy to step over yonder with you," The Misfit said, pointing to Bailey and John Wesley. "The boys want to ask you something," he said to Bailey. "Would you mind stepping back in them woods there with them?"

"Listen," Bailey began, "we're in a terrible predicament! Nobody realizes what this is," and his voice cracked. His eyes were as blue and intense as the parrots in his shirt and he remained perfectly still.

The grandmother reached up to adjust her hat brim as if she were going to the woods with him but it came off in her hand. She stood staring at it and after a second she let it fall on the ground. Hiram pulled Bailey up by the arm as if he were assisting an old man. John Wesley caught hold of his father's hand and Bobby Lee followed. They went off toward the woods and just as they reached the dark edge, Bailey turned and supporting himself against a gray naked pine trunk, he shouted, "I'll be back in a minute, Mamma, wait on me!"

"Come back this instant! " his mother shrilled but they all disappeared into the woods.

"Bailey Boy! " the grandmother called in a tragic voice but she found she was looking at The Misfit squatting on the ground in front of her. "I just know you're a good man," she said desperately. "You're not a bit common! "

"Nome, I ain't a good man," The Misfit said after a second as if he had considered her statement carefully, "but I ain't the worst in the world neither. My daddy said I was a different breed of dog from my brothers and sisters. 'You know,' Daddy said, 'it's some that can live their whole life out without asking about it and it's others has to know why it is, and this boy is one of the latters. He's going to be into everything!" He put on his black hat and looked up suddenly and then away deep into the woods as if he were embarrassed again. "I'm sorry I don't have on a shirt before you ladies," he said, hunching his shoulders slightly. "We buried our clothes that we had on when we escaped and we're just making do until we can get better. We borrowed these from some folks we met," he explained.

"That's perfectly all right," the grandmother said. "Maybe Bailey has an extra shirt in his suitcase."

"I'll look and see terrectly," The Misfit said.

"Where are they taking him?" the children's mother screamed.

"Daddy was a card himself," The Misfit said. "You couldn't put anything over on him. He never got in trouble with the Authorities though. Just had the knack of handling them."

"You could be honest too if you'd only try," said the grandmother. "Think how wonderful it would be to settle down and live a comfortable life and not have to think about somebody chasing you all the time."

The Misfit kept scratching in the ground with the butt of his gun as if he were thinking about it. "Yes'm, somebody is always after you," he murmured.

The grandmother noticed how thin his shoulder blades were just behind his hat because she was standing up looking down on him. "Do you every pray?" she asked.

He shook his head. All she saw was the black hat wiggle between his shoulder blades. "Nome," he said.

There was a pistol shot from the woods, followed closely by another. Then silence. The old lady's head jerked around. She could hear the wind move through the tree tops like a long satisfied insuck of breath. "Bailey Boy! " she called.

"I was a gospel singer for a while," The Misfit said. "I been most everything. Been in the arm service both land and sea, at home and abroad, been twict married, been an undertaker, been with the railroads, plowed Mother Earth, been in a tornado, seen a man burnt alive oncet," and he looked up at the children's mother and the little girl who were sitting close together, their faces white and their eyes glassy; "I even seen a woman flogged," he said.

"Pray, pray," the grandmother began, "pray, pray..."

I never was a bad boy that I remember of," The Misfit said in an almost dreamy voice, "but somewheres along the line I done something wrong and got sent to the penitentiary. I was buried alive," and he looked up and held her attention to him by a steady stare.

"That's when you should have started to pray," she said. "What did you do to get sent to the penitentiary that first time?"

"Turn to the right, it was a wall," The Misfit said, looking up again at the cloudless sky. "Turn to the left, it was a wall. Look up it was a ceiling, look down it was a floor. I forgot what I done, lady. I set there and set there, trying to remember what it was I done and I ain't recalled it to this day. Oncet in a while, I would think it was coming to me, but it never come."

"Maybe they put you in by mistake," the old lady said vaguely.

"Nome," he said. "It wasn't no mistake. They had the papers on me."

"You must have stolen something," she said.

The Misfit sneered slightly. "Nobody had nothing I wanted," he said. "It was a head-doctor at the penitentiary said what I had done was kill my daddy but I known that for a lie. My daddy died in nineteen ought nineteen of the epidemic flu and I never had a thing to do with it. He was buried in the Mount Hopewell Baptist churchyard and you can go there and see for yourself."

"If you would pray," the old lady said, "Jesus would help you."

"That's right," The Misfit said.

"Well then, why don't you pray?" she asked trembling with delight suddenly.

"I don't want no hep," he said. "I'm doing all right by myself."

Bobby Lee and Hiram came ambling back from the woods. Bobby Lee was dragging a yellow shirt with bright blue parrots in it.

"Throw me that shirt, Bobby Lee," The Misfit said. The shirt came flying at him and landed on his shoulder and he put it on. The grandmother couldn't name what the shirt reminded her of. "No, lady," The Misfit said while he was buttoning it up, "I found out the crime don't matter. You can do one thing or you can do another, kill a man or take a tire off his car, because sooner or later you're going to forget what it was you done and just be punished for it."

The children's mother had begun to make heaving noises as if she couldn't get her breath. "Lady," he asked, "would you and that little girl like to step off yonder with Bobby Lee and Hiram and join your husband?"

"Yes, thank you," the mother said faintly. Her left arm dangled helplessly and she was holding the baby, who had gone to sleep, in the other. "Hep that lady up, Hiram," The Misfit said as she struggled to climb out of the ditch, "and Bobby Lee, you hold onto that little girl's hand."

"I don't want to hold hands with him," June Star said. "He reminds me of a pig."

The fat boy blushed and laughed and caught her by the arm and pulled her off into the woods after Hiram and her mother.

Alone with The Misfit, the grandmother found that she had lost her voice. There was not a cloud in the sky nor any sun. There was nothing around her but woods. She wanted to tell him that he must pray. She opened and closed her mouth several times before anything came out. Finally she found herself saying, "Jesus. Jesus," meaning Jesus will help you, but the way she was saying it, it sounded as if she might be cursing.

"Yes'm, The Misfit said as if he agreed. "Jesus thown everything off balance. It was the same case with Him as with me except He hadn't committed any crime and they could prove I had committed one because they had the papers on me. Of course," he said, "they never shown me my papers. That's why I sign myself now. I said long ago, you get you a signature and sign everything you do and keep a copy of it. Then you'll know what you done and you can hold up the crime to the punishment and see do they match and in the end you'll have something to prove you ain't been treated right. I call myself The Misfit," he said, "because I can't make what all I done wrong fit what all I gone through in punishment."

There was a piercing scream from the woods, followed closely by a pistol report. "Does it seem right to you, lady, that one is punished a heap and another ain't punished at all?"

"Jesus!" the old lady cried. "You've got good blood! I know you wouldn't shoot a lady! I know you come from nice people! Pray! Jesus, you ought not to shoot a lady. I'll give you all the money I've got!"

"Lady," The Misfit said, looking beyond her far into the woods, "there never was a body that give the undertaker a tip."

There were two more pistol reports and the grandmother raised her head like a parched old turkey hen crying for water and called, "Bailey Boy, Bailey Boy!" as if her heart would break.

"Jesus was the only One that ever raised the dead," The Misfit continued, "and He shouldn't have done it. He thown everything off balance. If He did what He said, then it's nothing for you to do but thow away everything and follow Him, and if He didn't, then it's nothing for you to do but enjoy the few minutes you got left the best way you can – by killing somebody or burning down his house or doing some other meanness to him. No pleasure but meanness," he said and his voice had become almost a snarl.

"Maybe He didn't raise the dead," the old lady mumbled, not knowing what she was saying and feeling so dizzy that she sank down in the ditch with her legs twisted under her.

"I wasn't there so I can't say He didn't," The Misfit said. "I wisht I had of been there," he said, hitting the ground with his fist. "It ain't right I wasn't there because if I had of been there I would of known. Listen lady," he said in a high voice, "if I had of been there I would of known and I wouldn't be like I am now." His voice seemed about to crack and the grandmother's head cleared for an instant. She saw the man's face twisted close to her own as if he were going to cry and she murmured, "Why you're one of my babies. You're one of my own children!" She reached out and touched him on the shoulder. The Misfit sprang back as if a snake had bitten him and shot her three times through the chest. Then he put his gun down on the ground and took off his glasses and began to clean them.

Hiram and Bobby Lee returned from the woods and stood over the ditch, looking down at the grandmother who half sat and half lay in a puddle of blood with her legs crossed under her like a child's and her face smiling up at the cloudless sky.

Without his glasses, The Misfit's eyes were red - rimmed and pale and defenseless - looking. "Take her off and thow her where you thown the others," he said, picking up the cat that was rubbing itself against his leg.

"She was a talker, wasn't she?" Bobby Lee said, sliding down the ditch with a yodel.

"She would of been a good woman," The Misfit said, "if it had been somebody there to shoot her every minute of her life."

"Some fun! " Bobby Lee said.

"Shut up, Bobby Lee," The Misfit said. "It's no real pleasure in life."

Unit 12
William Styron (1925–2006)
威廉·斯泰伦

作者简介

威廉·斯泰伦，小说家，1925年出生于弗吉尼亚的纽波特纽斯(Newport News)。他的作品以激烈的悲剧性情节而著称。二战期间，他曾在美国海军陆战队服役。1947年，他从杜克大学毕业。1945年以来，斯泰伦开始发表短篇小说。作为“南方派”作家，他的作品既带有显著的南方特点，又不局限于南方小说的思想主题，写作风格变化多样，尤其擅长通过人物的千姿百态来戏剧化地表现时代特征。1951年，他的第一部长篇小说《在黑暗中躺下》(*Lie Down in Darkness*)讲述了生活在弗吉尼亚的一个富裕家庭的悲剧故事。主人公佩登，在充满自私、背叛、嫉妒、仇恨、报复和乱伦倾向的家庭中逐渐变得性格扭曲、行为变态，最终自杀身亡。小说运用象征、意识流等技巧，在修辞方面以福克纳为楷模，发表后赢得了评论界的高度评价，并获得美国文学艺术学会颁发的“罗马奖”。《纵火焚屋》(*Set This House on Fire*,1960)的发表引起了评论界褒贬不一的评价，但作品鲜明的存在主义倾向备受法国读者的青睐。1967年，斯泰伦发表《纳特·特纳的自白》(*The Confessions of Nat Turner*)，故事基于1831年发生在弗吉尼亚州的黑奴暴动的历史事实来展开。在这部小说中，他提出了许多探讨文学和历史真实性的复杂问题，并荣获“普利策奖”。1979年，他最杰出的作品《索菲的选择》(*Sophie's Choice*)问世，讲述波兰妇女索菲在奥斯维辛集中营里的悲惨遭遇，她被迫在自己的一对儿女中选择一个，把另一个送往焚尸炉。小说把纳粹的暴行与美国南方的蓄奴制并置，使读者对历史中践踏人性的罪行、善与恶的较量以及宗教信仰等问题进行深刻反思。这部小说结构精致，规模宏大，把事实与自传、历史与虚构结合在一起，标志着斯泰伦在文学创作生涯上的一次超越。小说获全国图书奖，并在1982年改拍成电影，斯泰伦再次受到世人瞩目。

他的作品还包括：《漫长的行程》(*The Long March*, 1953)，《看得见的黑暗》(*Darkness Visible: A Memoir*, 1998)，《潮汐镇的早晨》(*A Tidewater Morning: Three Tales of Youth*, 1993)。在艺术形式方面，他的作品受到南方文学传统和20世纪哲学、文学思潮的双重影响。一方面，福克纳的文学观和创作风格对斯泰伦的文学创作产生了深远的影响。和福克纳一样，斯泰伦着重描写和分析人物内心世界的冲突并围绕这一问题进行创作；另一方面，斯泰伦对他那一时代的文化思潮非常敏感。他从意识流、心理现实主义等新的写作技巧以及现代文学传统中汲取了丰富的营养。斯泰伦曾被评为“世界十大文化名人之一",曾是全美文学艺术院和科学艺术学会成员。2006 年 11 月 1 日,威廉·斯泰伦死于肺病,享年81 岁。

作品导读

The Confessions of Nat Turner, the novel by William Styron, was published in 1967 and awarded Pulitzer Prize. As the "Author's Note" to the novel indicates, Styron based his story on an early pamphlet, *The Confessions of Nat Turner*, transcribed from Turner's narrative to a white lawyer Thomas R. Gray about Turner's role in the 1831 slave rebellion. It stirs much controversy as soon as it is published, mainly from blacks, who consider the interpretation of Turner to be inaccurate. Presented as a first-person narrative from an African American rebel's point of view, the novel tells the story of an actual slave uprising organized by a slave named Nat Turner in the year 1831. William Styron calls the novel "a meditation on history".

In this novel, Styron allows himself great creative license in reconstructing events, developing the fictional Nat in opposite to the cultural portrait of Turner as a heroic slave. Imagining much of Turner's youth and early manhood before the rebellion that he headed at the age of 31, Styron in frequently rhetorical and pseudo-biblical style has Turner recall his religious faith and his power of preaching to other slaves. Embittered and frustrated by the evils of slavery, including the failure to obtain the freedom promised by his first master, Turner is portrayed as unable to find surcease in human relations, black or white, sexually or spiritually. Impelled by supernatural visions, on 21 August 1831 basically kind black minister Nat Turner (1800 - 1831) becomes the leader and raises a brief but bloody slave insurrection in Southampton County, Virginia. In about two days' time, Turner and a small band of slaves and free blacks kill fifty - five white people, including many women and children. Hundreds of local militiamen and vigilantes from Virginia and nearby North Carolina respond to crush the insurrection. The violent insurrection is put down with great speed and brutality, killing many of the participants plus dozens of innocent blacks. Surviving participants are captured and tried immediately; many are sentenced to death, with the exception of Turner, who evades capture for two months. He is eventually found and then executed on 11 November 1831.

The author's introduction consists of an excerpt from the historical document, *The Confessions of Nat Turner,* written by T. R. Gray in November of 1831, shortly after the capture of Nathaniel Turner. In the introduction to this document, titled "To the Public," Gray briefly summarizes the capture of Nat Turner on October 30, 1831 after the "band of savages" which he led had already been caught and dealt with by Southern justice. In the following excerpt, Part Ⅲ: Study War depicts Turner's inability to participate in the actual bloodshed once the rebellion gets under way. As his band of armed slaves moves from farm to farm, Nat finds himself in danger of losing his place as leader. He is nauseous at the sight of gore and unable to kill whites until, as narrated in the excerpt, he is taunted by his co-conspirator, the ex-wielding Will.

作品选读

The Confessions of Nat Turner
Author's Note

In August, 1831, in a remote region of southeastern Virginia, there took place the only effective, sustained revolt in the annals of American Negro slavery. The initial passage of this book, entitled "To the Public," is the preface to the single significant contemporary document concerning this insurrection – a brief pamphlet of some twenty pages called "The Confessions of Nat Turner," published in Richmond early in the next year, parts of which have been incorporated in this book. During the narrative that follows I have rarely departed from the known facts about Nat Turner and the revolt of which he was the leader. However, in those areas where there is little knowledge in regard to Nat, his early life, and the motivations for the revolt (and such knowledge is lacking most of the time), I have allowed myself the utmost freedom of imagination in reconstructing events – yet I trust remaining within the bounds of what meager enlightenment history has left us about the institution of slavery. The relativity of time allows us elastic definitions: the year 1831 was, simultaneously, a long time ago and only yesterday. Perhaps the reader will wish to draw a moral from this narrative, but it has been my own intention to try to re-create a man and his era, and to produce a work that is less an "historical novel" in conventional terms than a meditation on history.

WILLIAM STYRON

Roxbury, Connecticut

New Year's Day, 1967

To the Public

The late insurrection in Southampton has greatly excited the public mind and led to a thousand idle, exaggerated and mischievous reports. It is the first instance in our history of an open rebellion of the slaves, and attended with such atrocious circumstances of cruelty and destruction, as could not fail to leave a deep impression, not only upon the minds of the community where this fearful tragedy was wrought, but throughout every portion of our country in which this population is to be found. Public curiosity had been on the stretch to understand the origin and progress of this dreadful conspiracy, and the motives which influence its diabolical actors. The insurgent slaves had all been destroyed, or apprehended, tried and executed (with the exception of the leader) without revealing any thing at all satisfactory, as to the motives which governed them, or the means by which they expected to accomplish their object. Every thing connected with this sad affair was wrapt in mystery, until Nat Turner, the leader of this ferocious band, whose name has resounded throughout our widely extended empire was captured. This "great Bandit" was taken by a single individual, in a cave near the residence of his late owner, on Sunday, the thirtieth of October, without attempting to make the slightest resistance, and on the following day lodged in the jail of the County. His captor was Benjamin Phipps, armed with a shot gun well charged. Nat's only weapon was a small light sword which he immediately surrendered and begged that his life might be spared. Since his confinement, by permission of the Jailor, I have had ready access to him, and, finding that he was willing to make a full and free confession of the origin, progress and consummation of the insurrectory movements of the slaves of which he was the contriver and head, I determined for the gratification of public curiosity to commit his statements to writing and publish them, with little or no variation, from his own words. That this is a faithful record of his confessions, the annexed certificate of the County Court of Southampton, will attest. They certainly bear one stamp of truth and sincerity. He makes no attempt (as all the other insurgents who were examined did) to exculpate himself, but frankly acknowledges his full participation in all the guilt of the transaction. He was not only the contriver of the conspiracy, but gave the first blow toward its execution.

It will thus appear, that whilst every thing upon the surface of society wore a calm and peaceful aspect; whilst not one note of preparation was heard to warn the devoted inhabitants of woe and death, a gloomy fanatic was revolving in the recesses of his own dark, bewildered and overwrought mind schemes of indiscriminate massacre to the whites. Schemes too fearfully executed as far as his fiendish band proceeded in their desolating march. No cry for mercy penetrated their flinty bosoms. No acts of remembered kindness made the least impression upon these remorseless murderers. Men, women and children, from hoary age to helpless infancy, were involved in the same cruel fate. Never did a band of savages do their work of death more unsparingly. Apprehension for their own personal safety seems to have been the only principle of restraint in the whole course of their bloody proceedings. And it is not the least remarkable feature in this horrid transaction, that a band actuated by such hellish purposes, should have resisted so feebly, when met by the whites in arms. Desperation alone, one would think, might have led to greater efforts. Each individual sought his own safety either in concealment, or by returning home, with the hope that his participation might escape detection, and all were shot down in the course of a few days, or captured and brought to trial and punishment. Nat has survived all his followers, and the gallows will speedily close his career. His own account of the conspiracy is submitted to the public, without comment. It reads an awful, and it is hoped, a useful lesson as to the operations of a mind like his, endeavoring to grapple with things beyond its reach. How it first became bewildered and confounded, and finally corrupted and led to the conception and perpetration of the most atrocious and heart-rending deeds. It is calculated also to demonstrate the policy of our laws in restraint of this class of our population, and to induce all those entrusted with their execution, as well as our citizens generally, to see that they are strictly and rigidly enforced. If Nat's statements can be relied on, the insurrection in this county was entirely local, and his designs confident but to a few, and these in his immediate vicinity. It was not instigated by motives of revenge or sudden anger, but the results of long deliberation, and a settled purpose of mind. The offspring of gloomy fanaticism, acting upon materials but too well prepared for such impressions, it will be long remembered in the annals of our country and many a mother as she presses her darling infant to her bosom, will shudder at the recollection of Nat Turner, and his band of ferocious miscreants.

Believing the following narrative, by removing doubts and conjectures from the public mind which otherwise must have remained, would give general satisfactions, it is respectfully submitted to the public by their ob't serv't.

T. R. GRAY

Jerusalem, Southampton County, Va., Nov. 5, 1831

We the undersigned, members of the court convened at Jerusalem, on Saturday, the fifth day of Nov., 1831, for the trial of Nat, alias Nat Turner a negro slave, late the property of Putnam Moore, deceased, do hereby certify that the confessions of Nat, to Thomas R. Gray, was read to him in our presence, and that furthermore, when called upon by the presiding Magistrate of the Court, to state if he had anything to say, why sentence of death should not be passed upon him, replied he had nothing further than he had communicated to Mr. Gray. Given under our hands and seals at Jerusalem, this 5th day of November, 1831.

JEREMIAH COBB, [seal]
THOMAS PRETLOW, [seal]
JAMES W. PARKER, [seal]
CARR BOWERS, [seal]
SAMUEL B. HINES, [seal]
ORRIS A. BROWNE, [seal]

Part Ⅲ: Study War

["TO DRAW THE BLOOD OF WHITE MEN"]

Mist the color of pearl hung over the countryside several hours past dawn when a dozen of us stopped to have breakfast of bacon and fruit in the woods near Mrs. Whitehead's. The sun had begun to burn off the haze, cloaking the day in muggy heat. During the night we had successfully attacked six homesteads and plantations, and seventeen white people lay dead. Of these, Will had accounted for seven; the rest were apportioned among Hark, Henry, Sam, and Jack. No one had escaped our ax and sword, and thus no one had survived to raise the alarm. The surprise we had effected was stunning and complete. Our campaign so far had been perfectly silent, perfectly lethal. I knew that if we were by now blessed by good fortune to negotiate the upper loop of the "S" with as much thoroughness and quiet, murderous precision as we had managed so far, we might not have to risk using gunfire at all until we were very close to Jerusalem. Our present force had grown, as I had expected, to eighteen; nine of these men now had horses – including four magnificent Arabian stallions we had taken from the Reese plantation. We were bountifully supplied with swords; broadaxes, and guns. Two young Negroes who had joined us at the Newsom place were drunk and clearly terrified, but the remainder of the new recruits flexed themselves and strutted about beneath the trees in fighting mettle. Yet I was still restless and troubled. In desperation I wondered if ever a commander had been beset by such a wicked dilemma – his authority, his very being, threatened to its roots by the near-mutinous insolence of a subaltern whom he could not afford to lose, much less send away. Partly in an effort to free myself momentarily from Will's deranging presence, but also because the place was an objective in my plans, I had just before dawn sent Will and four others under the command of Sam to sack the Bryant estate, which lay three miles or so off to the east. Sam had of course grown up with Will at Nathaniel Francis's, and once or twice they had run off together; I thought that for a while at least, Sam might be able to control him and in the process calm him down. At the Bryant place there were half a dozen people who must be put to death, several recruits to get, and a number of swift, gallant quarter horses that would be invaluable for surprise attacks. Because of the isolation of the estate I told Sam that they could use guns. It should be easy work. We waited in the hushed hot woods for this group to rejoin us before we set out in full strength on the next stage of our attack.

I did not feel at all well; the long siege of vomiting that overcame me at the Reese place had left me sweaty and queasy and weak, with racking recurrent spasms of pain in my stomach. A catbird squawked and chattered close by in the woods. "Hush up!" my mind cried. It had become fearfully hot – the sun glowering down already through a canopy of haze no longer milky-pure but leaden, oppressive, hostile. Trying to conceal from the rest of the men the tremors that had begun to shake my body, I ate no bacon or peaches but withdrew alone with my map and plans into a clump of trees. I left Nelson and Henry in charge of the troops. A creek ran nearby and as I made brief notations of our progress on the map I heard the men watering the horses with the copper buckets that were part of our plunder. There was an air of excitement and high spirits among the Negroes in the clearing. I could hear their laughter; even though some were drunk, I wished that I might share their swagger and boisterousness, wished I could still the trepidation gnawing at the inside of me, slow the anxious beating of my heart. Finally I offered up a prayer, asking the Lord to strengthen my resolve as he had done with David, and some of the sickness and vertigo went away. When Sam's troops reappeared in the clearing at about half past eight I felt partially revived and I rose and strode out to greet them. Those six had now become ten – several mounted on the Bryants' dashing quarter horses – I could see by the sumptuous new leather boots which Sam wore that their errand had been successful in more ways than one. I had not actively discouraged a certain amount of looting; it was plain that to try and forbid any one of this disinherited and outcast army from grabbing baubles and trophies and plums would be like attempting to prevent a newly uncaged pigeon from seeking the air. At the same time I was determined to enforce limits: we must not be encumbered, we must not be impeded, and when I saw that Will had carried off from the

Bryant place an enormous gilt-framed wall mirror I knew that it was now or never again – I had to call him down at once.

As I walked toward the group I could tell that Will had made himself both hero and cynosure of the mission. Face and hands streaked with blood as he swung about in the saddle, he wore a blue jacket whose shoulders glittered with the epaulets of an army colonel, and an officer's braided cap rode piratically on his head, bobbing about as he harangued the new field-hand recruits with a triumphant jabber of disconnected words and sounds: "De axes you gotta keep shahp, man!" he crowed. "Shahp as piss-ice, das what! If'n de ax ain' shahp de red juice don'run! Das right! Das how come I got de mirrow, so's I can see how shahp is de ax!" The man and boys around him howled with laughter. They were flecked with dry strings of gore on pants and boots and bare black arms. They leaned forward toward him from their saddles or, dismounting, gazed up at him with flashing white teeth, in thrall to his mad and singsong apostrophe. The Bryant Negroes, three of whom I had never seen before, were joyously, seraphically drunk, flourishing half-gallon jugs of brandy. The mixture of bloodshed and freedom had set them afloat upon a cloud of delirium, their laughter and hysteria seemed to soar up an blow like a gust of wind through the very trees. To them Will, not I, was the black avatar of their deliverance. One of those boys, a light-skinned lad of around eighteen with rotted teeth, had so lost control of himself in laughter that he had wet his pants in a flood. "I'se runnin' de show now!" Will cried. "I'se de one dat make de ax sing 'Zip Coon.' Will he de gin'ral now!" He spurred his mount, one of the Arabians, and at the same time checked in his reins and the great foaming stallion like Pegasus leaped skyward with a frenzied scream. "Will he de gin'ral now!" he shouted once more, and as the horse's front legs came down to earth the satanic mirror snared the sun blindingly, threw back a shimmering vista of sky, leaves, earth, and a blur of black and brown faces that whirled in a glassy void, then vanished. "Whoa dere, Roscoe!" Will bellowed at the horse, stopping him. "I'se runnin' de show, hawse, not you! I boss ob de ruction!"

"No, I'se runnin' the show!" I called then. The Negroes fell silent. "We get that straight right now. You ain't runnin' no show. Now drop that mirror on the ground. White people can see that two miles off. I mean what I says."

From the saddle he regarded me with haughtiness and disdain. Against all will or desire I felt my heart pounding, and I knew that my voice had cracked, revealing fear. In vain I tried to keep tremor from coursing visibly along the length of my arms. For a long moment Will said nothing, casting down upon me his contemptuous gaze. Then he stuck out his tongue, red as a slice of watermelon, and made a long, slow, circular licking journey around the edges of his pink lips – a gesture of droll and lunatic derision. Some of the men behind me began to giggle, scuffling their feet in pleasure. "I doesn't has to gib you no mirrow," he said in a mincing, surly voice. "An' I isn't gwine gib you no mirrow. So stick dat in yo' ass, preacher man!"

"Drop that there mirror on the ground!" I commanded him again. I watched him tighten his grip on the haft of his broadax – naked threat – and panic swept over me in an icy wave. I

saw my whole mission burnt to ashes in the fire of his madman's insensate eyes. "Drop it!" I said.

"Preacher man," he drawled, rolling his eyes comically at the new men, "preacher man, you jes' better step aside an' let de ax man run de show. 'Cause, preacher man, less'n you can handle de ax you cain't handle de army." And he gave a vicious yank upward on the thick blood-drenched haft of the ax and pulled the mirror tightly, possessively against the saddle. "Preacher man" – and his voice became a snarl – "less'n you kin make de ax sing a tune you is *all done*."

I do not know what might have happened if at that point Nelson had not intervened, bringing to a halt this confrontation which had so nearly broken me. Perhaps my other close followers would have rallied to my aid and we would then have proceeded onward in much the same fashion as we had planned. Perhaps Will might have cut me down on the spot, then in demented command ridden off with the others to chaos; surely they could not have gotten far without my knowledge of a strategic route, and my mission would have been set down as a "localized disturbance" involving "a few disgruntled darkies" rather than the earthquake it truly became. Whatever, Nelson rescued the situation by donning at the critical moment the mantle of authority which – in Will's eyes, at least – I lacked or never had the right to own. I cannot explain his method, his charm's workings. It might have been Nelson's older age and manner – that methodical, muscular, laconic, self-assured air of experience he carried, his quality of brawny discretion and worldly wisdom: these were fatherly attributes in a way, and through some alchemy they had gained Will's loony respect if not his fear. Hardly before I was aware that he had come between us, I heard Nelson's voice and saw him reach up and clutch the bridle of Will's horse. "Slow down dere, sweet," he said sharply. "Nat he do run de show! Now slow down, sweet, and drap dat mirrow on de ground!" It was the tone one uses in addressing a likeable but headstrong child – a voice not so much enraged as vexed, cross, severe, unmistakably meant to be obeyed. It cut through to Will like a hickory stick – "Drap it!" he again commanded, and the mirror slid from Will's fingers and toppled unbroken to earth.

"Nat he still de gin'ral," Nelson rasped, bristling as he glared upward. "You better study 'bout dat, sweet, or me an' you's really gwine hab a rookus! Now you jes' cool off yo' black head!" Then he turned and lumbered back to the cooking fire beneath the trees, leaving Will briefly chastened, sulky-looking, and abashed.

Yet although this crisis had been disposed of, I could not rest easy. I was sure that Will's frightening competition for power had not been buried by the stand-off but simply deflected, put aside, and his bitter, contemptuous words – thrown at me, a challenge – had made me all the more panicky over the knowledge that I was unable to kill. Of the others of my force, only Nelson had failed to spill blood, and he not through any reluctance but because he had simply lacked the occasion. And as for the rest – Henry and Sam and Austin and Jack, my closest followers: was it only my imagination that caused me to feel in their manner toward me a coolness, to sense in the way they had spoken to me in the last hours a new-found suspicion and mistrust, a withdrawal, as if by failing to perform, even as ritual, that act which each of them had done I had somehow begun to lose a sure grip upon my rights and the respect due me as a commander? Certainly in days and weeks past I had never pretended that I would shirk this duty. Had I not told them so many times: To draw the blood of white men is holy in God's eyes? Now in my impotence and irresolution I felt beleaguered not only by Will's obscene jibes and threats but by fear that even those closest to me might abandon faith in my leadership if I persisted in this womanish failure to strike down white flesh. Heat blazed upon the clearing, still another catbird screeched in the humming woods. Dizzily, I stole off to retch dry spasms in the bushes. I felt mortally sick and the aching self beneath my skin pulsed and burned with fever. But at nine o'clock or thereabouts I returned to the clearing to assemble the company. And in this condition – shivering, ill, nearly torn apart by frights and apprehensions that I never thought God would permit – I was by providence hurried toward Margaret Whitehead, and our last meeting...

To Richard Whitehead on his path toward the hogpen, standing alone beneath the hot morning sun in a patch of green cotton, our approach was likely that of the hosts of Armageddon. Twenty Negroes and more in a jagged line – all mounted, light glistening from ax and gun and sword – who burst from the distant woods in a cloud of dust which, obscuring us at the same time that it revealed our relentless purpose and design, must have appeared to him borne from the hellish bowels of the earth: the sight was surely a reenactment of all the fears and visions of black devils and heathen hordes that had ever imperiled his Methodist sanctity. Yet he too, like Travis, like all the others lulled by a history which had never known our kind before, was doubtless touched with disbelief at the same time that a portion of his mind grappled with the horror – and who knows but whether this was not the reason that he stood rooted to the ground like a cotton plant, his bland divine's sun-pink face uptilted to the sky in vague bewilderment as we drew closer, perhaps hoping that this demonic apparition or vision or whatever, the result of undigested bad bacon or troubled sleep or August heat or all three, would go away. But the furor! The noise of pounding hooves and clanking steel and the panting lungs of horses and the hoots and harsh whispers of breath, closer now, from those grinning nigger faces! Merciful Lord! Such noise was a part of no apparition; besides, it was becoming almost intolerable! He seemed to raise his hands as if to stop up his ears, rattled a little in the legs, made no other motion, stood immobile and perplexed even as the two outriders, Hark and Henry, enveloped him on either side, and slackening pace only long enough to take aim, struck him dead with two swift hatchet chops to the skull. From the house I heard a woman shriek.

"First Troop!" I cried. "Secure the woods!" I had just seen the new overseer, a man named Pretlow, and his two young white helpers jump from the steaming still and streak for the woods, the boys running, Pretlow astride a crippled barrel-bellied mule. "Git after them!" I cried to Henry and his men. "They won't git far!" I wheeled and shouted to the others: "Second and Third Troops, take the gun room! On to the house! "

Ah God! At that moment I was overcome again by such dizziness that I pulled in my horse and got down instantly and stood there in the hot field, leaning with my head against the saddle. I shut my eyes; needlepoints of red light floated through the dark, my lungs were filled with dust. When the horse stirred, I rocked as if in a rowboat. Across the field screams of terror came from the house; one stricken female cry, prolonged and wavering, ceased with shocking suddenness. I heard a voice nearby, Austin's, and looked up to see him riding bareback one of the stallions, with a Bryant Negro seated behind. I gave the other boy my mount and told them both to join the troop chasing Pretlow and his helpers at the edge of the woods. I stumbled, fell to my knees, rose quickly.

"You's sick, Nat, isn't you?" said Austin, peering down.

"Go on," I replied, "go on! " They galloped off.

On foot now skirted Richard Whitehead's corpse lying face down between two rows of cotton. I walked unsteadily, following along the old familiar log fence which I myself had helped build, separating field and barnyard. My men in the house, in the stable, and in the barn, were making a barbaric racket. Still more screams erupted from the house: I remembered that Mrs. Whitehead's summer-visiting daughters were home. I clambered over the fence, nearly falling. As I grabbed for the post, I glimpsed the gross old house nigger Hubbard, at gunpoint, being forced into a wagon by Henry and another: captive eunuch, he would not go with us willingly, but tied up in the cart with other pet collected coons, would surely go. "Lawd, sweet Lawd! " he boohooed to the skies as they shoved him up into the wagon, and he sobbed as if his heart would perish. At that moment I rounded the corner of the oxen barn and looked toward the porch of the house. There deserted of all save those two acting out their final tableau – the tar-black man and the woman, bone-white, bone-rigid with fear beyond telling, pressed urgently together against the door in a simulacrum of shattered oneness and heartsick farewell – the porch seemed washed for an instant in light that flowed from the dawn of my own beginning. Then I saw Will draw back as if from a kiss and with a swift sideways motion nearly decapitate Mrs. Whitehead in a single stroke.

And he had seen me. "Dar she is, preacher man, dey's one left! " he howled. "An' she all your'n! Right by de cellah do'! Go git her, preacher man! " he taunted me in his wild rage. "If'n you cain't make de red juice run you cain't run de army! "

Soundless, uttering not a word, Margaret Whitehead rose up and scrambled from her hiding place beyond the sheltering wall of the cellar door and fled me – fled me like the wind. Fleet and light she ran, after the fashion of a child, with bare arms stiffly outstretched, brown hair tied with a bow and tossing this way and that above a blue taffeta dress, pressed to her back in a sweaty oblong of deeper blue. I had not caught sight of her face and realized it was she only when, disappearing around the corner of the house, the silk ribbon which I had seen before fell from her hair and rippled briefly on the air before fluttering to earth.

"Dar! She gone! " Will roared, gesturing with his broadax to the other Negroes, who had begun to straggle across the yard. "Does you want her, preacher man, or she fo' me?"

Ah, how I want her, I thought, and unsheathed my sword. She had run into the hayfield, and when I too rounded the corner of the house I thought she had slipped away, for there was no one in sight. But she had merely fallen down in the waist-high grass and as I stood there she rose again – a small and slender figure in the distance – and resumed her flight toward a crooked far-off fence. I ran headlong into the field. The air was alive with grasshoppers: they skimmed and flickered across my path, brushed my skin with brittle momentary sting. I felt the sweat streaming into my eyes. The sword in my right hand hung like the weight of all the earth. Yet I gained on Margaret quickly, for she had tired fast, and I reached her just as she was trying to clamber over the rotted pole fence. She made no sound, uttered no word, did not turn to plead or contend or resist or even wonder. Nor did I speak – our last encounter may have been the quietest that ever was. Beneath her foot one of the poles gave way in crunching powdery collapse and she tripped forward, bare arms still outthrust as if to welcome someone beloved and long-unseen. As she stumbled thus, then recovered, I heard for the first time her hurtful, ragged breathing, and it was with this sound in my ears that I plunged the sword into her side, just below and behind her breast. She screamed then at last. Litheness, grace, the body's nimble felicity – all fled her like ghosts. She crumpled to earth, limp, a rag, and as she fell I stabbed her again in the same place, or near it, where pulsing blood already encrimsoned the taffeta's blue. There was no scream this time although the echo of the first sang in my ears like a far angelic cry; when I turned aside from her fallen body I was troubled by a steady soughing noise like the rise and fall of a summer tempest in a grove of pines and realized that it was the clamor of my own breathing as it welled up in sobs from my chest.

I lurched away from her through the field, calling out to myself like one bereft of mind. Yet hardly had I taken a dozen steps when I heard her voice, weak, frail, almost without breath, not so much voice as memory – faint as if from some distant and half-forgotten lawn of childhood: Oh Nat I hurt so. Please kill me Nat I hurt so.

I stopped and looked back. "*Die*, God damn you white soul," I wept. "Die!"

Oh Nat please kill me I hurt so.

"Die! Die! Die! Die!"

The sword fell from my hand. I returned to her side and looked down. Her head was cradled against the inside of her arm, as if she had composed herself for sleep, and all the chestnut streaming luxuriance of her hair had fallen in a tangle amid the hayfield's parched and fading green. Grasshoppers stitched and stirred in restless fidget among the weeds, darting about her face.

"I hurt so," I heard her whisper.

"Shut your eyes," I said. I reached down to search with my fingers for a firm length of fence rail and I could sense once more her close girl-smell and the fragrance of lavender, bitter in my nostrils, and sweet. "Shut your eyes," I told her quickly. Then when I raised the rail above her head she gazed at me, as if past the imponderable vista of her anguish, with a grave and drowsy tenderness such as I had never known, spoke some words too soft to hear and, saying no more, closed her eyes upon all madness, illusion, error, dream, and strife. So I brought the timber down and she was swiftly gone, and I hurled the hateful, shattered club far up into the weeds.

For how long I aimlessly circled her body – prowled around the corners of the field in haphazard quest for nothing, like some roaming dog – how long this went on I do not recollect. The sun rose higher, boiling; my own flesh was incandescent, and when at the farm I heard the men call for me their voices were untold distances away. By the edge of the woods I found myself seated on a log, head in my hands, unaccountably thinking of ancient moments of childhood – warm rain, leaves, a whippoorwill, rushing mill wheels, jew's-harp strumming – centuries before. Then I arose again and resumed my meaningless and ordained circuit of her body, not near it yet ever within sight as if that crumpled blue were the center of an orbit around whose path I must make a ceaseless pilgrimage. And once in my strange journey I thought I heard again her whispery voice, thought I saw her rise from the blazing field with arms outstretched as if to a legion of invisible onlookers, her brown hair and innocent school gown teased by the wind as she cried: "Oh, I would fain swoon into an eternity of love!" But then she vanished before my eyes – melted instantly like an image carved of air and light – and I turned away at last and went back to join my men.

Unit 13 Reynolds Price (1933–)

雷诺兹·普莱斯

作者简介

雷诺兹·普莱斯，1933 年 2 月出生于北卡罗来纳州 (North Carolina)。美国南方小说家、诗人、剧作家、圣经翻译和随笔作家，擅长撰写回忆录，尤其以长篇小说创作著称。他的父亲所罗门·普莱斯 (William Solomon Price)是一个电器推销员。父亲的酗酒使全家经常陷入困境，普莱斯在贫穷和不稳定中度过了他的童年，在短篇小说《陪伴死者》(*The Company of the Dead*)中沃特斯(Kennon Walters)身上就有他父亲的影子。1951 年他进入杜克大学学习，并立志成为一名作家。1955 年他获得“罗氏奖学金(Rhodes Scholarship)”而进入牛津大学默顿学院(Merton College)研究英国文学。在学习期间发表了一篇研究米尔顿的论文和一些短篇小说。父亲因癌症去世后，普莱斯担负起照顾母亲及弟弟生活的重任。从 25 岁至今，普莱斯一直在杜克大学任教并从事小说创作。他的创作傲然沿袭南方小说的地域、家族等主题和传统的写作手法，传统守旧却不落俗套，他的作品在南方文学的沿革中占有非常重要的地位，他重新点亮了南方区域作家逐渐褪色的光环。

像珀西和奥康纳一样，普莱斯对基督教的笃信和对耶稣的迷恋与他患过的一场大病密切相关。1989 年普莱斯因脊髓癌症导致瘫痪，但普莱斯没有被病魔打倒，依旧笔耕不辍。普莱斯的小说大多以北卡莱罗纳州东部的家乡为背景，以那里的人民为原型，讲述过去与家庭之间的关系，并涉及原罪。1962 年他的第一部小说《长久而美好的生活》(*A Long and Happy Life*)出版后得到一致好评并多次再版，获“威廉·福克纳基金奖”第一名。他的长篇小说《凯特·维登》(*Kate Vaiden*,1986)描写爱情、家庭和责任，获“全国评论界书评奖”(*The National Book Critics Circle Award*)。而最能反映普莱斯创作雄心和家庭生活之苦恼的作品是他的小说三部曲《地衣之表》(*The Surface of Earth*,1975)及其两部续集《休息的承诺》(*The Promise of Rest*,1995)和《光明之源》(*The Source of Light*,1981)，讲述了梅菲尔德家族和肯德尔家族四代人近一个世纪的故事，小说中弥漫着过去以及逃离过去对个人和家庭造成的影响。

他的主要作品还包括：《短篇小说集》(*The Collected Stories*,1994)，该书获“普利策奖”；两部回忆录，《记忆犹新》(*Clear Pictures*,1989)和《重生：我打败了脊椎里的恶魔！》(*A Whole New Life*,1994)，后者主要讲述了作者与脊髓癌抗争的故事；小说《慷慨的人》(*A Generous Man*,1966)、《好心》(Good Hearts,1988)和小说三部曲《大圆弧》(*A Great*

Circle,1975, 1981, 1995);诗集《冰的法则》(*The Laws of Ice*,1985)和儿童小说《完美朋友》(*A Perfect Friend*,2000);等等。

作品导读

Price sets much of his fiction in his "home country" of eastern North Carolina, and believes, as did Flannery O'Connor, that the Southern grotesque is a realistic response to small-town life in which abnormity or eccentricity was not concealed. Price also observed in a 1990 interview: "So much of the Southern impulse in the arts has been comic, in the very broadest sense of the word 'comedy'. It's comedy that arises out of a tragic sense of life or a sense of the pain and difficulty in life."

The Company of the Dead narrates several tragedies, not the least of which is its narrator's long life lived without "the black heart's blood of actual love", and yet one leaves the story with a larger notion of what love can be. The story is about the protagonist Hubble's reminiscence about eighty years ago. Hubble recalls his experience of the three nights he companies the corpses of the dead with Simp. The first one they accompany is Miss Georgie, a former school teacher. After midnight when Simp unions the cameo from Miss Georgie's neck and opens three buttons to have a look at the corpse, something dreadful happens that Miss Georgie grins and blows a bubble which grows and shrinks. Both the boys are scared and learn some lessons. They are praised by people for their good job. The second corpse they accompany is General Husky, and this is a peaceful night that nothing particular happens. The third one they accompany is a beautiful woman, Mariana Adams. The woman is pregnant and falls from the horse when she goes to find her drunkard husband. Mariana looks as if she was asleep and like an angel. In the early morning Mariana's husband comes to ask Mariana if he lives, miraculously the woman answers "no". When asked the second time, she gives the same answer. Accordingly Mariana's husband cuts his throat that morning. Hubble learns his lesson: love is the height of virtue.

作品选读

The Company of the Dead

Eighty-some years ago when I was a boy, Simp Dockett and I were in modest demand as reliable and inexpensive all-night "setters." I'm talking of the early 1900s in a small country town; and when people died and the corpse came home from the mortuary, a member of the family was expected to "set up" all night by the coffin and keep the dead company. The coffin lid was open of course, though in hot weather there would be a veil of mosquito net to keep off moths and flies. I could always see what the flies were after, but the moths had me stumped.

They barely eat so it can't be food; I eventually wondered if it might be light. Do some corpses give off actual light that we can't see but moths love and flock to? Later below, I will give my witness, for what it's worth.

By the time Simp and I had our truly wild night – the one I must tell before too late – we were good-sized boys, fifteen years old. But we started our business when we were still twelve. I'd like to think that the fact we lasted through our first job says something about what guts we had, but I know it only describes our greed. We made a small piece of money that night, and we wanted more; so from that point on, we guaranteed gentlemanly conduct and no dozing off in the loved one's presence. We even wore celluloid collars silk ties. They made us look order and hurt so much they kept us awake.

What happened the first night is something my own children always loved to hear. The corpse in question was an elderly spinster who taught us in Sunday school, at age three or four, and later in grade school – Miss Georgie LaGrange. All times of the year, freeze or swelter, she brought a great bowl of warm apple float each Sunday and made us eat it in thin china bowls that had been her mother's. It was "good for our bowels," she'd promise in whispers. Simp and I had grown well out of her class when the elders finally had to retire her. She'd started weighing the children each week and recording the figures on a chart by the door. Nothing wrong with that, but then a few children told their mothers Miss Georgie would make them to peel to their step-ins before she weighed them. So the elders let a grace period lapse; then after six months they gently removed her.

Gentle to the elders; it killed Miss Georgie. Though well past seventy and too far-sighted to be helped by glasses, she advertised sketching and painting lessons – not a taker in town. So Javis, the yard man, found her cold at the wheel of her dead brother's Packard in the shed one Monday morning. Though she'd never driven a mile in her life, the coroner said she died of heart failure, no hint of suicide, and had been stone dead since at least Friday night. Knowing Miss Georgie's mind had softened, everybody believed it and I still do.

My father was the lawyer that drew her will. The yard man knew that and had nowhere else to turn. Miss Georgie's people were long since dead. Her only nephew was two states away; and everyone knew he was not in the will, given as he was to getting arrested in women's clothes. So all my family were well into smothered steak and biscuits that cool spring evening when the back door rattled; and there stood Jarvis with tears in his eyes, though we already knew he was Miss Georgie's heir.

The next evening Father went out again to be with Miss Georgie as they brought her body home. When he got back to us, we four children were doing our homework on the dining table by two oil lamps. I think this country might yet revive as a place where decent people dwell if the government turned off all the lights every evening at dark. At least it would force everybody back home, the ones who aren't already born-felons. And there, they'd gather in one or two rooms. It would be pressed on them by circumstance. Few people would have a great many oil lamps, and very few rooms in homes would be heated. All this mischief that's done now in basements – fathers and daughters, mothers and sons – could seldom occur. The crimes would be honest crimes of public passion, murders in the midst of family and friends, not faceless stranglings near the trash compactor at city landfills.

Anyhow Father stopped on the doorsill and called me – "Hubble."

I was his older son and worshiped his tracks. I still think he liked me, though he never confessed it. The sound of my name, even one odd as Hubble, was grand in his voice. I rose from my stool like mist from a pond and followed him out.

He didn't wait for me, didn't look or turn till he got to a standing water spigot far back in the yard. These dirty days, you'd need to go high in the Grand Teton range to see skies black as our sky was then, any moonless night. But the three million stars were beaming so clear, I could see my father waiting as I came. He stood a whole moment, staring straight up. I thought the starshine was burning his skin.

And seeming to confirm it, he looked down slowly, turned the spigot and waited. Then he washed his face in two hands of water.

By the time he looked up again, I was with him. I touched the flap of the left-side pocket in the coat to his suit.

He said, "Hub, I've got you a grown man's job."

He asked me regularly, Sunday nights, what I planned to be. I'd always tell him some job he admired-a doctor or something to do with problems, like a civil engineer. So what he'd said wasn't all that strange. I just said "Good" and stood there to hear it. Many boys back then quit school at fourteen and trekked up the road to the nearest real town for a regular wage.

But then he veered, "How old are you, son?"

"Twelve and four months, sir."

His enormous hands must have still been wet; he wheeled them around in the air above me and finally said, "Are you too young, you think?"

I should have said "For what?" but what boy would? I said, "No sir."

He said, "Then you and Simp can set up tonight with Miss Georgie's corpse."

I understood at once and it truly thrilled me. I'd already been to at least a dozen funerals, which meant that I'd also viewed the remains as they lay, banked with flowers, in a cool parlor or dining room. I'd always wanted to touch the skin – it looked so fragrantly powdered and needy, so ready to wake up and thank you for warmth – but there were always adults at hand, with forbidding eyes. Standing with Father outdoors in the dark, my next thought was that Simp and I would be the bosses, alone all night with a whole dead body to use our way. A friend of ours named Baxter Wade, just one year older, had worked last summer at the mortuary. And the stories he told nearly curled our hair.

He knew all about embalming fluid – how they pump it into a vein in your right arm and meanwhile drain out your blood on the left. The best news was, the fluid is green. So once the pickling replaces red blood, every inch of your skin is bright bottle-green. Then nothing is left but to make you up with flesh-colored paint and dusting powder. Every now and then, an embalmer slips and forgets a part. And family members have been known to fold on the parlor floor at the sight of a green earlobe on Mother. Baxter also said he knew one boy who claimed he fondled a pretty girl that died of the flu, and the boy didn't catch so much as a cold ("fondled" is my guess; Baxter claimed more). My next thought was, we could look at some hidden part of Miss Georgie, under the collar, to check for green. We weren't sure that we could take Baxter's word.

So I said, "Yes, sir. You can count on us." I knew Simp didn't have better plans; nobody we knew in those days had plans, for tonight or for life. Life was just forward motion, at the gentlest clip you could manage to take and still eat three meals a day and sleep dry.

Father told me to put on my black suit and his gray cravat; and as I bolted, he called me back. "Miss Georgie's estate will pay you, son – one dollar per boy."

The sum was handsome for those slim days, but I said "No sir." I'd have paid a good part of my savings for the chance.

He blared his eyes, the sign for Get serious. "You're a paid employee, this whole night, Hub. Miss Georgie's purchasing first-class care. Act according. Be respectful, no jokes; don't loosen your tie. You'll find some old biscuits in a bag by the stove, and I set out a jar of her fig preserves. Eat nothing else. Don't touch the coffin unless there's a fire, and don't shut an eye till I come by to spell you just after daybreak."

I said Simp and I would set right on as long as he needed; forget about school.

He smiled for the first time but said, "There you're wrong." Then he motioned me onward to dress and find Simp.

By the time we got to Miss Georgie's porch, it must have been nearly nine o'clock. But a small group of mourners had already gathered. It turned out that Jarvis, the sudden heir, had barred the door till our arrival, telling the world that we were "the family" and would be here shortly. Meanwhile he stood in front of the door in his own black suit and a wine-colored tie. Neither Simp nor I shared a drop of blood with Miss Georgie, and the mourners knew it, but even Simp bucked up at Jarvis's claim, and we took on the role. We'd known everybody in sight all our lives; they were loyal members of our church or were some of the older teachers at school. Miss Georgie had taught the second grade, including me and Simp, from roughly the year they invented fire till five years ago. So the two of us climbed up toward them proudly. Young as I was, I already liked standing tall and big-eyed with shoulders squared, daring all comers.

At the top, Mr. Pepper – the drunkard school-principal – stepped over and personally shook our hands. Simp glanced at me and nodded to mean "You do the talking." So I said, "Everybody step in. Miss Georgie's ready." I don't know what I thought she was ready for; and as Simp and I led the way to the door, I suddenly prayed it wouldn't be locked. I had no key.

In immediate answer Jarvis trotted ahead and turned the brass knob. Then he stepped inside what seemed a dark house and pressed his back to the open door to see us in. I consulted Simp's eyes for an instant. When I saw they were scared, I took the first step of our manly job. And yes, she was ready.

By ten-fifteen every mourner had seen the new Miss Georgie. The undertaker had painted her thick, the face and hands, which added a century or so to her age; but everybody said what they always say, "She looks so natural, just like she's asleep." I of course didn't say what I thought at once. The real Miss Georgie had looked cold-dead since the day they made her quit teaching school. And the only place where the paint she now wore would look half natural was in a plush whorehouse for truly weird gents with serious cash.

Jarvis hung around in the back of the house for another short while. We guessed he was starting an inventory of his new possessions. In fact we were wrong – he'd had no warning whatever of his luck; and after the funeral when my father told him he'd inherited everything, he pole-axed over on the floor, unconscious, and had to be revived. By the time he was ready to leave that night though, Simp and I were searching the room for a deck of cards or a checkerboard. I was on my knees, rummaging a cabinet, when I heard footsteps. I looked up and Jarvis was tall in the door.

"What the hell you doing?" His voice was rusty but every word cut me.

I instantly knew it had to be the first curse word these walls had heard since Miss Georgie's brother died, so it struck me dumb, and I couldn't answer.

Simp said "He's just hunting some kind of game to keep us awake. She got any cards?"

Jarvis's face went awful in a hurry. "She ain't got *nothing* now, no more. And if there was something as sinful as cards under this roof tonight, you think I'd tell you?"

By then I was ready to say "No sir."

Simp faced me and frowned; you didn't call black men sir back then. So he took over and said "Look, Jarvis. We're nothing but boys; we like our sleep. But we can't sleep tonight. We need some help and you know where things are hid around here – "

Jarvis stayed as dark as before. "You can goddamn well believe I know every curl of dust in the furtherest corners. So don't touch nothing. Stay wide awake and watch Miss Georgie – don't shut a damn eye. I'll see you at daybreak." Then he vanished. I truly mean vanished. I'd still swear to God he just disappeared. If he did, however he brought it off, I knew from that instant how Jarvis was still there with us in spirit, his big black eyes in the chilly air.

Simp plainly agreed since he waited ten seconds and whispered to me "I bet his spirit will spy all night."

Both of us turned then, went to hard chairs and sat down firmly. I can't speak for Simp; but as for me, to stay awake, I thought the hardest thoughts I could manage. Both my parents and the sister I liked were being dragged naked through a field of barbed wire by slow blind mules at a steady rate. And that was years before barbed wire came into its own in the First World War. But awful as it was to see and hear, the thoughts eventually had me nodding in a chair as rigid as any steel strut.

I didn't know at first what woke me; my eyes flew open on the mantle clock. It was twelve-twenty and my first response was pride to have finally passed midnight, alive and conscious. In a town small as ours, children barely saw moonrise, much less midnight. Then I heard a sound I recognized; I knew at once it was what had woke me.

Simp was back in the corner by the open coffin. His right hand seemed to be reaching in; and two more times he whispered "Whoa, whoa."

I whispered "Hush and sit your butt down." I'd already thought about Jarvis again and how I knew he was somehow with us like the Holy Ghost. Simp had agreed just awhile before, but now he was acting the fool again. I said "This all belongs to Jarvis now. He'll burn us up."

Simp said "That nigger won't burn dry cotton." Don't think exceptionally hard of Simp; back then we were less than a generation from the Civil War, something as common and flat-incredible as chattel slavery; and we lived in a town that had been scoured over, like hot lye-water flung in your eyes, by Sherman's men not forty years past. We may have deserved it; but you don't forgive rape, not in under a thousand years.

All Simp did next was reach his left hand round behind him and beckon me on while he still said "Whoa."

I thought maybe something was wrong with Miss Georgie; so being half of her guard for the night, I had no choice but to come up behind Simp and face the facts.

There were two hard facts. Simp had unpinned the cameo from Miss Georgie's neck and opened three buttons. I might have paused to think it was doubtless the first time a man, or a boy at least, had touched her anywhere else but the hand. Yet the sight itself held me. Below the collar where the paint line quit, she was green as Ireland. Simp's index finger was touching the ridge of her collarbone; he seemed to be stuck, like your tongue on ice. That was not the worst. After all we'd halfway hoped to see green. The worst part shone as new as creation, a dread to behold.

Miss Georgie was blowing a sizable bubble. Few men or boys had ever seen her smile, though your mother might admit she'd caught her at it a time or two. And now her lips were still thin as paper, but the corners were plainly lifting in a grin, and between them an actual bubble was growing.

I fell back a step; it shook me that hard. Then I said, "One of us has got to run, Simp, for reinforcements."

He didn't even face me. "The hell you say. I'm not leaving you, Hub; you can't leave me."

I understood him; the bubble had trapped us. As both of us stood there, it swelled on slowly to the size of a tangerine and more or less stopped. From that point forward it would sometimes grow a quarter-inch, then shrink back again. But it always stayed a little murky with a yellow hue, not the rainbow skin of a clean soap-bubble.

We had our work cut out for us then. Either it would keep on swelling and shrinking and keep us thinking Miss Georgie was somehow coming to life, green all over as we knew she was;

or any second, it would burst and be done, a final gas attack from a lady who launched a number of memorable such. If the latter, then fine; we could sit back down and continue the night. The former didn't even bear thinking through. What would Jarvis say when he walked in at sunrise and found Miss Georgie frying our breakfast?

Neither thing happened. Simp and I stood there, give or take a step backward, an hour more. When nothing dramatic occurred either way, I reminded Simp it was he who must button her collar again and pin the cameo. He heard the news with bald-faced terror; but knowing his duty, he shut both eyes and managed someway. The bubble survived. So finally we sat down again in easier chairs and took turns shutting our eyes to rest. While the other snoozed, the one on guard would stay awake by hook or crook (I mostly sang hymns) and make sporadic checks on the bubble. I dreaded my turns and prayed between them that, next time, the thing would have dried and burst. Simp must have done the same – everytime he woke and went on duty, he'd say first thing, "Hub, tell me it's gone" and turn ashy pale when I shook my head.

Toward the end of my truly last watch, toward dawn, I made one more check, found the bubble intact and Miss Georgie no less dead than before. Then I sat back to wait and fell into sleep like an open well in strange woods at night. I didn't even wake at the sound of Jarvis's key in the back door, his feet in the kitchen. Thank God, Simp did and shook me hard. So we were upright, if not clear-eyed, when Jarvis came up the long hall to meet us.

His disgusted face showed he knew we'd shirked, but what he said was "Is she all right?"

Simp looked at me.

I didn't know what Jarvis had in mind; so I said "First-rate," which was what Father said if you asked how he felt on a sunny day.

Jarvis all but spit on the floor, then swallowed his bile and stepped to the coffin. If we had both shot him at point-blank range, he couldn't have jerked any harder than he did. When his body calmed he didn't turn to face us. He kept looking at her; but he said "What please, in the name of Jesus, have you fools done?"

We faced each other and together said "Nothing." But when we joined him at the coffin rail; and oh Lord God, the bubble had grown since my last check to the size of a healthy navel orange. The surface was still a jaundice yellow, but the cloudy air inside had darkened like a captive storm. And as we watched, before even Jarvis could reach with his handkerchief and wipe it away, the bubble burst and spread its remains across Miss Georgie from brow to chin.

We got our money all the same; and a few years ago, I heard my own wife's undertaker say that such things were not that rare in the inner sanctums of mortuaries, though they seldom happen now that the trade has learned its lesson and sews lips shut. The odd thing was, for a first experience, you might have thought it would balk Simp and me from further such jobs. Not a bit, or so I thought at first. Once word on the bubble got out in town, we were pitied and praised for our ordeal; and within three weeks, we were called to "set" with Brigadier General Matthew Husky's enormous remains. I thought we were both stronger boys for the test.

But the second night – as the house stilled down except for the general's widow upstairs, snoring her way through thick plaster walls – Simp said to me, "Hub, did we learn our lesson?"

It was not his usual cast of mind; and while I' d always thought I was smarter, I knew Simp was some months nearer to manhood, so I asked what lesson he had in mind.

He was used to my being the wordsmith among us, and it took him awhile to fix his reply; but when I'd nearly forgot my question, Simp said, "Well, you can't turn your back on the dead."

I said, "If you're speaking of ghosts, forget it. Poor Miss Georgie didn't blow that bubble; it was gas, a normal chemical event." My older brother Tump was studying chemistry; the words were his. But the next was mine, prepared in private to steel my resolve, "And it's unchristian anyhow. God wouldn't let good souls hang back here to flummox boys and scare old Negroes."

Simp said, "I'm white and I'm scared to death. You've heard a lot more from God than me. The Bible's got way more ghosts than good women."

Simp was a Bible scholar; I knew he was right on the matter of women, so I didn't risk faulting his count of the ghosts. I waited awhile till Simp started nodding. By then I'd pulled my wisdom together. I said, "The lesson is nothing but this. Keep the corpse as cool as you can, no more bugs than you can help, and don't go touching their burial clothes."

Simp said, "I beg to God you're right; but until further notice, my eyes are peeled. One false move out of this old joker, and stand aside or I'll stampede you down."

I knew when to humor him and shut down a quarrel. But through that peaceful night by the general, I had more than one inspiration on the subject of what we ought to have learned from the bubble and its, after all, tempting hint at a prank by something out there, if not at a frank demonic stab at scaring us dead. But despite the fact that it filled the largest readymade coffin like melted wax, General Husky's corpse behaved with spotless dignity. The peace in fact was too great for me; and sad to report, I slept a good part of that second night.

Not Simp Dockett – he meant what he said; and for weeks to come, he would suddenly throw me a note in class with some new flash of purported memory from his sleepless watch: The general sang two bars of "Dixie" at first sunrise. I'd look back and laugh till the day I had to swallow one note (it bore the word fart) to keep Miss Miriam Bailey from seizing it – she taught us grammar and was martyred by flatulence. After that I made Simp keep his own so-called memories till recess.

But the time I started out to describe, and have yet to tell, was truly the last. We learned the lesson and it changed my life – I learned it anyhow and Simp was impressed at the very least. As we left the room on that bright morning after such a strange night, we eyed each other, white as paste. And both of us knew we'd silently retired. It had been that final, that wondrous and – worst – it has proved untellable in my life till now. I know Simp died with his half untold except to me; he confessed as much when I left his deathbed in 1939. Not one of his three chatterbox wives had prised a word about it from him, though each had tried.

Who died was a beautiful woman, a girl really. She was even a distant cousin of mine, Mariana Adams. She'd married at sixteen, three years before – an absolute scoundrel from up on the river, named Kennon Walters. The scoundrel part was owing to liquor; otherwise he was handsome as she was lovely, with his stiff black hair and eyes that could tell you a lie and make it stick like knives through your face. He was also at times a practicing lawyer, though honest to a fault in that respect. For all his regular quarterly drunks, nobody ever claimed Kennon was cruel. He was just so proud that once he was drinking, he'd ride away and hide his shame, till sanity returned, in an old fishing-camp his father had built ten miles from home on the Clannish River.

The last time Kennon rode off and left her, he stayed gone upward of two winter weeks. And finally Mariana lit out to find him. Her heart nor mind would let her wait longer; she had the news they'd both waited for. Kennon had always publicly said he would end his drinking the day his first child saw safe light, and now she was pregnant. Still she went on horseback alone in the cold. There was no other way to get there then, no passable rode for a gentler conveyance. She'd ridden brilliantly all her life, and the horse was as tame as a thornless rose. But she hadn't told anybody she was leaving, and she left at sunup with just two saddlebags of provisions and a smallish lantern in case dark overtook her return – she truly hoped to return with Kennon but was wise enough to allow for failure.

Whether she got there or not is unsure. Late the next morning when the horse came home and the searchers beat the woods and found her, her frozen body lay crosswise in the track, aimed neither way. And though her stiff right hand was pointed as if to aim herself at a goal, the way she had fallen, nobody could guess which way she meant. Some said they found her provisions by Kennon where he lay in a stupor; some say no, he was in his own filth, no food in sight and no memory of her.

It seemed cleared to me, though I barely knew her; that if Mariana had truly found him, she wouldn't have left with Kennon unconscious and in his own waste. But maybe he rallied and said something dreadful that cast her off, or maybe his mind was so far gone that he mistook her for some kind of threat and raised a hurtful hand against her. Her skin was not marked except at the temple; and that was a bruise she sustained in falling from the horse, whenever, and striking a white flint rock in the ground.

Whatever – and God alone still knows – when half of the search party brought her home, Kennon's brother Phil pushed on and found him, told him the worst and brought him back too. It was not till the doctor searched Mariana's body that anybody knew what had sent her off on a risky mission in weather that cold. She was somewhere between three and four months pregnant. When they told poor Kennon, he first tried to kill himself, then the horse; then the doctor laid him out with morphine. Nobody thought he would wake for the funeral; but Simp and I could vow, though we didn't, that he saw her body one final time and that she saw him or knew he was there.

Because Mariana's wealthy father was long since dead, and her mother was too overcome by grief, again we were summoned to watch through the night. By then Simp and I were so well-seasoned that we had no trouble spelling each other in staying awake and dignified. And since our premier night with Miss Georgie, we'd had no untoward incident to spook us. But every white male in town, from twelve up, knew that Mariana Adams was a beauty surpassing mythical perfection; and men and women, white and black, had joined in ruing the day she flung her life away at the feet of Kennon Walters. So however hardened Simp and I were, when we entered that parlor and took our instructions from the weeping mother, we were thrilled to the sockets at the near prospect of a chance to guard this famous beauty as her body spent its last night above ground.

Mariana's mother only thanked us profusely, then asked us not to disturb the netting. Since it was winter, with insects asleep, we didn't know why she took the precaution; but we nodded agreement and, once she was gone, sat back to do our calculus lesson (we were both near failing). We hadn't exchanged a word on the subject of viewing the corpse and had worked at least an hour in silence when Simp rose, stretched, silently walked to the coffin rail and stood a long minute before he said, "She's an angel by now; any fool could see –" Most Christians then as now believed that souls become bright angels in a flash at the moment of death, with harp and wings.

It was not their worst error; but it always disturbed me, even that young, and I told Simp the truth, "Right now her soul's in dreamless sleep and will stay that way till the trump of doom. Then God will shake her and decide where she goes." I was referring to Judgment Day; that far back, it was my favorite date. I expected it often and would search most sunsets for trumpet notes and the glint of wings. I felt that guilty, though I'd hurt nothing worse than bugs in the dirt beneath my shoes.

Simp didn't even turn. He gazed on at her and said, "No fool but a blind man with both hands missing, could say such a thing."

It made me mad and I stood up hot to see for myself.

She was every atom of what he said. Her mother had wanted her buried "as she lived," so the undertaker was not allowed to embalm and paint her. She lay before us in a white night-gown with her throat and shoulders bare. She'd always worn her black hair loose, not plaited or tucked; and it flared out beside her like a whole other creature, entirely alive. It was only her skin that assured us she was gone. Ever white, it was still paler now; and it all but quivered with a low phosphorescence that truly came from deep within her, a final remnant of the goodness she showed in every move. I thought through the moment in that way later, years later in fact; but even that night I felt no fear, no strange attraction – I was proud to be near her.

Nothing about her tempted me or Simp to lift the net and touch any part of that splendid a sight. I finally said, "Simp, angels wish they looked good as this." And with no more words, we both went back to the calculus lesson, though more than once we rose up separately and stood to watch her.

I can't speak for Simp, but I know I was memorizing the sight and also teaching myself a hard truth – that this much beauty can still be stopped by a stumbling horse or a limb from a tree. Till then I'd nursed a boy's common notion that beauty counts in the eyes of Nature and will be protected by the ground itself, if not bright angels.

It was four in the morning, my turn to guard while Simp caught a nap, when I thought I heard footfalls on the porch. They seemed to climb the eight high steps and stop at the door, then a long silent wait. I still wasn't scared. If you were white, in that town then, the chances of meeting with harm from a human were practically nil. I guessed it might be Talcot Briley, an affable moron who seldom slept and made late harmless inspection tours of yards and houses.

But the front door creaked, slowly opened and shut.

And before I could move or call to Simp, a man strode past me and went to the coffin. I didn't so much see him as smell him, a strong good scent of leather and the night. It was then I said my single word; I think it was "Please," some syllable that begged for mercy to Simp and me and for honor at least to dead Mariana.

He didn't look back but made a huge downward sweep with his hand that shut me up from five yards' distance and seated me fast. All I was good for after that was a silence reach to press Simp's knee. I wanted a witness.

Simp came to, saw my hushing finger and watched like me in frozen quiet from then on out.

I hadn't seen Kennon Walters for years, maybe not since my boyhood; but next I knew him. No man born around here since Kennon looks anything like as rank, wild and good. By good I only mean handsome, magnetic. You had to watch him and, as with Mariana, you worked to record his memory clearly as a future standard for strength and waste. Otherwise you knew he could take one hand and separate your leg from your hip; you also knew that he very well might.

By then he'd laid the netting back; and I almost thought Mariana's light, her peculiar shine, outlined his right profile that was toward me. He hadn't reached in and all he'd said so far was whispers that I couldn't catch. But finally, still not facing us, he said, "Come here."

Simp and I stayed put, astonished.

So Kennon said, "Come stand by me this instant, or I'll cut you both."

One way or the other, on liquid legs we both obeyed; and after what happened in the next long seconds, I've always guessed he meant us for witnesses, the way I'd wanted Simp with me. Kennon thought he could change the laws of Nature – he'd pretty well managed to do it till then – and he wanted us to judge. Whether he already knew the outcome, I still can't say. But he forced our hand; and hard as it's been to shut my lips on what I saw, I never once doubted I owed Kennon Walters at least that silence for the gift I got in sharing his deed.

Even that early in my long life, my sense of possibility could stretch. The fact that I did so badly in science, not to mention math, through all grades of school was my best early blessing. It kept me from stringing the barbedwire fences that rational men put up against truth, the shapeless grandeur of what may be.

Next Kennon put both hands on the coffin and kept on watching Mariana's face for maybe a minute. If I'd been watched with half that force, I'd have burst into flame in under a minute. But nothing changed. So then he spoke to the body in a whisper that was clear in the room as any shout, "Come back long enough to say if I live."

I know he said exactly that; he spoke very slowly in a clear bass voice. I seized each word as it came through the air and pressed it hard on my mind that then was still uncrowded. I thought, "He's planning to die if she fails him." I never wondered if he caused her death in direct fashion. That close to his shadow, his fine-smelling body, I knew he hadn't killed this Mariana, not against her will in any case.

Her eyes didn't open – Simp always agreed, the few times we ever mentioned it later. And for a good while she stayed dead still. Even the pulsing light from inside her withdrew and dimmed.

Kennon spoke again. This time I understood it was God he begged for help. He said, "I need this word. Let her answer." Desperate as he sounded, he never said please; it was all commands.

Then something obeyed him – our Maker or a demon or Mariana her shining self, wherever she roamed. She went on waiting till I quit hoping and knew that even Kennon couldn't summon her back with all the fury of his parched soul. But then her pale lips worked to part in what I thought would be a slow smile. It proved to be sound, her earthly voice. I'd heard her say my name four times in earlier years and will know her tones in Heaven if I get there. What she said was "No."

By then I'd nearly forgot Kennon's question.

He had not. He issued a sob like nothing I'd heard on Earth till then or have met with since, and I've heard much grief. He said "Again," another order.

Her lips moved again and – this time I had no question at all – she made a smile so lovely it soothed my heart for years. But she said again, "No." I remembered the question, *Should Kennon live*? No, twice No.

Simp and I looked at him.

We might have been air. Every lustrous hair on his head looked charged with newer force, and his wide dark eyes were fixed on her. Had they seen her the night she left home to find him? Had he repelled her and sent her out into freezing darkness? Or had she never reached him with her news of the child and perished, maybe lost and hunting the chance of safety at his crushing hands, wherever he lay – the father of what grew daily within her?

Now he laid a great broad hand on her mouth and pressed as though he'd press her through flooring, the ground, the mantling rock beneath our soil toward the world's red core of burning rock.

I took a step back in fear and dread. Would she fight; would bile press out of her gorge? Would God the Judge appear among us and burn Kennon down, maybe ruining me and Simp in the blaze?

Simp actually seized Kennon's bulky wrist and tried to tame it.

Kennon turned eyes on him that would swipe down a saint; and with one short swing of his weaker arm, he flung Simp off like water drops.

Simp landed by the settee and covered his head.

I crouched down by him in hopes of sparing myself worse damage.

When Kennon's steps crossed the front porch and left, I started to count. I told myself "If I get to a hundred and he's not back and fire hasn't struck us, I'll risk one more look out at the room." I truly counted to one hundred slowly – pure silence, still air. I took the look round. The room as before, no sign of strangeness. Simp was rousing too, not visibly bleeding. I said, "Is he gone?"

Simp said, "Hub, he's the least of our worries. He's bound to be dead." How Simp knew it, he didn't say. I thought of myself as the better detective, but of course he was right that one bad time.

They found Kennon Walters that morning at ten as Mariana's hearse drove up to her family plot with us all behind on ponies, in buggies. He had cut his throat and fallen in the hole that was meant for her grave.

I hadn't asked Simp that night, or ever, what the worst of our worries might be or become – maybe a thoroughly raised Mariana, bent on vengeance or a still deeper taste of the love she lacked and truly craved.

That at least was what I've kept from the night, my ultimate lesson. Love – this force commended by God and Christ his Son as the height of virtue – will freeze one life and char the next; no way to predict who lives or dies. No lover strives or ends with flesh and mind intact, uncharred and smiling. In the long years since, I've kept that lesson hid well within me, a guiding secret like no known light in the mounting hours of age and loss. And through this generous hapless republic – where, all the length of the twentieth century, the one word love has stoked life and commerce, disease and health, swans and owls, child-killers and dolphins – I've struggled by the instant to keep my own heart dry inside me, not launched on the pointed stakes of love.

I'm ninety-two years old, writing this line, a man at peace with what he's done and what comes next. I leave this story, in both its parts, as my best gift to a world I've liked and thank, here now, but have never pressed for the black heart's blood of actual love.

Unit 14
Anne Tyler(1941–)
安妮·泰勒

作者简介

安妮·泰勒，小说家，1941 年 10 月 25 日出生于明尼苏达州(Minnesota)的明尼阿波利斯市(Minneapolis)，在北卡罗来纳州的罗利长大。她自认为是一个地道的南方人。1961 年泰勒毕业于杜克大学，并在哥伦比亚大学完成研究生学业。随后在杜克大学图书馆工作一年。泰勒大部分时光是在马里兰州(Maryland)巴的摩尔(Baltimore)度过的，此地或南方小镇成为她小说创作的背景。泰勒是个多产的作家。从 20 世纪 60 年代开始，很多杂志，如《十七岁年华》(*Seventeen*)、《纽约客》(*New Yorker*)等，都刊登过她的作品。自从 1964 年出版第一部小说《倘若清晨来临》(*If Morning Ever Comes*)，泰勒平均两三年便有一部新作问世，迄今已经出版了 17 部小说。与此同时，她还撰写短篇小说及书评，已经发表的短篇小说有五十多篇，其中多部小说入选年度《美国最佳短篇小说选》(*Best American Short Stories*)，并且获得过“欧·亨利奖”。她的作品继承了南方作家一贯的写作内容，即以错综复杂的家庭关系为主题，描写地方小人物的生存状态，尤其是个人与家庭、社会之间的矛盾冲突。安妮·泰勒的作品文笔细腻，文风简朴，语言风趣幽默，心理描写深刻，塑造出了一个又一个具有鲜明个性的人物，赢得了评论界的好评及广大读者的喜爱。她的许多作品也荣获众多国内奖项，她的《摩根的去世》(*Morgan's Passing*, 1980)获得“珍妮特·海丁格·卡夫卡美国女作家小说奖”，同时还获得过“全国评论界书评奖”和“美国图书奖”的提名。《思乡餐厅的晚餐》(*Dinner at the Homesick Restaurant*, 1982)获得“普利策奖”的提名，并获得“福克纳文学奖”。《预产期》(*Breathing Lessons*, 1988)获得“普利策奖”。这些奖项既是对她作品的认可，也提高了她的知名度。她的主要作品还包括《世俗的财产》(*Earthly Possessions*)、《马口铁罐之树》(*The Tin Can Tree*)、《直线下滑的生活》(*The Slipping-down Life*)、《寻找凯莱布》(*Searching for Caleb*)、《次要旅行者》(*The Accidental Tourist*)、《圣人之举》(*Saint Maybe*, 1991)、《年龄的阶梯》(*Ladder of Years*)、《拼凑起来的行星》(*A Patchwork Planet*, 1998)、《回到我们成年的年代》(*Back When We Were Grownups*, 2001)、《业余婚姻》(*The Amateur Marriage*, 2004)等。

作品导读

Dinner at the Homesick Restaurant is Anne Tyler's ninth novel, telling of the long, often unhappy life of a deserted wife who is a possessive and domineering mother. The novel follows the lives of three siblings: Cody, Ezra, and Jenny, and explores their experiences and recollections of growing up with their mother, Pearl. After the family is abandoned by their father, Beck. The novel ends with Pearl's funeral, and a surprise occurrence. Anne Tyler considers it her best work.

Married to Beck, a traveling salesman, and having three children, Pearl Tull is a rather rigid perfectionist. After Beck abandons the family, Pearl struggles to maintain a front as if nothing is wrong, yet is prone to angry outbursts when her children misbehave. Cody, the oldest, is wild and adventurous, but is envious of his brother Ezra who he believes is Pearl's favorite. As they are growing up, this plays out in endless pranks. Ezra is passive, and never tries to get back at Cody. He is nurturing and sweet, and these traits often interest Cody's girlfriends, which furthers Cody's resentment. Ezra goes to work at a restaurant which he later manages and ultimately inherits, while Cody becomes a wealthy and successful efficiency expert. When Ezra becomes engaged to Ruth, his star cook, Cody becomes obsessed with luring her away, and ultimately succeeds but his marriage to Ruth is not easy. Ezra never recovers and remains at home with Pearl. Jenny is the youngest and most scholarly of the Tulls, but in college she marries on an impulse and ends with unhappy results. Only in her third marriage to a man with six children whose wife has abandoned him does she find stability in family life and in her successful if harried career as a pediatrician.

At 87 Pearl is blind and dying. She recalls her family members but most of all she remembers her own children. She recalls Cody, her oldest son, as a "troublemaker", "a difficult baby". Ezra, her second child, is "so sweet and clumsy that he could break your heart". And Jenny, the girl, in Pearl's mind, is a kind of "luxury". Pearl realizes that she is an angry sort of mother, being abandoned, who always feels too burdened to be alone in raising her children. Now at her deathbed, she dreams of her three young children at the beach, laughing and running toward her across the sand in sunlight. The pain and anger of their troubled relationships are all but forgotten.

A recurring scene in the novel involves Ezra's unsuccessful attempts to bring the family together for a meal at his "Homesick Restaurant", reflecting his desire to unite and mend the family. At Pearl's funeral Beck returns to the family for the first time. However, they never seem to be able to get through a single dinner without conflict, this time with Cody facing down his father.

作品选读

Dinner at the Homesick Restaurant
Chapter 10

When Pearl Tull died, Cody was off on a goose hunt and couldn't be reached for two days. He and Luke were staying in a cabin owned by his business partner. It didn't have a telephone, and the roads were little more than logging trails.

Late Sunday, when they returned, Ruth came out to the driveway. The night was chilly, and she wore no sweater but hugged herself as she walked toward the car, her white, freckled face oddly set and her faded red hair standing up in the wind. That was how Cody guessed something was wrong. Ruth hated cold weather, and ordinarily would have waited inside the house.

"It's bad news," she said. "I'm sorry."

"What happened?"

"Your mother's passed away."

"Grandma died?" asked Luke, as if correcting her.

Ruth kissed Luke's cheek but kept her eyes on Cody, maybe trying to gauge the damage. Cody himself, wearily closing the car door behind him, was uncertain of the damage. His mother had been a difficult woman, of course. But even so...

"She died in her sleep, early yesterday," Ruth said. She took Cody's hand in both of hers and gripped it, tightly, so that the pain he felt right then was purely physical. He stood for a while, allowing her; then he gently pulled away and went to open the car trunk.

They had not bagged any geese – the hunt had been a lame excuse, really, to spend some time with Luke, who was now a senior in high school and would not be around for much longer. All Cody had to unload was the rifles in their canvas cases and a duffel bag. Luke brought the ice chest. They walked toward the house in silence. Cody had still not responded.

"The funeral's tomorrow at eleven," said Ruth. "I told Ezra we'd be there in the morning."

"How is he taking it?" Cody asked.

"He sounded all right."

Inside the front door, Cody set down the duffel bag and propped the rifles against the wall. He decided that he felt not so much sad as heavy. Although he was lean bodied, still in good shape, he imagined that he had suddenly sunk in on himself and grown denser. His eyes were weighty and dry, and his step seemed too solid for the narrow, polished floorboards in the hall.

"Well, Luke," he said.

Luke seemed dazed, or perhaps just sleepy. He squinted palely under the bright light.

"Do you want to go to the funeral?" Cody asked him.

"Sure, I guess," said Luke.

"You wouldn't have to."

"I don't mind."

"Of course he's going," said Ruth. "He's her grandson."

"That doesn't obligate him," Cody told her.

"Of course it obligates him."

This was where they differed. They could have argued about it all night, except that Cody was so tired.

For their journey south, Cody drove Ruth's car because his own was still spattered with mud from the geese hunt. He supposed they would have to ride in some shiny, formal funeral procession. But when he happened to mention this to Ruth, halfway down the turnpike, she told him that Ezra had said their mother had requested cremation. ("Golly," Luke breathed.) There would only be the service, therefore – no cemetery trip and no burial. "Very sensible," Cody said. He thought of the tidy framework of his mother's bones, the crinkly bun on the back of her head. Did that fierce little figure exist any more? Was it already ashes?" Ah, God it's barbaric, however you look at it," he told Ruth.

"What, cremation?" she asked.

"Death."

They sped along – Cody in his finest gray suit, Ruth in still black beside him. Luke sat in the rear, gazing out the side window. They were traveling the Beltway now, approaching Baltimore. They passed trees ablaze with red and yellow leaves and shopping malls full of ordinary, Monday morning traffic. "When I was a boy, this was country," Cody said to Luke.

"You told me."

"Baltimore was nothing but a little harbor town."

There was no answer. Cody searched for Luke in the rear-view morrow. "Hey," he said. "You want to drive the rest of the way?"

"No, that's all right."

"Really. You want to?"

"Let him be," Ruth whispered.

"What?"

"He's upset."

"What about?"

"Your mother, Cody. You know he always felt close to her."

Cody couldn't figure how anyone could feel close to his mother – not counting Ezra, who was thought by some to be a saint. He checked Luke's face in the mirror again, but what could you tell from that impassive stare? "Hell," he said to Ruth, "all I asked was did he want to drive."

The city seemed even more ruined than usual, tumbling under a wan, blue sky. "Look at there," Cody said, "Linsey's Candy and Tobacco. They sold cigarettes to minors. Bobbie Jo's Barbecue. And there's my old school."

On Calvert Street, the row houses stood in two endless lines. "I don't see how you knew which one was home," Luke had told him once, and Cody had been amazed. Oh, if you lived here you knew. They weren't alike at all, not really. One had dozens of roses struggling in its tiny front yard, another an illuminated Madonna glowing night and day in the parlor window. Some had their trim painted in astonishing colors, assertively, like people with their chins thrust out. The fact that they were attached didn't mean a thing.

He parked in front of his mother's house. He slid from the car and stretched, waiting for Ruth and Luke.

By now, Pearl would have been out the door and halfway down the steps, reaching for the three of them with those eager, itchy fingers of hers.

"Is that your sister's car?" Ruth asked him.

"I don't know what kind of car she drives."

They climbed the steps. Ruth had her hand hooked in the back of Luke's belt. He was too tall for her to cup the nape of his neck, as she used to do.

When Cody first left home, he would knock when he returned for a visit. It was a delicious, planned act; it was an insult to his mother. She had known that and objected. "Can't you walk straight in? Do you have to act like company?" "But company is what I am," he'd said. She had started outwitting him; she had lain in wait, rushing to meet him at the very first sound of his shoes on the sidewalk. (So it was, perhaps, not solely love that had sent her plunging down the steps.) Now, crossing the porch, Cody didn't know whether to knock or just open the door. Well, he supposed this house belonged to Ezra now. He knocked.

Ezra looked sad and exhausted, loosely filling a lightweight khaki suit that only he would have thought appropriate. As always, he seemed whiskerless, boy faced. There was a space between his collar and the knot of his tie. A handkerchief bunched messily out of his jacket pocket. "Cody. Come in," he said. He touched Cody's arm in that tentative way he had – something more than a handshake less than a hug. "Ruth? Luke? We were starting to worry about you."

From the gloomy depths of the house, Jenny steeped forward to kiss everyone. She smelled of some complicated perfume but had her usual hastily assembled look – her tailored coat unbuttoned, her dark hair rough and tossed. Her husband ambled behind her, fat and bearded, good-natured. He clapped Cody on the shoulder. "Nice to see you. Too bad about your mother."

"Thank you, Joe."

"We're supposed to be starting for the church this very minute," Jenny said. "We have to leave early because we're picking up some of the children on the way."

"I'm all set," Cody said.

Ezra asked, "But don't you want coffee first?"

"No, no, let's get going."

"See," Ezra said, "I had planned on coffee and pastries before we started out. I'd assumed you'd be coming earlier."

"We've already had breakfast," Cody told him.

"But everything's on the table."

Cody felt his old, familiar irritation beginning. "Ezra – "he said.

"That was thoughtful of you," Ruth told Ezra, "but really, we're fine, and we wouldn't want to hold people up."

Ezra checked his watch. He glanced behind him, toward the dining room. "It's only ten-fifteen," he said. He walked over to a front window and lifted the curtain.

Now that it was apparent he had something on his mind, the others stood waiting. (He could be maddeningly slow, and all the slower if pushed.)

"It's like this," he said finally.

He coughed.

"I was kind of expecting Dad," he said.

There was a blank, fat pause.

"Who?" Cody asked.

"Our father."

"But how would he know?"

"Well, ah, I invited him."

"Ezra, for God's sake," Cody said.

"It wasn't my idea." Ezra said. "It was Mother's said. She talked about it when she got so sick. She said, 'Look in my address book. Ask everybody in it to my funeral.' I wondered who she meant, at first. You know she never wrote anyone, and most of her relatives are dead. But as soon as I opened the address book I saw it: Beck Tull. I didn't even realize she knew where he had run off to."

"He wrote her; that's how she knew," Cody said.

"He did?"

"From time to time he sent these letters, boasting, bragging. *Doing fine...expecting a raise...* I peeked inside when Mother wasn't looking."

"I never even guessed," said Ezra.

"What difference would it have made?"

"Oh, I don't know..."

"He ditched us," Cody said, "when we were kids. What do you care about him now?"

"Well, I don't," said Ezra. And Cody, who had so often been exasperated by Ezra's soft heart, saw that in this case, it was true: he really didn't care. He looked directly at Cody with his peculiarly clear, light-filled eyes, and he said, "It was Mother who asked; not me. All I did was call him up and say, 'This is Ezra. Mother has died and we're holding her funeral Monday at eleven.' "

"That was all?" Cody said.

"Well, and then I told him he could stop by the house first, if he got here early."

"But you didn't ask, 'How are you?' or 'Where're you been?' or 'Why'd you go?'"

"I just said, 'This is Ezra. Mother has died and – '"

Cody laughed.

"At any rate," Jenny said, "it doesn't seem he's coming."

"No," said Cody, "but think about it. I mean, don't you get it? First he leaves and Mother pretends he hasn't. Out of pride, or spite, or something, she never says a word about it, makes believe to all of us that he's only on a business trip. A thirty-five-year business trip. Then Ezra calls him on the phone and does the very same thing. 'This is Ezra,' he say, as if he'd seen Dad just yesterday –"

Jenny said, "Can we get started now? My children will be freezing to death."

"Oh, surely," Ruth told her. "Cody, honey, her children are waiting on us."

"Mother would have done that, just exactly," Cody said. "If Dad had walked in she would have said, 'Ah, yes, there you are. Can you tell me if my slip is showing?'"

Joe gave a litter bark of laughter. Ezra smiled, but his eyes filmed over with tears. "That's true," he said. "She would have. You know? She really would have."

"Fine, then, she would have," Jenny said. "Shall we go?"

She had been so young when their father left, anyhow. She claimed to have forgotten all about him.

At the funeral, the minister, who had never met their mother, delivered a eulogy so vague, so general, so universally applicable that Cody thought of that parlor game where people fill in words at random and then giggle hysterically at the story that results. Pearl Tull, the minister said, was a devoted wife and a loving mother and a pillar of the community. She had lived a long, full life and died in the bosom of her family, who grieved for her but took comfort in knowing that she'd gone to a far finer place.

It slipped the minister's mind, or perhaps he hadn't heard, that she hadn't been anyone's wife for over a third of a century; that she'd been a frantic, angry, sometimes terrifying mother; and that she'd never shown the faintest interest in her community but dwelt in it like a visitor from a superior neighborhood, always wearing her hat when out walking, keeping her doors tightly shut when at home. That her life had been very long indeed but never full; stunted was more like it. Or crabbed. Or...what was the word Cody wanted? Espaliered. Twisted and flattered to the wall – all the more so as she'd aged and wizened, lost her sight, and grown to lean too heavily on Ezra. That she was not at all religious, hadn't set foot in this church for decades; and thought in certain wistful moods she might have mentioned the possibility of paradise, Cody didn't take much comfort in the notion of her residing there, fidgeting and finding fault and stirring up dissatisfactions.

Cody sat in the right front pew, the picture of a bereaved and dutiful son. But skeptical thoughts flowed through his head so loudly that he almost believed they might be heard by the congregation. He was back to his boyhood, it seemed, fearing that his mother could read his mind as unhesitatingly as she read the inner temperature of a roasting hen by giving its thigh a single, contemptuous pinch. He glanced sideways at Ruth, but she was listening to the minister.

The minister announced the closing hymn, which Pearl had requested in her funeral instructions: "We'll Understand It All By and By." Raising his long, boneless face to lead the singing, Reverend Thurman did appear bewildered – perhaps less by the Lord's mysterious ways than by the unresponsive nature of this group of mourners. Most were just staring into open hymnbooks, following each stanza silently. And there were so few of them: a couple of Ezra's co-workers, some surly teen-aged grandchildren sulking in scattered pews, and five or six anonymous old people, who were probably there as church members but gave the impression of having wandered in off the streets for shelter, dragging their string-handed shopping bags.

When the service was finished, the minister descended from the pulpit and stopped to offer Cody, as firstborn, a handshake and condolences. "All my sympathy...know what a loss..."

"Thank you," said Cody, and he and Ruth and the minister proceeded down the aisle. Jenny and Joe followed, and last came Ezra, blowing his nose. By rights the grandchildren should have risen too, but if they had there would have been hardly any guests remaining.

Outside, the cold was a relief, and Cody was grateful for the lumbering noise of the traffic in the street. He stood between Jenny and Ruth and accepted the murmurs of strangers. "Beautiful service," they told him.

"Thank you," he said.

He heard a woman say to Ezra, over by the church doorway, "I'm so sorry for your trouble," and Ezra said, kindly, "Oh, that's all right" – although for Ezra alone, of the three of them, this death was clearly not all right. What would he fill his life with now? He had been his mother's eyes. Lately, he had been her hands and feet as well. Now that she was gone he would come home every night and...do what? What would he do? Just sit on the couch by himself, Cody pictured; or lie on the bed, fully dressed, staring into the swarming, brownish air above his bed.

Jenny said, "Did Ezra tell you we're meeting at his restaurant afterward?"

Cody groaned. He shook an old man's hand and said to Jenny, "I knew it. I just knew it." Hadn't he told Ruth, in fact? In the car coming down, he'd said, "Oh, God, I suppose there'll be one of those dinners. We'll have to have one of those eternal family dinners at Ezra's restaurant."

"He's probably too upset," Ruth said. "I doubt he'd give a dinner now."

This showed she didn't know Ezra as well as she'd always imagined. Certainly he would give a dinner. Any excuse would do – wedding or engagement or nephew's name on the honor roll. "Dinner at the Homesick Restaurant! Everyone in the family! Just a cozy family gathering" – and he'd rub his hands together in that annoying way he had. He no doubt had his stuff at work even at this moment, preparing the...what were they called? The funeral baked meats. Cody sighed. But he suspected they would have to attend.

The old man must have spoken; he was waiting for Cody to answer. He tilted his flushed, tight-skinned face beneath an elaborate plume of silver hair that let the light shine through. "Thank you," Cody said. Evidently, this was the wrong response. The old man made some disappointed adjustment to his mouth. "Um..."said Cody.

"I said," the old man told him, "I said, 'Cody? Do you know me?'"

Cody knew him.

It shouldn't have taken him so long. There were clues he should have picked up at once: that fan-shaped pompadour, still thick and sharply crimped; the brilliant blue of his eyes; the gangsterish air of his pinstriped, ill-fitting navy blue suit.

"Yes," the old man said, with a triumphant nod. "It's your father speaking, Cody."

Cody said to Jenny, "I'm not sure if Ezra remembered to set a place for Dad."

"What?" Jenny said. She looked at Beck Tull. "Oh," she said.

"At the restaurant. Did he remember?"

"Oh, well, probably," she said.

"Nothing fancy," Cody told Beck.

Beck gaped at him.

"Just a light repast at the Homesick."

"What are you talking about?" Beck asked.

"Dinner afterward, of course, at the Homesick Restaurant."

Beck passed a hand across his forehead. He said, "Is this here Jenny?"

"Yes," Jenny told him.

"Jenny, last time I set eyes on you you were just about eight years old," said Beck. "Was it eight? Or nine. Your favorite song was 'Mairzy Doats.' You babbled that thing night and day."

"Oh, yes," Jenny said distantly. "And little lambs eat ivy."

Beck, who had drawn a breath to go on speaking, paused and shut his mouth.

"You remember Ruth," said Cody.

"Ruth?"

"My wife."

"Why should I remember her? I've been away! I haven't been here!"

Ruth stepped forward to offer her hand. "So Cody's married," said Beck. "Fancy that. Any children?"

"Well, Luke, of course," Cody said.

"I'm a grandfather!" He turned to Jenny. "How about you? Are you married?"

"Yes, but he's left to pick up the little ones," Jenny said. She waved goodbye to somebody.

"And Ezra?" Beck asked. "Where's Ezra?"

"Over there by the steps," Cody said.

"Ah."

Beck set off jauntily, running a hand through his crest of hair. Jenny and Cody gazed after him.

"If I just saw him on the street," Jenny said, "I would have passed him by."

"We are just seeing him on the street," Cody told her.

"Well. Yes."

They watched Beck arrive before Ezra with a bounce, like a child presenting some accomplishment. Ezra bent his head courteously to hear Beck's words, then gave him a mild smile and shook his hand.

"Imagine! " they heard Beck say. "Look at you! Both my sons are bigger than I am."

"Dinner is at my restaurant," Ezra told him calmly.

Beck's expression faltered once again, but recovered itself. "Wonderful! " he said. He moved toward the teen-agers, who had got wind of what was going on and stood in a clump nearby – silent, staring, hostile as usual. Beck seemed not to notice. "I'm your grandpa," he told them. "Your Grandpa Tull. Even heard of me?" Probably they hadn't, unless they'd thought to inquire. He moved down the line, beaming. "I'm your long-lost grandpa. And you are – What a handsome young fellow! "

He pumped the hand of the tallest teen-ager, who unfortunately was not a grandson at all but one of Ezra's salad boys.

Cody and Ruth and Jenny led the way to the restaurant on foot. The others lagged behind untidily. The first group turned onto St. Paul Street and passed various bustling little building – a dry cleaner's and a drugstore and a florist. All the other pedestrians were black; most held jangling radios to their ears, so that scraps of songs about love and jealousy and hardhearted women kept approaching and fading away. Then Ezra's wooden sign swung overhead, and the three of them climbed the steps and walked in.

In the chilly light from the windows, the restaurant seemed glaringly empty. One long table was covered with white linen, set with crystal and china. Thirteen places, Cody counted; for Jenny's Joe would be bringing more children, those too small to have sat through the service. A sweet-faced, plump waitress in a calico smock was drawing up a high chair for the baby. When she saw them come in, she stopped to give Jenny a hug. "I'm so sorry for your trouble," she said. "You and all your family, hear?"

"Thank you, Mrs. Potter," Jenny said. "Do you know my brother Cody? And this is Ruth, his wife."

Mrs. Potter clicked her tongue. "It's a terrible day for you," she said.

Cody turned toward the door in time to see Beck and Ezra enter, trailed by teen-agers. Ezra had obviously relaxed and grown talkative; he never could be cool to anyone for long. "So

I tore out that wall there..."he was saying.

"Very nice. Very classy," said Beck.

"Stripped down these floors..."

"I hope you don't serve that kind of food a fellow can't identify."

"Oh, no."

"A mishmash of food, one thing not separate from another."

"No, never," Ezra said.

Cody watched with interest. (Ezra very often served such food.) Ezra led Beck through the room, waving an arm here and there. "See, these tables can be moved together if anyone should...and this is the kitchen...and these are two of my cooks, Sam and Myron. They've come in especially for our dinner. At night I have three more: Josiah, Chenille, and Mohammad."

"Quite an operation," said Beck.

The others, meanwhile, hung around their table. No one took a seat. Cody's son, Luke, and Jenny's son Peter – both unnaturally formal in white shirts and ties – wrestled together in an aimless, self-conscious way, tossing hidden glances at Beck. Probably these children saw him as a brand-new chance – a fresh start, someone to appreciate them at last. Yet when they finally sat down, no one chose a place near Beck. It was shyness, maybe. Even Ezra settled some distance away. Since Joe and the younger ones had still not arrived, this meant that Beck found himself flanked by several empty chairs. He didn't seem to notice. Kinglike, he sat alone, folding his hands before his plate and beaming around at the others. A tracery of red veins, distinct as mapped rivers and tributaries, showed in his cheeks. "So," he said. "My son owns a fancy restaurant."

Ezra looked pleased and embarrassed.

"And my daughter's a doctor," said Beck. "But Cody? What about you?"

Cody said, "Why, you know: I'm an efficiency consultant."

"Ah, how's that?"

Cody didn't answer. Ezra said, "He checked out factories. He tells them how to do things more efficiently."

"Ah! A time-study man."

"He's one of the very best," said Ezra. "He's always getting written up in articles."

"Is that so. Well, I sure am proud of you, son."

Cody had a sudden intimation that tomorrow, it would be more than he could manage to drag himself off to work. His success had finally filled its purpose. Was this all he had been striving for – this one brief moment of respect flitting across his father's face?

"I often wondered about you, Cody," Beck said, leaning toward him. "I often thought about you after you I went away."

"Oh?" said Cody, politely. "Have you been away?"

His father sat down.

"Anyhow," Ezra said. He cleared his throat. "Well. Dad. Are you still working for the

Tanner Corporation?"

"No, no, I'm retired. Retired in sixty-five. They gave me a wonderful banquet and a sterling silver pen-and-pencil set. Forty-two years of service I put in."

Ruth murmured – an admiring, womanly sound. He turned to her and said, "To tell you the truth, I kind of miss it. Miss the contacts, miss the life...A salesman's life has a lot of action, know what I mean? Lot of activity. Oftentimes now it doesn't seem there's quite enough to keep me busy. But I do a bit of socializing, cardplaying. Got a few buddies at my hotel. Got a lady friend I see." He peeked around at the others from under his tufted eyebrows. "I bet you think I'm too old for such things," he said. "I know what you're thinking! But this is a really fine lady; she puts a lot of stock in me. And you understand I mean no disrespect to your mother, but now that she's gone and I'm free to remarry..."

Somehow, it had never occurred to Cody that his parents were still married. Jenny and Ezra, too, blinked and drew back slightly.

"Only trouble is this lady's daughter," Beck told them. "She's got this daughter, no-good daughter, thirty-five years old if she's a day but still residing at home. Eustacia Lee. No good whatsoever. Lost two fingers in a drill press years ago and never worked since, spent her compensation money on a snowmobile. I'm not too sure I want to live with her."

No one seemed able to think of any comment.

Then Joe arrived. He burst through the door, traveling in an envelope of fresh-smelling air, carrying the baby and towing a whole raft of children. Really there were only three, but it seemed like more; they were so chattery and jumbled. "Mrs. Nesbitt almost didn't let me out of school," and "You'll never guess what the baby ate," and "Phoebe had to stay in for being prejudiced in math." "Who's this?" a child asked, facing Beck.

"Your Grandpa Tull."

"Oh," she said, taking a seat. "Do us kids get wine?"

"Joe, I'd like you to meet my father," Jenny said.

"Really?" said Joe. "Gosh." But then he had to figure out the highchair strap.

The last two children slipped into the empty chairs on either side of Beck. They twined their feet through the rungs, set pointy elbows on the table. Surrounded, Beck gazed first to his left and then to his right. "Will you look at this! " he said.

"Pardon?" Jenny asked.

"This group. This gathering. This...assemblage! "

"Oh," said Jenny, taking a bib from her purse. "Yes, it's quite a crowd."

"Eleven, twelve, thirteen...counting the baby, it's fourteen people! "

"There would have been fifteen, but Slevin's off at college," Jenny said.

Beck shook his head. Jenny tied the bib around the baby's neck.

"What we've got," said Beck, "is a...well, a crew. A whole crew."

Phoebe, who was religious, started loudly reciting a blessing. Mrs. Potter set a steaming bowl of soup before Beck. He sniffed it, looking doubtful.

"It's eggplant soup," Ezra told him.

"Ah, well, I don't believe..."

"Eggplant Soup Ursula. A recipe left behind by one of my very best cooks."

"On this day of death," Phoebe said, "the least some people could do is let a person pray in silence."

"She cooked by astrology," Ezra said. "I'd tell her, 'let's have the endive salad tonight,' and she'd say, 'Nothing vinegary, the stars are wrong,' and up would come some dish I'd never thought of, something I would assume was a clear mistake, but it worked; it always worked. There might be something to this horoscope business, you know? But last summer the stars advised her to leave, and she left, and this place has never been the same."

"Tell us the secret ingredient," Jenny teased him.

"Who says there's a secret ingredient? Some special, surprising trick that you'd only share with blood skin?"

"Well," said Ezra. "It's bananas."

"Aha."

"Without bananas, this soup is nothing."

"On this day of death," Phoebe said, "do we have to talk about food?"

"It is not a day of death," Jenny told her. "Use your napkin."

"The thing is," Beck said. He stopped. "What I mean to say," he said, "it looks like this is one of those great big, jolly, noisy, rambling...why, families!"

The grown-ups looked around the table. The children went on slurping soup. Beck, who so far hadn't even dipped his spoon in, sat forward earnestly. "A clan, I'm talking about," he said, "like something on TV. Lots of cousins and uncles, jokes, reunions – "

"It's not really that way at all," Cody told him.

"How is that?"

"Don't let them mislead you. It's not the way it appears. Why, not more than two or three of these kids are even related to you. The rest are Joe's, by a previous wife. As for me, well, I haven't been with these people in years – couldn't tell you what that baby's name is. Is it a boy or girl, by the way? Was I even informed of its birth? So don't count me in your clan. And Becky down there, at the end of the table –"

"Becky?" said Beck. "Does she happen to be named for me, by any chance?"

Cody stopped, with his mouth open. He turned to Jenny.

"No," said Jenny, wiping the baby's chin. "Her name's Rebecca."

"You think we're a family," Cody said, turning back. "You think we're some jolly, situation-comedy family when we're in particles, torn apart, torn all over the place, and our mother was a witch."

"Oh, Cody," Ezra said.

"A raving, shrieking, unpredictable witch," Cody told Beck. "She slammed us against the wall and called us scum and vipers, said she wished us dead, shook us till our teeth rattled, screamed in our faces. We never knew from one day to the next, was she all right? Was she not? The tiniest thing could set her off. 'I'm going to throw you through that window,' she used to tell me. 'I'll look out that window and laugh at your brains splashed all over the pavement.'"

The main course was set before them, on tiptoe, by Mrs. Potter and another woman who smiled steadily, as if determined not to hear. But nobody picked up his fork. The baby crooned softly to a mushroom button. The other children watched Cody with horrified, bleached faces, while the grown-ups seemed to be thinking of something else. They kept their eyes lowered. Even Beck did.

"It wasn't like that," Ezra said finally.

"You're going to deny it?" Cody asked him.

"No, but she was not always angry. Really she was angry very seldom, only a few times, widely spaced, that happened to stick in your mind."

Cody felt drained. He looked at his dinner and found pink-centered lamb and bright vegetables – a perfect arrangement of colors and textures, one of Ezra's masterpieces, but he couldn't take a bite.

"Think of the other side," Ezra told him. "Think of how she used to play Monopoly with us. Listened to Fred Allen with us. Sang that little song with you – what was the name of that song you two sang? *Ivy, sweet sweet Ivy*...and you'd do a little soft-shoe. The two of you would link arms and soft-shoe into the kitchen."

"Is that right! " said Beck. "I didn't remember Pearl could soft-shoe."

Mrs. Potter poured wine into Cody's glass. He set his fingers around the stem but then couldn't lift it. He was conscious of Ruth, to his right, watching him with concern.

Then Ezra said, "So! What do you think of this wine, Dad?"

"Oh, afraid I'm not much for wine, son," said Beck.

"This is a really good one."

"Little shot of bourbon is more my style," said Beck.

"And best of all's the dessert wine. They make it with these grapes that have suffered from a special kind of mold, you see –"

"Well, wait now," Beck said. "Mold?"

"You're going to love it."

"And what is this here whitish stuff?"

"It's kasha."

"I don't believe I've heard of that."

"You'll love it," Ezra said.

Beck shook his head, but he looked gratified, as if he liked to think that Ezra had traveled so far beyond him.

Then Cody pushed his plate away. "I've got this partner, Sloan," he said. "A bachelor all his life. He never married."

Everyone took on an exaggerated attentiveness – even the children.

"Last year," Cody said, "Sloan ran into some old girlfriend, a woman he'd known years ago, and she had her little daughter with her. They were celebrating the daughter's birthday. Sloan asked which birthday it was, just making conversation, and when the woman told him, something rang a bell. He calculated the dates, and he said, 'Why! My God! She must be mine!' The woman looked over at him, sort of vaguely, and then she collected her thoughts and said, 'Oh. Yes, she is, as a matter of fact.'"

They waited. Cody smiled and gave them a little salute, implying that they could go back to their food.

"Well. What a strange lady," Beck said finally.

"Not at all," Cody told him.

"You'd think she'd at least have –"

"What she was saying was, the man had nothing to do with them. He wasn't even there, you see, so he didn't count. He wasn't part of the family."

Beck drew back sharply. His eyes no longer seemed so blue; they had darkened to a color nearer navy.

Then Joe said, "The baby!"

The baby was struggling soundlessly, convulsively, mouth open and face going purple. "She's strangling," Jenny said. Several people leapt up and a wineglass overturned. Joe was trying to pull the baby from the high chair, but Jenny stopped him. "Never mind that! Let me at her!" It seemed the tray was strapped in place and they couldn't get the baby out from under it. An older child started crying. Something crashed to the floor. Jenny punched the baby in the midriff and a mushroom button shot onto the table. The baby wailed and turned pink. Hiccuping, she was dragged from the high chair and placed on her mother's lap, where she settled down cheerfully and started pursuing a pea around the rim of Jenny's plate.

"Will I live to see them grown?" Jenny asked others.

"He's gone," said Ezra.

They knew instantly whom he meant. Everyone looked toward Beck's chair. It was empty. His napkin was tossed aside, one corner dipping into his plate and soaking up gravy.

"Wait here," Ezra said.

They not only waited; they suspended talk, suspended movement, while Ezra rushed across the dining room and out the front door. There was a pause, during which even the baby said nothing. Then Ezra came back, running his fingers distractedly through his hair. "He's nowhere in sight," he said. "But it's only been a minute. We can catch him! Come on, all of you."

Still, no one moved.

"Please!" said Ezra. "Please. For once, I want this family to finish a meal together. Why, every dinner we've ever had, something has gone wrong. Someone has left in a huff, or in tears, everything's fallen apart...Come on! Everybody out, cover the area, track him down!

We could gather back here when we find him and take up where we left off."

"Or," Cody pointed out, "we could finish the meal without him. That's always a possibility."

But it wasn't; even he could see that. One empty place at the table ruined everything. The chair itself, with its harp-shaped wooden back, had a desolate, reproachful look. Slowly, people rose. The children grouped around Ezra, who was issuing directives like a military strategist. "You and the little ones try Bushnell Street...rendezvous with Joe on Prima..." Then Ruth stood up too, to take the baby while Jenny put her coat on. They headed for the door. "Good hunting!" Cody called, and he tipped his chair back expansively and asked Mrs. Potter for another glass of wine.

Inwardly, though, he felt chastened. He thought of times in grade school when he'd teased some classmate to tears, taken things a little too far, and then looked around to find that all of his friends had stopped laughing. Wasn't there the same hollow silence in this dining room, among these sheeted tables? Mrs. Potter replaced the wine bottle upon a silver-rimmed coaster. She stepped back and folded her hands across her stomach.

"I believe I'll just go check on how they're doing," Cody told her.

Outside, the sky had deepened to a blue that was almost gaudy. A weak sun lit the tops of the buildings, and it didn't seem so cold. Cody stood with his hands at his hips, his feet spread wide – unperturbed, to all appearances – and looked up and down the street. One section of the search party was just disappearing around a corner: Joe and the teen-agers. A stately black woman with her head wrapped in bandannas had stopped to redistribute the contents of the two grocery bags.

Cody took the alley to the right of the doorway, a narrow strip of concrete lined with old packing crates and garbage cans battered shapeless. He passed the restaurant's kitchen window, where an exhaust fan blew him a memory of Ezra's lamb. He skirted a spindly, starved cat with a tail as matted as a worn-out bottle-brush. The back of his neck took on that special alertness required on Baltimore streets, but he walked at an easy, sauntering pace with his hands in his trouser pockets.

"Always have a purse," his father used to tell him. "Act like you're heading someplace purposeful, and none of the lowlife will mess with you," He had also said, "Never trust a man who starts his sentences with 'Frankly,'" and "Nine tenths of a good sidearm pitch is in the flick of the wrist," and, "If you want to sell a person something, look off elsewhere as you're speaking, not straight into his eyes."

"All we have is each other," Ezra would say, justifying one of his everlasting dinners. "We've got to stick together; nobody else has the same past that we have." But in that meager handful of advice offered by Beck Tull – truly the sole advice Cody could remember from him – there didn't seem much of a past to build on. From the sound of it, you would imagine that the three of them shared only a purposeful appearance, a mistrust of frankness, a deft wrist, and an evasive gaze.

Cody suddenly longed for his son – for Luke's fair head and hunched shoulders. (He would rather die than desert a child of his. He had promised himself when he was a boy: anything but that.) He thought back to their goose hunt, where they hadn't had much to say to each other; they had been shy and standoffish together. He wondered whether Sloan would lend him the cabin again next weekend, so they could give it another try.

He came out on Bushnell – sunnier than the alley and almost empty. He shaded his eyes with his hand and looked around him and – why! There was Luke, as if conjured up, sitting for some reason on the stoop of a boarded-over building. Cody started toward him, walking fast. Luke heard his footsteps and raised his head as Cody arrived. But it wasn't Luke. It was Beck. His silver hair appeared yellow in the sunlight, and he had taken off his suit coat to expose his white shirt and his sharp, cocked shoulders so oddly like Luke's. Cody came to a halt.

"I was just looking for the Trailways station," Beck told him. "I thought I could make it walking, but now I'm not so sure."

Cody took out his handkerchief to wipe his forehead.

"See, Claudette will be expecting me," said Beck. "That's the lady friend I mentioned. I figured I better go on and find a bus. Sorry to eat and run, but you know how it is with women. I told her I'd be home before supper. She's depending on me."

Cody replaced the handkerchief.

"I guess she'll want to get married, after this," said Beck. "She knows about Pearl's passing. She's sure to be making plans."

He held up his jacket, as if inspecting it for flaws. He folded it carefully, inside out, and laid it over his arm. The lining was something silky, faintly rainbow hued, like the sheen on aging meat.

"To tell the truth," Beck said, "I don't much want to marry her. It's not only that daughter; it's me. It's really me. You think I haven't had girlfriends before? Oh, sure, and could have married almost any one of them. Lots have begged me, 'Write your wife. Get a divorce. Let's tie the knot.' 'Well, maybe in a while,' I'd tell them, but I never did. I don't know, I just never did."

"You left us in her clutches," Cody said.

Beck looked up. He said, "Huh?"

"How could you do that?" Cody asked him. "How could you just dump us on our mother's mercy?" He bent closer, close enough to smell the camphorish scent of Beck's suit. "We were kids, we were only kids, we had no way of protecting ourselves. We looked to you for help. We listened for your steps at the door so we'd be safe, but you just turned your back on us. You didn't lift a finger to defend us."

Beck stared past Cody at the traffic.

"She wore me out," he told Cody finally.

"Wore you out?"

"Used up my good points. Used up all my good points."

Cody straightened.

"Oh, at the start," Beck said, "she thought I was wonderful. You ought to have seen her face when I walked into a room. When I met her, she was an old maid already. She'd given up. No one had courted her for years; her girlfriends were asking her to baby-sit; their children called her Aunt Pearl. Then I came along. I made her so happy! There's my downfall, son. I mean with anyone, any one of these lady friends, I just can't resist a person I make happy. Why, she might be gaptoothed, or homely, or heavyset – all the better! I expect that if I'd got that divorce from your mother I'd have married six times over, just moving on to each new woman that cheered up some when she saw me, moving on again when she got close to me and didn't act so pleased any more. Oh, it's closeness that does you in. Never get too close to people, son – did I tell you that when you were young? When your mother and I were first married, everything was perfect. It seemed I could do no wrong. Then bit by bit I guess she saw my faults. I'd never hid them, but now it seemed they mattered after all. I made mistakes and she saw them. She saw that I was away from home too much and not enough support to her, didn't get ahead in my work, put on weight, drank too much, talked wrong, ate wrong, dressed wrong, drove a car wrong. No matter how hard I tried, seemed like everything I did got muddled. Spoiled. Turned into an accident, I'd bring home a simple toy, say, to cheer you all up when I came, and it would somehow start a fight – your mother saying it was too expensive or too dangerous or too difficult, and the three of you kids bickering over who got to play with it first. Do you recall the archery set? I thought it would be such fun, set up a target on a tree trunk and shoot our bows and arrows. But it didn't work out like I'd planned. First Pearl claims she's not athletic, then Jenny says it's too cold, then you and Ezra get in some kind of, I don't know, argument or quarrel, end up scuffling, shoot off an arrow, and wing your mother."

"I remember that," said Cody.

"Shot her through the shoulder. A disaster, a typical disaster. Then next week, while I'm away, something goes wrong with the wound. I come home from a sales trip and she tells me she nearly died. Something, I don't know, some infection or other. For me, it was the very last straw. I was sitting over a beer in the kitchen that Sunday evening and all at once, not even knowing I'd do it, I said, 'Pearl, I'm leaving.'"

Cody said, "You mean that was when you left?"

"I packed a bag and walked out," said Beck.

Cody sat down on the stoop.

"See," said Beck, "what it was, I guess: it was the grayness; grayness of things; half-right-and-half-wrongness of things. Everything tangled, mingled, not perfect any more. I couldn't take that. Your mother could, but not me. Yes sir, I have to hand it to your mother."

He sighed and stroked the lining of his jacket.

"I'll be honest," he said, "when I left I didn't think I'd ever care to see you folks again. But later, I started having these thoughts. 'What do you suppose Cody's doing now? What's Ezra up to, and Jenny?' 'My family wasn't so much,' I thought, 'but it's all there really is, in the end.' By then, it was maybe two, three years since I'd left. One night I was passing through Baltimore and I packed a block away, got out and walked to the house. Pretty near froze to death, standing across the street and waiting. I guess I was going to introduce myself or something, if anybody came out. It was you that came. First I didn't even know you, wondered if someone else had moved in. Then I realized it was just that you had grown so. You were almost a man. You came down the walk and you bent for the evening paper and as you straightened, you kind of flipped it in the air and caught it again, and I saw that you could live without me. You could do that carefree a thing, you see – flip a paper and catch it. You were going to turn out fine. And I was right, wasn't I? Look! Haven't you all turned out fine – leading good lives, the three of you? She did it; Pearl did it. I knew she would manage it. I turned and walked back to my car.

"After that, I just stuck to my own routine. Had a few pals, a lady friend from time to time. Somebody's start to think the world of me and I would tell myself, 'I wish Pearl could see this.' I'd even write her a note, now and then. I'd write and give her my latest address, anyplace I moved to, but what I was really writing to say was, 'There's this new important boss we've got who regards me very highly.' Crazy, isn't it? I do believe that all these years, anytime I had any success, I've kind of, like, held it up in my imagination for your mother to admire. Just take a look at this, Pearl, I'd be thinking. Oh, what will I do now she's gone?"

He shook his head.

Cody, searching for something to say, happened to look toward Prima Street and see his family rounding the corner, opening like a fan. The children came first, running, and the teen-agers loped behind, and the grow-ups – trying to keep pace – were very nearly running themselves, so that they all looked unexpectedly joyful. The drab colors of their funeral clothes turned their faces bright. The children's arms and legs flew out and baby bounced on Joe's shoulders. Cody felt surprised and touched. He felt that they were pulling him toward them – that it wasn't they who were traveling, but Cody himself.

"They've found us," he told Beck. "Let's go finish our dinner."

"Oh, well, I'm not so sure," Beck said. But he allowed himself to be helped to his feet. "Oh, well, maybe this one last course," he said, "but I warn you, I plan to leave before that dessert wine's poured."

Cody held on to his elbow and let him toward the others. Overhead, seagulls drifted through a sky so clear and blue that it brought back all the outings of his boyhood – the drives, the picnics, the autumn hikes, the wildflower walks in the spring. He remembered the archery trip, and it seemed to him now that he even remembered that arrow sailing in its graceful, fluttering path. He remembered his mother's upright from along the grasses, her hair lit gold, her small hands smoothing her bouquet while the arrow journeyed on. And high above, he seemed to recall, there had been a little brown airplane, almost motionless, droning through the sunshine like a bumblebee.

Unit 15
Richard Ford(1944–)
理查德·福特

作者简介

理查德·福特,美国短篇小说家。出生于美国密西西比州杰克逊市(Jackson),8岁那年父亲患心脏病,年幼的福特便经常在父母所在的杰克逊市和外祖母所在的小石城(Little Rock)之间来回穿梭。他16岁时,父亲病逝。中学毕业后,福特考入密西根州立大学学习,起初学习酒店管理,后来转向文学。1966年他毕业后与大学时期的恋人克里斯蒂娜(Kristina Hensley)结婚。他曾创办法律学校,担任警察,甚至从事情报工作。这些尝试均以失败告终后,福特转向写作,并在友人的鼓励下考入加利福尼亚大学攻读硕士学位。毕业后,福特为纽约一家名为《内部体育》(*Inside Sports*)的杂志撰稿,然而该杂志于1982年停刊,福特陷入失业困境。他再次萌生写作的念头,并以自己当时的经历为蓝本,历时4年创作出长篇小说《体育记者》(*The Sportswriter*)。该作品于1986年出版后,被《时代》杂志评为年度最优秀的5部小说之一,并获"笔友/福克纳小说奖(the Pen/Faulkner Award for Fiction)"的提名。1995年,被认为是《体育记者》姊妹篇的长篇小说《独立日》(*Independence Day*)出版,该作品不仅使福特获得"笔友/福克纳小说奖",也为他赢得了"普利策奖"。

福特多才多艺,著作颇丰,以《体育记者》和其姊妹篇《独立日》最为出名。他还著有长篇小说《我的一片心》(*A Piece of My Heart*,1976)、《终极好运》(*The Ultimate Good Luck*,1981)和《野性生活》(*Wildlife*,1990);短篇小说集《石泉》(*Rock Spring*,1987)、《男人和女人》(*Women with Men*,1997)以及《多重罪恶》(*A Multitude of Sins*,2002)。此外,他还担任电影《美丽天使》(*Bright Angel*)的编剧,参与编选《美国最佳短篇小说集》(*Best American Short Stories*, 1990);在1992年和2007年他曾两次编纂《格兰塔书美国短篇小说》(*Granta Book of the American Short Story*),并经常为《纽约人》和《纽约时报》撰稿。同时,他还在密歇根大学、普林斯顿大学等多个大学执教,现任美国艺术与文学院院士。福特的作品大都以蒙大拿州和怀俄明州为背景,从第一人称的角度进行叙述。其作品中的主人公多为居无定所或被家族驱逐的人,他们相互之间以及他们与某个地方之间建立起来的是一种临时短暂、无法永恒的关系,因此,"短暂无常"(Transience)也就成为福特小说的一大主题。所以,评论界认为福特的作品颠覆了旧南方文学的传统,表现出后现代文学的特点,他的作品反映出对南方传统历史意识的解构、地域情节的淡化以及家族观念的消解。

作品导读

The Sportswriter is an introspective novel about a sportswriter, Frank Bascombe, who has worked as a sportswriter for a glossy New York sports magazine for 12 years. But at the age of 38, he is in so-called "mid-life, post-divorce crisis", to be specific, he suffers from incurable dreaminess and the occasional pounding of the heart at first, and then he is in face of a series of losses – losses of his profession, his son and his marriage during a short period. Standing at the crossroad of his life, he does not know which fork to take. He is in complete despair.

Despair is a principle theme. First of all, Frank himself is not good at communicating with others, let alone establishing social contact. Moreover, he distrusts closeness or intimacy any more because of his experience of divorce. Besides, from the author we know Frank comes from Biloxi, Mississippi, and then from Frank we know something about his ex-wife, X – she is described as a northerner and "always expresses a 'perfect Michigan attitude' to his friend, Walter's suicide." After their divorce, Frank is in urgent need of establishing a new family in order to end exploring his own fault and shortcomings. He is desperate to find a direction in his life through the life of someone else. Later, he finds a new girlfriend, Vicki, who comes from Texas and often takes pride in her sense of southern cultural identity. To his disappointment, the woman Frank chooses to live together with doesn't want to spend her rest life with him. What's more, to overcome despair and find comfort, he falls back on sports and writing about sports, by which he can struggle for emotional survival and cultural connectedness. Frank is depicted as seeking small consolations in retreat from existential despair. He tries to find comfort in ordinary things, and ordinary things appear in the novel as mysterious and extraordinary.

As a critic says that "Frank is a Babbit for the 1980s, a White Man Without a Clue, cut off from his culture, exiled from his family, and distant from his own emotional life; he wanders the suburbs of contemporary America completely adrift from anything that might wake him from his 'dreaminess' or help establish meaning social contact." Ford invites us to see through the self-censorship of his first-person narrator, and to interrogate myths of writing and identity which expose problems about American cultural life more fundamental than the social surface of the novel might suggest.

作品选读

The Sportswriter

1

My name is Frank Bascombe. I am a sportswriter.

For the past fourteen years I have lived here at 19 Hoving Road, Haddam, New Jersey, in a large Tudor house bought when a book of short stories I wrote sold to a movie producer for a lot of money, and seemed to set my life and me and our three children – two of whom were not even born yet – up for a good life.

Just exactly what that good life was – the one I expected – I cannot tell you now exactly, though I wouldn't say it has not come to pass, only that much has come in between. I am no longer married to X, for instance. The child we had when everything was starting has died, though there are two others, as I mentioned, who are alive and wonderful children.

I wrote half of a short novel soon after we moved here from New York and then put it in the drawer, where it has been ever since, and from which I don't expect to retrieve it unless something I cannot now imagine happens.

Twelve years ago, when I was twenty-six, and in the blind way of things then, I was offered a job as a sportswriter by the editor of a glossy New York sports magazine you have all heard of, because of a free-lance assignment I had written in a particular way he liked. And to my surprise and everyone else's I quit writing my novel and accepted.

And since then I have worked at nothing but that job, with the exception of vacations, and one three-month period after my son died when I considered a new life and took a job as an instructor in a small private school in western Massachusetts where I ended up not liking things, and couldn't wait to leave and get back here to New Jersey and writing sports.

My life over these twelve years has not been and isn't now a bad one at all. In most ways it's been great. And although the older I get the more things scare me, and the more apparent it is to me that bad things can and do happen to you, very little really worries me or keeps me up at night. I still believe in the possibilities of passion and romance. And I would not change much, if anything at all. I might not choose to get divorced. And my son, Ralph Bascombe, would not die. But that's about it for these matters.

Why, you might ask, would a man give up a promising literary career – there were some good notices – to become a sportswriter?

It's a good question. For now let me say only this: if sportswriting teaches you anything, and there is much truth to it as well as plenty of lies, it is that for your life to be worth anything you must sooner or later face the possibility of terrible, searing regret. Though you must also manage to avoid it or your life will be ruined.

I believe I have done these two things. Faced down regret. Avoided ruin. And I am still here to tell about it.

I have climbed over the metal fence to the cemetery directly behind my house. It is five o'clock on Good Friday morning, April 20. All other houses in the neighborhood are shadowed, and I am waiting for my ex-wife. Today is my son Ralph's birthday. He would be thirteen and starting manhood. We have met here these last two years, early, before the day is started, to pay our respects to him. Before that we would simply come over together as man and wife.

A spectral fog is lifting off the cemetery grass, and high up in the low atmosphere I hear the wings of geese pinging. A police car has murmured in through the gate, stopped, cut its lights and placed me under surveillance. I saw a match flare briefly inside the car, saw the policeman's face looking at a clipboard.

At the far end of the "new part" a small deer gazes at me where I wait. Now and then its yellow tapetums blink out of the dark toward the old part, where the trees are large, and where three singers of the *Declaration of Independence* are buried in sight of my son's grave.

My next-door neighbors, the Deffeyes, are playing tennis, calling their scores in hushed-polite early-morning voices. "Sorry." "Thanks." "Forty-love." Pock. Pock. Pock. "Ad to you, dear." "Yes, thank you." "Yours." Pock, pock. I hear their harsh, thrashing nose breaths, their feet scraping. They are into their eighties and no longer need sleep, and so are up at all hours. They have installed glowless barium-sulphur lights that don't shine in my yard and keep me awake. And we have stayed good neighbors if not close friends. I have nothing much in common with them now, and am invited to few of their or anyone else's cocktail parties. People in town are still friendly in a distant way, and I consider them fine people, conservative, decent.

It is not, I have come to understand, easy to have a divorced man as your neighbor. Chaos lurks in him – the viable social contract called into question by the smoky aspect of sex. Most people feel they have to make a choice and it is always easier to choose the wife, which is what my neighbors and friends have mostly done. And though we chitter-chatter across the driveways and hedges and over the tops of each other's cars in the parking lots of grocery stores, remarking on the condition of each other's soffits and down-drains and the likelihood of early winner, sometimes make tentative plans to get together, I hardly ever see them, and I take it in my stride.

Good Friday today is a special day for me, apart from the other specialness. When I woke in the dark this morning, my heart pounding like a tom-tom, it seemed to me as though a change were on its way, as if this dreaminess tinged with expectation, which I have felt for some time now, were lifting off of me into the cool tenebrous dawn.

Today I am leaving town for Detroit to begin a profile of a famous ex-football player who lives in the city of Walled Lake, Michigan, and is confined to a wheelchair since a waterskiing accident, but who has become an inspiration to his former teammates by demonstrating courage and determination, going back to college, finishing his degree in communication arts, marrying his black physiotherapist and finally becoming honorary chaplain for his old team. "Make a contribution" will be my angle. It is the kind of story I enjoy and find easy to write.

Anticipation rises higher, however, because I'm taking my new girlfriend Vicki Arcenault with me. She has recently moved up to New Jersey from Dallas, but I am already pretty certain I'm in love with her (I haven't mentioned anything about it for fear of making her wary). Two months ago, when I sliced up my thumb sharpening a lawnmower blade in my garage, it was Nurse Arcenault who stitched me up in the ER at Doctors Hospital, and things have gone on from there. She did her training at Baylor in Waco, and came up here when her marriage gave out. Her family, in fact, lives down in Barnegat Pines, not far away, not far away, in a subdivision close to the ocean, and I am scheduled to be exhibit A at Easter dinner – a vouchsafe to them that she has made a successful transition to the northeast, found a safe and good-hearted man, and left bad times including her dagger-head husband Everett far behind. Her father, Wade, is a toll-taker at Exit 9 on the Turnpike, and I cannot expect he will like the difference in our ages. Vicki is thirty. I am thirty-eight. He himself is only in his fifties. But I am in hopes of winning him over and eager as can be under the circumstances. Vicki is a sweet, saucy little black-hair with a delicate width of cheekbone, a broad Texas accent and a matter-of-factness with her raptures that can make a man like me cry out in the night for longing.

You should never think that leaving a marriage sets you loose for cherry womanizing and some exotic life you'd never quite grasped before. Far from true. No one can do that for long. The Divorced Men's Club I belong to here in town has proven that to me if nothing else – we don't talk much about women when we are together and feel relieved just to be men alone. What leaving a marriage released me – and most of us – to, was celibacy and more fidelity than I had ever endured before, though with no one convenient to be faithful to or celibate for. Just a long empty moment. Though everyone should live alone at some time in a life. Not like when you're a kid, summers, or in a single dorm room in some crappy school. But when you're grown up. Then be alone. It can be all right. You can end up more within yourself, as the best athletes are, which is worth it. (A basketball player who goes for his patented outside jumper becomes nothing more than the simple wish personified that the ball go in the hole.) In any case, doing the brave thing isn't easy and isn't supposed to be. I do my work and do it well and remain expectant of the best without knowing in the least what it will be. And the bonus is that a little bundle like Nurse Arcenault seems sent straight from heaven.

For several months now I have not taken a trip, and the magazine has found plenty for me to do in New York. It was started in court by X's sleaze-ball lawyer, Alan, that my travel was the cause of our trouble, especially after Ralph died. And though that isn't technically true – it was a legal reason X and I invented together – it is true that I have always loved the travel that accompanies my job. Vicki has only seen two landscapes in her entire life: the flat, featureless gloom-prairies around Dallas, and New Jersey – a strange unworldliness these days. But I will soon show her the midwest, where old normalcy floats heavy on the humid air, and where I happen to have gone to college.

It is true that much of my sportswriter's work is exactly what you would think: flying in airplanes, arriving and departing airports, checking into and out of downtown hotels, waiting hours in corridors and locker rooms, renting cars, confronting unfriendly bellman. Late night drinks in unfamiliar bars, up always before dawn, as I am this morning, trying to get a perspective on things. But there is also an assurance to it that I don't suppose I could live happily without. Very early you come to the realization that nothing will ever take you away from yourself. But in these literal and anonymous cities of the nation, your Milwaukees, your St. Louises, your Seattles, your Detroits, even your New Jerseys, something hopeful and unexpected can take place. A woman I met at the college where I briefly taught, once told me I had too many choices, that I was not driven enough by dire necessity. But that is just an illusion and her mistake. Choices are what we all need. And when I walked out into the bricky warp of these American cities, that is exactly what I feel. Choices aplenty. Things I don't know anything about but might like are here, possibly waiting for me. Even if they aren't. The exhilaration of a new arrival. Good light in a restaurant that especially pleases you. A cab driver with an interesting life history to tell. The casual, lilting voice of a woman you don't know, but that you are allowed to listen to in a bar you've never been in, at a time when you would otherwise have been alone. These things are waiting for you. And what could be better? More mysterious? More worth anticipating? Nothing. Not a thing.

The barium-sulphur lights die out over the Deffeyes' tennis court. Delia Deffeyes' patient and troubleless voice, still hushed, begins assuring her husband Caspar that he played well, while they walk toward their dark house in their pressed whites.

The sky has become a milky eye and though it is spring and nearly Easter, the morning has a strangely winter cast to it, as though a high fog is blotting its morning stars. There is no moon at all.

The policeman has finally seen enough and idles out the cemetery gate onto the silent streets. I hear a paper slap on a sidewalk. Far off, I hear the commuter train up to New York making its belling stop at our station – always a consoling sound.

X's brown Citation stops at the blinking red light at Constitution Street, across from the new library, then inches along the cemetery fence on Plum Road, her lights on high beam. The deer has vanished. I walked over to meet her.

X is an old-fashioned, solidly Michigan girl from Birmingham, whom I met in Ann Arbor. Her father, Henry, was a Soapy Williams best-of-his-generation liberal who still owns a plant that stamps out rubber gaskets for a giant machine that stamps out car fenders, though he is now a Republican and rich as a Pharaoh. Her mother, Irma, lives in Mission Viejo, and the two of them are divorced, though her mother still writes me regularly and believes X and I will eventually reconcile, which seems as possible as anything else.

X could choose to move back to Michigan if she wanted to, buy a condominium or a ranch-style home or move out onto the estate her father owns. We discussed it at the divorce, and I did not object. But she has too much pride and independence to move home now. In addition, she is firmly behind the idea of family and wants Paul and Clarissa to be near me, and I'm happy to think she has made a successful adjustment of her new life. Sometimes we do not really become adults until we suffer a good whacking loss, and our lives in a sense catch up with us and wash over us like a wave and everything goes.

Since our divorce she has bought a house in a less expensive but improving section of Haddam called The Presidents by the locals, and has taken a job as teaching pro at Cranbury Hills C. C. She co-captained the Lady Wolverines in college and has lately begun entering some of the local pro-ams, now that her short game has sharpened up, and even placed high in a couple last summer. I believe all her life she has had a yen to try something like this, and being divorced has given her the chance.

What was our life like? I almost don't remember now. Though I remember it, the space of time it occupied. And I remember it fondly.

I suppose our life was the generic one, as the poet said. X was a housewife and had babies, read books, played golf and had friends, while I wrote about sports and went here and there collecting my stories, coming home to write them up, mooning around the house for days in old clothes, taking the train to New York and back now and then. X seemed to take the best possible attitude to my being a sportswriter. She thought it was fine, or at least she said she did and seemed happy. She thought she had married a young Sherwood Anderson with movie possibilities, but it didn't bother her that it didn't turn out that way, and certainly never bothered me. I was happy as a swallow. We went on vacations with our three children. To Cape Cod (which Ralph called Cape God), to Searsport, Maine, to Yellowstone, to the Civil War battlefields at Antietam and Bull Run. We paid bills, shopped, went to movies, bought cars and cameras and insurance, cooked out, went to cocktail parties, visited schools and romanced each other in the sweet, cagey way of adults. I looked out my window, stood in my yard sunsets with a sense of solace and achievement, cleaned my rain gutters, eyed my shingles, put up storms, fertilized regularly, computed my equity, spoke to my neighbors in an interested voice – the normal applauseless life of us all.

Though toward the end of our marriage I became lost in some dreaminess. Sometimes I would wake up in the morning and open my eyes to X lying beside me breathing, and not recognize her! Not even know what town I was in, or how old I was, or what life it was, so dense was I in my particular dreaminess. I would lie there and try as best I could to extend now knowing, feel that pleasant soaring-out-of-azimuth-and-attitude sensation I grew to like as long as it would last, while twenty possibilities for who, where, what went by. Until suddenly I would get it right and feel a sense of – what? Loss, I think you would say, though loss of what I don't know. My son had died, but I'm unwilling to say that was the cause, or that anything is ever the sole cause of anything else. I know that you can dream your way through an otherwise fine life, and never wake up, which is what I almost did. I believe I have survived that now and nearly put dreaminess behind me, though there is a resolute sadness between X and me that our marriage is over, a sadness that does not feel sad. It is the way you feel at a high school reunion when you hear an old song you used to like played late at night, only you are all alone.

X appears out of the agate cemetery light, loose-gaited and sleepy, wearing deck shoes, baggy corduroys and an old London Fog I gave her years ago. Her hair has been cut short in a new-style way I like. She is a tall girl, big and brown-haired and pretty, who looks younger than she is, which is only thirty-seven. When we met fifteen years ago in New York, at a dreary book signing, she was modeling at a Fifth Avenue clothing store, and sometimes even now she has a tendency to slouch and walk about long-stride in a loose-limbed, toes-out way, though when she takes a square stance up over a golf ball, she can smack it a mile. In some ways she has become as much of a genuine athlete as anyone I know. Needless to say, I have the greatest admiration for her, and love her in every way but the strictest one. Sometimes I see her on the street in town or in her car without expecting to and without her knowing it, and I am struck by wonder: what can she want from life now? How could I have ever loved her and let her go.

"It's chilly, still," she says, in a small, firm voice when she is close enough to be heard, her hands stuffed down deep inside her raincoat. It is a voice I love. In many ways it was her voice I loved first, the sharpened midwestern vowels, the succinct glaciated syntax: Binton Herbor, himburg, Gren Repids. It is a voice that knows the minimum of what will suffice, and banks on it. In general I have always liked hearing women talk more than men.

I wonder, in fact, what my own voice will sound like. Will it be a convincing, truth-telling voice? Or a pseudo-sincere, phony, ex-husband one that will stir up trouble? I have a voice that is really mine, a frank, vaguely, rural voice more or less like a used car salesman a no-frills voice that hopes to uncover simple truth by a straight-on application of the facts. I used to practice it when I was in college. "Well, okay, look at it this way," I'd say right out loud. "All right, all right." "Yeah, but look here." As much as any, this constitutes my sportswriter voice, though I have stopped practicing by now.

X leans herself against the curved marble monument of a man named Craig – at a safe distance from me – and presses her lips inward. Up to this moment I have not noticed the cold. But now that she said it, I feel it in my bones and wish I'd worn a sweater.

These pre-dawn meetings were my idea, and in the abstract they seem like a good way for two people like us to share a remaining intimacy. In practice they are as uncomfortable as a hanging, and it's conceivable we will just forgo it next year, though we felt the same way last year. It is simply that I don't know how to mourn and neither does X. Neither of us has the vocabulary or temperament for it, and so we are more prone to pass the time chatting, which isn't always wise.

"Did Paul mention our rendezvous last night?" I say. Paul, my son, is ten. Last night I had an unexpected meeting with him standing in the dark street in front of his house, when his mother was inside and knew nothing of it, and I was lurking about outside. We had a talk about Ralph, and where he was and about how it might be possible to reach him – all of which caused me to go away feeling better. X and I agree in principle that I shouldn't sneak my visits, but this was not that way.

"He told me Daddy was sitting in the car in the dark watching the house like the police." She stares at me curiously.

"It was just an odd day. It ended up fine, though." It was in fact much more than an odd day.

"You could've come in. you're always welcome."

I smile a winning smile at her. "Another time I will." (Sometimes we do strange things and say they're accidents and coincidences, though I want her to believe it was a coincidence.)

"I just wondered if something was wrong," X says.

"No. I love him very much."

"Good," X says and sighs.

I have spoken in a voice that pleases me, a voice that is really mine.

X brings a sandwich bag out of her pocket, removes a hard-boiled egg and begins to peel it into the bag. We actually have little to say. We talk on the phone at least twice a week, mostly about the children, who visit me after school while X is still out on the teaching tee. Occasionally I bump into her in the grocery line, or take a table next to hers at the August Inn, and we will have a brief chairback chat. We have tried to stay a modern, divided family. Our meeting here is only by way of a memorial for an old life lost.

Still it is a good time to talk. Last year, for instance, X told me that if she had her life to live over again she would probably wait to get married and try to make a go of it on the LPGA tour. Her father had offered to sponsor her, she said, back in 1966 – something she had never told me before. She did not say if she would marry me when the time came. But she did say she wished I had finished my novel, that it would have probably made things better, which surprised me. (She later took that back.) She also told me, without being particularly critical, that she considered me a loner, which surprised me too. She said that it was a mistake to have made as few superficial friends as I have done in my life, and to have concentrated only on the few things I have concentrated on – her, for one. My children, for another. Sportswriting and being an ordinary citizen. This did not leave me well enough armored for the unexpected, was her opinion. She said this was because I didn't know my parents very well, had gone to a military school, and grown up in the south, which was full of betrayers and secret-keepers and untrustworthy people, which I agree is true, though I never knew any of them. All that originated, she said, with the outcome of the Civil War. It was much better to have grown up, she said, as she did, in a place with no apparent character, where there is nothing ambiguous around to confuse you or complicate things, where the only thing anybody ever thought seriously about was the weather.

"Do you think you laugh enough these days?" she finishes peeling her egg and puts the sack down deep in her coat pocket. She knows about Vicki, and I've had one or two other girlfriends since our divorce that I'm sure the children have told her about. But I do not think she thinks they have turned my basic situation around much. And maybe she's right. In any case I am happy to have this apparently intimate, truth-telling conversation, something I do not have very often, and that a marriage can really be good for.

"You bet I do," I say. "I think I'm doing all right, if that's what you mean."

"I suppose it is," X says, looking at her boiled egg as if it posed a small but intriguing problem. "I'm not really worried about you." She raises her eyes at me in an appraising way. It's possible my talk with Paul last night has made her think I've gone off my bearings or started drinking.

"I watch Johnny. He's good for a laugh," I say. "I think he gets funnier as I get older. But thanks for asking." All this makes me feel stupid. I smile at her.

X takes a tiny mouse bite out of her white egg. "I apologize for prying into your life."

"It's fine."

X breathes out audibly and speaks softly. "I woke up this morning in the dark, and I suddenly got this idea in my head about Ralph laughing. It made me cry, in fact. But I thought to myself that you have to strive to live your life to the ultimate. Ralph lived his whole life in nine years, and I remember him laughing. I just wanted to be sure you did. You have a lot longer to live."

"My birthday's in two weeks."

"Do you think you'll get married again?" X says with extreme formality, looking up at me. And for a moment what I smell in the dense morning air is a swimming pool! Somewhere nearby. The cool, aqueous suburban chlorine bouquet that reminds me of the summer coming, and all the other better summers of memory. It is a token of the suburbs I love, that from time to time a swimming pool or a barbecue or a leaf fire you'll never ever see will drift provocatively to your nose.

"I guess I don't know," I say. Thought in truth I would love to be able to say "Couldn't happen, not on a bet, not this boy". Except what I do say is nearer to the truth. And just as quick, the silky-summery smell is gone, and the smell of dirt and stolid monuments has won back its proper place. In the quavery gray dawn a window lights up beyond the fence on the third floor of my house. Bosobolo, my African boarder, is awake. His day is beginning and I see his dark shape pass the window. Across the cemetery in the other direction I see yellow lights in the caretaker's cottage, beside which sits the green John Deere backhoe used for dredging graves. The bells of St. Leo the Great begin to chime a Good Friday prayer call. "Christ Died Today, Christ Died Today" (though I believe it is actually "Stabat Mater Dolorosa").

"I think I'll get married again," X says matter-of-factly. Who to, I wonder?

"Who to?" Not – please – one of the fat-wallet 19th-hole clusters, the big hale 'n' hearty, green-sports-coat types who're always taking her on weekends to the Trapp Family Lodge and getaways to the Poconos, where they take in new Borscht Belt comedians and make love on weaterbeds. I hope against all hope not. I know all about those guys. The children tell me. They all drive Oldsmobiles and wear tasseled shoes. And there is every good reason to go out with them, I grant you. Let them spend their money and enjoy their discretionary time. They're decent fellows, I'm sure. But they are not to be married.

"Oh, a software salesman, maybe," X says. "A realtor. Somebody I can beat at golf and bully." She smiles at me a mouth-down smirky smile of unhappiness, and bunches her shoulders to wag them. But unexpectedly she starts to cry through her smile, nodding toward me as if we both knew about it and should've expected this, and that in a way I am to blame, which in a way I am.

The last time I saw X cry was the night our house was broken into, when, in the search for what might've been stolen, she found some letters I'd been getting from a woman in Blanding, Kansas. I don't know why I kept them. They really didn't mean anything to me. I hadn't seen the woman in months and then only once. But I was in the thickest depths of my dreaminess then, and needed – or thought I did – something to anticipate away from my life, even though I had no plans for ever seeing her and was in fact intending to throw the letters away. The burglars had left Polaroid pictures of the inside of our empty house scattered about for us to find when we got back from seeing *The Thirty-Nine Steps at the Playhouse*, plus the words, "We are the stuffed men," spray-painted onto the dining room wall. Ralph had been dead two years. The children were with their grandfather at the Huron Mountain Club, and I was just back from my teaching position at Berkshire College, and was hanging around the house more or less dumb as a cashew, but otherwise in pretty good spirits. X found the letters in a drawer of my office desk while looking for a sock full of silver dollars my mother had left me, and sat on the floor and read them, then handed them to me when I came in with a list of missing cameras, radios and fishing equipment. She asked if I had anything to say, and when I didn't, she went into the bedroom and began tearing apart her hope chest with a claw hammer and a crowbar. She tore it to bits, then took it to the fireplace and burned it while I stood outside in the yard mooning at Cassiopeia and Gemini and feeling invulnerable because of dreaminess and an odd amusement I felt almost everything in my life could be subject to. It might seem that I was "within myself" then. But in fact I was light years away from everything.

In a little while X came outside, with all the lights in the house left shining and her hope chest going up the chimney in smoke – it was June – and sat in a lawn chair in another part of the dark yard from where I was standing and cried loudly. Lurking behind a large rhododendron in the dark, I spoke some hopeful and unconsoling words to her, but I don't think she heard me. My voice had gotten so soft by then as to be inaudible to anyone but myself. I looked up at the smoke of what I found out was her hope chest, full of all those precious things: menus, ticket stubs, photographs, hotel room receipts, place cards, her wedding veil, and wondered what it was, what in the world it could've been drifting off into the clear spiritless New Jersey nighttime. It remained me of the smoke that announced a new Pope – *a new Pope*! – if that is believable now, under those circumstances. And in four months I was divorced. All this seems odd now, and far away, as if it had happened to someone else and I had only read about it. But that was my life then, and it is my life now, and I am in relatively good spirits about it. If there's another thing that sportswriting teaches you, it is that there are no transcendent themes in life. In all cases things are here and they're over, and that has to be enough. The other view is a lie of literature and the liberal arts, which is why I did not succeed as a teacher, and another reason I put my novel away in the drawer and have not taken it out.

"Yes, of course," X says and sniffs. She has almost stopped crying, though I have not tried to comfort her (a privilege I no longer hold). She raises her eyes up to the milky sky and sniffs again. She is still holding the nibbled egg. "When I cried in the dark, I thought about what a big nice boy Ralph Bascombe should be right now, and that I was thirty - seven no matter what. I wondered about what we should all be doing." She shakes her head and squeezes her arms tight against her stomach in a way I have not seen her do in a long time. "It's not your fault, Frank. I just thought it would be all right if you saw me cry. That's my idea of grief. Isn't that womanish?"

She is waiting for me to say a word now, to liberate us from that old misery of memory and life. It's pretty obvious she feels something is odd today, some freshening in the air to augur a permanent change in things. And I am her boy, happy to do that very thing – let my optimism win back a day or at least the morning or a moment when it all seems lost to grief. My one redeeming strength of character may be that I am good when the chips are down. With success I am worse.

"Why don't I read a poem," I say, and smile a happy old rejected suitor's smile.

"I guess I was supposed to bring it, wasn't I?" X says, wiping her eyes. "I cried instead of bringing a poem." She has become girlish in her tears.

"Well, that's okay," I say and go down into my pants pockets for the poem I have Xeroxed at the office and brought along in case X forgot. Last year I brought Housman's "To An Athlete Dying Young" and made the mistake of not reading it over beforehand. I had not read it since I was in college, but the title made me remember it as something that would be good to read. Which it wasn't. If anything, it was much too literal and dreamily so about real athletes, a subject I have strong feelings about. Ralph in fact had not been much of an athlete. I barely got past"townsman of a stiller town," before I had to stop and just sit staring at the little headstone of red marble, incised with the little words RALPH BASCOMBE.

"Housman hated women, you know," X had said into the awful silence while I sat. "That's nothing against you. I just remembered if from some class. I think he was an old pederast who would've loved Ralph and hated us. Next year I'll bring a poem if that's okay."

"Fine," I had answered miserably. It was after that she told me about my writing a novel and being a loner, and having wanted to join the LPGA back in the sixties. I think she felt sorry for me – I'm sure of it, in fact – though I also felt sorry for myself.

"Did you bring another Housman poem?" she says now and smirks at me, then turns and throws her nibbled egg as far as she can off into the graveness and elms of the old part, where it hits soundlessly. She throws as a catcher would, snapping it by her car in a gainly way, on a tape-line into the shadows. I admire her positive form. To mourn the loss of one child when you have two others is a hard business. And we are not very practiced, though we treat it as a matter of personal dignity and affection so that Ralph's death and our loss will not get entrapped by time and events and ruin our lives in a secret way. In a sense, we can do no wrong here.

Out on Constitution Street an appliance repair truck has stopped at the light. Easler's Philio Repair, driven by Sid(formerly of Sid's Service, a bankrupt). He has worked on my house many times and is heading toward the village square to have a cup at The Coffee Spot before plunging off into the day's kitchens and basements and sump pumps. The day is starting in earnest. A lone pedestrian – a man – walks along the sidewalk, one of the few Negroes in town, walking toward the station in a light-colored, wash-and-wear suit. The sky is still milky, but possibly it will burn off before I leave for the Motor City with Vicki.

"No Housman today," I say.

"Well," X says and smiles, and seats herself on Craig's stone to listen. "If you say so." Lights are numerous and growing dim with the daylight along the backs of houses on my street. I feel warmer.

It is a "Meditation" by Theodore Roethke, who also attended the University of Michigan, something X will be wise to, and I start it in my best, most plausible voice, as if my dead son could hear it down below:

"I have gone into the waste lonely places behind the eye..."

X has already begun to shake her head before I am to the second line, and I stop and look to her to see where the trouble is.

She puches out her lower lip and sits her stone. "I don't like that poem," she says matter-of-factly.

I knew she would know it and have a strong opinion about it. She is still an opinionated Michigan girl, who thinks about things with certainty and is disappointed when the rest of the world doesn't. Such a big strapping things-in-order girl should be in every man's life. They alone are reason enough for the midwest's existence, since that's where most of them thrive. I feel tension rising off me like a fever now. It is possible that reading a poem over a little boy who never cared about poems is not a good idea.

"I thought you'd know it," I say in a congenial voice.

"I shouldn't really say I don't like it," X says coldly. "I just don't believe it, is all."

It is a poem about letting the everyday make you happy – insects, shadows, the color of a woman's hair – something else I have some strong beliefs about. "When I read it, I always think it's me talking," I say.

"I don't think those things in that poem would make anybody happy. They might not make you miserable. But that's all," X says and slips down off the stone. She smiles at me in a manner I do not like, tight-lipped and disparaging, as if she believes I'm wrong about everything and finds it amusing. "Sometimes I don't think anyone can be happy anymore." She puts her hands in her London Fog. She probably has a lesson at seven, or a follow - through seminar, and her mind is ready to be far, far away.

"I think we're all released to the rest of our lives, is my way of looking at it," I say hopefully. "Isn't that true?"

She stares at our son's grave as if he were listening and would be embarrassed to hear us. "I guess."

"Are you really getting married?" I feel my eyes open wide as if I knew the answer already. We are like brother and sister suddenly, Hansel and Gretel, planning their escape to safety.

"I don't know." She wags her shoulders a little, like a girl again, but in resignation as much as anything else. "People want to marry me. I might've reached an age, though, when I don't need men."

"Maybe you should get married. Maybe it would make you happy." I do not believe it for a minute, of course. I'm ready to marry her again myself, get life back on track. I miss the sweet specificity of marriage, its firm ballast and sail. X misses it too, I can tell. It's the thing we both feel the lack of. We are having to make everything up now, since nothing is ours by right.

She shakes her head. "What did you and Pauly talk about last night? I felt like it was all men's secrets and I wasn't in on it. I hated it."

"We talked about Ralph. Paul has a theory we can reach him by sending a carrier pigeon to Cape May. It was a good talk."

X smiles at the idea of Paul, who is as dreamy in his own way as I ever was. I have never thought X much liked that in him, and preferred Ralph's certainty since it was more like hers and, as such, admirable. When he was fiercely sick with Reye's, he sat up in bed in the hospital one day, in a delirium, and said, "Marriage is a damnably serious business, particularly in Boston" – something he'd read in Bartlett's, which he used to leaf through, memorizing and reciting. It took me six weeks to track the remark down to Marquand. And by then he was dead lying right here. But X liked it, thought it proved his mind was working away well underneath the deep coma. Unfortunately it became a kind of motto for our marriage from then till the end, and unmeant malediction Ralph pronounced on us.

"I like your new hair," I say. The new way was a thatch along the back that is very becoming. We are past the end of things now, but I don't want to leave.

X fingers a strand, pulls it straight away from her head and cuts her eyes over at it. "It's dikey, don't you think?"

"No." And indeed I don't.

"Well. It'd gotten to a funny length. I had to do something. They screamed at home when they saw it." She smiles as if she's realized this moment that children become our parents, and we just become children again. "You don't feel old, Frank?" She turns and stares away across the cemetery. "I don't know why I've got all these shitty question. I feel old today. I'm sure it's because you're going to be thirty-nine."

The black man has come to the corner of Constitution Street and stands waiting as the traffic light from red to green across from the new library. The appliance truck is gone, and a yellow minibus stops and lets black maids out onto the same corner. They are large women in white, tentish maid-dresses, talking and swinging big banger purses, waiting for their white ladies to come and pick them up. The man and women do not speak. "Oh, isn't that the saddest thing you ever saw." X says, staring at the women. "Something about that breaks my heart. I don't know why."

"I really don't feel a bit old," I say, happy to be able to answer a question honestly, and possibly slip in some good advice on the side. "I have to wash my hair a little more often. And sometimes I wake up and my heart's pounding to beat the band - though Fincher Barksdale says it isn't anything to worry about. I think it's a good sign. I'd say it was some kind of urgency, wouldn't you?"

X stares at the maids who are talking in a group of five, watching up the street where their rides will come from. Since our divorce she has developed the capability of complete distraction. She will be talking to you but be a thousand miles away. "You're very adaptable," she says airily.

"I am. I know you don't have a sleeping porch in your house, but you should try sleeping with all your windows open and your clothes on. When you wake up, you're ready to go. I've been doing it for a while now."

X smiles at me again with a tight-lipped smile of condescension, a smile I don't like. We are not Hansel and Gretel anymore. "Do you still see your palmist, what's-her-name?"

"Mrs. Miller. No, less often." I'm not about to admit I tried to see her last night.

"Do you feel you're at the point of understanding everything that's happened - to us and our life?"

"Sometimes. Today I feel pretty normal about Ralph. It doesn't seem like it's going to make me crazy again."

"You know," X says, looking away. "Last night I lay in bed and thought bats were flying around my room, and when I closed my eyes I just saw a horizon line a long way off, with everything empty and flat like a long dinner table set for one. Isn't that awful?" She shakes her head. "Maybe I should lead a life more like yours."

A small resentment rises in me, though this is not the place for resentment. X's view of my life is that it is a jollier, more close to the grain business than hers, and certainly more that way than I know it to be. She'd probably like to tell me again that I should've gone ahead and written a novel instead of quitting and being a sportswriter, and that she should've done some things differently herself. But that would not be right, at least about me - there were even plenty of times when she thought so herself. Everything looks old gloomy to her now. One strain in her character that our divorce has touched is that she is possibly less resilient than she has been before in her life, and worry about getting older is proof of it. I'd cheer her up if

I could, but that is one of the talents I lost a long time ago.

"I'm sorry again," she says. "I'm just feeling blue today. There's something about your going away that makes me feel like you're leaving for a new life and I'm not."

"I hope I am," I say, "though I doubt it. I hope you are." Nothing, in fact, would I like better than to have a whole new colorful world open up to me today, though I like things pretty well as they are. I will settle for a nice room at the Pontchartrain, a steak Diane and a salad bar in the rotating rooftop restaurant, seeing the Tigers under the lights. I am not hard to make happy.

"Do you ever wish you were younger?" X says moodily.

"No. I'm fairly happy this way."

"I wish it all the time," she says. "That seems stupid, I know."

I have nothing I can say to this.

"You're an optimist, Frank."

"I hope I am." I smile a good yeoman's smile at her.

"Sure, sure," she says, and turns away from me and begins making her way quickly out through the tombstones, her head up toward the white sky, her hands deep in her pockets like any midwestern girl who's run out of luck for the moment but will soon be back as good as new. I hear the bells of St. Leo the Great chime six o'clock, and for some reason I have a feeling I won't see her for a long time, that something is over and something begun, though I cannot tell you for the life of me what those something might be.

Unit 16
Truman Capote (1924–1984)
杜鲁门·卡波特

作者简介

杜鲁门·卡波特，小说家、剧作家，1924年9月30日出生于新奥尔良（New Orleans）。幼时父母离婚，他被送到南方的远房亲戚家寄养。孤独的童年成就了他的写作，他与另一位来自南方的剧作家田纳西·威廉姆斯（Tennessee Williams）齐名，在美国文学界素有“神童”之称。从17岁开始他就在《纽约客》（*New Yorker*）、《大西洋月刊》（*Atlantic Monthly*）等刊物上发表作品。1945年他发表的短篇小说《米丽亚姆》（Miriam）引起了评论界的关注，并获得了“欧·亨利纪念奖”。他的早期作品体现出美国南方文学的传统。第一部长篇小说《其他的声音，其他的房间》（*Other Voices, Other Rooms*）（1948），讲述了一个有同性恋倾向的男孩到南方寻找亲生父亲和自我价值的艰难成长经历。短篇小说集《黑夜之树及其他故事》（*A Tree of Night and Other Stories*，1949）主要描写美国南部乡村人们的心理世界。代表作《冷血》（*In Cold Blood*，1966）根据作者六年实地调查堪萨斯城连环凶杀案的记录材料写成，记录了作者对生活在正常社会边缘的罪犯的内心世界的研究，也记录了美国司法机构的运作情况。这部非虚构小说集传统小说的想象力与新闻报道的纪实性于一体，出版后引起很大轰动，进入畅销书之列，这种新颖的文学形式成为人们效仿的对象，真正奠定了卡波特在文坛上的地位。

卡波特曾前往意大利积累写作素材，旅居国外期间，他格外怀念自己的童年生活，由此写出了半自传体小说《草竖琴》（*The Grass Harp*，1957）。20世纪50年代初，他开始改编、撰写剧本，对非虚构小说进行实验和探索。他陪同黑人演出团体进行了一次旅苏之行，其中的所见所闻被写成了《听到了缪斯》（*Muses Are Heard*，1956）。此后，卡波特发表了小说《蒂凡尼家的早餐》（*Breakfast at Tiffany's*，1958）。作品讲述了纽约一个年轻而天真的妓女的故事。这是一部以第一人称的叙述反映现实生活的作品，不像《其他的声音，其他的房间》那样集中描述人们的精神孤独，属于色调相对比较明朗的作品。女主人公霍利也成为卡波特笔下众多人物中最吸引读者的一个。卡波特晚年荒淫纵欲、不知节制，与许多曾经才华横溢却不可一世的艺术家一样，他的人生舞台谢幕得并不精彩，1984年8月25日晚卡波特因用药过度猝死于女友家中，享年59岁。卡波特的后期作品还包括小说《圣诞节的回忆》（*A Christmas Memory*，1966）和短篇小说集《犬吠》（*The Dogs Bark*，1973）等。

作品导读

Published when Truman Capote was only 23 years old, *Other Voices, Other Rooms* is a literary touchstone of the mid-20th century. It is a southern gothic where hidden motives and dark secrets bubble and steam like a swamp at high noon on summer's longest day.

This semiautobiographical novel mainly tells the story of a 13-year-old boy called Joel Knox. After the death of his mother, Joel goes to live with his father, who abandoned him at the time of his birth. After he receives a letter from his father inviting him to live with him, Joel travels alone to Skully's Landing and meets lots of people on the way. But when Joel arrives at Skully's Landing, the decaying mansion in rural Alabama, his father is nowhere to be found. Instead, Joel meets his morose stepmother, Amy, eccentric cousin Randolph, and a defiant little girl named Idabel, who soon offers Joel the love and approval he seeks and becomes his friend.

The dilapidated mansion in the middle of swampy nowhere, the sort of place with peeling walls and opulent Persian carpets, the rooms packed with the curios of several generations, are none more mysterious than the current inhabitants, and no mystery greater than why his father, after having sent for him, refuses to see him. Whenever Joel brings it up, meaningful glances are exchanged by the grown-ups. The house belongs to Amy, a prissy and overdressed spinster. She's given refuge to both Joel's father and her cousin Randolph, a prime example of dissipated southern gentry. Amy doesn't seem pleased to see Joel, but Randolph is enraptured. Despite Joel's queries, the whereabouts of his father remain a mystery. When he finally is allowed to see his father, Joel is stunned to find his father is a quadriplegic, having tumbled down a flight of stairs after being inadvertently shot by Randolph. Joel runs away with Idabel but catches pneumonia and eventually returns to the Landing where he is nursed back to health by Randolph. Finally Joel accepts his new family and finds his place.

Other Voices, Other Rooms has a moral on the pain and necessity of needing other people delivered in the flowery language, visual and spoken, of southern storytelling, embellished by just the right touch of mysticism. It deserves to be savored.

This chapter selected tells the reasons why Joel chooses to live with his father and the journey form New Orleans to Skully's Landing. The chapter describes Joel's ride with the truck driver Sam Radclif and the people he meets in the cafe, and finally arrives at Skully's Landing.

作品选读

Other Voices, Other Rooms
Chapter 1

Now a traveler must make his way to Noon City by the best means he can, for there are no buses or trains heading in that direction, though six days a week a truck from the Chuberry Turpentine Company collects mail and supplies in the next - door town of Paradise Chapel: occasionally a person bound for Noon City can catch a ride with the driver of the truck, Sam Radclif. It's a rough trip no matter how you come, for these washboard roads will loosen up even brandnew cars pretty fast; and hitchhikers always find the going bad. Also, this is lonesome country; and here in the swamplike hollows where tiger lilies bloom the size of a man's head, there are luminous green logs that shine under the dark marsh water like drowned corpses; often the only movement on the landscape is winter smoke winding out the chimney of some sorry - looking farmhouse, or a wing - stiffened bird, silent and arrow - eyed, circling over the black deserted pinewoods.

Two roads pass over the hinterlands into Noon City; one from the north, another from the south; the latter, known as the Paradise Chapel Highway, is the better of the pair, though both are much the same: desolate miles of swamp and field and forest stretch along either route, unbroken except for scattered sighs advertising Red Dot 5φ Cigars, Doctor Pepper, NEHI, Grove's Chill Tonic, and 666. Wooden bridges spanning brackish creeks named for long - gone Indian tribes rumble like far - off thunder under a passing wheel; herds of hogs and caws roam the roads at will; now and then a farm family pauses from work to wave as an auto whizzes by, and watch sadly till it disappears in red dust.

One sizzling day in early June the Turpentine Company's driver, Sam Radclif, a big balding six - footer with a rough, manly face, was gulping a beer at the Morning Star Café in Paradise Chapel when the proprietor came over with his arm around this stranger - boy.

"Hiya, Sam," said the proprietor, a fellow called Sydney Katz. "Got a kid here that'd be obliged if you could give him a ride to Noon City. Been trying to get there since yesterday. Think you can help?"

Radclif eyed the boy over the rim of his beer glass, not caring much for the looks of him. He had his notions of what a "real" boy should look like, and this kid somehow offended him. He was too pretty, too delicate and fair - skinned; each of his features was shaped with a sensitive accuracy, and a girlish tenderness softened his eyes, which were brown and very large. His brown hair, cut short, was streaked with pure yellow strands. A kind of tired, imploring expression masked his thin face, and there was an unyouthful sag about his shoulders. He wore long, wrinkled white linen breeches, a limp blue shirt, the collar of which was open at the throat, and rather scuffed tan shoes.

Wiping a mustache of foam off his upper lips, Radclif said: "What's your name, son?"

"Joel. Jo-el Har-ri-son Knox." He separated the syllables explicitly, as though he thought the driver deaf, but his voice was uncommonly soft.

"That so?" drawled Radclif, placing his dry beer glass on the counter. "A mighty fancy name, Mister Knox."

The boy blushed and turned to the proprietor, who promptly intervened: "This is a fine boy, Sam. Smart as a whip. Knows words you and me never heard of."

Radclif was annoyed. "Here, Katz," he ordered, "fillerup." After the proprietor trundled away to fetch a second beer, Sam said kindly, "Didn't mean to tease you, son. Where bouts you from?"

"New Orleans," he said. "I left there Thursday and got here Friday...and that was as far as I could go; no one come to meet me."

"Oh, yeah," said Radclif. "Visiting folks in Noon City?"

The boy nodded. "My father. I'm going to live with him."

Radclif raised his eyes ceilingward, mumbled "Knox" several times, then shook his head in a baffled manner.

"Nope, don't think I know anybody by that name. Sure you're in the right place?"

"Oh, yes," said the boy without alarm. "Ask Mister Katz, he's heard about my father, and I showed him the letters and...wait." He hurried back among the tables of the gloomy café, and returned toting a huge tin suitcase that, judging by his grimace, was extremely heavy. The suitcase was colorful with faded souvenir stickers from remote parts of the globe: Paris, Cairo, Venice, Vienna, Naples, Hamburg, Bombay, and so forth. It was an odd thing to see on a hot day in a town the size of Paradise Chapel.

"You been all them places?" asked Radclif.

"No-o-o," said the boy, struggling to undo a wornout leather strap which held the suitcase together. "It belonged to my grandfather; that was Major Knox: you've read about him in history books, I guess. He was a prominent figure in the Civil War. Anyway, this is the valise he used on his wedding trip around the world."

"Round the world, eh?" said Radclif, impressed. "Musta been a mighty rich man."

"Well, that was a long time ago." He rummaged through his neatly packed possessions till he found a slim package of letters. "Here it is," he said, selecting one in a watergreen envelope.

Radclif fingered the letter a moment before opening it; but presently, with clumsy care, he extracted a green sheet of tissue-like paper and, moving his lips, read:

Edw. R. Sansom, Esq.

Skully's Landing

May 18, 19 –

My dear Ellen Kendall,

I am in your debt for answering my letter so quickly; indeed, by return post. Yes, hearing from me after twelve years must have seemed strange, but I can assure you sufficient reason prompted this long silence. However, reading in the Times-Picayune, to the Sunday issue of which we subscribe, of my late wife's passing, may God the Almighty rest her gentle soul, I at once reasoned the honorable thing could only be to again assume my paternal duties, forsaken, lo, these many years. Both the present Mrs Sansom and myself are happy (nay, overjoyed!) to learn you are willing to concede our desire, though, as you remark, your heart will break in doing so. Ah, how well I sympathize with the sorrow such a sacrifice may bring, having experienced similar emotions when, after that final dreadful affair, I was forced to take leave of my only child, whom I treasured, while he was still no more than an infant. But that is all of the lost past. Rest assured, good lady, we here at the Landing have a beautiful home, healthful food, and a cultured atmosphere with which to provide my son.

As to the journey: we are anxious Joel reach here no later than June First. Now when he leaves New Orleans he should travel via train to Biloxi, at which point he must disembark and purchase a bus ticket for Paradise Chapel, a town some twenty miles south of Noon City. We have at present no mechanical vehicle; therefore, I suggest he remain overnight in P.C. where rooms are let above the Morning Star Café, until appropriate arrangements can be made. Enclosed please find a cheque covering such expenses as all this may incur.

Yrs. Respct.

Edw. R. Sansom

The proprietor arrived with the beer just as Radclif, frowning puzzledly, sighed and tucked the paper back in its envelope. There were two things about this letter that bothered him; first of all, the handwriting: penned in ink the rusty color of dried blood, it was a maze of curlicues and dainty i's dotted with daintier o's. What the hell kind of a man would write like that? And secondly: "If your Pa's named Sansom, how come you call yourself Knox?"

The boy stared at the floor embarrassedly. "Well," he said, and shot Radclif a swift, accusing look, as if the driver was robbing him of something, "they were divorced, and mother always called me Joel Knox."

"Aw, say, son," said Radclif, "you oughtn't to have let her done that! Remember, your Pa's your Pa no matter what."

The proprietor avoided a yearning glance for help which the boy now cast in his direction by having wandered off to attend another customer. "But I've never seen him," said Joel, dropping the letters into his suitcase and buckling up the strap. "Do you know where this place is? Skully's Landing?"

"The Landing?" Radclif said. "Sure, sure I know all about it." He took a deep swallow of beer, let forth a mighty belch, and grinned. "Yes sir, if I was your Pa I'd take down your britches and muss you up a bit." Then draining the glass, he slapped a half-dollar on the counter, and stood meditatively scratching his hairy chin till a wall clock sounded the hour four: "O.K., son' let's shove," he said, starting briskly towards the door.

After a moment's hesitation the boy lifted his suitcase and followed.

"Come see us again," called the proprietor automatically.

The truck was a Ford of the pick-up type. Its interior smelled strongly of sun-warmed leather and gasoline fumes. The broken speedometer registered a petrified twenty. Rainstreaks and crushed insects blurred the windshield, of which one section was shattered in a bursting-star pattern. A toy skull ornamented the gear shift. The wheels bump-bumped over the rising, dipping, curving Paradise Chapel Highway.

Joel sat scrunched in a corner of the seat, elbow propped on window frame, chin cupped in hand, trying hard to keep awake. He hadn't had a proper hour's rest since leaving New Orleans, for when he closed his eyes, as now, certain sickening memories slid through his mind. Of these, one in particular stood out: he was at a grocery counter, his mother waiting next him, and outside in the street January rain was making icicles on the naked tree limbs. Together they left the store and walked silently along the wet pavement, he holding a calico umbrella above his mother, who carried a sack of tangerines. They passed a house where a piano was playing, and the music sounded sad in the grey afternoon, but his mother remarked what a pretty song. And when they reached home she was humming it, but she felt cold and went to bed, and the doctor came, and for over a month he came everyday, but she was always cold, and Aunt Ellen was there, always smiling, and the doctor, always smiling, and the uneaten tangerines shriveled up in the icebox; and when it was over he went with Ellen to live in a dingy two-family house near Pontchartrain.

Ellen was a kind, rather gentle woman, and she did the best she knew how. She had five school-aged children, and her husband clerked in a shoe store, so there was not a great deal of money; but Joel wasn't dependent, his mother having left a small legacy. Ellen and her family were good to him, still he resented them, and often felt compelled to do hateful things, such as tease the older cousin, a dumb-looking girl named Louise, because she was a little deaf: he'd cup his ear and cry "Aye? Aye?" and couldn't stop till she broke into tears. He would not joke or join in the rousing after-supper games his uncle inaugurated nightly, and he took odd pleasure in bringing to attention a slip of grammar on anyone's part, but why this was true puzzled him as much as the Kendalls. It was as if he lived those months wearing a pair of spectacles with green, cracked lenses, and had wax-plugging in his ears, for everything seemed to be something it wasn't, and the days melted in a constant dream. Now Ellen liked to read Sir Walter Scott and Dickens and Hans Andersen to the children before sending them upstairs, and one chilly March evening she read "The Snow Queen." Listening to it, it came to Joel that he had a lot in common with Little Kay, whose outlook was twisted when a splinter from the Sprite's evil mirror infected his eye, changing his heart into a lump of bitter ice: suppose, he thought, hearing Ellen's gentle voice and watching the firelight warm his cousins' faces, suppose, like Little Kay, he also were spirited off to the Snow Queen's frozen palace? What living soul would then brave robber barons for his rescue? And there was no one, really no one.

During the last weeks before the letter came he skipped school three days out of five to loaf around the Canal Street docks. He got into a habit of sharing the boxlunch Ellen fixed for him with a giant Negro stevedore who, as they talked together, spun exotic sea - life legends that Joel knew to be lies even as he listened; but this man was a grown - up, and grown - ups were suddenly the only friends he wanted. And he spent solitary hours watching the loading and unloading of banana boats that shipped to Central America, plotting of course a stowaway voyage, for he was certain in some foreign city he could land a good - paying job. However, on his thirteenth birthday, as it happened, the first letter from Skully's Landing arrived.

Ellen had not shown him this letter for several days. It was peculiar, the way she'd behaved, and whenever her eyes had met his there was a look in them he'd never seen before: a frightened, guilty expression. In answering the letter she'd asked assurance that, should Joel find himself discontented, he would be at once allowed to return; a guarantee his education would be cared for; a promise he could spend Christmas holidays with her. But Joel could sense how relieved she was when, following a long correspondence, Major Knox's old honeymoon suitcase was dragged down from the attic.

He was glad to go. He could not think why, nor did he bother wondering, but his father's more or less incredible appearance on a scene strangely deserted twelve years before didn't strike him as in the least extraordinary, in as much as he'd counted on some such happening all along. The miracle he'd planned, however, was in the nature of a kind old rich lady who, having glimpsed him on a street - corner, immediately dispatched an envelope stuffed with thousand - dollar bills; or a similar Godlike action on the part of some goodhearted stranger. And this stranger, as it turned out, was his father, which to his mind was simply a wonderful piece of luck.

But afterwards, as he lay in a scaling iron bed above the Morning Star Café, dizzy with heat and loss and despair, a different picture of his father and of his situation asserted itself: he did not know what to expect, and he was afraid, for already there were so many disappointments. A panama hat, newly bought in New Orleans and worn with dashing pride, had been stolen in the train depot in Biloxi; then the Paradise Chapel bus had run three hot, sweaty hours behind schedule; and finally, topping everything, there had been no word from Skully's Landing waiting at the café. All Thursday night he'd left the electric light burning in the strange room, and read a movie magazine till he knew the latest doings of the Hollywood stars by heart, for if he let his attention turn inward even a second he would begin to tremble, and the mean tears would not stay back. Toward dawn he'd taken the magazine and torn it to shreds and burned the pieces in an ashtray one by one till it was time to go downstairs.

"Reach behind and hand me a match, will you, boy?" said Radclif. "Back there on the shelf, see?"

Joel opened his eyes and looked about him dazedly. A perfect tear of sweat was balanced on the tip of his nose. "You certainly have a lot of junk," he said, probing around the shelf, which was littered with a collection of yellowed newspapers, a slashed inner tube, greasy tools, an air pump, a flashlight and...a pistol. Alongside the pistol was an open carton of ammunition; bullets the bright copper of fresh pennies. He was tempted to take a whole handful, but ended by artfully dropping just one into his breast pocket. "Here they are."

Radclif popped a cigarette between his lips, and Joel, without being asked, struck a match for him.

"Thanks," said Radclif, a huge drag of smoke creeping out his nostrils. "Say, ever been in this part of the country before?"

"Not exactly, but my mother took me to a Gulfport once, and that was nice because of the sea. We passed through there yesterday on the train."

"Like it round here?"

Joel imagined a queerness in the driver's tone. He studied Radclif's blunt profile, wondering if perhaps the theft had been noticed. If so, Radclif gave no sign. "Well, it's...you know, different."

"Course I don't see any difference. Lived hereabouts all my life, and it looks like everywhere else to me, ha ha! "

The truck hit suddenly a stretch of wide, hard road, unbordered by tree-shade, though a black skirt of distant pines darkened the rim of a great field that lay to the left. A far-off figure, whether man or woman you could not tell, rested from hoeing to wave, and Joel waved back. Farther on, two little white-haired boys astride a scrawny mule shouted their delight when the truck passed, burying them in a screen of dust. Radclif honked and honked the horn at a tribe of hogs that took their time in getting off the road. He could swear like nobody Joel had ever heard, except maybe the Negro dockhand.

A while later, scowling thoughtfully, Joel said: "I'd like to ask you something, O.K.?" He waited till Radclif nodded consent. "Well, what I wanted to ask was, do you know my...Mister Sansom?"

"Yeah, I know who he is, sure," said Radclif, and swabbed his forehead with a filthy handkerchief. "You threw me off the track with those two names, Sansom and Knox. Oh sure, he's the guy that married Amy Skully." There was an instant's pause before he added: "But the real fact is, I never laid eyes on him."

Joel chewed his lip, and was silent a moment. He was crazy with questions he wanted answered, but the ideas, but the idea of asking them embarrassed him, for to be so ignorant of one's own blood-kin seemed shameful. Therefore he said what he had to in a very bold voice: "What about this Skully's Landing? I mean, who all lives there?"

Radclif squinted his eyes while he considered. "Well," he said at last, "they've got a coupla niggers out there, and I know them. Then your daddy's wife, know her: my old lady does dressmaking for her now and again; used to, anyway." He sucked in cigarette smoke, and flipped the butt out the window. "And the cousin...yes, by God, the cousin! "

"Oh?" said Joel casually, though never once in all the letters had such a person been mentioned, and his eyes begged the driver to amplify. But Radclif merely smiled a curious smile, as if amused by a private joke too secret for sharing.

And that was as far as the matter went.

"Looking sharp now," said Radclif presently, "we're coming into town."

A house. A grey clump of Negro cabins. An unpainted clapboard church with a rain-rod steeple, and three Holy panes of ruby glass. A sign: The Lord Jesus Is Coming! Are You Ready? A little black child wearing a big straw hat and clutching tight a pail of blackberries. Over all the sun's stinging glaze. Soon there was a short, unpaved and nameless street, lined with similar one-floored houses, some nicer-looking than others; each had a front porch and a yard, and in some yards grew scraggly rose bushes and crepe myrtle and China trees, from a branch of which very likely dangled a child's play swing made of rope and an old rubber tire. There were Japonica trees with waxy blackgreen polished leaves. And he saw a fat pink girl skipping rope, and an elderly lady ensconced on a sagging porch cooling herself with a palmetto fan. Then a red-barn livery stable: horses, wagons, buggies, mules, men. An abrupt bend in the road: Noon City.

Radclif braked the truck to a halt. He reached across and opened the door next to Joel. "Too bad I can't ride you out to the Landing, son," he said hurriedly. "The company'd raise hell. But you'll make it fine; it's Saturday, lotsa folks living out thataway come into town on Saturday."

Joel was standing alone now, and his blue shirt, damp with sweat, was pasted to his back. Toting the sticker-covered suitcase, he cautiously commenced his first walk in the town.

Noon City is not much to look at. There is only one street, and on it are located a General Merchandise store, a repair shop, a small building which contains two offices, one lodging a lawyer, the other a doctor; a combination barbershop-beautyparlor that is run by a one-armed man and his wife; and a curious, indefinable establishment known as R. V. Lacey's Princely Place where a Texaco gasoline pump stands under the portico. These buildings are grouped so closely together they seem to form a ramshackle palace haphazardly thrown together overnight by a half-wit carpenter. Now across the road in isolation stand two other structures: a jail, and a tall queer tottering ginger-colored house. The jail has not housed a white criminal in over four years, and there is seldom a prisoner of any kind, the Sheriff being a lazy no-good, prone to take his ease with a bottle of liquor, and let trouble-makers and thieves, even the most dangerous type of cutthroats, run free and wild. As to the freakish old house, no one has lived there for God knows how long, and it is said that once three exquisite sisters were raped and murdered here in a gruesome manner by a fiendish Yankee bandit who rode a silvergrey horse and wore a velvet cloak stained scarlet with the blood of Southern womanhood; when told by antiquated ladies claiming one-time acquaintance with the beautiful victims, it is a tale of Gothic splendor. The windows of the house are cracked and shattered, hollow as eyeless sockets; a rotted balcony leans perilously forward, and yellow sunflower birds hide their nests in its secret places; the scaling outer walls are ragged with torn, weather-faded posters that flutter when there is a wind. Among the town kids it is a sign of great valor to enter these black rooms after dark and signal with a matchflame from a window on the topmost floor. However, the porch of this house is in pretty fair condition, and on Saturdays the visiting farm-families make it their headquarters.

New people rarely settle in Noon City or its outlying parts; after all, jobs are scarce here. On the other hand, seldom do you hear of a person leaving, unless it's to wend his lonesome way up onto the dark ledge above the Baptist church where forsaken tombstones gleam like stone flowers among the weeds.

Saturday is of course the big day. Shortly after daylight a procession of mule-drawn wagons, broken-down flivvers, and buggies begins wheeling in from the countryside, and towards midmorning a considerable congregation is gathered. The men sport their finest shirts and store-bought breeches; the women scent themselves with vanilla flavoring or dime-store perfume, of which the most popular brand is called Love Divine; the girls wear dodads in their cropped hair, inflame their cheeks with a lot of rouge, and carry five-cent paper fans that have pretty pictures painted on them. Though barefoot and probably half-naked, each little child is washed clean and given a few pennies to spend on something like a prize-inside box of molasses popcorn. Finished poking around in the various stores, the womenfolk assemble on the porch of the old house, while their men mosey on over to the livery stable. Swift and eager, saying the same things over and over, their voices hum and weave through the long day. Sickness and weddings and courting and funerals and God are the favorite topics on the porch. Over at the stable the men joke and drink whiskey, talk crops and play jackknife: once in a while there are terrible fights, for many of these men are hot-tempered, and if they hold a grudge against somebody they like to wrestle it out.

When twilight shadows the sky it is as if a soft bell were tolling dismissal, for a gloomy hush stills all, and the busy voices fall silent like birds at sunset. The families in their vehicles roll out of the town like a sad, funeral caravan, and the only trace they leave is the fierce quiet that follows. The proprietors of the different Noon City establishments remain open an hour longer before bolting their doors and going home to bed; but after eight o'clock not a decent soul is to be seen wandering in this town except, maybe, a pitiful drunk or a young swain promenading with his ladylove.

"Hey, there! You with the suitcase! "

Joel whirled round to find a bandy-legged, little one-armed man glowering at him from the doorway of a barbershop; he seemed too sickly to be the owner of such a hard, deep voice. "Come here, kid," he commanded, jerking a thumb at his aproned chest.

When Joel reached him, the man held out his hand and in the open palm shone a nickel. "See this?" he said. Joel nodded dumbly. "O.K.," said the man, "now look up the road yonder. See that little gal with the red hair?"

Joel saw whom he meant all right. It was a girl with fiery dutchboy hair. She was about his height, and wore a pair of brown shorts and a yellow polo shirt. She was prancing back and forth in front of the tall, curious old house, thumbing her nose at the barber and twisting her face into evil shapes. "Listen," said the barber, "you go collar that nasty youngun for me and this nickel's yours for keeps. Oh-oh! Watch out, here she comes again..."

Whooping like a wildwest Indian, the redhead whipped down the road, a yelling throng of young admirers racing in her wake. She chunked a great fistful of rocks when she came opposite the spot where Joel was standing. The rocks landed with a maddening clatter on the barbershop's tin roof, and the one-armed man, his face an apoplectic color, hollered: "I'll getcha, Idabel! I'll getcha sure as shooting; you just wait!" A flourish of female laughter floated through the screen door behind him, and a waspish-voiced woman shrilled: "Sugar, you quit actin the fool, and hie yourself in here outa that heat." Then, apparently addressing a third party: "I declare but what he ain't no better'n that Idabel; ain't neither one got the sense God gave'em. Oh shoot, I says to Miz Potter (she was in for a shampoo a week ago today and I'd give a pretty penny to know how she gets that mop so filthy dirty), well, I says: 'Miz Potter, you teach that Idabel at the school,' I says, 'now how come she's so confounded mean?' I says: 'It do seem to me a mystery, and her with that sweet ol sister – speakin of Florabel – and them two twins, and noways alike. Wellsir, Miz Potter answers me: 'Oh, Miz Caulfield, that Idabel sure do give me a peck of trouble and it's my opinion she oughta be in the penitentiary.' Uh huh, that's just what she said. Well, it wasn't no revelation to me cause I always knew she was a freak, no ma'am, never saw that Idabel Thompkins in a dress yet. Sugar, you come on in here outa that heat..."

The man made a yoke with his fingers and spit fatly through it. He gave Joel a nasty look, and snapped, "Are you standing there wanting my money for doing nothing whatsoever, is that it, eh?"

"Sugar, you hear me?"

"Hush your mouth, woman," and the screen door whined shut.

Joel shook his head and went on his way. The redheaded girl and her loud gang were gone from sight, and the white afternoon was ripening towards the quiet time of day when the summer sky spills soft color over the drawn land. He smiled with chilly insolence at the interested stares of passers-by, and when he reached the establishment known as R. V. Lacey's Princely Place, he stopped to read a list that was chalked on a tiny, battered blackboard which stood outside the entrance: Miss Roberta V. Lacey Invites You to Come in and Try Our Tasty Fried Catfish and Chicken – Yummy Dixie Ice Cream – Good Delicious Barbecue – Sweet Drinks & Cold Beer.

"Sweet drinks," he said half-aloud, and it seemed as if frosty Coca-Cola was washing down his dry throat. "Cold beer." Yes, a cold beer. He felt the lumpy outline of the change purse in his pocket, then pushed the swinging screen door open and stepped inside.

In the box-shaped room that was R. V. Lacey's Princely Place there were about a dozen people standing around, mostly overalled boys with rawboned, sunbrowned faces, and a few young girls. A hubbub of talk faded to nothing when Joel entered and self-consciously sat himself down at a wooden counter which ran the length of the room.

"Why, hello, little one," boomed a muscular woman who immediately strode forward and propped her elbows on the counter before him. She had long ape-like arms that were covered with dark fuzz, and there was a wart on her chin, and decorating this wart was a single antenna-like hair. A peach silk blouse sagged under the weight of her enormous breasts; a zany light sparkled in the red-rimmed eyes she focused on him. "Welcome to Miss Roberta's." Two of her dirty-nailed fingers reached out to give his cheek a painful pinch. "Say now, what can Miss Roberta do for this cute-lookin fella?"

Joel was overwhelmed. "A cold beer," he blurted, deafly ignoring the titter of giggles and guffaws that sounded in the background.

"Can't serve no beer to minors, babylove, even if you are a mighty cute-lookin fella. Now what you want is a nice NEHI grapepop," said the woman, lumbering away.

That giggles swelled to honest laughter, and Joel's ears turned a humiliated pink. He wondered if the woman was a lunatic. And his eyes scanned the sour-smelling room as if it were a madhouse. There were calendar portraits of toothy bathing beauties on the walls, and a framed certificate which said: This is to certify that Roberta Velma Lacey won Grand Prize in Lying at the annual Double Branches Dog Days Frolic. Hanging from the low ceiling were several poisonous streamers of strategically arranged flypaper, and a couple of naked lightbulbs that were ornamented with shredded ribbons of green-and-red crepe paper. A water pitcher filled with branches of towering pink dogwood sat on the counter.

"Here y'are," said the woman, plunking down a dripping wet bottle of purple sodapop. "I declare, little one, you sure are hot and dusty-lookin." She gave his head a merry pat. "Know somethin, you must be the boy Sam Radclif brung to town, say?"

Joel admitted this with a nod. He took a swallow of the drink, and it was lukewarm. "I want...that is, do you know how far it is from here to Skully's Landing?" he said, realizing every ear in the place was tuned to him.

"Ummn," the woman tinkered with her wart, and walled her eyes up into her head till they all but disappeared. "Hey, Romeo, how far you spec it is out to The Skulls," she said, and grinned crazily. "I call it The Skulls on accounta..." but she did not finish, for at that moment the Negro boy of whom she'd asked the information, answered: "Two miles, more like three, maybe, ma'am."

"Three miles," she parroted. "But if I was you, babylove, I wouldn't go traipsin over there."

"Me neither," whined a yellow-haired girl.

"Is there anyway I could get a ride out?"

Somebody said, "Ain't Jesus Fever in town?"

"Yeah, I saw Jesus - Jesus, "he parked round by the Livery - "What? Y'all mean old Jesus Fever? Christamighty, I thought he was way gone and buried! - Nah, man. He's past a hundred but alive as you are. –Sure, I seen Jesus - Yeah, Jesus is here..."

The woman grabbed a flyswatter and slammed it down with savage force. "Shut up that gab. I can't hear a thing this boy says."

Joel felt a little surge of pride, tinged with fright, at being the center of such a commotion.

The woman fixed her zany eyes on a point somewhere above his head, and said: "What business you got with The Skulls, babylove?"

Now this again! He sketched the story briefly, omitting all except the simplest events, even to excluding a mention of the letters. He was trying to locate his father, that was the long and short of it. Could she help him?

Well, she didn't know. She stood silent for some time, toying with her wart and staring off into space. "Hey, Romeo," she said finally, "you say Jesus Fever's in town?"

"Yes'm." The boy she called Romeo was colored, and wore a puffy, stained chef's cap. He was stacking dishes in a sink behind the counter.

"Come here, Romeo," she said, beckoning, "I got something to discuss." Romeo joined her promptly in a rear corner. She began whispering excitedly, glancing over her shoulder now and then at Joel, who could not hear what they were saying. It was quiet in the room, and everyone was looking at him. He took out the bullet thefted from Sam Radclif and rolled it nervously in his hands.

Suddenly the door swung open. The skinny girl with fiery, chopped-off red hair swaggered inside, and stopped dead still, her hands cocked on her lips. Her face was flat, and rather impertinent; a network of big ugly freckles spanned her nose. Her eyes, squinty and bright green, moved swiftly from face to face, but showed none a sign of recognition; they paused a cool instant on Joel, then traveled elsewhere.

Hi, Idabel – Whatchasay, Idabel?

"I'm hunting sister," she said. "Anybody seen her?" her voice was boy-husky, sounding as though strained through some rough material: it made Joel clear his throat.

"Seen her sitting on the porch a while back," said a chinless young man.

The redhead leaned against the wall, and crossed her pencil-thin, bony-kneed legs. A ragged bandage stained with mercurochrome covered her left knee. She pulled out a blue yo-yo and let it unwind slowly to the floor and spin back. "Who's that?" she asked, jerking her head towards Joel. When nobody answered, she looptylooped the yo-yo, shrugged and said: "Who cares, pray tell?" But she continued to watch him cagily from the corners of her eyes. "Hey, hows about a dope on credit, Roberta?" she called.

"Miss Roberta," said the woman, momentarily interrupting her confab with Romeo. "I don't need to tell you you have a right smart tongue, Idabel Thompkins, and always did have. And till such time as you learn a few ladylike manners, I'd be obliged if you'd keep outa my place, hear? Besides, since when have you got all this big credit? Ha! March now...and don't come back till you put on some decent female clothes."

"You know what you can do," sassed the girl, stomping out the door. "This old dive'll have a mighty long wait before I bring my trade here again, you betcha." Once outside, her silhouette darkened the screen as she paused to peer in at Joel.

And now dusk was coming on. A sea of deepening green spread the sky like some queer wine, and across this vast green, shadowed clouds were pushed sluggishly by a mild breeze.

Presently the trek homeward would commence, and afterwards the stillness of Noon City would be almost a sound itself: the sound a football might make among the mossy tombs on the dark ledge. Miss Roberta had lent Romeo as Joel's guide. The two kept duplicate pace; the Negro boy carried Joel's bag; wordlessly they turned the corner by the jail, and there was the stable, a barnlike structure of faded red which Joel had noticed earlier that day. A number of men who looked like a gang of desperadoes in a Western picture-show were congregated near the hitching post, passing a whiskey bottle from hand to hand; a second group, less boisterous, played a game with a jackknife under the dark area of an oak tree. Swarms of dragonflies quivered above a slime-coated watertrough; and a scabby hound dog padded back and forth, sniffing the bellies of tied-up mules. One of the whiskey drinkers, an old man with long white hair and a long white beard, was feeling pretty good evidently, for he was clapping his hands and doing a little shuffle-dance to a tune that was probably singing in his head.

The colored boy escorted Joel round the side of the stable to a backlot where wagons and saddled horses were packed so close a swinging tail was certain to strike something. "That's him," said Romeo, pointing his finger, "there's Jesus Fever."

But Joel had seen at once the pygmy figure huddled atop the seatplank of a grey wagon parked on the lot's further rim: a kind of gnomish little Negro whose primitive face was sharp against the drowning green sky. "Don't less us be fraid," said Romeo, leading Joel through the maze of wagons and animals with timid caution. "You best hold tight to my hand, white boy: Jesus Fever, he the oldest ol buzzard you ever put eyes on."

Joel said, "But I'm not afraid," and this was true.

"Shhh! "

As the boys approached, the little pygmy cocked his head at a wary angle; then slowly, with the staccato movements of a mechanical doll, he turned sideways till his eyes, yellow feeble eyes dotted with milky specks, looked down on them with dreamy detachment. He had a funny derby hat perched rakishly on his head, and in the candy-striped ribbon-band was jabbed a speckled turkey feather.

Romeo stood hesitantly waiting, as if expecting Joel to take the lead; but when the white child kept still, he said: "You lucky you come to town, Mister Fever. This here little gentman's Skully kin, and he going out to the Landing for to live."

"I'm Mister Sansom's son," said Joel, though suddenly, gazing up at the dark and fragile face, this didn't seem to mean much. Mr. Sansom. And who was he? A nothing, a nobody. A name that did not appear even to have particular significance for the old man whose sunken, blind-looking eyes studied him without expression.

Then Jesus Fever raised the derby a respectful inch. "Say I should find him here: Miss Amy say," he whispered hoarsely. His face was like a black withered apple, and almost destroyed; his polished forehead shone as though a purple light gleamed under the skin; his sickle curved posture made him look as though his back were broken: a sad little brokeback dwarf crippled with age. Yet, and this impressed Joel's imagination, there was a touch of the wizard in his yellow spotted eyes: it was a tricky quality that suggested, well, magic and things read in books. "I here yestiday, day fore, cause Miss Amy, she say wait," and he trembled under the impact of a deep breath. "Now I can't talk no whole lot: ain't got the strenth. So up, child. Gettin towards night, and night's misery on my bones."

"Right with you, Mister Jesus," said Joel without enthusiasm. Romeo gave him a boost into the wagon, and handed up the suitcase. It was an old wagon, wobbly and rather like an oversized peddler's cart; the floor was strewn with dry cornhusks and croquer sacks which smelled sweetly sour.

"Git, John Brown," urged Jesus Fever, gently slapping the reins against a tan mule's back. "Lift them feet, John Brown, lift them feet..."

Slowly the wagon pulled from the lot and groaned up a path onto the road. Romeo ran ahead, gave the mule's rump a mighty whack and darted off; Joel felt a quick impulse to call him back, for it came to him all at once that he did not want to reach Skully's Landing alone. But there was nothing to be done about it now. Out in front of the stable the bearded drunk had quit dancing, and the hound dog was squatting under the water trough scratching fleas. The wagon's rickety wheels made dust clouds that hung in the green air like powdered bronze. A bend in the road: Noon City was gone.

It was night, and the wagon crept over an abandoned country road where the wheels ground softly through deep fine sand, muting John Brown's forlorn hoofclops. Jesus Fever had so far spoken only twice, each time to threaten the mule with some outlandish torture: he was going to skin him raw or split his head with an axe, possibly both. Finally he'd given up and, still hunched upright on the seatplank, fallen asleep. "Much further?" Joel asked once, and there was no answer. The reins lay limply entwined round the old man's wrists, but the mule skillfully guided the wagon unaided.

Relaxed as a rag doll, Joel was stretched on a croquersack mattress, his legs dangling over the wagon's end. A vein-like latticework of stars frosted the southern sky, and with his eyes he interlinked these spangled vines till he could trace many ice-white resemblances: a steeple, fantastic flowers, a springing cat, the outline of a human head, and other curious designs like those made by snowflakes. There was a vivid, slightly red three-quarter moon; the evening wind eerily stirred shawls of Spanish moss which draped the branches of passing trees. Here and there in the mellow dark fireflies signaled one another as though messaging in code. He listened contented and untroubled to the remote, singing-saw noise of night insects.

Then presently the music of a childish duet came carrying over the sounds of the lonesome countryside: "What does the robin do then, poor thing..." Like specters he saw them hurrying in the moonshine along the road's weedy edge. Two girls. One walked with easy grace, but the other moved as jerky and quick as a boy, and it was she that Joel recognized.

"Hello, there," he said boldly when the wagon overtook them.

Both girls had watched the wagon's approach, and slowed their step perceptibly; but the one who was unfamiliar, as if startled, cried, "Gee Jemima! " She had long, long hair that fell past her hips, and her face, the little he could see of it, smudged as it was in shadow, seemed very friendly, very pretty. "Why, isn't it just grand of you to come along this way and want to give us a ride?"

"Help yourself," he said, and slid over to make a seat.

"I'm Miss Florabel Thompkins ," she announced, after she'd hopped agilely up beside him, and pulled her dresshem below her knees. "This is the Skullys' wagon? Sure, that's Jesus Fever...is he asleep? Well, don't that beat everything." She talked rapidly in a flighty, too birdlike manner, as if mimicking a certain type of old lady. "Come on, sister, there's oodles of room."

The sister trudged on behind the wagon. "I've got two feet and I reckon I'm not such a flirt I can't find the willpower to put one in front of the other, thanks all the same," she said, and gave her shorts an emphatic hitch.

"You're welcome to ride," said Joel weakly, not knowing what else to do; for she was a funny kid, no doubt about it.

"Oh, folderol," said Florabel Thompkins, "don't you pay her no mind. That's just what Mama calls Idabel Foolishness. Let her walk herself knock-kneed for what it means to the great wide world. No use trying to reason with her: she's got willful ways, Idabel has. Ask anybody."

"Huh," was all Idabel said in her defense.

Joel looked from one to the other, and concluded he liked Florabel the best; she was so pretty, at least he imagined her to be, though he could not see her face well enough to judge fairly. Anyway, her sister was a tomboy. And he'd had a special hatred of tomboys ever since the days of Eileen Otis. This Eileen Otis was a beefy little roughneck who had lived on the same block in New Orleans, and she used to have a habit of waylaying him, stripping off his pants, and tossing them high into a tree. That was years gone by, but the memory of her could infuriate him still. He pictured Florabel's redheaded sister as a regular Eileen Otis.

"We've got us a lovely car, you know," said Florabel. "It's a green Chevrolet that six persons can ride in without anybody sitting on anybody's lap, and there are real windowshades you can pull up or down with darling toy babies. Papa won this lovely Chevrolet from a man at a cock-fight, which I think was real smart of him, only Mama says different. Mama's as honest as the day is long, and she don't hold with the cock-fights. But what I'm trying to say is: we don't usually have to hitch rides, and with strangers, too...course we do know Jesus Fever... kinda. But what's your name? Joel? Joel what? Knox...well, Joel Knox, what I'm trying to say is my Papa usually drives us to town in our lovely car..." She jabbered on and on, and he was content to listen till, turning his head, he saw her sister, and thought she was looking at him peculiarly. As this exchange of stares continued, a smileless but amused look that passed between them was lighted by the moon; it was as if each were saying: *I don't think so much of you, either*. "...but one time I just happened to slam the door on Idabel's hand," Florabel was still talking of the car, "and now her thumbnail won't grow the least bit: it's all lumpy and

black. But she didn't cry or take on, which was very brave on her part; now me, I couldn't stand to have such a nasty old...show him your hand, sister."

"You let me alone or I'll show it to you O.K.: in a place you're not expecting."

Florabel sniffed, and glanced peevishly at Joel because he laughed. "It don't pay to treat Idabel like she was a human being," she said ominously. "Ask anybody. The tough way she acts you'd never suppose she came from a well-to-do family like mine, would you?"

Joel held his peace, knowing no matter what he said it would be the wrong thing.

"That's just what I mean," said Florabel, turning the silence to her own advantage, "you'd never suppose. Naturally she is as we're twins: born the same day, me ten minutes first, so I'm elder; both of us twelve, going on thirteen. Florabel and Idabel. Isn't it tacky the way those names kinda rhyme? Only Mama thinks it's real cute, but..."

Joel didn't hear the rest, for he suddenly noticed Idabel had stopped trailing the wagon. She was far back and running, running like a pale animal through the lake of weeds lining the wayside towards a flowering island of dogwood that bloomed lividly some distance off like seashore foam on a black beach. But before he could point this out to Florabel, her twin was gone and lost between the shining trees. "Isn't she afraid to be out there all alone in the dark?" he interrupted, and with a gesture indicated where Idabel had disappeared.

"The child is afraid of nothing," stated Florabel flatly. "Don't you fret none over her; she'll catch up when she gets to feeling like it."

"But out in those woods..."

"Oh, sister takes her notions and there's no sense in asking why. We were born twins, like I told you, but Mama says the Lord always sends something bad with the good." Florabel yawned and leaned back, the long hair sprawling about her shoulders. "Idabel will take any kind of a dare; even when we were real little she'd go up and poke around the Skullys' and peek in all the windows. One time she even got a good look at Cousin Randolph." Lazily she reached up and seized a firefly that was pulsing goldenly in the air above her head, then: "Do you like living at that place?"

"What place?"

"The Landing, silly."

Joel said: "I may, but I haven't seen it yet." Her face was close to his, and he could tell she was disappointed with the answer. "And you, where's your house?"

She waved an airy hand. "Just a little ways up yonder. It's not far from the Landing, so maybe you could come visit sometime." She tossed the firefly into the air where it hung suspended like a small moon. "Naturally I didn't know whether to think you lived at the Landing or not. Nobody ever sees any of them Skullys. Why, the Lord himself could be living there with none the wiser. Are you kin to..." but this was cut short by a terrible, paralyzing wail, and wild crashing in the all-around darkness.

Idabel bounded into the road from the underbrush. She was flailing her arms and howling loud and fierce.

"You darn fool!" her sister screamed, but Joel did nothing, for his heart was lodged somewhere in his throat. Then he turned to check Jesus Fever's reaction, but the old man still snoozed; and strangely the mule had not bolted with fright.

"That was pretty good, eh?" said Idabel. I'll bet you thought the devil was hot on your trail."

Frorabel said: "Not the devil, sister...he's inside you." And to Joel: "She'll catch it when I tell Papa, cause she couldn't have got up here without us seeing unless she cut through the hollow, and Papa's told her and told her about that. She's all the time snooping around in there hunting sweetgum: some day a big old moccasin is going to chew off her leg right at the hip, mark my word."

Idabel had returned carrying a spray of dogwood, and now she smelled the blooms exultantly. "I've already been snakebit," she said.

"Yes, that's the truth," her sister admitted. "You should've seen her leg, Joel Knox. It swelled up like a watermelon; all her hair fell out; oh, she was dogsick for two months, and Mama and me had to wait on her hand and foot."

"It's lucky she didn't die," said Joel.

"I would've if I was you and didn't know how to take care of myself," said Idabel.

"She was smart, all right," conceded Florabel. "She just went smack in the chicken yard and snatched up this rooster and ripped him wide open; never heard such squawking. Hot chicken blood draws the poison."

"You ever been snakebit, boy?" Idabel wanted to know.

"No," he said, feeling somehow in the wrong, "but I was nearly run over by a car once."

Idabel seemed to consider this. "Run over by a car," she said, her woolly voice tinged with envy.

"Now you oughtn't to have told her that," snapped Florabel. "She's liable to run straight off and throw herself in the middle of the highway."

Below the road and in the shallow woods a close-by creek's sliding, pebble-tinkling rush underlined the bellowed comments of hidden frogs. The slow-rolling wagon cleared a slope and started down again. Idabel picked the petals from the dogwood spray, dripping them in her path, and tossed the rind aside; she tilted her head and faced the sky and began to hum; then she sang: "When the northwind doth blow, and we shall have snow, what does the robin do then, poor thing?" Florabel took up the tune: "He got to the barn, to keep he-self warm, and hide he-self under he wing, poor thing!" It was a lively song and they sang it over and over till Joel joined to make a trio; their voices pealed clear and sweet, for all three were sopranos, and Florabel vivaciously strummed a mythical banjo. Then a cloud crossed the moon and in the black the singing ended.

Florabel jumped off the wagon. "Our house is over in there," she said, pointing toward what looked to Joel like an empty wilderness. "Don't forget...come to visit."

"I will," he called, but already the tide of darkness had washed the twins from sight.

Sometime later a thought of them echoed, receded, left him suspecting they were perhaps what he'd first imagined: apparitions. He touched his cheek, the cornhusk, glanced at the sleeping Jesus – the old man was trance like but for his body's rubbery response to the wagon's jolting – and was reassured. The guide reins jangled, the hoofbeats of the mule made a sound as drowsy as a fly's bzzz on a summer afternoon. A jungle of stars rained down to cover him in blaze, to blind and close his eyes. Arms akimbo, legs crumpled, lips vaguely parted – he looked as if sleep had struck him with a blow.

Fence posts suddenly loomed; the mule came alive, began to trot, almost to gallop down a graveled lane over which the wheels spit stone; and Jesus Fever, jarred conscious, tugged at the reins: "Whoa, John Brown, whoa! " And the wagon presently came to a spiritless standstill.

A woman slipped down the steps leading from a great porch; delirious white wings sucked round the yellow globe of a kerosene lantern that she carried high. But Joel, scowling at a dream demon, was unaware when the woman bent so intently towards him and peered into his face by the lamp's smoky light.

Appendix 1

The South

The South is the region including the present states of Maryland, Virginia, North Carolina, South Carolina, Georgia, Kentucky, Tennessee, Louisiana, Mississippi, Alabama, Missouri, Arkansas, Florida, West Virginia, eastern Texas, and formally, Delaware. The area was explored and colonized by the French and Spanish during the 16th century. The first settlement was made as St. Augustine, Fla. (1565), and the Franciscan and Jesuit missionaries were prominent in the early colonization, although the settlers also included Huguenots. Roanoke and Jamestown were the first English settlements, the latter being founded by the Virginia Company. Except for the books of Sandys and John Smith, the English writing of this period was mainly promotional or descriptive, e.g. the works of Whitakers, Pory, Alsop, Hammond, Strchey, Hariot, and the authors of the Burwell Papers.

From the beginning, the South was characteristically agrarian, and the second wave of colonists, including wealthy Cavaliers who came during the interregnum, stimulated the growth of the aristocratic plantation system, in which the staple crops of tobacco, rice, and later cotton were worked under the institution of slavery. There was little popular education, and, even after the founding of William and Mary (1693), education was mostly restricted to the upper classes. Southern culture thus tended to follow the aristocratic Cavalier tradition. The dominant Episcopal Church crushed dissent in most of the colonies, although Catholicism flourished in Maryland under the Calverts, Oglethorpe's Georgia was nonsectarian, and in the 18th century Virginia became comparatively tolerant. As a result of various restraining forces, art and literature in the early South were of little consequence. Most of the writing was historical, as in the works of Beverley, Lawson, Blair, Smith, and Hugh Jones, although there were also the satires of Tailfer and Ebenezer Cook, and the charming journals of Byrd. Southern patriot leaders in the Revolutionary struggle included Patrick Henry, Washington, Jefferson, the Lees, Madison, the Randolphs, Francis Marion, George Mason, and Pickens, and many battles in the later phases of the war took place in the South. These men continued as leaders of the new Republic; of the first five presidents, four were Southerners, while Washington D.C., became the capital of the U.S.

During the 19th century, however, the economic system of the South, based on slave labor, separated the region from the North, which became increasingly industrial, and, with the frontier West, assumed greater political and financial power. Such differences as had appeared in the Federal Constitutional Convention led to the Southern emphasis on states' rights, especially after the Louisiana Purchase (1803), which brought within the U.S. the whole region of the

Mississippi River. The widening schism was marked by such crises as the Missouri Compromise (1820), Calhoun's opposition to the Northern "Tariff of Abominations", the conflict over the Mexican War and its spoils, the Compromise of 1850, the struggles in Kansas and Nebraska, and the Dred Scott case. The survival of Spanish and French traditions, especially among the Creoles and Cajuns of Louisiana, made for distinctions, as did the tendency of the Border States to share the interests of the North. Southern aristocrats tended towards statesmanship rather than literature.

The agrarian emphasis may been seen in Jefferson and John Taylor of Carolina, the feudal gentility in J. P. Kentucky and the laudatory biographies by Marshall, Wirt, and Weems. The English Augustan tradition appears in the Tuesday Club of Annapolis, the Delphian Club of Baltimore, and the Russell's Bookstore Group in Charleston, influenced both by neoclassical views and by the romanticism of Scott, as is evident in the writings of Legare Simms, and others. The fiction of N. B. Tucker was based on Cahoun's philosophy; William J. Grayson was an apologist for slavery; W. A. Caruthers and J. E. Cooke were slight historical romancers; Lamar shows the influence of Byron; and Poe and Chivers represent Southern romanticism carried into the realm of metaphysical mysticism. Regional periodicals included the *Southern Literary Messenger, Be Bow's Review*, and the *Southern Quarterly Review*. The sectional feelings expressed through these and other media reached its peak in the Civil War, when the South seceded from the Union, to form the temporary political association of the Confederacy. During this time the enslaved blacks of the region, kept from education, rarely had an opportunity to express themselves in the written words, although it was occasionally achieved, often by freed persons, like Benjamin Banneker, Martin Delany, and David Walker. With secession came increased chauvinistic literature from white authors. Among the poets of the war and its sequel were Hayne, Timrod, J. R. Randall, Father Ryan, Lanier, J. R. Thompson, and Margaret Preston.

During the period of Reconstruction, the formal social and economic framework was overturned by the abolition of slavery and the new status of blacks. Something of the Southern situation in this period was depicted by the Northerner Albion Tourgee. The local - color movement included such Southern authors as Joel Chandler Harris, Richard M. Johnston, George W. Cable, Kate Chopin, Mary Murfree, John Fox, Lafcadio Hearn, and John T. Moore.

In the 20th century the literature of the South has become not only distinguished but very diverse, yet it has often laid stress on regionalism. The most outstanding fiction, like Faulkner's Yoknapatawpha saga, has used precisely delineated local settings and situations to create a microcosm for the treatment of universal issues. Some fiction has emphasized romance, the past, and fantasy, as in different ways the novels of Margaret Mitchell, Hervey Allen, and Cabell have. Some fiction has concerned itself with the problems of a new industrialism, like the novels of Olive Dargan and T. S. Stribling. Some of the novels and plays have concentrated on the ways of life and folklore of blacks, as have the works of Roark Bradford, Paul Green, DuBose Heyward, and Julia Peterkin. At long last black writers have been able to treat their own heritage in significant works of literature, although in many instances the authors have been from the South but have not remained residents of the region. Black writers who have depicted the South or its impact on their lives and their culture are very various and include William Attaway, Arna Bontemps, Sterling Brown, C. W. Chesnutt, William Demby, W. E. B. DuBois, P. L. Dunbar, Ernst Gaines, Alex Haley, Chester Himes, Langston Hughes, Zora Neale Hurston, Ishmael Reed, Albery Whitman, and Richard Wright. But the 20th century South is too large, its writers are too many, to individual, and too important to be grouped according to subject, school, or heritage.

Appendix 2

The Southern Renascence

For some reasons that no one seems to understand completely, at specific periods in the nation's history many of the most significant literary figures seem to have resided in the same georgraphic region. From about 1790 to 1830, with Washington Irving, James Fenimore Cooper, James Kirke Paulding, and William Cullen Bryant furnishing the nucleus, New York was the literary capital of the U. S. About 1830 it moved to Boston where it remained until the beginning of the Civil War. Between 1830 and 1860 almost every literary figure of any importance lived within a few miles of that New England city – James Russell Lowell, Oliver Wendell Holmes, and William Wadsworth Longfellow at Cambridge; Ralph Waldo Emerson, Henry David Thorreau, and Nathaniel Hawthorne at Concord; and Herman Melville at the height of his career in nearby Pittsfield, Massachusetts. Certainly that area had no serious challenger to being the literary center of the country. From 1860 to 1900, because of Civil War and its aftermath, the U. S. had no literary capital. There were distinguished writers – Walt Whitman, Emily Dickinson, and Mark Twain – but they lived miles apart and had little communication with each other. There is no evidence that any one of them read seriously the writing of either of the other two. About 1912 important writers began again to congregate in the same vicinity. This time, with Hamlin Garland, Theodore Dreiser, Carl Sandburg, and Edgar Lee Masters leading the way, and assisted by Poetry magazine, many persons with literary aspirations migrated toward Chicago. When the young Ernest Hemingway wanted to find a sympathetic audience for his plans for a career in literature, he had merely to ride a streetcar from his home in suburban Oak Park to the downtown Loop.

Although there is broad disagreement on the reason why, the compass needle moved again in about 1920 – and pointed South. For thirty years or more that region dominated literary activity in America. During this period, three of the most significant literary groups in 20thcentury America were centered in the South – the Fugitives, the Agrarians, and the New Critics – and some of the nation's most enduring writers lived and wrote there – William Faulkner, Eudora Welty, Robert Penn Warren, John Crowe Ransom, Allen Tate, Thomas Wolfe, Caroline Gordon, Cleanth Brooks, and Andrew Lytle. Ellen Glasgow and James Branch Cabell, because their literary careers were launched before World War I, are not included in Southern Renascence, though some of their most important work was done in the 1930s, and even later.

Most literary historians and critics would agree that there is no clear sociological explanation for the Southern Renascence. The South in the 1920s was the last place one would expect significant literary activity to occur. According to Howard W. Odum and Harry Estelle Moore's influential study, *Regionalism: A Culture - Historical Approach to National Integration*

(1938), during the 1920s the cultural index or plane of living of the South was the lowest in the nation. It was the bottom of the list in almost everything: Ownership of automobiles, radios, residence telephones; income per capita; bank deposits; homes with electricity, running water, and indoor plumbing. Its residents subscribed to the fewest magazines and newspapers, read the fewest books; they also provided the least support for education, public libraries, and art museums. It would not appear to have produced an economic and intellectual climate conducive to the creation of significant literature. As Donald Davidson once remarked, one wonders how "Faulkner managed to survive, much less write." Apparently there was little change even in the 1930s; in one of his fireside chats President Roosevelt proclaimed the South the nation's number one economic problem.

Despite these adverse circumstances, however, the Renascence did occur. The South, as Randall Stewart once observed, suddenly became a "nest of the singing birds." Many explanations for this phenomenon have been offered. One of the most interesting and illuminating is Allen Tate's: "With the war of 1914–1918, the South reentered the world – but gave a backward glance as it slipped over the border: that backward glance gave us the Southern Renascence, a literature conscious of the past in the present" (*The New Provincialism*[1965]). He and his friends, he wrote in the *The Profession of letters in the South* (1935), came to realize that the Southern attitude was different from the dominant American one, which he defined as "a social point of view", one that did not require a literature of "conviction and experience" but one supported by "statistical survey." The total purpose of Donald Davidson and his fellow Agrarians, Davidson wrote in *Still Rebels, Still Yankees* (1957), was "to seek the image of the South which we could charge with high conviction and to give it, wherever we could, the finality of art." The Southern writers whose best work began to appear in the period between the two wars attempted to find, as Lewis Simpson writes in *The Dispossessed Garden* (1975), "the meaning of the past," to discover or reconstruct some viable relationship to the Southern tradition as it differed from that of other sections of America. The specific characteristics of this tradition, as it was presented in the poems, essays, novels and stories of the third, fourth, and fifth decades of this century, are summarized by Cleanth Brooks in *The Southern Renascence: a Traditionalist View*: a feeling for the concrete and the specific, an awareness of conflict, a sense of community and of religious wholeness, a belief in human imperfection, and a genuine and never wavering disbelief in perfection ever developing as a result of human effort and planning; a deep-seated sense of the tragic, and a conviction that nature is mysterious and contingent. Any attempt to harness nature and make it a servant of man will always be doomed to failure. "This is the ground," Richard King writes in *The Southern Renascence* (1980), in which the South's artistic promptings took root and flourished."

Locating the origins of the Southern Renascence in 1929, the year that saw the publication of Thomas Wolfe's *Look Homeward, Angel* and William Faulkner's *The Sound and the Fury*, C. Vann Woodward, the leading historian of the South in the post-World War II era, characterized it as s flowering of the " literary arts – poetry, fiction and drama." Although Woodward suggested no point at which the literary well ran dry, one might conveniently locate the end of the main phase of the Renaissance somewhere around 1955. After that the South was preoccupied with "other voices, other rooms."

The Southern Renascence was not "just" a literary movement. It was certainly that, but it also represented an outpouring of history, sociology, political analysis, autobiography, and innovative forms of journalism. W. J. Cash, James Agee, Lillian Smith, Howard Odum, and William Alexander Percy were as central to Southern Renascence as William Faulkner, Robert Penn Warren, John Crowe Ransom and Allen Tate.

Appendix 3

The Mind of the South

Preview to Understanding

– Wilbur Joseph Cash

There exists among us by ordinary – both North and South – a profound conviction that the South is another land, sharply differentiated from the rest of the American nation, and exhibiting within itself a remarkable homogeneity.

As to what its singularity may consist in, there is, of course, much conflict of opinion, and especially between Northerner and Southerner. But that it is different and that it is solid – on these things nearly everybody is agreed. Now and then, to be sure, there have arisen people, usually journalists or professors, to tell us that it is all a figment of the imagination, that the South really exists only as a geographical division of the United States and is distinguishable from New England or the Middle West only by such matters as the greater heat and the presence of a larger body of Negroes. Nobody, however, has ever taken them seriously. And rightly.

For the popular conviction is indubitably accurate: the South is, in Allen Tate's phrase, "Uncle Sam's other province." And when Carl Carmer said of Alabama that "The Congo is not more different from Massachusetts, or Kansas or California," he fashioned a hyperbole which is applicable in one measure or another to the entire section.

This is not to suggest that the land does not display an enormous diversity within its borders. Anyone may see that it does simply by riding along any of the great new motor roads which spread across it – through brisk towns with tall white buildings in Nebraska Gothic; through smart suburbs, with their faces newly washed; through industrial and Negro slums, medieval in dirt and squalor and wretchedness, in all but redeeming beauty; past sleepy old hamlets and wide fields and black men singing their sad songs in the cotton, past log cabin and high grave houses, past hill and swamp and plain... "The distance from Charleston to Birmingham is in some respects measurable only in sidereal terms, as is the distance from the Great Smokies to Lake Pontchartrain. And Howard Odum has demonstrated that the economic and social difference between the Southeastern and Southwestern states is so great and growing that they have begun to deserve to be treated, for many purposes, as separate regions.

Nevertheless, if it can be said there are many Souths, the fact remains that there is also one South. That is to say, it is easy to trace throughout the region (roughly delimited by the boundaries of the former Confederate States of America, but shading over into some of the border states, notably Kentucky, also) a fairly definite mental pattern, associated with a fairly definite social pattern – a complex of established relationships and habits of thought, sentiments, prejudices, standards and values, and associations of ideas, which, if it is not common strictly to every group of white people in the South, is still common in one appreciable measure or another, and in some part or another, to all but relatively negligible ones.

It is no product of Cloud - Cuckoo - Town, of course, but proceeds from the common American heritage, and many of its elements are readily recognizable as being simply variations on the primary American theme. To imagine it existing outside this continent would be quite impossible. But for all that, the peculiar history of the South has so greatly modified it from the general American norm that, when viewed as a whole, it decisively justifies the notion that the country is – not quite a nation within a nation, but the next thing to it.

To understand it, it is necessary to know the story of its development. And the best way to begin that story, I think, is by disabusing our minds of two correlated legends – those of the Old and the New Souths.

What the Old South of the legend in its classical form was like is more or less familiar to everyone. It was a sort of stage piece out of the eighteenth century, wherein gesturing gentlemen move soft - spokenly against a background of rose gardens and dueling grounds, through always gallant deeds, and lovely ladies, in farthingales, never for a moment lost that exquisite, remoteness which has been the dream of all men and the possession of none. Its social pattern was manorial, its civilization that of the Cavalier, its ruling class an aristocracy coextensive with the planter group – men often entitled to quarter the royal arms of St. George and St. Andrew on their shields, and in every case descended from the old gentlefolk who for many centuries had made up the ruling classes of Europe.

They dwelt in large and stately mansions, preferably white and with columns and Grecian entablature. Their estates were feudal baronies, their slaves quite too numerous ever to be counted, and their social life a thing of Old World splendor and delicacy. What had really happened here, indeed, was that the gentlemanly idea, driven from England by Cromwell, had taken refuge in the South and fashioned for itself a world to its heart's desire: a world singularly polished and mellow and poised, wholly dominated by ideals of honor and chivalry and noblesse – all those sentiments and values and habits of action which used to be, especially in Walter Scott, invariably assigned to the gentleman born and the Cavalier.

Beneath these was a vague race lumped together indiscriminately as the poor whites – very often, in fact, as the "white - trash." These people belonged in the main to a physically inferior type, having sprung for the most part from the convict servants, redemptioners, and debtors of old Virginia and Georgia, with a sprinkling of the most unsuccessful sort of European peasants and farm laborers and the dregs of the European town slums. And so, of course, the gulf between them and the master classes was impassable, and their ideas and feelings did not enter into the make-up of the prevailing Southern civilization.

But in the legend of the New South the Old South is supposed to have been destroyed by the Civil War and the thirty years that followed it, to have been swept both socially and mentally into the limbo of things that were and are not, to give place to a society which has been rapidly and increasingly industrialized and modernized both in body and in mind – which now, indeed, save for a few quaint survivals and gentle sentimentalities and a few shocking and inexplicable brutalities such as lynching, is almost as industrialized and modernized in its outlook as the North. Such an idea is obviously inconsistent with the general assumption of the South's great difference, but paradox is the essence of popular thinking, and millions – even in the South itself – placidly believe in both notions.

These legends, however, bear little relation to reality. There was an Old South, to be sure, but it was another thing than this. And there is a New South. Industrialization and commercialization have greatly modified the land, including its ideology, as we shall see in due course. Nevertheless, the extent of the change and of the break between the Old South that was and the South of our time has been vastly exaggerated. The South, one might say, is a tree with many age rings, with its limbs and trunk bent and twisted by all the winds of the years, but with its tap root in the Old South. Or, better still, it is like one of those churches one sees in England. The facade and towers, the windows and clerestory, all the exterior and superstructure are late Gothic of one sort or another, but look into its nave, its aisles, and its choir and you find the old mighty Norman arches of the twelfth century. And if you look into its crypt, you may even find stones cut by Saxon, brick made by Roman hands.

The mind of the section, that is, is continuous with the past. And its primary form is determined not nearly so much by industry as by the purely agricultural conditions of that past. So far from being modernized, in many ways it has actually always marched away, as to this day it continues to do, from the present toward the past.

It follows, therefore, that to get at its nature we shall have first of all to examine into the question of exactly what the Old South was really like.

From Chapter I
Of Time And Frontiers

Nobody of any considerable information, of course, any longer believes in the legend of the Old South precisely as, for purposes of relief, I have sketched it in my introduction. Nobody can. For during the last twenty-five years the historians, grown more sober since the days when John Fiske could dispense with discretion and import whole fleets packed to the bowsprits with Prince Rupert's men, have been steadily heaping up a mass of evidence that actual Cavaliers or even near-Cavaliers were rare among Southern settlers.

And indeed, even though no such body of evidence existed, the thing would still be obvious. Men of position and power, men who are adjusted to their environment, men who find life bearable in their accustomed place – such men do not embark on frail ships for a dismal frontier where savages prowl and slay, and living is a grim and laborious ordeal. The laborer, faced with starvation; the debtor, anxious to get out of jail; the apprentice, reckless, eager for a fling at adventure, and even more eager to escape his master; the peasant, weary of the exactions of milord; the small landowner and shopkeeper, faced with bankruptcy and hopeful of a fortune in tobacco; the neurotic, haunted by failure and despair; and once in a blue moon some wealthy bourgeois, smarting under the snubs of a haughty aristocracy and fancying himself in the role of a princeling in the wilderness – all these will go. But your fat and moneyed squire, your gentleman of rank and connection, your Cavalier who is welcome in the drawing-rooms of London–almost never. Not even, as a rule, if there is a price on his head, for across the Channel is France, and the odds are that Cromwell can't last.

But though, in view of such considerations, nobody any longer holds to the Cavalier thesis in its overt form, it remains true that the popular mind still clings to it in essence. Explicit or implicit in most considerations of the land, and despite a gathering tendency on the part of the more advanced among the professional historians, and lately even on the part of popular writers, to cast doubt on it, the assumption persists that the great South of the first half of the nineteenth century – the South which fought the Civil War – was the home of a genuine and fully realized aristocracy, coextensive and identical with the ruling class, the planters; and sharply set apart from the common people, still pretty often lumped indiscriminately together as the poor whites, not only by economic condition but also by the far vaster gulf of a different blood and a different (and long and solidly established) heritage.

To suppose this, however, is to ignore the frontier and that *sine qua non* of aristocracy everywhere – the dimension of time. And to ignore the frontier and time in setting up a conception of the social state of the Old South is to abandon reality. For the history of this South throughout a very great part of the period from the opening of the nineteenth century to the Civil War (in the South beyond the Mississippi until long after that war) is mainly the history of the roll of frontier upon frontier – and on to the frontier beyond.

Prior to the close of the Revolutionary period the great South, as such, has little history. Two hundred years had run since John Smith had saved Jamestown, but the land which was to become the cotton kingdom was still more wilderness than not. In Virginia – in the Northern Neck, all along the tidewater, spreading inland along the banks of the James, the York, the Rappahannock, flinging thinly across the redlands to the valley of the Shenandoah, echoing remotely about the dangerous water of Albemarle – in South Carolina and Georgia – along a sliver of swamp country running from Charleston to Georgetown and Savannah – and in and around Hispano-Gallic New Orleans, there was something which could be called effective settlement and societal organization.

Here, indeed, there was a genuine, if small, aristocracy. Here was all that in aftertime was to give color to the legend of the Old South. Here were silver and carriages and courtliness and manner. Here were great houses – not as great as we are sometimes told, but still great houses: the Shirleys, the Westovers, the Stratfords. Here were the names that were some time to flash with swords and grow tall in thunder – the Lees, the Stuarts, and the Beauregards. Charleston, called the most brilliant of American cities by Crevecoeur, played a miniature London, with overtones of La Rochelle, to a small squirarchy of the rice plantations. In Virginia great earls played at Lord Bountiful, dispensing stately hospitality to every passer-by – to the barge captain on his way down the river, to the slaver who had this morning put into the inlet with a cargo of likely Fulah boys, to the wandering Yankee peddling his platitudinous wooden nutmeg, and to other great earls, who came, with their ladies, in canopied boats or in coach and six with liveried outriders. New Orleans was a pageant of dandies and coxcombs, and all the swamplands could show a social life of a considerable pretension.

2

It is well, however, to remember a thing or two about even these Virginians. (For brevity's sake, I shall treat only of the typical case of the Virginians, and shall hereafter generally apply the term as embracing all these little clumps of colonial aristocracy in the lowlands.) It is well to remember not only that they were not generally Cavaliers in their origin but also that they did not spring up to be aristocrats in a day. The two hundred years since Jamestown must not be forgotten. It is necessary to conceive Virginia as beginning very much as New England began – as emerging by slow stages from a primitive backwoods community, made up primarily of farmers and laborers. Undoubtedly there was a sprinkling of gentlemen of a sort - minor squires, younger sons of minor squires, or adventurers who had got themselves a crest, a fine coat, and title to huge slices of the country. And probably some considerable part of the aristocrats at the end of the Revolution are to be explained as stemming from these bright-plumed birds. It is certain that the great body of them cannot be so explained.

The odds were heavy against such gentlemen – against any gentlemen at all, for that matter. The land had to be wrested from the forest and the intractable red man. It was a harsh and bloody task, wholly unsuited to the talents which won applause in the neighborhood of Rotten Row and Covent Garden, or even in Hants or the West Riding. Leadership, for the great part, passed inevitably to rough and ready hands. While milord tarried at dice or languidly directed his even more languid workmen, his horny-palmed neighbors increasingly wrung profits from the earth, got themselves into position to extend their holdings, to send to England for redemptioners and convict servants in order to extend them still further, rose steadily toward equality with him, attained it, passed him, were presently buying up his bankrupt remains.

The very redemptioners and convict servants were apt to fare better than the gentleman. These are the people, of course, who are commonly said to explain the poor whites of the Old South, and so of our own time. It is generally held of them that they were uniformly shiftless or criminal, and that these characters, being inherent in the germ plasm, were handed on to their progeny, with the result that the whole body of them continually sank lower and lower in the social scale. The notion has the support of practically all the standard histories of the United States, as for example those of John Bach McMaster and James Ford Rhodes. But, as Professor G. W. Dyer, of Vanderbilt University, has pointed out in his monograph, Democracy in the South before the Civil War, it has little support in the known facts.

In the first place, there is no convincing evidence that, as a body, they came of congenitally inferior stock. If some of the convicts were thieves or cutthroats or prostitutes, then some of them were also mere political prisoners, and so, ironically, may very well have represented as good blood as there was in Virginia. Perhaps the majority were simply debtors. As for the redemptioners, the greater number of them seem to have been mere children or adolescents, lured from home by professional crimps or outright kidnapped. It is likely enough, to be sure, that most of them were still to be classed as laborers or the children of laborers; but it is an open question whether this involves any actual inferiority, and certainly it involved no practical inferiority in this frontier society.

On the contrary. Most of them were freed while still in their twenties. Every freeman was entitled to a headright of fifty acres. Unclaimed lands remained plentiful in even the earliest-settled areas until long after the importation of bound servants had died out before slavery. And to cap it all, tobacco prices rose steadily. Thus, given precisely those qualities of physical energy and dogged application which, in the absence of degeneracy, are pre-eminently the heritage of the laborer, the former redemptioner (or convict, for that matter) was very likely to do what so many other men of his same general stamp were doing all about him: steadily to build up his capital and become a man of substance and respect. There is abundant evidence that the thing did so happen. Adam Thoroughgood, who got to be the greatest planter in Norfolk, entered the colony as an indentured servant. Dozens of others who began in the same status are known to have become justices of the peace, vestrymen, and officers of the militia – positions reserved, of course, for gentlemen. And more than one established instance bears out Moll Flanders.

In sum, it is clear that distinctions were immensely supple, and that the test of a gentleman in seventeenth-century Virginia was what the test of a gentleman is likely to be in any rough young society – the possession of a sufficient property.

Aristocracy in any real sense did not develop until after the passage of a hundred years – until after 1700. From the foundations carefully built up by his father and grandfather, a Carter, a Page, a Shirley began to tower decisively above the ruck of farmers, pyramided his holdings in land and slaves, squeezed out his smaller neighbors and relegated them to the remote Shenandoah, abandoned his story-and-a-half house for his new "hall," sent his sons to William and Mary and afterward to the English universities or the law schools in London. These sons brought back the manners of the Georges' and more developed and subtle notions of class. And the sons of these in turn began to think of themselves as true aristocrats and to be accepted as such by those about them – to set themselves consciously to the elaboration and propagation of a tradition.

But even here the matter must not be conceived too rigidly, or as having taken place very extensively. The number of those who had moved the whole way into aristocracy even by the time of the Revolution was small. Most of the Virginians who counted themselves gentlemen were still, in reality, hardly more than superior farmers. Many great property-holders were still almost, if not quite, illiterate. Life in the greater part of the country was still more crude than not. The frontier still lent its tang to the manners of even the most advanced, all the young men who were presently to rule the Republic having been more or less shaped by it. And, as the emergence of Jeffersonian democracy from exactly this milieu testifies, rank had not generally hardened into caste.

3

But this Virginia was not the great South. By paradox, it was not even all of Virginia. It was a narrow world, confined to the areas where tobacco, rice, and indigo could profitably be grown on a large scale – to a relatively negligible fraction, that is, of the Southern country. All the rest, at the close of the Revolution, was still in the frontier or semi-frontier stage. Here were no baronies, no plantations, and no manors. And here was no aristocracy nor any fully established distinction save that eternal one between man and man.

In the vast backcountry of the seaboard states, there lived unchanged the pioneer breed – the unsuccessful and the restless from the older regions; the homespun Scotch-Irish, dogged out of Pennsylvania and Maryland by poverty and the love of freedom; pious Moravian brothers, as poor as they were pious; stolid Lutheran peasants from northern Germany; ragged, throat-slitting Highlanders, lusting for elbow-room and still singing hotly of Bonnie Prince Charlie, all that generally unpretentious and often hard-bitten crew which, from about 1740, had been slowly filling up the region. Houses, almost without exception, were cabins of logs. Farms were clearings, on which was grown enough corn to meet the grower's needs, and perhaps a little tobacco which once a year was "rolled" down to a landing on a navigable stream. Roads and trade hardly yet existed. Life had but ceased to be a business of Indian fighting. It was still largely a matter of coon-hunting, of "painter" tales and hard drinking.

Westward, Boone had barely yesterday blazed his trail. Kentucky and Tennessee were just opening up. And southward of the Nashville basing the great Mississippi Valley, all that country which was to be Alabama, Mississippi, western Georgia, and northern Louisiana, was still mainly a wasteland, given over to the noble savage and peripatetic traders with an itch for adventure and a taste for squaw seraglios.

Then the Yankee, Eli Whitney, interested himself in the problem of extracting the seed from a recalcitrant fiber, and cotton was on its way to be king. The despised backcountry was coming into its own – but slowly at first. Cotton would release the plantation from the narrow confines of the coastlands and the tobacco belt, and stamp it as the reigning pattern on all the country. Cotton would end stagnation, beat back the wilderness, mow the forest, pour black men and plows and mules along the Yazoo and the Arkansas, spin out the railroad, freight the yellow waters of the Mississippi with panting stem-wheelers – in brief, create the great South. But not in a day. It was necessary to wait until the gin could be proved a success, until experience had shown that the uplands of Carolina and Georgia were pregnant with wealth, until the rumor was abroad in the world that the black-lands of the valley constituted a new El Dorado.

It was 1800 before the advance of the plantation was really under way, and even then the pace was not too swift. The physical difficulties to be overcome were enormous. And beyond the mountains the first American was still a dismaying problem. It was necessary to wait until Andrew Jackson and the men of Tennessee could finally crush him. 1810 came and went, the battle of New Orleans was fought and won, and it was actually 1820 before the plantation was fully on the march, striding over the hills of Carolina to Mississippi – 1820 before the tide of immigration was in full sweep about the base of the Appalachians.

From 1820 to 1860 is but forty years – a little more than the span of a single generation. The whole period from the invention of the cotton gin to the outbreak of the Civil War is less than seventy years – the lifetime of a single man. Yet it was wholly within the longer of these periods, and mainly within the shorter, that the development and growth of the great South took place. Men who, as children, had heard the war-whoop of the Cherokee in the Carolina backwoods lived to hear the guns at Vicksburg. And thousands of other men who had looked upon Alabama when it was still a wilderness and upon Mississippi when it was still a stubborn jungle, lived to fight – and to fight well, too – in the ranks of the Confederate armies.

The inference is plain. It is impossible to conceive the great South as being, on the whole, more than a few steps removed from the frontier stage at the beginning of the Civil War. It is imperative, indeed, to conceive it as having, remained more or less fully in the frontier stage for a great part – maybe the greater part of its antebellum history. However rapidly the plantation might advance, however much the slave might smooth the way, it is obvious that the mere physical process of subduing the vast territory which was involved, the essential frontier process of wresting a stable foothold from a hostile environment, must have consumed most of the years down to 1840.

It is plain, too, in the light of these things, that if one is to maintain that the ruling class of the great South was really an aristocracy, one must suppose either that it somehow rose up from the frontier and got to be such in forty or fifty years at best, or that it represented an extension of the Virginia aristocracy – that these Virginians (using the term for all the old colonial groups, mind you) migrated in great numbers to the new regions, and are to be taken as accounting for most of the great estates which presently grew up from cotton.

……

5

How account for the ruling class, then? Manifestly, for the great part, by the strong, the pushing, the ambitious, among the old coon-hunting population of the backcountry. The frontier was their predestined inheritance. They possessed precisely the qualities necessary to the taming of the land and the building of the cotton kingdom. The process of their rise to power was simplicity itself. Take a concrete case.

A stout young Irishman brought his bride into the Carolina upcountry about 1800. He cleared a bit of land, built a log cabin of two rooms, and sat down to the pioneer life. One winter, with several of his neighbors, he loaded a boat with whisky and the coarse woolen cloth woven by the women, and drifted down to Charleston to trade. There, remembering the fondness of his woman for a bit of beauty, he bought a handful of cotton seed, which she planted about the cabin with the wild rose and the honey-suckle – as a flower. Afterward she learned, under the tutelage of a new neighbor, to pick the seed from the fiber with her fingers and to spin it into yarn. Another winter the man drifted down the river, this time to find the half-way station of Columbia in a strange ferment. There was a new wonder in the world – the cotton gin – and the forest which had lined the banks of the stream for a thousand centuries was beginning to go down. Fires flared red and portentous in the night – to set off an answering fire in the breast of the Irishman.

Land in his neighborhood was to be had for fifty cents an acre. With twenty dollars, the savings of his lifetime, he bought forty acres and set himself to clear it. Rising long before day, he toiled deep into the night, with his wife holding a pine torch for him to see by. Aided by his neighbors, he piled the trunks of the trees into great heaps and burned them, grubbed up the stumps, hacked away the tangle of underbrush and vine, stamped out the poison ivy and the snakes. A wandering trader sold him a horse, bony and half-starved, for a knife, a dollar, and a gallon of whisky. Every day now – Sundays not excepted – when the heavens allowed, and every night that the moon came, he drove the plow into the earth, with uptorn roots bruising his shanks at every step. Behind him came his wife with a hoe. In a few years the land was beginning to yield cotton – richly, for the soil was fecund with the accumulated mold of centuries. Another trip down the river, and he brought home a mangy black slave – an old and lazy fellow reckoned of no account in the rice-lands, but with plenty of life in him still if you knew how to get it out. Next year the Irishman bought fifty acres more, and the year after another black. Five years more and he had two hundred acres and ten Negroes. Cotton prices swung up and down sharply, but always, whatever the return, it was almost pure velvet. For the fertility of the soil seemed inexhaustible.

When he was forty-five, he quit work, abandoned the log house, which had grown to six rooms, and built himself a wide-spreading frame cottage. When he was fifty, he became a magistrate, acquired a carriage, and built a cotton gin and a third house – a "big house" this time. It was not, to be truthful, a very grand house really. Built of lumber sawn on the place, it was a little crude and had not cost above a thousand dollars, even when the marble mantel was counted in. Essentially, it was just a box, with four rooms, bisected by a hallway, set on four more rooms bisected by another hallway, and a detached kitchen at the back. Wind-swept in winter, it was difficult to keep clean of vermin in summer. But it was huge, it had great columns in front, and it was eventually painted white, and so, in this land of wide fields and pinewoods it seemed very imposing.

Meantime the country around had been growing up. Other "big houses" had been built. There was a county seat now, a cluster of frame houses, stores, and "doggeries" about a red brick courthouse. A Presbyterian parson had drifted in and started an academy, as Presbyterian parsons had a habit of doing everywhere in the South – and Pompeys and Caesars and Ciceros and Platos were multiplying both among the pickaninnies in the slave quarters and among the white children of the "big houses." The Irish-man had a piano in his house, on which his daughters, taught by a vagabond German, played as well as young ladies could be expected to. One of the Irishman's sons went to the College of South Carolina, came back to grow into the chief lawyer in the county, got to be a judge, and would have been Governor if he had not died at the head of his regiment at Chancellorsville.

As a crown on his career, the old man went to the Legislature, where he was accepted by the Charleston gentlemen tolerantly and - with genuine liking. He grew extremely mellow in age and liked to pass his time in company, arguing about predestination and infant damnation, proving conclusively that cotton was king and that the damyankee didn't dare do anything about it, and developing a notable taste in the local liquors. Tall and well-made, he grew whiskers after the Galway fashion - the well-kept whiteness of which contrasted very agreeably with the brick red of his complexion - donned the long-tailed coat, stove-pipe hat, and string tie of the statesmen of his period, waxed innocently pompous, and, in short, became a really striking figure of a man.

Once, going down to Columbia for the inauguration of a new Governor, he took his youngest daughter along. There she met a Charleston gentleman who was pestering her father for a loan. Her manner, formed by the Presbyterian parson, was plain but not bad, and she was very pretty. Moreover, the Charleston gentleman was decidedly in hard lines. So he married her.

When the old man finally died in 1854, he left two thousand acres, a hundred and fourteen slaves, and four cotton gins. The little newspaper which had recently set up in the county seat spoke of him as "a gentleman of the old school" and "a noble specimen of the chivalry at its best"; the Charleston papers each gave him a column; and a lordly Legare introduced resolutions of respect into the Legislature. His wife outlived him by ten years - by her portrait a beautifully fragile old woman, and, as I have heard it said, with lovely hands, knotted and twisted just enough to give them character, and a finely transparent skin through which the blue veins showed most aristocratically.

1941

Appendix 4

I'll Take My Stand: The South and Agrarian Tradition

Introduction: A Statement of Principles

The authors contributing to this book are Southerners, well acquainted with one another and of similar tastes, though not necessarily living in the same physical community, and perhaps only at this moment aware of themselves as a single group of men. By conversation and exchange of letters over a number of years it had developed that they entertained many convictions in common, and it was decided to make a volume in which each one should furnish his views upon a chosen topic. This was the general, background. But background and consultation as to the various topics were enough; there was to be no further collaboration. And so no single author is responsible for any view outside his own article. It was through the good fortune of some deeper agreement that the book was expected to achieve its unity. All the articles bear in the same sense upon the book's title-subject: all tend to support a Southern way of life against what may be called the American or prevailing way; and all as much as agree that the best terms in which to represent the distinction are contained in the phrase, Agrarian versus Industrial.

But after the book was under way it seemed a pity if the contributors, limited as they were within their special subjects, should stop short of showing how close their agreements really were. On the contrary, it seemed that they ought to go on and make themselves known as a group already consolidated by a set of principles which could be stated with a good deal of particularity. This might prove useful for the sake of future reference, if they should undertake any further joint publication. It was then decided to prepare a general introduction for the book which would state briefly the common convictions of the group. This is the statement. To it every one of the contributors in this book has subscribed.

Nobody now proposes for the South, or for any other community in this country, an independent political destiny. That idea is thought to have been finished in 1865. But how far shall the South surrender its moral, social, and economic autonomy to the victorious principle of Union? That question remains open. The South is a minority section that has hitherto been jealous of its minority right to live its own kind of life. The South scarcely hopes to determine the other sections, but it does propose to determine itself, within the utmost limits of legal action. Of late, however, there is the melancholy fact that the South itself has wavered a little and shown signs of wanting to join up behind the common or American industrial ideal. It is against that tendency that this book is written. The younger Southerners, who are being converted frequently to the industrial gospel, must come back to the support of the Southern tradition. They must be persuaded to look very critically at the advantages of becoming a "new South" which will be only an undistinguished replica of the usual industrial community.

But there are many other minority communities opposed to industrialism, and wanting a much simpler economy to live by. The communities and private persons sharing the agrarian tastes are to be found widely within the Union. Proper living is a matter of the intelligence and the will, does not depend on the local climate or geography, and is capable of a definition which is general and not Southern at all. Southerners have a filial duty to discharge to their own section. But their cause is precarious and they must seek alliances with sympathetic communities everywhere. The members of the present group would be happy to be counted as members of a national agrarian movement.

Industrialism is the economic organization of the collective American society. It means the decision of society to invest its economic resources in the applied sciences. But the word science has acquired a certain sanctitude. It is out of order to quarrel with science in the abstract, or even with the applied sciences when their applications are made subject to criticism and intelligence. The capitalization of the applied sciences has now become extravagant and uncritical; it has enslaved our human energies to a degree now clearly felt to be burdensome. The apologists of industrialism do not like to meet this charge directly; so they often take refuge in saying that they are devoted simply to science! They are really devoted to the applied sciences and to practical production. Therefore it is necessary to employ a certain skepticism even at the expense of the Cult of Science, and to say, It is an Americanism, which looks innocent and disinterested, but really is not either.

The contribution that science can make to a labor is to render it easier by the help of a tool or a process, and to assure the laborer of his perfect economic security while he is engaged upon it. Then it can be performed with leisure and enjoyment. But the modern laborer has not exactly received this benefit under the industrial regime. His labor is hard, its tempo is fierce, and his employment is insecure. The first principle of a good labor is that it must be effective, but the second principle is that it must be enjoyed. Labor is one of the largest items in the human career; it is a modest demand to ask that it may partake of happiness.

The regular act of applied science is to introduce into labor a labor-saving device or a machine. Whether this is a benefit depends on how far it is advisable to save the labor. The philosophy of applied science is generally quite sure that the saving of labor is a pure gain, and that the more of it the better. This is to assume that labor is an evil, that only the end of labor or the material product is good. On this assumption labor becomes mercenary and servile, and it is no wonder if many forms of modern labor are accepted without resentment though they are evidently brutalizing. The act of labor as one of the happy functions of human life has been in effect abandoned, and is practiced solely for its rewards.

Even the apologists of industrialism have been obliged to admit that some economic evils follow in the wake of the machines. These are such as overproduction, unemployment, and a growing inequality in the distribution of wealth. But the remedies proposed by the apologists are always homeopathic. They expect the evils to disappear when we have bigger and better machines, and more of them. Their remedial programs, therefore, look forward to more industrialism. Sometimes they see the system righting itself spontaneously and without direction: they are Optimists. Sometimes they rely on the benevolence of capital, or the militancy of labor, to bring about a fairer division of the spoils: they are Cooperationists or Socialists. And sometimes they expect to find super-engineers, in the shape of Boards of Control, who will adapt production to consumption and regulate prices and guarantee business against fluctuations: they are Sovietists. With respect to these last it must be insisted that the true Sovietists or Communists – if the term may be used here in the European sense – are the Industrialists themselves. They would have the government set up an economic super-organization, which in turn would become the government. We therefore look upon the Communist menace as a menace indeed, but not as a Red one; because it is simply according to the blind drift of our industrial development to expect in America at last much the same economic system as that imposed by violence upon Russia in 1917.

Turning to consumption, as the grand end which justifies the evil of modern labor, we find that we have been deceived. We have more time in which to consume, and many more products to be consumed. But the tempo of our labors communicates itself to our satisfactions, and these also become brutal and hurried. The constitution of the natural man probably does not permit him to shorten his labor-time and enlarge his consuming-time indefinitely. He has to pay the penalty in satiety and aimlessness. The modern man has lost his sense of vocation.

Religion can hardly expect to flourish in an industrial society. Religion is our submission to the general intention of a nature that is fairly inscrutable; it is the sense of our role as creatures within it. But nature industrialized, transformed into cities and artificial habitations, manufactured into commodities, is no longer nature but a highly simplified picture of nature. We receive the illusion of having power over nature, and lose the sense of nature as something mysterious and contingent. The God of nature under these conditions is merely an amiable expression, a superfluity, and the philosophical understanding ordinarily carried in the religious experience is not there for us to have.

Nor do the arts have a proper life under industrialism, with the general decay of sensibility which attends it. Art depends, in general, like religion, on a right attitude to nature; and in particular on a free and disinterested observation of nature that occurs only in leisure. Neither the creation nor the understanding of works of art is possible in an industrial age except by some local and unlikely suspension of the industrial drive.

The amenities of life also suffer under the curse of a strictly-business or industrial civilization. They consist in such practices as manners, conversation, hospitality, sympathy, family life, romantic love – in the social exchanges which reveal and develop sensibility in human affairs. If religion and the arts are founded on right relations of man-to-nature, these are founded on right relations of man-to-man.

Apologists of industrialism are even inclined to admit that its actual processes may have upon its victims the spiritual effects just described. But they think that all can be made right by extraordinary educational efforts, by all sorts of cultural institutions and endowments. They would cure the poverty of the contemporary spirit by hiring experts to instruct it in spite of itself in the historic culture. But salvation is hardly to be encountered on that road. The trouble with the life-pattern is to be located at its economic base, and we cannot rebuild it by pouring in soft materials from the top. The young men and women in colleges, for example, if they are already placed in a false way of life, cannot make more than an inconsequential acquaintance with the arts and humanities transmitted to them. Or else the understanding of these arts and humanities will but make them the more wretched in their own destitution.

The "Humanists" are too abstract. Humanism, properly speaking, is not an abstract system, but a culture, the whole way in which we live, act, think, and feel. It is a kind of imaginatively balanced life lived out in a definite social tradition. And, in the concrete, we believe that this, the genuine humanism, was rooted in the agrarian life of the older South and of other parts of the country that shared in such a tradition. It was not an abstract moral "check" derived from the classics – it was not soft material poured in from the top. It was deeply founded in the way of life itself – in its tables, chairs, portraits, festivals, laws, marriage customs. We cannot recover our native humanism by adopting some standard of taste that is critical enough to question the contemporary arts but not critical enough to question the social and economic life which is their ground.

The tempo of the industrial life is fast, but that is not the worst of it; it is accelerating. The ideal is not merely some set form of industrialism, with so many stable industries, but industrial progress, or an incessant extension of industrialization. It never proposes a specific goal; it initiates the infinite series. We have not merely capitalized certain industries; we have capitalized the laboratories and inventors, and undertaken to employ all the labor-saving devices that come out of them. But a fresh labor-saving device introduced into an industry does not emancipate the laborers in that industry so much as it evicts them. Applied at the expense of agriculture, for example, the new processes have reduced the part of the population supporting itself upon the soil to a smaller and smaller fraction. Of course no single labor-saving process is fatal; it brings on a period of unemployed labor and unemployed capital, but soon a new industry is devised which will put them both to work again, and a new commodity is thrown upon the market. The laborers were sufficiently embarrassed in the meantime, but, according to the theory, they will eventually be taken care of. It is now the public which is embarrassed; it feels obligated to purchase a commodity for which it had expressed no desire, but it is invited to make its budget equal to the strain. All might yet be well, and stability and comfort might again obtain, but for this: partly because of industrial ambitions and partly because the repressed creative impulse must break out somewhere, there will be a stream of further labor-saving devices in all industries, and the cycle will have to be repeated over and over. The result is an increasing disadjustment and instability.

It is an inevitable consequence of industrial progress that production greatly outruns the rate of natural consumption. To overcome the disparity, the producers, disguised as the pure idealists of progress, must coerce and wheedle the public into being loyal and steady consumers, in order to keep the machines running. So the rise of modern advertising – along with its twin, personal salesmanship – is the most significant development of our industrialism.

Advertising means to persuade the consumers to want exactly what the applied sciences are able to furnish them. It consults the happiness of the consumer no more than it consulted the happiness of the laborer. It is the great effort of a false economy of life to approve itself. But its task grows more difficult every day.

It is strange, of course, that a majority of men anywhere could ever as with one mind become enamored of industrialism: a system that has so little regard for individual wants. There is evidently a kind of thinking that rejoices in setting up a social objective which has no relation to the individual. Men are prepared to sacrifice their private dignity and happiness to an abstract social ideal, and without asking whether the social ideal produces the welfare of any individual man whatsoever. But this is absurd. The responsibility of men is for their own welfare and that of their neighbors, not for the hypothetical welfare of some fabulous creature called society.

Opposed to the industrial society is the agrarian, which does not stand in particular need of definition. An agrarian society is hardly one that has no use at all for industries, for professional vocations, for scholars and artists, and for the life of cities. Technically, perhaps, an agrarian society is one in which agriculture is the leading vocation, whether for wealth, for pleasure, or for prestige – a form of labor that is pursued with intelligence and leisure, and that becomes the model to which the other forms approach as well as they may. But an agrarian regime will be secured readily enough where the superfluous industries are not allowed to rise against it. The theory of agrarianism is that the culture of the soil is the best and most sensitive of vocations, and that therefore it should have the economic preference and enlist the maximum number of workers.

These principles do not intend to be very specific in proposing any practical measures. How may the little agrarian community resist the Chamber of Commerce of its county seat, which is always trying to import some foreign industry that cannot be assimilated to the life-pattern of the community? Just what must the Southern leaders do to defend the traditional Southern life? How may the Southern and the Western agrarians unite for effective action? Should the agrarian forces try to capture the Democratic party, which historically is so closely affiliated with the defense of individualism, the small community, the state, the South? Or must the agrarians – even the Southern ones – abandon the Democratic party to its fate and try a new one? What legislation could most profitably be championed by the powerful agrarians in the Senate of the United States? What anti-industrial measures might promise to stop the advances of industrialism, or even undo some of them, with the least harm to those concerned? What policy should be pursued by the educators who have a tradition at heart? These and many other questions are of the greatest importance, but they cannot be answered here.

For, in conclusion, this much is clear: If a community, or a section, or a race, or an age, is groaning under industrialism, and well aware that it is an evil dispensation, it must find the way to throw it off. To think that this can not be done is pusillanimous. And if the whole community, section, race, or age thinks it cannot be done, then it has simply lost its political genius and doomed itself to impotence.

参考文献

Anderson, John Dennis. Student Companion to William Faulkner. Westport, Connecticut · London: Greenwood Press, 2007:1.

Andrews, William L. The Literature of the American South: A Norton Anthology. New York ·London: W.W. Norton & Company, 1998.

Capote, Truman. Other Voices, Other Rooms. Vintage Books ·A Division of Random House, Inc.·New York: Vintage International, 1994.

Mc Cullers, Carson. Complete Novels: The Ballad of the Sad Café. New York: Literary Classics of the United States, Inc. 2001.

Cassill, R.V. The Norton Anthology of Short Fiction. New York ·London: W.W. Norton & Company, 1995.

Cooper, William J. JR, Terrill, Thomas E. The American South: A History. New York: Alfred A. Knopf, INC.

Daniel, Thomas Young. The Past in the Present: A Thematic Study of Modern Southern Fiction. Baton Rouge & London: Louisiana State University Press, 1981.

Flora, Joseph M. Relocating Southerners in the West. The Southern Literary Journal, Vol. 33, No.2, (Spring, 2001).

Ford, Richard. The Sportswriter. Vintage Books·A Division of Random House·New York: Vintage Contemporaries, 1986.

Gray, Richard, Robinson, Owen. A Companion to the Literature and Culture of the American South. Blackwell Publishing Ltd., 2004.

King, Richard. A Southern Renaissance: The Cultural Awakening of the American South 1930–1955. New York: Oxford University Press, 1980.

Percy, Walker. The Moviegoer. Vintage Books·A Division of Random House, Inc. ·New York: Vintage International, 1998.

Rubin, Louis D.JR. (ed.). The History of Southern Literature. Baton Rouge & London: Louisiana State University Press, 1985.

Tate, Allen. The Fathers. Baton Rouge and London: Louisiana State University Press, 1996.

Tyler, Anne. Four Complete Novels: Dinner at the Homesick Restaurant. New York: Wings Books, 1990.